POLITICAL ECONOMY IN
WESTERN DEMOCRACIES

POLITICAL ECONOMY IN WESTERN DEMOCRACIES

Edited by Norman J. Vig
and Steven E. Schier

HOLMES & MEIER
New York   London

First published in the United States of America 1985 by
Holmes & Meier Publishers, Inc.
30 Irving Place
New York, N.Y. 10003

Great Britain:
Hillview House
One Hallswelle Parade
London NW11 ODL, England

Book design by Ellen Foos

LIBRARY OF CONGRESS CATALOGING IN PUBLICATION DATA
Main entry under title:

Political economy in western democracies.

Includes bibliographies and index.
1. Economics—Political aspects—Addresses, essays,
lectures.   2. Economic policy—Addresses, essays,
lectures.   3. Welfare state—Addresses, essays, lectures.
I. Vig, Norman J.   II. Schier, Steven E.
HB73.P625   1985   338.9   84-25320
ISBN 0-8419-0989-X
ISBN 0-8419-0990-3 (pbk.)

Manufactured in the United States of America

For
Nora S. Vig
and
Marjorie I. Schier

CONTENTS

COMPARATIVE MACROECONOMIC POLICIES

ECONOMIC CONDITIONS AND POLITICAL BEHAVIOR

List of Tables

List of Figures

PREFACE

It is no longer realistic to study politics and economics in isolation from each other. Virtually everything the state does has some impact on economic markets, while the behavior of private business firms and other corporate bodies severely constrains the social and economic choices available to government. One result of this growing interdependence has been a phenomenal revival of interest in political economy—the study of relationships between economic and political life that once dominated Western social philosophy. In the past decade political scientists, economists, and sociologists have begun to reintegrate their disciplines in an effort to comprehend and perhaps ameliorate the critical problems that mature industrial societies face in the late twentieth century.

The advanced capitalist democracies have experienced more than a decade of political and economic turmoil in the aftermath of the first OPEC oil price shock of 1973. Since then the "economic miracle" that had brought unprecedented growth and prosperity to Western Europe for a quarter century after World War II has given way to inflation, unemployment, pessimism, and renewed ideological conflict. As public revenues have fallen behind expenditures, the welfare state itself has come under attack from both left and right. Economic issues have returned to the center of politics, and new, more conservative, governments have been elected in several countries. In the United States the Reagan administration has revitalized the capitalist "engine of growth" in the mid-1980s, but only at the cost of new social inequalities and enormous trade and budgetary deficits that may further jeopardize national and international stability.

This volume is an effort to meet the need for a text that analyzes these dramatic developments both comparatively and from the perspective of political economy. The editors and the dozen other contributors are all political scientists actively engaged in teaching and research on political economy, and the book is designed for use in undergraduate as well as graduate level political science and political economy courses. With this in mind, technical notation, reference citation, and methodological discussion have been intentionally kept to a minimum, and in several chapters data has been presented in simplified form. An introductory chapter on the study of political economy and shorter essays on the issues raised in each section are included to aid students. But the collection addresses fundamental issues of politics and economics that should be of interest to a wider audience as well.

Norman J. Vig
Steven E. Schier

POLITICAL ECONOMY IN
WESTERN DEMOCRACIES

1 INTRODUCTION: POLITICAL SCIENCE AND POLITICAL ECONOMY

Norman J. Vig

Political economy is both older and younger than political science. It is older because it was the precursor to modern economics, political science, and sociology. In eighteenth- and nineteenth-century England, "political economy" was considered the branch of moral philosophy most relevant to the everyday affairs of men. Economic and political philosophers such as Adam Smith, John Stuart Mill, and Karl Marx treated social relationships holistically, showing how economic arrangements affected political life and vice versa. It was only in the late nineteenth and early twentieth centuries that economics, sociology, and eventually politics came to be viewed as distinct scientific disciplines. As theory and research became increasingly specialized and detailed, the social sciences drifted apart to the point where, after World War II, their practitioners came to speak almost different languages. The linkages among political, economic, and social phenomena were more obscure in the 1950s and 1960s than to the political economists of a century earlier.

With relatively few exceptions, economic development and even economic policy making were ignored by political scientists in this period. Economic development was relegated to the status of a Third World problem, and steady economic growth and affluence were taken for granted as stabilizing elements in the politics of advanced capitalist democracies. Much of the new "behavioral" political science was devoted to exploring the sociological and psychological roots of partisan voting and similar activities. Political outcomes were assumed to reflect these constants together with the benign interplay and competition among pluralistic interest groups representing all sectors of society. Democratic

3

politics came to be viewed largely as "the politics of collective bargaining" (Lipset, 1964), in which each sector competed for its share of the growing economic pie within a consensual framework of Keynesian economic management. The "welfare state" and "mixed economy" were assumed to have eliminated most of the historic ideological and class conflicts over fundamental political values. The concept of "postindustrial society" also implied that "postmaterial" values were displacing traditional economic concerns, especially among young people (Inglehart, 1977).

The past decade has seen a revival of political economy as this rosy conceptualization of advanced industrial societies has fallen apart (Andrain, 1984; Vig, 1981). The primary reason is that in the 1970s economic stagnation, inflation, and unemployment reappeared in all of the industrial democracies and brought economic issues and policies to the center of political controversy as they had not been since the 1930s (Dahrendorf, 1982). A few statistics tell the story. The economic growth rate of the European Community fell from 4.6 percent annually during 1960–73 to 2.3 percent for 1974–80 and 0.1 percent in 1981–83 (Albert and Ball, 1984, 7–11). Inflation, which had averaged about 3 percent in Western nations as late as 1967, jumped to 12 percent during 1974–75 and 11 percent during 1980–81 in the wake of the massive oil price increases by the Organization of Petroleum Exporting Countries (OPEC). Perhaps worst of all, the unemployment rate in Europe rose from 2.1 percent during 1960–70 to an estimated 10.8 percent in 1983—a level also reached in the United States during 1982.

In the 1930s it became abundantly clear that capitalist markets did not necessarily operate at anything like the full-employment equilibrium posited by neoclassical economists. The result was a rejection—or at the very least, a profound modification—of prevailing theoretical orthodoxy and a turn toward more active government intervention to prevent chronic underinvestment and unemployment. John Maynard Keynes's *General Theory of Employment, Interest, and Money* (1936) provided a new analytical foundation for macroeconomic management and political choice—in other words, it established the basis for a new political economy. As the late Joan Robinson once put it:

> By making it impossible to believe any longer in an automatic reconciliation of conflicting interests into a harmonious whole, the *General Theory* brought out into the open the problem of choice and judgment that the neoclassicals had managed to smother. The ideology to end ideologies broke down. Economics once more became Political Economy (Robinson, 1962, 76).

As Professor Robinson lamented, after World War II "Keynesian" economics was translated into a new set of economic orthodoxies known as the "neoclassical synthesis" of Paul Samuelson et al. Economists once again narrowed their focus to the more technical and theoretical avenues of research, while at the same time claiming a near monopoly on expertise as economic policy advisers. National economies came to be treated as closed market systems in need of only limited "fine-tuning" to maintain equilibrium. Political forces and institutions were largely excluded from consideration as external "givens" that, like the weather, were beyond the scope of rational analysis and prediction. Political economy once again fell into disrepute as a less-than-scientific endeavor.

This has begun to change in the past decade. Something like the breakdown of ideology described by Robinson has again occurred in a period of economic crisis and uncertainty. This time political scientists and sociologists, as well as economists and other academics concerned with public policy, have begun to refocus attention on the study of political economy as it has become evident that "economic" problems can no longer be understood in isolation from other social realities and that no discipline or school of experts has a monopoly on such complex phenomena as structural unemployment and internationally transmitted inflation. Thus a "new political economy" is developing that is interdisciplinary and draws on a wide range of scholarly and philosophical traditions. Although no consensus has been achieved, new and often eclectic thinking about the relationships between "politics" and "markets" (Lindblom, 1977) has stimulated the growth of a new field of discourse and research that promises to occupy a central place in the social sciences for the remainder of this century.

This book is intended to bring to the reader—especially the undergraduate with some background in political science and economics—a collection of writings by political scientists that both illustrates the nature and the range of the new research and sheds light on many important contemporary issues in political economy. Most of the contributions have been written specifically for this volume with this student audience in mind but should be of interest to the general reader as well. The remainder of this introduction will attempt to set the stage by outlining some of the main concerns of and approaches to political economy and by explaining the organization and content of the book.

WHAT IS POLITICAL ECONOMY?

As already suggested, political economy is not a fixed subject or discipline but a recurrent mode of conceptualizing social life. Its scope or field of vision has broadened and narrowed at different times as economic belief systems have alternately displaced or rekindled interest in fundamental issues such as human equality and growth. Thus it tends to be rediscovered, as Joan Robinson suggests, when prevailing ideologies and thought patterns are called into question by events.

That is presumably why the field appears to defy precise definition or conceptualization. In two recent works, each entitled *Modern Political Economy,* the closest we get to a general definition is the statement, "Political economy studies the interdependence between the economy and the polity of a country or countries" (Frey, 1978, vii; cf. Frohlich and Oppenheimer, 1978). Another states that "the central issues are those concerning the relationship between the state, or its government, and the economy: what that relationship *is,* both generally and in particular cases; and, most critically, what that relationship *ought* to be" (Jones, 1983, 4). Still others avoid the term (and convey differing emphases) by speaking of "the politicized economy" (Best and Connolly, 1982) or "political economics" (Alt and Chrystal, 1983).

If political economy is something like the proverbial elephant that can be described by some of its parts but not really pictured in its entirety, some distinctions can be made that may help to delineate it. First, it is both *normative* and *empirical.* Second, it is *policy-oriented* but not simply a branch of policy analysis. Third, it incorporates both *structural* and *behavioral* levels of analysis. Finally, it emphasizes the importance of *international* as well as national political-economic structures.

Joseph Schumpeter distinguished political economy from economics in his *History of Economic Analysis* (1954). He defined political economy as "an exposition of a comprehensive set of economic policies that its author advocates on the strength of certain unifying normative principles, such as the principles of economic Liberalism, Socialism" (quoted in Gamble, 1983, 64). The distinction between political economy as a field of normative discourse and economics as a value-free science is a traditional one based on the philosophical origins of classical political economy. To some extent it still holds, since political economy raises fundamental value questions about the proper role of the state and private markets and often gives rise to critical evaluations of existing arrangements. Indeed, "critical political economy" is usually rooted in Marxian interpretations of capitalism and its presumed failings (Gamble, 1983). But the "science" of microeconomic choice and market equilibrium also favors the moral order of liberal bourgeois society, and it is increasingly recognized in the philosophy of social science that no field of inquiry can be entirely "value-free" (see, e.g., Myrdal, 1969). Much of contemporary political economy is explicitly derived from value orientations dating back to nineteenth-century socialism or liberalism (see next section).

At the same time, however, the current revival of political economy has generated a great deal of new empirical research to test normative theories and hypotheses. This is in part due to the availability of far more sophisticated tools and methodologies for quantitative research. Younger political scientists and others with advanced training in mathematics and statistics have begun to analyze such phenomena as the determinants of public sector growth and the influence of economic conditions on voting behavior in ways that cast doubt on many of the conventional assumptions about economics and politics. Modeling techniques adapted from econometrics are now applied to a wide range of "political" questions (see, e.g., Whitely, 1980; Hibbs and Fassbender, 1981). Thus it is no longer possible to write political economy off as a field for amateur economists and moralists; through mutual interest and the cross-fertilization of disciplines it is now pressing forward at the boundaries of social science research.

The motivation, we have suggested, lies in the need to resolve critical economic problems that now threaten national and international social stability. Political economists have focused much of their attention on efforts to explain the multiple political and social causation of such apparently "economic" phenomena as inflation (see, e.g., Hirsch and Goldthorpe, 1978; Peretz, 1983). Although the *proximate* causes may be found in such technical factors as the supply and circulation rate of the money stock ($MV = PT$), it is now widely recognized (even by economists) that we have to answer the question of *why* the money supply is expanded, or what political and social pressures have in the past led monetary authorities to accommodate values other than price stability. At the same time, political institutions and processes can no longer be seen as irrelevant to the formulation and execution of economic policies. Many of the new political economists—including the "public choice" theorists to be mentioned below—now recognize that policy choices are constrained by incentives built into the routines of public and private organizations and into the democratic process itself. The role of such traditional "political" institutions as elections, interest groups, and parties now takes on central relevance for economic policy making.

Because political economy seeks to broaden and deepen the study of public policy by probing its structural and behavioral antecedents, it is not merely a branch of "policy studies" or "policy science." It is not primarily concerned with the specifics of decision making in particular fields of policy—such as defining a particular array of options from which a policy maker may select the most efficient alternative. That is perhaps best regarded as a specialized branch of applied econometrics or decision theory. Political economy is oriented toward the ends as well as the means of public policy. It does not necessarily assume that diverse policy goals can be harmonized or even "traded off" in some optimal manner; political conflict is thus accepted as inevitable. (It is perhaps here, more than anywhere else, that the political economist differs from the economist whose thinking is premised on the idea of some optimal allocation of resources generated by market exchange.)

What we continually come back to in political economy is the realization that economic and political activities are not really governed by separate social systems but are integral parts of a common "regime" for allocating rewards and legitimizing certain kinds of social behavior. The structures for accomplishing this make a great deal of difference, obviously. If private economic groups are free to organize and pursue their interests in the political arena, one gets a very different outcome than if all sectors and industries are owned and regulated by the state. But even in relatively open democratic systems such as those of Western Europe there is a good deal of variation in the relationships between public and private authority or, more specifically, in the organization of interest groups and their linkages to the state. The degree of "pluralism" or "corporatism" is an important structural variable in the operation of national economies, as is the relative size and strength of the organized labor movement. These structural differences have important policy implications and may lead to normative conclusions about the legitimacy and effectiveness of the regime. For example, one might advocate institutional or policy reforms in the direction of more centralized corporatist bargaining or toward free market competition, depending on one's assessment of the current power structure.

Finally, many political economists are concerned with the interactions between international politics and economics. While international trade and finance have long been studied by economists, they have tended to ignore the political importance of institutions such as multinational corporations and banks which often dominate host countries (Gilpin, 1975). More broadly, political economists recognize the existence of world market systems and structures that serve the interests of some nations and groups at the expense of others, particularly insofar as they create relationships of dependency between the developing nations and the advanced centers of capitalism (Wallerstein, 1979; Frank, 1980a, 1980b). Others focus on the economic consequences of changes in world politics, e.g., the effects of collapsing American "hegemony" in the Western alliance since the late 1960s and the rapid development of the Asian periphery (Calleo, 1982; Keohane, 1984). The "Japanese model" has inspired a new interest in "industrial policy" (Reich and Magaziner, 1982; Reich, 1983) in part because it is recognized that no country—even the United States—is immune to the pressures of foreign economic competition or the "internationalization of markets."

NORMATIVE AND ANALYTICAL APPROACHES

It is evident from the preceding discussion that political economy is a very diverse field of inquiry in which many different approaches are taken. These approaches often reflect ideological predispositions or value preferences. The deepest divisions are still between those influenced by the "classical liberal" (now conservative) laissez-faire school of economics and those in the Marxist socialist tradition. Both classical liberal and neo-Marxian concepts have inspired new analytical frameworks that provide many valuable insights into contemporary problems. However, between these two poles we also find a variety of neoconservative and reformist perspectives and a good deal of eclectic empirical research. Although this book emphasizes the latter, we should briefly comment on the normative orientations of the "right" and the "left."

Classical Liberalism and Public Choice

Nineteenth-century liberals advocated individual liberty, free trade, and limited government. Following Adam Smith and his utilitarian disciples, liberal economists argued that social welfare was maximized by the free play of market forces. Individuals pursuing their self-interest (or utility preferences) in the marketplace would, through a multitude of separate transactions, allocate resources to their highest use. This assumed that individual market participants behaved rationally in seeking to maximize their utilities and that all markets remained open, competitive, and self-equilibrating. In addition to maximizing efficiency and thus social welfare, it was argued, the protection of private property and free markets was an essential defense against political tyranny.

These fundamental behavioral, structural, and normative propositions have been adopted and elaborated by contemporary conservative economists and political theorists such as Friedrich Hayek and Milton Friedman. They are reflected in current economic doctrines, such as monetarism, but also in new theoretical approaches to political economy (Usher, 1981). For example, "public choice theory" extends the logic of classical microeconomics to political behavior, that is, individuals are assumed to act "rationally" (i.e. pursue their utilities) in elections and other "nonmarket" contexts just as they do in economic decision making (Mueller, 1979). The result in politics, however, will not be an optimal allocation of resources if people are allowed to use the authority of the state to obtain benefits for themselves while shifting the costs to others (e.g. through differential taxation). Many of these theorists thus argue that unless the role of government is strictly limited, it will be dominated by special interests and drain capital resources away from the more efficient allocational mechanisms of the private marketplace. Hence, public choice theorists point to the potentially irrational economic consequences of democracy in the absence of further constitutional limitations or other constraining rules (Brittan, 1975; Buchanan and Wagner, 1977).

Classical (or, strictly speaking, neoclassical) liberalism of this kind should obviously not be confused with political "liberalism" as that term is used in the United States to connote left-of-center politics. It is the Republican rather than the Democratic party that is liberal in the sense employed here (although both parties share many principles from the liberal political tradition). In many European countries conservative political parties have long had other bases of support (e.g. religion, nationalism), and neoclassical liberalism is often stronger among "bourgeois" center parties representing small business, professionals, and white collar employees. However, market-oriented approaches to political economy are now receiving more attention in Western Europe. They inspire Margaret Thatcher's Britain as well as Ronald Reagan's America.

Neo-Marxism

If neoclassical liberal analysis has largely been developed by economists and extended to politics, neo-Marxist approaches owe more to sociologists and social philosophers who reject the capitalist economic paradigm. Although they do not necessarily acknowledge all of Marx's postulates—such as the inevitability of class warfare and revolutionary change—neo-Marxists follow his lead in holding that political power can be understood only in relation to the underlying structure of economic production and the social class interests it serves. Capitalist modes of production are viewed as inherently exploitative in that they allocate disproportionate wealth to one group—the owners of capital—and prevent the majority (i.e. workers) from exercising effective democratic control. The result is periodic "accumulation crises" (overproduction of some goods and underinvestment in other sectors necessary to maintain economic growth and full employment) and "legitimation crises" (loss of support for the political regime).

Many of these perspectives have been used in analyzing the economic crises of the 1970s. James O'Connor (1973), for example, portrayed the "fiscal crisis of the state" as a manifestation of the need in capitalist systems to spend ever more public money on welfare programs to buy off political discontent. Some of the most important Marxist contributions concern the theory of the state. Poulantzas (1973, 1978) elaborated the concept of the "relative autonomy of the state," i.e., the idea that governments in capitalist democracies needed to maintain a certain degree of independence from particular capitalist interests or "class fractions" in order to serve the interests of the capitalist system as a whole. Thus concessions could be made to workers and other democratic forces in the welfare state without sacrificing the essential interests of the dominant class (see also Offe, 1975, 1980; Gough, 1979). The German Marxist, Jurgen Habermas (1973), drew on another strand of Marxist sociology in emphasizing popular alienation and the delegitimation of public institutions. For different reasons, then, both the neoclassical liberals and the neo-Marxists are severe critics of the social democratic welfare state.

Neo-Marxists have also helped to direct attention to many of the exploitative features of international economic development. Many of them have employed "dependency theory" in analyzing historical and contemporary relations between countries and their impacts on domestic political structures. Some very important theoretical and comparative work has also been done on the causes and failures of revolutions from this political-economic perspective (see especially Skocpol, 1979).

Other Perspectives

Some additional normative positions can be identified even though they are not as sharply delineated as the neoclassical and neo-Marxist. A group of *neoconservatives,* including Daniel Bell, Samuel Huntington, and Richard Rose, is concerned with the "overloading" and "governability" of democratic systems due to the decay of political parties, rise of special interest groups, and growth of the public sector (Crozier, Huntington, and Watanuki, 1975; Bell, 1976; Rose and Peters, 1978). Their arguments against the growth of the welfare functions of the state are based less on the alleged efficiency of the private sector or oppressive character of government than on the need to restore confidence in public authority by limiting it to those functions it can perform effectively (cf. Birch, 1984).

Toward the other side of the political spectrum a diverse collection of disillusioned pluralists, "post-Keynesians," and neocorporatists advocate a stronger role for the state in economic planning, usually in the form of new "industrial policies." Much of their analysis focuses on the pernicious consequences of "interest group liberalism" (Lowi, 1979) or "pluralistic stagnation" brought on by the ability of private interest groups to veto effectively public policies affecting them. Some see the privileged position of business as the problem (Lindblom, 1977), while others simply argue that pluralistic interest group competition no longer serves as a fair and effective basis for economic policy making (Dahl, 1982). Some economists as well as political scientists now see specialized interest associations as a major impediment to economic growth (see especially Olson, 1982).

Neocorporatist thinking deserves special mention. The term "corporatism" came into vogue in the 1970s to denote a form of limited competition and cooperation among centralized institutions representing large sectors of business, industry, labor, and government. Such organized sectoral representation and bargaining were seen as an emerging form of "intermediation" in advanced capitalist systems that promoted effective national economic policy making in countries such as Austria, Sweden, and West Germany (Lehmbruch and Schmitter, 1982; Wilson, 1983). Although it now appears that trends in this direction were exaggerated, many advocates of national industrial policies call for new forms of "partnership" between government, industry, and labor (e.g. Reich, 1983).

Contributions by Political Scientists

Although political scientists are found in all of the foregoing categories, they have been less identified with the dominant normative schools than economists or sociologists and more eclectic in their approaches to political economy. Perhaps because many concepts and methods in their own field have been borrowed from the other social sciences, they may find it easier to deal with issues that cross disciplinary boundaries. But the traditional subfields of political science are also highly relevant to many conceptual issues in political economy. For example, most of the underlying normative issues have been central to political theory for a long time. Political scientists have also devoted a great deal of attention to institutions such as elections, bureaucracies, political parties, and interest groups that now appear to constrain the operation of economies in many unforeseen ways (see, e.g., Martin, 1977). They have led the way in analyses of the changing nature of pluralism and corporatism, and in comparative systems analysis generally. Their behavioral methods put them in the forefront of the study of public opinion and its relationship to economic conditions, while their rapidly growing interest in policy studies (including comparative public policy) now directs their attention to many of the most pressing substantive problems in political economy. Finally, no other discipline has contributed so much to the study of international relations.

It is thus not surprising that political scientists are actively engaged in political-economic research and publication. Political economy panels are now a regular feature at political science conferences, and a separate professional association, the Conference Group on the Political Economy, now meets annually with the American Political Science Association. Most of the authors of this book have presented papers before this group, and their contributions here represent several important areas of scholarship. But no claim is made that the authors are fully representative of the profession or the diverse opinions held by political economists.

PLAN OF THE BOOK

The main purpose of this book is to bring a sample of such writings to a wider audience in a form that will also help to meet pressing needs for undergraduate teaching material in political economy. Although all areas cannot be covered in a single text, we have chosen a broad, comparative focus. The chapters span the major Western democracies, within a framework highlighting four principal areas of discourse and research: normative and empirical theories of state–market relations; the growth and crisis of the welfare state; comparative macroeconomic policies; and economic voting, or the impact of economic conditions on government popularity and support.

The first part contains essays of broad theoretical and normative import. The question of the proper economic role of the state is an ancient one that has become critical once again as consensus on economic and social policy has broken down. Keynesian economic management and welfare state expansion provided the basis for political compromise between capital and labor after World War II, but by the 1970s this "postwar settlement" had come under attack from both right and left. At the same time, the relationships between government and society have evolved in response to changes in the structure of industrial economies and in the organization and functions of interest groups. The essays in the first section explore the new criticisms of the liberal welfare state, the changing linkages between state and social structures, and the potential consequences of the collapse of the Keynesian paradigm.

The second part then looks at the crisis of the welfare state in more detail. The "fiscal crisis of the state" in the 1970s and 1980s is linked most directly to growth of the public sector and, more specifically, to the financing of "welfare" programs. Democratic governments now consume or transfer between one-third and two-thirds of national income, the largest share of which is spent on health, education, and social security programs. But the causes of welfare state expansion and the criteria for determining an optimal level of social welfare spending raise extremely complex and difficult issues for all industrial democracies. Part II focuses on these issues and on the relative performance of different nations in balancing conflicting demands for growth, stability, and welfare provision in the past decade.

Following this survey, the chapters in the third section then focus more sharply on the particular macroeconomic policies that are being followed in four major nations: Great Britain, the United States, West Germany, and France. These nations have all responded somewhat differently to the economic crises of the 1970s, suggesting a range of alternatives for coping with "stagflation" and industrial renewal. The "hypercapitalist" regimes of Margaret Thatcher and Ronald Reagan can be contrasted to the more cautious crisis management of the Schmidt and Kohl governments in West Germany and to the neo-Keynesian socialist experiment of François Mitterrand in France. The nature of the choices and trade-offs facing Western democracies in the 1980s and beyond is suggested by these case studies.

Finally, students of political economy need to ask themselves what the public will support, that is, whether democratic capitalist governments can mobilize and hold the support of popular majorities for social and economic adjustments that may be necessary even though they require sacrifice. In the 1970s many statesmen and scholars questioned the future survival of democratic systems on grounds that special interest groups and myopic electorates would prevent transition to a more rational, efficient, and equitable economic order. The fourth part thus examines detailed empirical evidence on the relationships between economic conditions and government popularity and voting behavior. Although the conclusions are mixed, they suggest that incumbent governments must indeed convince the public of the current and future success of their economic strategies if they are to retain power.

Overall, the four sections progress stepwise from the abstract philosophical debate over the proper role of the state, to the general problems of welfare provision and public finance, to the particular macroeconomic responses of different countries, and finally to the response of individual citizens as voters. It is hoped that the reader will perceive linkages—many of his own creation—between these levels of human action and analysis. We regret that we cannot explore other dimensions, especially international, of what has become a global political economy. The research agenda for the future is open—and immense.

REFERENCES

Albert, M., and Ball, J. 1984. "Toward European Economic Recovery in the 1980's: Report to the European Parliament." *The Washington Papers* (No. 109).

Alt, J. E., and Chrystal, K. A. 1983. *Political Economics*. Berkeley: University of California Press.

Andrain, C. F. 1984. "Capitalism and Democracy Reappraised: A Review Essay." *Western Political Quarterly* 37 (Dec.): 652–64.

Bell, D. 1976. *The Cultural Contradictions of Capitalism*. New York: Basic Books.

Best, M. H., and Connolly, W. E. 1982. *The Politicized Economy*. 2nd ed. Lexington, Mass.: Heath.

Birch, A. 1984. "Overload, Ungovernability and Delegitimation: The Theories and the British Case." *British Journal of Political Science* 14:135–60.

Brittan, S. 1975. "The Economic Consequences of Democracy." *British Journal of Political Science* 5:129–59.

Buchanan, J. M., and Wagner, R. E. 1977. *Democracy in Deficit: The Political Legacy of Lord Keynes*. New York: Academic Press.

Calleo, D. P. 1973. *America and the World Political Economy: Atlantic Dreams and National Realities*. Bloomington: Indiana University Press.

———. 1982. *The Imperious Economy*. Cambridge: Harvard University Press.

Crozier, M., Huntington, S., and Watanuki, J. 1975. *The Crisis of Democracy*. New York: New York University Press.

Dahl, R. A. 1982. *Dilemmas of Pluralist Democracy: Autonomy vs. Control*. New Haven: Yale University Press.

Dahrendorf, R.', ed. 1982. *Europe's Economy in Crisis*. New York: Holmes & Meier.

Frank, A. G. 1980a. *Crisis in the Third World*. New York: Holmes & Meier.

———. 1980b. *Crisis in the World Economy*. New York: Holmes & Meier.

Frey, B. S. 1978. *Modern Political Economy*. New York: Wiley.

Frohlich, N., and Oppenheimer, J. A. 1978. *Modern Political Economy*. Englewood Cliffs, N.J.: Prentice-Hall.

Gamble, A. 1983. "Critical Political Economy." In *Perspectives on Political Economy*, ed. R. J. B. Jones. New York: St. Martin's Press.

Gilpin, R. 1975. *U.S. Power and the Multinational Corporation*. New York: Basic Books.

Gough, I. 1979. *The Political Economy of the Welfare State*. London: Macmillan.

Habermas, J. 1973. *Legitimation Crisis*. Boston: Beacon Press.

Hibbs, D. A., Jr., and Fassbender, H., eds. 1981. *Contemporary Political Economy: Studies on the Interdependence of Politics and Economics*. Amsterdam: North–Holland.

Hirsch, F., and Goldthorpe, J. E., eds. 1978. *The Political Economy of Inflation*. Cambridge: Harvard University Press.

Inglehart, R. 1977. *The Silent Revolution*. Princeton: Princeton University Press.

Jones, R. J. Barry, ed. 1983. *Perspectives on Political Economy*. New York: St. Martin's Press.

Keohane, R. O. 1984. *After Hegemony*. Princeton: Princeton University Press.

Lehmbruch, G., and Schmitter, P. C., eds. 1982. *Patterns of Corporatist Policy-Making*. London: Sage.

Lindblom, C. E. 1977. *Politics and Markets: The World's Political-Economic Systems.* New York: Basic Books.

Lipset, S. M. 1964. "The Changing Class Structure and Contemporary European Politics." *Daedalus* 93 (Winter):271–303.

Lowi, T. 1979. *The End of Liberalism.* Rev. ed. New York: Norton.

Martin, A. 1977. "Political Constraints on Economic Strategies in Advanced Industrial Societies." *Comparative Political Studies* 10:323–54.

Mueller, D. C. 1979. *Public Choice.* Cambridge: Cambridge University Press.

Myrdal, G. 1969. *Objectivity in Social Research.* New York: Pantheon.

O'Connor, J. 1973. *The Fiscal Crisis of the State.* New York: St. Martin's Press.

Offe, C. 1975. "The Theory of the Capitalist State and the Problem of Policy Formation." In *Stress and Contradiction in Modern Capitalism,* ed. L. N. Lindberg, C. Crouch, and C. Offe. Lexington, Mass.: Heath.

———. 1980. "The Separation of Form and Content in Liberal Democratic Politics." *Studies in Political Economy* 3:5–16.

Olson, M. 1982. *The Rise and Decline of Nations: Economic Growth, Stagflation, and Rigidities.* New Haven: Yale University Press.

Peretz, P. 1983. *The Political Economy of Inflation in the United States.* Chicago: University of Chicago Press.

Poulantzas, N. 1973. *Political Power and Social Classes.* London: New Left Books.

———. 1978. *State, Power, Socialism.* London: New Left Books.

Reich, R. B. 1983. *The Next American Frontier.* New York: Times Books.

Reich, R. B., and Magaziner, I. 1982. *Minding America's Business: Decline and Rise of the American Economy.* New York: Harcourt Brace Jovanovich.

Robinson, J. 1962. *Economic Philosophy.* Chicago: Aldine.

Rose, R., and Peters, B. G. 1978. *Can Government Go Bankrupt?* New York: Basic Books.

Schumpeter, J. A. 1954. *History of Economic Analysis.* New York: Oxford.

Skocpol, T. 1979. *States and Revolutions: A Comparative Analysis of France, Russia, and China.* Cambridge: Cambridge University Press.

Usher, D. 1981. *The Economic Prerequisite to Democracy.* New York: Columbia University Press.

Vig, N. J. 1981. "Post-Keynesian Economics and Politics: Toward an Expectationist Theory of Democracy?" *World Politics* 34 (Oct.):62–89.

Wallerstein, I. 1979. *The Capitalist World-Economy.* New York: Cambridge University Press.

Whitely, P., ed. 1980. *Models of Political Economy.* London: Sage.

Wilson, F. L. 1983. "Interest Groups and Politics in Western Europe: The Neocorporatist Approach." *Comparative Politics* 16:105–23.

THEORIES OF STATE AND ECONOMY

At the most fundamental level, political economy is concerned with the basic nature of the state and its relationship to economic life. Although this has long been the subject of philosophical debate, current interest centers on the theory and practice of the hybrid capitalist order that has evolved in Western democracies since World War II. Since the late 1960s, critics on both the left and the right have attacked the fundamental premises of the postwar "mixed economy" or "liberal welfare state." The chapters in this section present normative and analytical perspectives on the role of the state and challenge many of the new critics on both sides of the debate.

In Chapter 2, Catherine Zuckert illuminates the contemporary debate by lucidly summarizing and evaluating the critiques of such writers as Hayek, Nozick, Rawls, and Dahl. Whereas rightist critics conceive the problem in terms of the inhibition of individual liberty and economic efficiency by the state, those on the left view the political and social structures of managed capitalism as exploitative of the poor and the working class. Zuckert finds that critics on the two sides make parallel arguments that largely cancel each other out. She defends the logic of the liberal welfare state by explaining how the costs of controlling irresponsible private power are counterbalanced by the costs of increased public power, how neither markets nor popular majorities alone can adequately represent popular preferences, and how the current mix of markets and democratic procedures in advanced capitalist systems can serve to limit the abuses of each. Which elements of the critiques summarized here are most compelling? How sound are Zuckert's arguments in defense of the contemporary system?

Gary Marks, in Chapter 3, then shifts from normative theory to one of the

17

principal concerns of recent empirical theory: the nature of interest group structures and their relationship to government policy making. Much of the attention here has centered on the alleged advantages of "neocorporatist" representation in certain European countries. Focusing on labor relations, Marks finds that political and policy success depends largely upon the degree to which the state can gain interest group acquiescence to policies imposing immediate costs in order to achieve long-term benefits. Although he identifies four distinct patterns of group–state interaction—neocorporatism, pluralism, quasi-corporatism, and dirigism—Marks argues that none is ideal for all nations. Rather, each nation should seek to adopt the approach that is best suited to its circumstances. Which elements of the left and right critiques identified by Zuckert apply to each of the patterns identified by Marks? Which mode of group–state interaction seems most desirable in the abstract? How do pluralist structures limit policy alternatives in a country like the United States?

The selection by Adam Przeworski and Michael Wallerstein, Chapter 4, stresses the political importance of economic theories. The authors assert that the economic crisis in advanced capitalist countries is at root a crisis of Keynesian economic theory. They describe Keynesianism in neo-Marxist terminology as a "class compromise"—one that allowed both profit accumulation and income redistribution but broke down as a capital shortage developed in the 1970s. They argue that greatly expanded public control of investment is much preferable to circumscribing democracy in the name of capital accumulation, as implied by the conservative doctrines now being followed by governments in Britain and America. Is this analysis of the grand alternatives valid? Is there a fundamental conflict between capitalism and democracy? What are the long-term implications of the collapse of the Keynesian paradigm?

These essays probe fundamental aspects of the relationship between state and economy, politics and markets, freedom and accountability. Current preoccupations with industrial growth and efficiency should not obscure the underlying ethical and political choices raised here. They will lie at the root of political economy for many years to come.

2 ON THE THEORY OF POLITICAL ECONOMY: IS LIBERALISM REALLY DEAD?

Catherine H. Zuckert

For the twenty-five years immediately following World War II, a widespread consensus reigned in both the United States and Western Europe: the social welfare state was the *only* viable form of liberal democracy. When Robert A. Dahl and Charles Lindblom declared in 1953 that there were no longer any "grand alternatives," they meant that both communism and fascism had been discredited by the World War II experience. Both "isms" had been shown to be unacceptably oppressive. "Laissez-faire" capitalism had also been discredited by the Great Depression, for the "free play" of the market destroyed producers as well as unemployed workers.

Constitutional protections of individual civil and political rights were necessary, but not sufficient, to preserve "liberal democracy." The economic benefits of the capitalistic system of production also had to be extended to all members of society. Whether that extension of welfare was a matter of humane charity, of right, or of political expediency remained a fundamental but subdued issue as long as the remarkable European economic recovery spurred by the Marshall Plan and a booming American economy made gradual, but steady, extension of social services relatively easy. John Maynard Keynes had shown that government intervention in the economy was necessary to mitigate the disastrous effects of business cycles, not merely by providing support for the victims in the form of unemployment compensation, food, health care, or other welfare benefits, but also by stimulating the economy to a full-employment level.

I wish to thank Michael P. Zuckert for his assistance in writing this chapter.

In 1960 Daniel Bell therefore announced "the end of ideology"; and a few years later even Richard Nixon declared, "We are all Keynesians." Among Western liberals there were no fundamental disagreements about the basic form of government, economy, or the relation between the two.

Ironically, the consensus began to break up just as the United States commenced a "war on poverty," an explicit attempt to extend the benefits of the system to the disadvantaged. For in the late 1960s attacks on the liberal welfare state appeared from both left and right. Although these critics began merely by suggesting that the mix of market economy and popular political responsibility characteristic of the liberal welfare state be altered somewhat—to obtain greater fairness or efficiency—opposition on both sides gradually became deeper and more thoroughgoing. On the right, as we shall see, the "economic" critique of the liberal welfare state on the grounds of its inefficiency led to a political critique, both procedural and principled. The more principled the critique, the more the state appeared to be a coercive agent whose oppressive potential must be limited as much as possible in order to preserve individual liberty. Where critics from the right pointed to an ever narrower range of legitimate governmental action with ever broader scope for the play of market forces, commentators from the left argued that more public supervision of private activity is necessary to achieve the egalitarian goals of liberal democracy. Beginning with an attempt to organize the poor and disadvantaged so that they, too, could obtain the benefits of "the system," leftist criticism also became more radical, as we shall see, to the point that some "New Left" writers concluded that any mix of market with democracy undermines the latter. After reviewing the apparently devastating criticism leveled at the liberal welfare state from both left and right, I will nevertheless argue that the uneasy mixture of market, popular responsibility, and bureaucracy characteristic of all current liberal democracies remains superior to either of its hypothetical alternatives.

THE RIGHT CRITIQUE

Criticism of the extensive governmental intervention in the economy characteristic of the liberal welfare state occurs on three different levels or grounds. "Right" critics fault the liberal welfare state first for being inefficient, second for distorting expressions of popular preferences, and third for curtailing freedom.

Using the Market to Increase Efficiency

Contemporary economists have pointed out the inefficiency involved not only in specific welfare policies like health or unemployment insurance but also in the articulation of macroeconomic policy itself. Former director of the Bureau of the Budget and chairman of the Council of Economic Advisors under President Carter, Charles L. Schultze, provides a preeminent example. The political institutions of the United States, or any participatory democracy, are "well-suited for generating compromises and accommodations about national issues needed in a large and heterogeneous society. [They are] especially designed to settle issues of value conflict" (Schultze, 1977, 88). But they often do not represent the most effective means of implementing the decisions. Even when market failures make governmental intervention necessary to achieve common goals, government may often succeed better if it utilizes economic incentives.

Economists who advocate the use of market mechanisms to implement public policy argue that economic incentives tend to work better than direct regulation or command for three related reasons. First, although all government regulations rest on the threat of coercion, economic transactions take place on the basis of consent. One trades only when one thinks that an exchange is, on balance, in one's interest, and the resulting action is hence voluntary. Since it takes two to trade, all trade agreements are unanimous as well as voluntary.

Second, government regulation or direction often presupposes knowledge that is not actually available (like the total energy resources of the nation or planet). Lack of reliable or accurate information is, indeed, one of the major reasons policies often fail to achieve their intended effects. By decentralizing decisions into the hands of profit-seeking producers and price-conscious consumers, market exchanges minimize the information any individual decision maker needs, while generating systemwide information about both supply and demand registered in prices. Rewarding producers of a desired public good with higher profits if they lower costs gives them an incentive to discover new modes of production, organization, or delivery of services. Such competitive, entrepreneurial experimentation also generates additional information, which makes better decisions possible.

Finally, the decentralization of market decisions, spread among millions of consumers and producers, makes it much more difficult for the group most hurt by any change to block innovation or adjustment in the relations of the economic factors of production. All such changes impose costs, for the short run at least, on some people, very often in the form of unemployment. To the extent to which the government manages or regulates economic enterprise, it will be subject to pressure from these people to protect their interests, to guarantee them a job or an income, and so to forestall or divert the adjustment that would take place in the absence of regulation. How can a popularly elected representative from Pittsburgh or Detroit convince his constituents that they ought to bear the major burden of enabling the nation as a whole to benefit from new technologies in steel or automobile production when they will demand that he seek protective measures to ensure their jobs and spread the cost in terms of higher prices throughout the nation?

Mancur Olson (1982) extended this critique to the "macro" level when he argued that the larger number of interest or potential "veto" groups in long-established polities like the United States or Great Britain has been the major cause of their relatively low rate of growth. Japan, West Germany, and France have had much higher rates of growth, Olson argued, because established groups were destroyed or their ability to influence policy severely limited in the immediate aftermath of World War II. The longer these nations have stable governments, however, the more their interests become organized and their productivity falls.

Olson, Schultze, and many other economists conclude that policies produced through the logrolling of special interests impose rigidities or artificial constraints on economic exchange that are necessarily costly— not simply in terms of economic production, but also in terms of employment. A classic example is the minimum wage. By imposing a floor on wages, most economists argue, labor unions have in effect deprived many teenagers and unskilled workers of potential income. These workers would be hired for less, but at the minimum wage their services cost more than they are worth to an employer.

Public Choice Analysis

Insight into the economic costs or inefficiencies caused by interest group politics leads rather directly to questioning the rationality of the legislative decision-making process itself: the economic critique quickly becomes a political critique also. If economic exchanges constitute such a superior way of implementing public policy, might they not constitute a more voluntaristic, rational, and efficient way of making political decisions also? The market-oriented critique of political decision making, it was seen, not only applied to policy implementation but also logically extended to policy determination as well.

Such a market-oriented analysis and evaluation of various possible procedures for making "collective choices" did not necessarily entail the antistatist conclusion that political decision making should be curtailed as far as possible. On the contrary, "public choice" theorists, as they came to be called, generally began from the admission of market failures characteristic of "welfare economics" (e.g. Buchanan and Tulloch, 1962). They began by recognizing situations in which the preferences or utilities of all members of the collectivity could not be maximized without coercive state action. Taking the maximization of popular preferences as an unquestioned goal, these theorists did not concern themselves so much with the substantive question of what the state should do as with the procedural question of how to determine the preferences, and hence the general direction, of the collectivity and its agent, the state.

Voting had traditionally been conceived as an expression of such preferences. The difficulty, Kenneth Arrow (1959) pointed out, was that there were situations when a majority vote would not reflect the actual preferences of the majority. Such results occurred when limited alternatives were considered in sequence—a procedure that proved to be quite analogous to the "logrolling" or "pork barrel" legislation characteristic of elected legislatures in large, heterogeneous societies. The problem then was to design political institutions so that they would approach the full expression, range, and ranking of individual (or, in a summative sense only, "collective") preferences and result in conditions of "Pareto optimality," when all individual utilities are maximized, or the condition at which no one can gain except at greater cost in utility to another.

Measured by the "economic" criteria of unanimous, completely voluntary agreement and Pareto optimality, most political decisions appeared questionable. Unanimity was easily seen to be an impossible rule for collective decisions because the veto, and hence the virtually insuperable bargaining position, it gave any dissenter makes the potential cost of decision too high. Any state action under such circumstances tends to be at least as costly for the vast majority that desires the legislation as no action at all. Utilities would not, therefore, be apt to be maximized under such circumstances. Rules requiring less than unanimity, on the other hand, make it rational for individuals to organize in order to be able to bargain more effectively with others. And it turns out to be rational for groups to conceal the true extent and intensity of their preferences in the process of bargaining, thereby creating problems of information and accuracy with regard to expression of the "popular will." Groups may either understate their preferences in the hope of making a better bargain by giving up less in order to get the results they dearly want, or they may overstate their desire in the hope of blackmailing the opposition into giving way. The rationality of organization for the individual leads, moreover, to overinvestment in organization from the perspective of the whole society; more time is spent lobbying than producing. The economic analysis of public choice thus increasingly tended to constitute a critique of politics as generally experienced in liberal democracies and pointed toward the rationality of substituting a more marketlike process of making decisions by assigning new rights, in clean air or traffic space, for example, and allowing individuals to trade these rights as they do more traditional forms of property (see Buchanan, 1976).

For individuals to trade rights in air or traffic space, however, they had to be granted such rights, and the allocation of such rights proved, upon examination, to be immensely difficult. Air could easily be conceived of as belonging to everyone in common, but how could or should individual assignments be made? On the basis of need? Labor or appropriation? Force? Convention or agreement? Why is or ought air to be treated differently from land? What about the generational problem? Can the father legitimately trade away the rights of his son to breathe?

Determination of economic policy through market exchange was already subject to persistent criticism on the grounds of the unequal distribution of the goods to be exchanged. If each individual does not possess an equal amount to exchange, the market does not express the preferences of individuals equally. On the contrary, for every "vote" or exchange decision the "dollar-a-year" man can make on his salary, the millionaire has a million. The more noneconomic goods were transformed into propertylike, exchangeable "rights," therefore, the more pressure would grow for active state intervention in the exchange process in order to redistribute "rights" equally. Since redistributive action would cancel both the efficiency and the expression of differential individual preferences achievable through market exchanges, Buchanan and others began to conclude, the state should *not* step in where the market "fails." Rather, the state should limit itself, e.g., through constitutional amendments requiring a balanced budget or prohibiting protective tariffs, in order to secure both the economic and political benefits of market exchange in as large an arena as possible.

Recent experience with Keynesian macroeconomic policy appeared, moreover, to support the very same conclusion. In the first place, fine-tuning proved not to be a feasible strategy for elected legislatures, which worked too slowly under too much pressure from specific interests. For example, although economists in the Johnson administration saw that the economy was heating up as early as 1965, it took two years to convince Congress to pass a surtax, which was then too little, too late. Moreover, Keynesian policies turned out to have an interventionist bias, with an emphasis on spending (Buchanan and Wagner, 1977). Whether that bias came from the moral, intellectual, or programmatic commitments of people in government, from a distortion of prices so that public goods appeared cheaper than they really were, or from the discrepancy between public desires defined as the sum of the demands of many specific interest groups or constituencies and general public desires for less bureaucracy and lower taxes, the conclusion drawn by the critics was the same: We should have less government, and the best, perhaps only way to achieve this would be through constitutional amendment (Friedman, 1980; Buchanan, 1976; Wildavsky, 1980). Government with all its inefficiency and irrationality would continue to expand if logrolling politics continued unabated. Finally, "rational-expectationist" theorists pointed out that government could not stimulate the economy by increasing spending repeatedly or over the long term, in any case. The "stimulative" effect depended essentially on workers continuing to work at their old rate of pay, for a time, so that investment or employment by firms would come out of rising profits. As soon as workers realized the effect of government spending, they would demand their "fair share," with the result that wages and prices moved up in line with public economic predictions. A policy that depended for its success on depriving laborers of relevant information concerning their conditions of employment appeared immoral as well as ineffective.

Limiting Government to Protect Liberty

Economic analyses of specific regulatory policies, of the political process, and of manipulative macroeconomic policy thus all pointed to the same conclusion: government should be reduced. Since public services had originally been extended on humanitarian grounds—to provide jobs for all who would work, to care for those who could not take care of themselves, to overcome the effects of past discrimination—reduction of government had to face the charge that it was simply inhumane. "Individualism" or freedom had to be defended as the primary political end or concern, which mandated limits on government. Three quite different defenses of liberty emerged.

The first, associated most prominently with the names of Milton Friedman and Ronald Reagan, looks primarily to the American political tradition to support the claim that individual liberty is and ought to be our primary political goal. Liberty is maximized, these men argue, when there is least government. And when government cannot be altogether avoided, it should be as decentralized as possible. Individuals have greater access to and potential influence upon small governments than on big; and where the policies of local governments vary, a resident can dissent by moving into another jurisdiction, if he does not like the policies of the government under which he presently lives. The accusation that minimal government rests solely on human selfishness and hence is immoral is, moreover, truly unfounded, according to the advocates of limited government. That accusation could more properly be made of the welfare state itself. Can one realistically speak of humane feeling, much less generosity, when help is provided through taxation and coercion? Those unable to care for themselves should be assisted, but most social services should and would be better provided by private agencies. More extensive government simply produces more extensive dependency. Higher welfare benefits not merely reduce incentives to work or produce, but they also undermine the individual's belief in his ability as well as his responsibility to care for himself and others, a condition altogether unsuitable for citizens of a self-governing nation.

The difficulty with an appeal to tradition is, of course, that it is only tradition. To say that it is "the American way" is not to establish its moral superiority. Why not sacrifice some freedom, a skeptic might ask, in order to obtain more equality, generosity, humanity, or justice?

In *The Constitution of Liberty* Friedrich Hayek attempts to meet that challenge by arguing that freedom must be the primary goal because it constitutes the necessary condition for the attainment of all others, moral as well as material. We express our moral judgments in terms of praise or blame, and it does not make sense to praise someone for acting well unless he could have acted badly. Moral judgments thus presuppose liberty of action.

Liberty is most clearly and fundamentally understood in terms of its opposite, slavery. To be free means simply not to be under the coercive power of another. Freedom so defined is a negative condition, but, Hayek observes, that does not make it less good. Peace is also negatively defined as the absence of war, and its negative definition does not make peace any less desirable. Freedom does not guarantee happiness; liberty alone will not enable men to rule themselves, but it is the absolutely necessary prerequisite for both.

To the extent to which they lack knowledge, people will make mistakes, do evil things, and suffer as a consequence. To live better, they need to increase their knowledge. Freedom is again the prerequisite, because human beings acquire knowledge only through trial and error, and people can undertake experiments or try to innovate only when and where they live in freedom.

Unlike many libertarians, Hayek does not regard the maximization of individual choice as the most important manifestation of human freedom. Nor does he think that it is accurate to conceive of market exchange as an expression of individual preferences, as if either individuals or their preferences have a set, stable, independent existence. Rather, he observes, individuals develop their particular talents, characteristics, preferences, or "utilities" only in the society of others. Their morals, indeed their personalities, are to a large extent products of that society. They preserve themselves and prosper only with the cooperation and on the basis of the knowledge and experience of others. The more civilized the society, the greater the division of labor or specialization. The more civilized the society, therefore, the more differentiation or individuation. The more specialization, however, the more each individual depends on the knowledge of others. Rationality does not exist so much in the individual decision maker or choice as in the broader system of exchange. Social exchange extends beyond the market, moreover; it includes the experiential, practical wisdom embedded in customs and laws that have grown up over generations. This emphatically social possession is less easily recognized as knowledge than the more theoretical sciences individuals learn in school, but it is nevertheless much more fundamental and important to their happiness.

Critics object to unregulated economic exchange, Hayek recognizes, not because they wish to constrain liberty or to restrict productivity but because they believe the distribution of goods that results is unjust. But, he responds, a just distribution of goods is not possible because we cannot know enough about each person's situation to reward each according to his moral merit. Market value does not reflect intrinsic value; it merely reflects "the perceived value of a person's actions and services to others." There is nothing wrong with a productive society deciding to help its less fortunate or less profitable members; Hayek simply insists that those benefited do not have a right to part of the results of the labor of others absent the consent of those others.

Hayek's agnostic approach to the problem of distributive justice has been challenged recently by the libertarian thinker Robert Nozick. "People will not long accept a distribution they believe is *unjust*" (1968, 158). To argue, as Hayek does, that market distribution merely reflects the perceived value of a person's services to others ignores the fact that some have more wealth or income with which to express their perceptions of value than do others. Market value reflects the distribution of resources as well as perceptions or preferences, and resources are divided unequally as a result not merely of market exchange but also of inheritance or even pure chance. The market does not, therefore, operate as a system of proportional representation in which each group registers its preferences without coercing others, as Friedman and Hayek claim, because the distribution of goods or income determines the extent to which any individual can express his desires.

Hayek uses a rather traditional notion of justice as giving each his or her due. In fact, Nozick argues, there is no ground upon which we can agree to regard one human being superior to another, i.e., as deserving more as a matter of right. Nozick thus concludes that redistributive policies are altogether unjustifiable on the basis of the Kantian principle that no man should be treated solely as a means to another's ends.

Why should one man not sacrifice some part of his income in order to maximize the common good? Nozick gives two reasons. First, the empirical: "There is no *social entity* with a good that undergoes some sacrifice for its own good. *There are only individual people. . . .* with their own individual lives" (emphasis added). Second, the moral: "Using one of these people for the benefit of others, uses him and benefits the others.

Nothing more. . . . He does not get some overbalancing good from his sacrifice, and no one is entitled to force this upon him" (1968, 32–33).

Since there are only individuals, the only justification for governmental "services" or coercion must be found in the desires or consent of the individuals concerned. Taxing one to benefit another is the equivalent of taking someone's labor or imposing partial slavery. No one and hence no one's labor (or its product) can justly be sacrificed to someone else, and thus no redistributive social policy can be just.

Nozick's own critique of redistributive welfare state policies is particularly impressive because it proceeds on the grounds egalitarians usually employ to attack the market and to justify intervention: justice and human dignity. But Nozick's critique of redistributive welfare policies ignores the social foundations of the development of individuality itself, which Hayek stresses. Recognition of the social matrix of all individual development and effort gives rise, in fact, to the left rebuttal of the individualistic assumptions characteristic of the right critique along with a demand for more social control of economic enterprise.

THE LEFT CRITIQUE

A market economy is not properly conceived merely as a string of individual acts or decisions, critics on the left tend to argue; exchange is rather an essentially social process. It takes at least two parties to trade, and the interaction of many more to get the advantages of specialization or an extensive division of labor. Economic activity is not an inherently satisfying activity. People do not engage in commerce or manufacture for its own sake so much as for the extrinsic rewards. If the benefits of economic exchange presuppose social interaction, however, these benefits cannot be explained, nor should they be distributed solely on the basis of individual effort, talent, or mere good fortune. If economic interaction involves all the members of a given society, the benefits ought to be attributed to the community as a whole. Where a large portion of the populace remains economically disadvantaged, especially in the midst of prosperity, the legitimacy of the existing mode of political and economic organization comes seriously into question.

To view the market abstractly, simply as a way of "optimizing" individual "utilities," obscures the fact that those who have the most resources to express their preferences also have the most power to see them established. It is a mistake to see market exchange merely as a mode of production; by distributing goods and services unequally, the market also allocates power to some to control the lives of others.

Because the market produces such great disparities in income and wealth, it does not truly reflect popular preferences or adequately serve essential human needs. The distribution of benefits and burdens through a market can obviously be altered through political action, however. The market or price system is, after all, only one of several possible ways of making *social* decisions about the allocation of *social* resources, commentators like Dahl and Lindblom argue. It does not always produce the most efficient, much less the most just, results. There is such a thing as market failure, for example, when neither the manufacturers nor the consumers of goods produced through a polluting process pay the costs, whether measured in terms of health or cleanup charges; these costs are borne rather by the public at large. It is therefore rational to experiment with other modes of decision making as well.

Bargaining represents an alternative mode of allocating social resources. The laws facilitating unionization, for example, were intended to substitute bargaining among organized groups for exchanges among discrete individuals in the marketplace. But organizing labor or consumer groups to counteract the concentrated economic power of corporations has not worked, critics like Frances Fox Piven and Richard Cloward (1971) argue, because the economic, organizational, and political resources of the respective groups are too unequal. More direct public ownership and control are necessary, they conclude, to achieve real social responsibility in economic enterprise.

Critics on the left thus call for more governmental interference in the economy in three different degrees of intensity, in order to achieve three somewhat different ends. First, left critics generally wish the government to act to improve the lot of the disadvantaged or to equalize income. Second, more severe critics of the welfare state wish to make the political process itself more truly democratic or to equalize power and influence. Third, some of the more radical critics argue that it is impossible to have a truly cooperative community until the competition and specialization associated with market exchange are entirely abolished.

Securing Greater Benefits for the Least Advantaged

The welfare state claims to remedy at least the worst effects of a market economy by protecting people from involuntary unemployment, disability, or other sources of earning incapacity. It does not tend to redistribute income per se. Baldly redistributive policies are, in fact, rather difficult to enact and execute in majoritarian liberal democracies where the poor are a minority and the majority stands to lose by the redistribution.

During the 1960s liberal governments therefore attempted to increase both the level and extent of welfare benefits without increasing the tax burden of the relatively advantaged. Rather than finance more extensive social services by raising taxes, these governments attempted to fund more generous welfare programs through the additional revenues generated by a growing economy. In the United States the Kennedy administration even lowered taxes in order to stimulate further economic growth. Increased governmental spending is a more effective stimulus than decreased taxation, liberal Keynesian economists like Walter Heller argued, because the poor tend to spend all their incremental income whereas the rich tend to hoard it. Increased transfer payments could therefore be justified as contributing to the general health of the economy, not as penalizing the rich (or middle) classes in order to help the poor.

Although benefits to those who could not work increased in the context of active full-employment policies, vast disparities in income, wealth, education, and health remained. In the United States, for example, critics were shocked to discover that nearly 25 percent of the population lived in poverty; expanded transfer programs reduced the number to 15 percent, but millions still lived in poverty in the wealthiest nation in history! Even in Sweden, where the "safety net" is much larger (including medical and dental services as well as housing and a family allowance), studies in the late 1960s showed that over a third of the working force earned less than $2,000 a year, and nearly 300,000 Swedes had an annual income below $600—surely less than subsistence in that nation's high-priced economy (Furniss and Tilton, 1977, 148). Why this destitution in the midst of general prosperity? critics asked.

In the liberal welfare state, the distribution of wealth and income is determined partly by direct governmental policies of taxation and redistributive transfer payments and partly by market outcomes, themselves heavily dependent on political settlements regarding such things as property ownership and investment policy. To some extent, then, the distribution of wealth and income is determined politically. When the disadvantaged fail to gain their fair share of the national product, left critics reasoned, it is not merely because they cannot compete successfully in the market. They suffer more fundamentally from an inability to act on their own behalf politically. What is necessary, these critics concluded, is to organize the poor so that they will be able to press their demands on elected officials more effectively. In the United States the "war on poverty" was thus accompanied by the "community action program" (Moynihan, 1969).

Ironically, the "organizational strategy" came under fire at just the time the CAP was being designed and implemented. Organization is not the way to improve the situation of poor or otherwise disadvantaged citizens, critics began to argue, because organization itself produces serious inequities. For members, labor unions, farm bureaus, commodity groups, etc. are instrumental in acquiring higher incomes or other benefits. They have little or no interest in the organization per se. For the officers, on the other hand, the organization itself becomes the source of income, prestige, and power. They thus acquire a stake in the status and perpetuity of the organization and its connections to other organizations of influence, independent of the desires of the members. As full-time employees in contrast to members who have to spend their time earning a living in a different fashion, paid staff are able not only to acquire more information about relevant policies and procedures but also to control the agenda of membership meetings and so, to a certain extent, to determine which issues come up for debate on what terms. Even where laws guarantee elections of interest group representatives, as in labor unions, these laws fail to tie the officers to the interests of their members in the absence of competing parties, effective guarantees of individual free speech (without reprisals), and full disclosure of financial and other organizational information (McConnell, 1966).

But the more the state regulates the internal operations of private interest groups, critics like Theodore J. Lowi pointed out (1967), the less the interaction of such groups operates as a check on public power. On the contrary, as more recent neocorporatist thinkers have concluded, the state finds it extremely useful to bring representatives of various groups into both the policy-making and administrative processes in order to secure their members' cooperation and consent. Even those who see corporatist structures as adding stability and governability to Western democracies think these advantages are "purchased at the price of organizational sclerosis, rigidification of differentials, perpetuation of inequalities, and most of all, disregard for the individualistic norms of citizen participation and accountability characteristic of a liberal democratic order" (Schmitter, 1981, 323). Not merely the effects of organization itself but even the increased benefits attained through pressure politics began to look more and more like means of manipulation, which served to mollify the dispossessed and so to maintain established forms of power and influence (Piven and Cloward, 1971).

So, it appeared to many critics, merely organizing the disadvantaged would not suffice to produce a truly just or democratic society; the interaction of interest groups is not a substitute for popular electoral control of public policy. Popular control had not resulted in an adequate redistribution of income, these critics began to conclude, because excessive reliance on the market for making economic decisions not only produces unnecessarily great inequalities of income but also pollutes the democratic political process itself. More directly and explicitly redistributive political action would be required to achieve real equality of power as well as of wealth.

Achieving Real Democracy

"One person, one vote" is *the* principle of democratic government. Voting means more than mechanically pushing a lever, however; the effective meaning of the principle ˙is that each citizen ought to have an equal chance to affect the outcome of a contested election or policy decision. Where some have the power to hire lawyers to lobby, to propagate their views through advertising, and to contribute heavily to the campaigns of legislators who support them, and where others cannot even read, the ability of each citizen to influence the outcome of a debate about public policy is obviously not equal. And the major source of this political inequality is clearly the economic inequality generated by a largely unregulated market economy.

To institute truly democratic control over economic policy, Dahl (1977) thus concludes, it will be necessary not merely to redistribute income on a massive scale but also to reorganize industrial production to give workers a real voice in the allocative or investment decisions that affect their livelihood so massively and immediately. More public control, especially of the national media, will also be necessary, Lindblom (1977) suggests, because "the privileged position of business" does not rest simply on its superior material resources. Elected legislators hesitate to press either regulation or nationalization too far because they fear they will lose their constituents' jobs (and hence their constituents' electoral support). No one wants to hurt business. But "business" is not the only possible mode of organizing or directing economic activity, Lindblom objects; liberal democracies ought to be experimenting more with planning and public ownership. There has been very little such experimentation in the United States since the New Deal and the TVA, however, because control of the media has enabled corporations to convince both the public and their representatives that private enterprise is the only proven means of producing prosperity.

As long as a majority of the populace does not own or control the majority of the wealth and the income it generates, that state cannot be truly democratic, these procedural critics argue. In a democracy, the majority has the power to control the economy and so to redistribute income in its own favor. Where no such redistribution occurs, therefore, the majority must not actually rule. The character of the process is to be determined by the results.

Unfortunately, the relation of equal rights (or liberties, e.g. of speech) to equal economic results is left fundamentally unclear in the democratic procedural critique. Would it be legitimate for the majority simply to expropriate the goods of the wealthy minority? How much inequality in income or wealth is legitimate for the sake of maintaining productive incentives? How much differentiation in knowledge, information, or occupation? Like the procedural critique of the welfare state posed by public choice theorists, the democratic critique ultimately needs to be grounded in a moral argument concerning the nature and foundation of individual rights.

John Rawls promised to offer just such a moral justification for a more egalitarian version of the liberal welfare state in his much acclaimed *A Theory of Justice* (1971). The rationale for the expanded social services characteristic of the liberal welfare state is usually stated in terms of "equal opportunity," Rawls observes; we provide education, housing, and even income assistance to ensure each citizen a chance to develop his or her own talents. No one's fate should be determined merely by family or class. Since native talents differ, however, so will incomes and positions.

But, Rawl presses, what exactly is wrong with letting one's family background determine one's economic position, or buying a degree in order to qualify as a teacher or lawyer? Is not the notion that one should advance only on the basis of his or her own talents, not the gifts or wealth of others, essentially the notion that one should be rewarded only on the basis of his or her own merit or desert as opposed to accidental or external qualities? If a person does not choose and hence is not responsible for his or her family, so one should not be rewarded or penalized on the basis of family. But if effort, or, more broadly, the character that leads some to work harder than others, is itself a product of one's family background, as many sociologists think, then no one should be rewarded or penalized for effort. Even more radically, if one is not responsible for one's natural potential, if native talents are distributed accidentally, acquired without choice or control, then no one deserves a reward for the exercise of these accidental qualities (see M. Zuckert, 1981).

Nevertheless, Rawls concludes, such abstract equality does not mandate simply equal results. To determine what abstract equality does require, he constructs a hypothetical mode of decision making. Assuming that all human beings desire their own welfare (or are self-interested), Rawls argues, we can determine what equality requires by imagining a human being without knowledge of his own particular (accidental) attributes or circumstances (behind the "veil of ignorance") and ask him to determine the method of distribution for all citizens (i.e., by putting him in "the original position"). Such a man (or mind) will approve only those policies that will benefit him. Since he does not know his own actual position, he will (rather conservatively) have to assume that he may be on the very bottom. He will therefore approve only policies that benefit the least advantaged along with everyone else. Differential rewards in terms of income or prestige are legitimate if and only if they serve as incentives that increase the total resources of society in which all (not merely most but even the least advantaged) share.

The Need to Abolish Both Market and Bureaucracy

Rawls's theory does not effectively overcome the damaging and estranging effects of the division of labor by revealing the moral foundations of a "just social union . . . in which all can freely participate" (Rawls, 1971, 529), Marxist critics respond, because the very assumptions upon which he constructs "the original position" perpetuate the competitive, self-interested ethic of corporate capitalism. In order to institute a truly just society, these critics argue, we must replace calculations of individual self-interest with truly communitarian norms and institutions.

Since actual Marxist regimes have failed so abysmally to protect the civil rights of their citizens, Marxist critics expect to meet objections on these grounds. Due process (e.g. in trials and imprisonment), and freedom of speech are important, Ralph Miliband (1969; 1982) thus assures his readers, but civil rights will not suffice to attain real liberty and equality. As long as a part of any nation controls the means of production, it controls the livelihood and hence the lives of others, and under such circumstances, individuals cannot really be free. Legal rights are not at all the same as effective powers. Individual stockholders officially own large corporations, for example, but they do not effectively control the salaried management. And workers find it difficult to resist manipulation by either their corporate or their labor bosses.

Without complete public control, Miliband thus suggests, society will continue to be characterized by class conflict based on the real difference of interest between the bosses and their subordinates. Since conflict and distrust hamper rather than further human endeavor, there is reason to believe that a truly communitarian society will be much more productive. Radical experimentation is hampered, however, by popular attachment to such bourgeois means of manipulation and mollification as unionization, increased welfare benefits, or "labor party" coalition governments.

Although Miliband admits that there are important differences in the interests and attitudes of career civil servants, professionals (lawyers and doctors), politicians, journalists, and corporate executives, he nevertheless insists that the managers of modern industrial societies have even more important commonalities in background, education, associations, and expectations. Most important, as a class they possess a disproportionate amount of influence and wealth. To be sure, they have had to share some of their power with labor leaders, not only in contract negotiations but also in parliamentary politics. By increasing the influence of the more moderate representatives of the working classes as well as by extending public services, the managers have primarily served their own interests in maintaining the established order by discouraging radical revolution.

Somewhat ironically, Miliband thus comes to the same conclusion Hayek had twenty years earlier in *The Road to Serfdom:* socialist parties will never achieve their goals through parliamentary maneuver and legislative reform. The bureaucratic management that necessarily grows with the extension of public services characteristic of the liberal welfare state is an inherently unegalitarian, antirevolutionary phenomenon. Like some right critics of the welfare state, some radical egalitarian reformers seek therefore to minimize state control by decentralizing the power to make social decisions. Where "right" critics would decentralize decisions to individuals or firms in a market, however, radical left critics wish to establish small egalitarian communities.

Trying to avoid the oppression they see in present "Marxist" as well as "capitalist" societies, "New Left" critics like the Cohn-Bendits argue that it is necessary to put an end to "the division of labor *and of knowledge,* which serves only to isolate people one from the others" (1968, emphasis added). As Alain Touraine (1971, 63) observes, differences in knowledge and organizational skill can create even greater estrangement and inequality than differences in wealth and income. To establish a true community in the place of self-interested competition, it thus appears necessary not only to abolish private property but also to destroy the differences of interest, opinion, occupation, and information that now separate man from man.

Proposals to do away with the division of labor entirely appear to be rather utopian or naive, however. A community in which there is no differentiation in knowledge, property, or occupation would have to live a very primitive life indeed. Such communities would clearly lack the marvels of advanced medical technology, for example, to say nothing of the productive advances connected with chemical fertilization. As Marx himself points out, such small communities cannot effectively defend themselves from being absorbed by larger political or economic systems. As Rawls recognizes, people do not really want to be equal merely at a subsistence or "starvation" level, and to have a prosperous society it is necessary to maintain both incentives and specialization. Bureaucracy may be hierarchical, but as Furniss and Tilton point out, it is difficult to imagine an egalitarian government run on the basis of favoritism or incompetence, i.e., nonbureaucratically: "Precisely the values that Max Weber attributed to bureaucracy—efficiency, rationality, and impersonality—make it indispensable" (1977, 90). Democracy defined as complete equality of condition—income, occupation, influence, and information—

is thus not merely inefficient but fundamentally unfeasible. A more balanced and accurate view of the real political possibilities of advanced industrial societies would thus seem to be in order.

In Defense of the Liberal Welfare State

To a large extent, the three levels of criticism of the liberal welfare state on the left parallel the three on the right. Both left and right agree that organized groups have an invidious effect on public policy, especially with regard to the production and distribution of economic goods. Both extend their criticism of the policy results of group influence to the legislative process characteristic of Western liberal democracies because both sides agree that this process does not produce results truly reflective of the will of the majority. Not surprisingly then, both sides finally conclude that the liberal welfare state is unjust. Upon examination, however, neither critique proves tenable. Rather, the factors or concerns emphasized by the right tend to counterbalance those stressed by the left—and vice versa.

Checking the Power of "Special Interests"

The economic critique of the invidious effects of organized interests in terms of "efficiency" can be and has easily been transformed into a critique on the grounds of justice: those able to organize and lobby to protect their own interests impose costs on the weak and unorganized, whether they be consumers, taxpayers, or welfare recipients. Since any attempt to abolish organized pressure groups would have unacceptably high political costs in lost freedom of speech and assembly (as well as unacceptably high economic costs in the loss of corporate efficiency), it is not really desirable or feasible to think in terms of the abolition of interest groups. The only practical response to problems of organized influence must be some means of counteracting its harmful effects.

Unfortunately, as the pluralists discovered, it simply is not possible to organize all interests or to represent all opinions in a large and diverse society, and all advanced industrial societies are large and diverse as a result of the extensive division of labor or specialization. Since organized groups are not equal, their jostling does not necessarily produce an equilibrium approximating the common interest. But to limit government in order to limit the influence of organized pressure groups, as Friedman suggests (1980), is to leave organized economic power unchecked. There is, moreover, considerable evidence to show that corporate managers do not seek to maximize productivity or efficiency so much as personal and corporate security; corporate organization itself can produce the kinds of inefficiencies attributed to political lobbying. Reliance on informal mechanisms—whether in the form of market exchanges or group bargaining—will not suffice to achieve optimal outcomes; intentional political action will also be necessary at times to protect the interests of the whole from the machinations or even merely mistaken calculations of a part.

When the economy does not perform to popular satisfaction, the majority rationally seeks to use its political muscle to make economic power more responsive to its wishes. This is precisely what public regulations in the United States, or partial public ownership in more socialistic European nations, represents. Put in more dynamic terms, the liberal welfare state represents a balance between two kinds of threats: irresponsible (whether by virtue of inefficiency, inhumanity, or sheer arrogance) economic management is threatened with public control (whether in the form of regulation or ownership) when it does not produce satisfactory results, whereas the extension of public control is limited by the potential costs of increasing an essentially unproductive public bureaucracy and diminishing private incentives. Since this "balance" is by no means self-equilibrating, it can be achieved only through an intentional, if often somewhat experimental, extension or limitation of public power.

The Limits of Popular Preference

Both public choice theorists and more egalitarian left critics like Dahl and Lindblom object to current welfare policies primarily on the grounds that these policies do not accurately reflect the preferences, interests, or desires of the majority. In stressing the importance of having policy reflect majority opinion, however, both procedural critiques of the liberal welfare state tend to ignore the need for independence of judgment, information, and practical political experience in the formulation of legislation or policy.

Left critics like Dahl bring out the distributional difficulty in the public choice theorists' argument that the market reflects popular preferences more clearly than brokered votes in a legislature. Unless each "voter" or buyer has equal resources, market exchange weighs the preferences of each according to his or her resources. However, the economic analyses of political decision making also bring out some of the difficulties in Dahl's understanding of democracy as simple majoritarianism.

If advanced industrial societies are not homogeneous or simply divided into two classes of owners and workers, as Dahl himself admits, there is no simple, uniform "majority." On the contrary, "majorities" have to be constructed; they vary from issue to issue; on some, perhaps many issues, it is probably inaccurate even to speak of the view of "the majority," since few citizens have enough information or concern even to formulate an opinion. If, as Arrow argues, "majority" votes often reflect the way the alternatives are posed more than the actual viewpoint(s) of the voters, the legitimacy of "majority rule" becomes extremely problematic. Why should this particular majority decide the issue for the whole community when there are other possible majorities within it? What gives the greater number a right, in any case, simply to impose its view(s) on others?

In fact, neither the reality nor the requirements of political decision making in advanced industrial societies can be captured in terms merely of the expression of preferences or pure majoritarianism. In the first place, as Hayek argues, the "preferences" of individuals are not "givens," derived in abstraction from interaction with others simply to be registered in votes. There is, or at least can be, a process of deliberation in which individuals modify their views, in part simply as a result of hearing others. Certainly there is an observable difference between an immediate reaction to a question on the basis of one's presuppositions, preferences, or prejudices and an informed judgment reached only after a review of all the available evidence, expert testimony from several points of view, as well as popular, partisan pressures. That is one of the reasons public opinion polls have validity only for the moment at which they are taken and do not constitute a reliable basis for predicting future electoral results, much less grounding future policy. It is one of the reasons polls show that a majority of the American public does not want to govern by poll; they wish rather to elect more knowledgeable representatives with time to study the issues before they make specific policy decisions.

The notion that "the majority" ought to rule, always and directly, thus also ignores the effects of the division of labor or specialization in politics as well as economics. Direct democracy is possible only in very small communities where the population is homogeneous and the issues of public policy not very complex. It is doubtful that the majority of the population of any large industrialized nation would willingly accept the enormous economic costs of dividing the nation into small governing units. It is also doubtful that the members of these units would retain their civil liberties. Where there is not complete homogeneity, James Madison observed, both in *The Federalist Papers* and in a letter to Jefferson, the majority simply imposes its will and interests on the minority. Unless there is a very strict system of frequent rotation in office, moreover, differences of interest, information, and organizational ability develop as soon as some are elected to office. Frequent rotation in office means, however, that no public official has much experience or expertise in performing his or her particular job. Both the economic and the political costs of direct democracy or pure majoritarianism are apt, therefore, to be very high.

Advanced industrial nations are not and cannot be strictly and directly governed by majority rule because the formulation of public policy in these complex societies requires not only a great deal of expert information but also time to absorb it. Since all citizens cannot work at different occupations and have time to acquire all the information relevant to specific policy decisions, they have no real choice but to trust officials to make the best decisions possible and then vote these officials in or out at the next election, according to the results. Voters can do more than choose among competing elites in elections; they can also communicate general, but only very general, policy preferences. They cannot possibly transform these preferences accurately or effectively into specific laws and regulations. That is and must be the task of professionals.

The complex relationship between representative institutions and appointed bureaucracies in the governments of advanced industrial societies arises, in fact, from just this need to combine popular with knowledgeable "responsibility." "Responsibility" is most often defined in debates about elected or party government in terms of responsiveness to popular or majoritarian desires. But it is clearly not responsible for an official (elected or appointed) to advocate a policy he knows will have enormous costs that the public fails to recognize, i.e., it is not responsible for an official to act against information he possesses and knows the public at large lacks. Responsible government means more than being responsive to or reflective of the majority's "will."

Neither the market nor the majoritarian model serves as an adequate explanation or standard whereby to judge the performance of large liberal democracies because both models take one and only one relevant factor into account. The same proves true of the more principled critiques of the liberal welfare state—whether on grounds of imperfect equality or liberty—because neither perfect equality (even simply economic equality) nor minimal government is actually possible or desirable in a large industrial society.

The Need to Balance Different Kinds of Goods and Processes

Even if all wealth and income were redistributed, Nozick (1968) and Michael Walzer (1983) point out, both would quickly become unequal again as long as people are allowed to buy what they want. (Would one really want to prohibit people from paying a modest fee to see Larry Bird play basketball, to parody Nozick's example, even though Bird would thus amass a great fortune based entirely on voluntary exchange? The government could, to be sure, try to equalize incomes again at the end of the year through steeply progressive taxation, but would Bird then be willing to play as often as the fans want?) It is not possible to allow individuals a wide range of choice in buying, much less voting, and to maintain strict economic equality, because some persons and goods will emerge as more valuable (or at least desired) than others. There is, therefore, a reason for the great constriction of choice, both consumer and electoral, in Marxist regimes, but there is also a well-known price in loss of civil liberties as well as productivity for their attempts to achieve economic equality. And the effects of the division of labor in the form of bureaucratic privileges still destroy real equality of income. Pure, simple, or unqualified equality can only mean enforced standardization at the lowest common denominator, which is not what anyone wants.

Because advanced industrial societies are necessarily characterized by differentiation, they will necessarily be characterized by inequality, disagreement, and potential conflict. All these differences are not economic, moreover, either in origin or manifestation. As the radical critics see, information and organizational skill can be even more important sources of influence than income or wealth, and individual differences in native potential are particularly important in both intellectual endeavors and positions of leadership. Equalizing incomes will not produce equal political power, whereas attempts to "standardize" opinions and occupations are clearly oppressive.

As both right and left critics of the liberal welfare state show, the demands of equality stand in tension with the requirements of efficiency, but this is by no means the only tension. Effective governmental regulation of economic activity requires both organizational and expert knowledge, yet, as Hayek argues, governmental regulation must be limited in order to generate the necessary knowledge. Bureaucratic organization may create both inefficiency and inequality, but as Furniss and Tilton argue, bureaucratic organization is an essential component of any nonpersonalistic or abstractly egalitarian regime. Lawyers are among the most specialized of the technocrats characteristic of advanced industrial societies, yet where there are no regulations or lawyers to contest them, civil liberties have no effective guarantees.

Michael Walzer's contention that there is an irreducible plurality of "goods" to be allocated in any society and that these "goods" are necessarily distributed through different kinds of procedures is truer to observed facts than the abstract individualistic egalitarianism of either Rawls or Nozick. Unfortunately, Walzer does not think through the implications of his particularistic pluralism with the analytic rigor both philosophers employ.

Market exchange is only one kind of social interaction suitable only for the distribution of certain kinds of goods, Walzer sees, because there really are things money cannot buy. For example, he suggests, one could bribe the judges for the Pulitzer prize, but if their "price" became public (as it would have to in a "market"), or even if the secret corruption continued, the prize would lose its value. Even if bought once in secret, the prize lacks the value for its possessor that it would have if properly bestowed. Prizes for best performances cannot be divided among many like food, and they can be allocated only by a panel with specialized knowledge.

There are also winners of popular elections, but electoral victories differ from prizes in two respects. First, the voters do not possess expert or detailed knowledge of a representative's activity or platform. The larger the number of electors, the more general and ill informed the judgment is apt to be. Second, elections concern anticipated outcomes as well as past performance; they express popular desires for future governmental policy as well as confidence (or lack thereof) in a particular candidate's record. In order to get a majority, moreover, the alternatives must be limited. Political decisions thus most properly concern indivisible goods. There can be only one "government" or "administration," for example; the nation cannot go to war in parts. When the decision is an "either/or," "right or wrong," which all members of a society will be forced to follow, voting is an appropriate mode of expressing popular consent (or rejection). Where goods are disaggregable and nonessential, however, markets provide both more accurate and less coercive ways of expressing popular tastes.

Not only are there different "goods" in every polity that have to be both produced and allocated in different ways, but the requirements of producing and allocating these goods often conflict. Dahl is unfortunately correct when he observes that daily employment in a huge hierarchy where one's very livelihood depends upon pleasing superiors does not render a person fit for self-rule or exercising democratic control. However efficient or stabilizing, corporate economic organization thus imposes political costs. Likewise, as Hayek argues, every governmental regulation of economic endeavor necessarily discourages experimentation and innovation because even the best-designed regulations must employ existing knowledge or "state of the art" technology, which they then impose on the future. To be legitimate, laws have to be passed by a majority, but experiments are almost always undertaken by minorities. Because popular opinion must at best rest on existing knowledge, it is always inherently and necessarily conservative. (Most men have difficulty imagining things they have not experienced, as Machiavelli notes in *The Prince*.)

Neither of these "costs" can be accurately measured, moreover. (They can, of course, be assigned quantitative values for the purpose of "measurement" or analysis, but these "values" are at best "guesstimates," since they correspond to unknowns. How can one ever accurately or precisely determine how many experiments were not undertaken because of regulation? Human creativity is essentially unpredictable.) Nor is it accurate to regard political and economic considerations as simple "trade-offs," as in Okun's "equality vs. efficiency." If, as de Tocqueville argues, participation in local government provides individuals with both the organizational skills and the self-confidence to undertake new projects, democracy positively contributes to the entrepreneurial spirit and thereby to economic productivity. People who prosper in their private lives tend to support the established public regime, so productivity contributes to political stability. There is, therefore, no escape from either complexity or conflict in the politics of advanced industrial societies.

Once we recognize not only that every polity has several different goals but also that the means of securing these goals often conflict, we can also see the way in which the different processes can be set against each other to counteract the worst effects of each. For example, a market is probably the most effective means of maximizing productivity, but the self-interested and morally corruptive tendencies of the market need to be counteracted by political participation in order to preserve a liberal polity. Democratic participation has its own characteristic vices, however, chief of which is the tendency of the majority to force dissenting minorities to conform. Private ownership, particularly of the major avenues of communication, does constitute an important check on politically coerced conformity to the views of the majority, as Friedman (1962) argues. The particular balance between individual effort and social obligation, democratic participation and economic productivity, will vary from individual to individual, from nation to nation. Nevertheless, whenever the different processes check each other's worst abuses, the combination or "compromise" will be more than the sum of its parts.

Any existing balance of the different "goods" and procedures involved in the politics of an advanced industrial society will be open to challenge, however, because none of the officially recognized goods or standards will be maximized, nor will either democratic or legal procedures be pure. There is no noncoercive end or "solution" to political debate or partisan opposition because most "interests" can legitimately claim to be supplying real, although different goods to the community as a whole. They differ primarily on the weight or priority they think the nation should give to their particular contributions or concerns. Because these goods are incommensurable, there is no quantitative science that can tell anyone precisely how much deliberation, how much knowledge, how much participation, or how much productivity is right or even merely desirable. It is no accident, therefore, that the liberal welfare state appears to be a piecemeal, pragmatic development, moving between two untenable extremes. It is and it should be. Upon examination, most of the criticism arises from a desire to maximize one *partial* good—individual autonomy,

economic efficiency, knowledge or innovation, participation or equality—
at the expense of all others.

Where the extremely individualistic understanding of market exchange characteristic of the "right" critique of the liberal welfare state
ignores the importance of both the given distribution of resources and the
social prerequisites of both production and individual development, the
simply egalitarian understanding of democracy characteristic of the left
underestimates the importance of preserving individual differences. The
liberal welfare state does represent a compromise, as Przeworski and
Wallerstein claim in Chapter 4, but it is not merely a compromise between the interests of two antagonistic classes. Rather, the untidy combination of market exchange, plurality voting, representative government,
and bureaucratic administration we call the liberal welfare state constitutes an attempt to achieve an optimal mix of inherently irreducibly
different "goods" or goals.

It is possible, however, to be clearer about the fundamental principles informing liberal welfare politics, especially as they bear on practice.
If the extensive division of labor in advanced industrial societies necessarily produces diverse opinions and interests, Miliband's Marxist dream of a
purely "cooperative," nonconflicting, "classless" society represents an im-
possibility.

If human beings develop their distinctive characteristics and talents
only through interaction with others, however, it is also unrealistic and
empirically invalid to talk of "individuals" outside of "society" contracting
for specified services or treatment. Granted, the contractarian models
Rawls and Nozick offer are not intended to be descriptions of the actual
process of state formation so much as to provide norms, to show what
individuals should or should not consent to. Nozick himself recognizes
that no actual state can be based entirely on explicit individual contracts
when he proceeds to justify the move from privately hired "protective
associations" that serve only their employers or contributors to states that
offer legal protection to conscientious objectors and taxpayers alike on the
basis of "indifference curves." Nozick argues that the individual incurs no
obligation for social services, his family upbringing, for example, which
are rendered before he has the opportunity to consent. But this denial of
obligation for services rendered without consultation or consent does not
follow from Nozick's own principle that no individual may rightly be used
for another's benefit *when he receives no compensating benefit.*

Nozick does show, however, that libertarians and egalitarians, indi-
vidualists and Marxists, actually ascribe to the same fundamental moral
proposition: no person is legitimately treated simply as a means to
another's good. On the basis of this principle, it is clear that workers
displaced by technological innovation do have a right for assistance or

compensation from the rest of society, which benefits generally from increased efficiency and productivity as a result of labor "mobility." Surely it is not just to impose all the costs on the worker who is displaced through no fault of his own. On the other hand, according to this principle, no human being has a right or claim to part of the products of the labor of others without somehow contributing himself to the common enterprise. This is the reason "welfare" benefits in Europe are generally tied to employment. The peculiar and unfortunate history of race relations in the United States makes that particular connection difficult to insist upon here.

Because part of his product can be traced to a socially provided foundation, every individual owes the community something for services received. It is a mistake, however, to think of differential treatment or rewards solely in terms of incentives, as Rawls does, because market exchange is only one of several possible forms of interaction among citizens. Indeed, the tendency in liberal societies to conceive of most interpersonal relations in economic, materialistic, or exchange terms is one of the major forces undermining the fundamental moral principle of modern liberalism because "economizing" leads individuals to view others simply in terms of their "utility" rather than their intrinsic worth.

REFERENCES

Arrow, Kenneth. 1959. "Rational Choice Functions and Ordering." *Economica* 26 (May):121–27; very well explicated in Norman Frohlich and Joe A. Oppenheimer, *Modern Political Economy* (Englewood Cliffs, N.J.: Prentice-Hall, 1978), 15–31.

Bell, Daniel. 1960. *The End of Ideology.* New York: Free Press.

Buchanan, James. 1976. *Limits of Liberty.* Chicago: University of Chicago Press.

Buchanan, James, with Tullock, Gordon. 1962. *Calculus of Consent.* Ann Arbor: University of Michigan Press.

Buchanan, James, with Wagner, Richard E. 1977. *Democracy in Deficit.* New York: Academic Press.

Cohn-Bendit, Daniel and Gabriel. 1968. *Obsolete Communism.* New York: McGraw-Hill.

Dahl, Robert A. 1977. "On Removing Certain Impediments to Democracy in the United States." *Political Science Quarterly* 92: 1–20.

Dahl, Robert A., and Lindblom, Charles. 1976. *Politics, Economics and Welfare.* Chicago: University of Chicago Press.

Friedman, Milton. 1962. *Capitalism and Freedom.* Chicago: University of Chicago Press.

——. 1980. *Free to Choose.* New York: Harcourt Brace Jovanovich.

Furniss, Norman, and Tilton, Timothy. 1977. *The Case for the Social Welfare State*. Bloomington: Indiana University Press.

Hayek, Friedrich. 1960. *The Constitution of Liberty*. Chicago: University of Chicago Press.

Lindblom, Charles. 1977. *Politics and Markets*. New York: Basic Books.

Lowi, Theodore J. 1967. "The Public Philosophy: Interest Group Liberalism." *American Political Science Review* 41 (March): 5–24.

McConnell, Grant. 1966. *Private Power and American Democracy*. New York: Knopf.

Miliband, Ralph. 1969. *The State in Capitalist Society*. New York: Basic Books.

———. 1982. *Capitalist Democracy in Britain*. New York: Oxford University Press.

Moynihan, Daniel Patrick. 1969. *Maximum Feasible Misunderstanding*. New York: Free Press.

Nozick, Robert. 1968. *Anarchy, State, and Utopia*. New York: Basic Books.

Okun, Arthur. 1975. *Equality and Efficiency: The Big Tradeoff*. Washington, D.C.: Brookings Institution.

Olson, Mancur. 1982. *The Rise and Decline of Nations*. New Haven: Yale University Press.

Piven, Frances Fox, and Cloward, Richard. 1971. *Regulating the Poor*. New York: Vintage.

Rawls, John. 1971. *A Theory of Justice*. Cambridge: Harvard University Press.

Schmitter, Phillip. 1981. "Interest Intermediation and Regime Governability." In *Organizing Interests in Western Europe*, ed. Suzanne Berger. Cambridge: Cambridge University Press.

Schultze, Charles L. 1977. *The Public Use of Private Interest*. Washington, D.C.: Brookings Institution.

Touraine, Alain. 1971. *The Post-Industrial Society*. New York: Random House.

Walzer, Michael. 1983. *Spheres of Justice*. New York: Basic Books.

Wildavsky, Aaron. 1980. *How to Limit Government Spending*. Berkeley: University of California Press.

Zuckert, Michael. 1981. "Justice Deserted: A Critique of Rawls." *Polity* 13 (Spring): 421–42.

3   STATE–ECONOMY LINKAGES IN ADVANCED INDUSTRIALIZED SOCIETIES

Gary W. Marks

Governments in Western democracies are perceived as responsible for economic performance, yet they lack authoritative control of market decision making. This was not a problem in the two decades following World War II, when governments claimed success for unparalleled economic growth, over which they really had very little control. But in more recent years, governments in all Western societies have had to cope with deteriorating economic performance and its unsettling political fallout.

From the 1960s, governments in many Western societies experimented with a range of microeconomic policies designed to extend their influence over private economic decision making. They devised various kinds of incomes policies and industrial policies to coordinate the activities of the major economic organizations of capital and labor in order to achieve overarching "national" objectives. These microeconomic policies extended the role of the state beyond aggregate fiscal and monetary controls but stopped short of the politically unpopular measure of nationalizing the means of production. A middle way was sought, a means of exerting political influence in the economy without undermining the institution of private property.

Arguments for such a strategy were grounded in economic hypotheses linking various kinds of economic planning and incomes policy to economic outcomes, particularly economic growth, full employment, and price stability. But the ability of the state to coordinate economic decision making is a political ability based on a political relationship between the state and the organizations that structure the economy. In this field, as in some others, the conventional wisdom concerning the relative "hardness" of economic science and the "softness" of political science is misleading. Economics enable us to analyze the probable economic consequences of policies, but we must turn to the systematic study of politics to understand if, and how, they may be achieved.

This chapter will analyze the influence of political constraints on microeconomic policies that attempt to coordinate organized economic decision making. The analytical framework developed here should apply to the range of microeconomic policies that go under the headings of industrial policy, structural policy, investment policy, incomes policy, etc. However, in using this framework as a basis for comparing societies, I have chosen to focus on one policy sector, for the individual policy sector seems to be the logical unit for intersocietal comparison. This has the advantage of making no assumption about the homogeneity of the political constraints operating in different policy sectors. In other words, it allows for the possibility that there may be significant variations in individual policy sectors within societies, as between them. Here I have decided to compare microeconomic policy in the field of industrial relations, which may be defined as relations among workers, employers, and the state concerned with the regulation of the labor market. Industrial relations is a core sector of the economy, and it is in the field of industrial relations that governments have tried most often, and most ambitiously, to influence economic outcomes directly through various forms of incomes policy.

TYPES OF STATE–ECONOMY LINKAGES

The terms *state* and *economy* are abstractions from a vast complex of human activities. We can conceptualize them by referring to their distinctive institutions: the state consisting of the political executive, legislature, judiciary, armed forces, etc.; the economy consisting of firms, corporations, banks, etc. Or more subtly, we can do so by referring to the kinds of activity that take place in them: the state as oriented to the exercise of authority in society; the economy as oriented to the production and consumption of scarce resources. Both conceptualizations suggest an essential problem in public economic policy: How can the state gain influence over the institutions that make up the economy? How can authority be exercised over the production and consumption of scarce resources? The questions arise because economic organizations and the state possess very different sources of power. Max Weber made this a central theme in his discussion of the nature of "domination" exercised by the state: "[There are] two diametrically contrasting types of domination, viz., domination by virtue of a constellation of interests (in particular: by virtue of a position of monopoly) and domination by virtue of authority, i.e., power to command and duty to obey" (Weber, 1978, 943).

The power of economic organizations is grounded in their domination of critical aspects of the production and allocation of scarce economic resources within society and as such is independent from state authority in a liberal capitalist society. This is an obvious constraint on a government determined to cast society in a fixed political image. However, the organized private economy poses problems even for governments that are not in principle opposed to the existence of concentrations of nonpublic power. Inflation and the competition among organized economic groups for a limited economic pie; strikes and other manifestations of conflict among labor market organizations; pollution and other unintended negative externalities of economic decision making—each is a consequence of the organized private economy for which governments are, in one way or another, held responsible.

The organized private economy is thus a competitive, sometimes overtly conflictual, externality-creating realm of decision making beyond the direct control of the state. From this perspective, economic policy in the context of liberal capitalist society tries to elicit a particular response from organized constellations of interests dominating the performance of various economic functions.

On the other hand, the organization of economic interests also presents an opportunity for public economic policy. Labor unions, employer associations, and other economic interest groups may provide predictable and coherent means for implementing economic policy as well as channels for expressing demands. The question of microeconomic policy is thus not simply, How may the state negate the independent power of private economic organizations? but, Under what conditions can the state harness private organizations to public purposes by coordinating interest group decision making in line with governmental priorities?

This question refers to an ability rather than a capacity, for it turns on the linkages between the state and organized interests rather than inherent strengths or limitations of the state viewed in isolation. The pursuit of this kind of economic policy is a political pursuit and depends on the extent to which the state can gain the support or acquiescence of interest groups to policies that impose selective or short-term costs to achieve general or longer-term benefits.

This question may be analyzed in two parts. First is the issue of *interest group political leverage,* the extent to which the relevant economic interest groups may block or defuse attempts to coordinate their sectoral claims in line with the government's priorities. The ability of interest groups to exercise overt pressure is influenced by their political resources, most importantly their relative size and coverage of potential members, internal unity, financial strength, prestige, militancy, voting power, and strategic location in the economy (Finer, 1976, 363–64). But the ability to resist government economic policy initiatives also depends on the degree to which the political process is fragmented and hence open to interest group influence. The political leverage of interest groups is thus also influenced by the accessibility of relevant policy-making or policy-adjudicating arenas in which they may exert an effective veto over the executive.

Political leverage is not always the result of overt pressure, though. Businessmen exert a kind of political leverage because of their position as decision makers in the economy, even though they may lack the kinds of organizational representation that we generally associate with interest group activity. Whereas the political might of employees as an interest constituency is closely tied to their ability to create and maintain some form of organized control over the supply of their labor, that of employers is only partially expressed in formal organization (Offe, 1981; Lindblom, 1977, ch. 13). This does not mean that employers always have the upper hand. The balance of power between workers and employers is a variable, not a constant. But it does mean that it is not possible to diagnose the political weakness of businessmen by looking at their organized representation. Generally speaking, the more highly organized *both* sides of industry, the greater the relative political strength of labor; the less organized both sides of industry, the less the relative strength of labor.

Second is the issue of *interest group concertation*, i.e., the extent to which the relevant economic interest groups are willing and able to coordinate their sectoral claims in line with the government's priorities. Under what conditions will interest groups sacrifice sectional or short-term interests for national or longer-term considerations? This question is particularly important for labor unions, which are the interest groups usually called upon to moderate their claims in microeconomic policies designed to reduce wage inflation and increase investments while at the same time moderating unemployment. Here we are on ground well traveled by scholars of neocorporatism. Two conditions have been emphasized as especially important in creating and sustaining an exchange between interest groups and the state: interest group centralization, which conditions the ability of interest groups to implement bargains struck with the state at the national level; and a relationship of trust between the relevant interest groups and the government, which serves to assure that the state will actually compensate interest groups for their short-term sacrifices (Lange, 1981; Marks, 1983; Schmitter and Lehmbruch, 1979).

Figure 3.1 dichotomizes interest group political leverage and concertability, defined as the ability of the state to coordinate affected interests

FIGURE 3.1

Types of State–Interest Group Linkages

Interest Group Political Leverage

		High	Low
Concertability	High	NEOCORPORATISM	QUASI-CORPORATISM
	Low	PLURALISM	DIRIGISM

within the process of policy making and policy implementation. This yields four potential types of state–economy linkages. The combination of high political leverage and high concertability are distinguishing characteristics of policy sectors in which interest group intermediation and policy making are described in the growing literature on the subject as *neocorporatist*. In the sphere of industrial relations, the societies that most closely approximate neocorporatist state–economy linkages are Austria, Norway, Sweden, and, to a lesser extent, Belgium, Finland, and the Netherlands up to the mid-1960s. In these liberal democracies, the political strength and concertability of interest groups, particularly labor unions, have sustained consensual incomes policies in the post–World War II period and have provided the state with a means to influence organizational decision making in line with its own priorities.

The combination of high interest group political leverage and low concertability describes key features of the classic model of *pluralist* politics, based on multiple opportunities for interest group influence in an open and competitive setting. In industrial relations, as in most other policy sectors, pluralist state–economy linkages are seen most clearly in the Anglo-American societies, where labor unions and employers' associations have significant political leverage but little internal cohesion. Economic policy making in such pluralist contexts has been constrained by the veto power exercised by fractionalized groupings over attempts to concert their demands in microeconomic policy.

The analysis of neocorporatist and pluralist state–economy linkages can draw on an established comparative literature concerned with variations in economic policy making in Western Europe. Conceptualizations of "corporatism," with a variety of prefixes, were developed in explicit contradistinction to that of "pluralism," in an attempt to account for the diversity of interest group forms and participation in public policy that was found in liberal capitalist societies. Both conceptualizations, however, share the assumption that interest groups, and particularly the major functional interest groups entrenched in the economy, have considerable political leverage. This need not be so. State–economy linkages under unconcertable interest groups having low political leverage—which I have termed *dirigism*—are approximated in French industrial relations, and the combination of concertable interest groups having low political leverage—termed *quasi-corporatism*—is approximated in Swiss industrial relations. Both types of state–economy linkages allow the state potential influence over organized economic decision making: under dirigism because the state may exclude interest groups from policy making; under quasi-corporatism because the state may incorporate them on its own terms.

The types of state–economy linkages outlined here—neocorporatism, pluralism, dirigism, and quasi-corporatism—are intended to make explicit the logical and empirical connections between interest group strength and organizational structure, the permeability of the political process, interest group–governing party relations, and the scope for state influence over organized economic decision making in that policy sector. Table 3.1 hypothesizes a set of associations between types of state–economy linkages and the following broad characteristics of economic policy making as applied to the field of industrial relations:

Policy formulation: Policy making may be an outcome of a bargaining process, encompassing the major economic groups, or it may be imposed unilaterally by the state.

Policy scope: Policy making may form part of a coordinated intersectoral policy mix, or it may be segmented among autonomous policy sectors.

Policy implementation: Responsibility for implementing policy may be extended to the relevant interest groups as a quasi-public function, or may be monopolized by the state and carried out statutorily.

Key decision-making arenas: Policy making may tend to be focused in one decision-making arena of the political process or may be dispersed in several arenas.

Policy instruments: The state may attempt to play a large role in influencing organized economic decision making, through incomes policy, industrial policy, etc., or it may avoid such a strategy by relying on aggregate fiscal and/or monetary instruments.

NEOCORPORATIST STATE–ECONOMY LINKAGES

In societies where interest groups, and particularly trade unions, are both politically strong and concertable, consensual incomes policy has been a durable nexus between the state and the economy, a means of state

TABLE 3.1
State–Economy Linkages and Characteristics of Economic Policy

TYPE OF STATE–ECONOMY LINKAGE	POLICY FORMULATION	POLICY SCOPE	POLICY IMPLEMENTATION	KEY DECISION-MAKING ARENA	POLICY INSTRUMENTS
Neocorporatism	bargained	intersectoral	self-imposed	focused on national bargaining among employers, unions, state	consensual incomes policy
Pluralism	mostly bargained, sometimes unilateral	sectoral	statutory	dispersed among executive and other contending actors	reliance on macroeconomic instruments occasionally supplemented by incomes policy
Dirigism	unilateral	intersectoral	statutory	focused on executive and bureaucracy	prices policy and centralized planning
Quasi-corporatism	bargained	sectoral	self-imposed	focused on encompassing policy network	reliance on macroeconomic instruments to create consensual economic climate

influence over a vital sphere of economic decision making. In Austria, Norway, Sweden, and, to a lesser extent, Belgium, Finland, and the Netherlands (up to the mid-1960s), trade unions have been strong enough to make it difficult for the state to enforce labor market policies against their wishes, yet centralized enough to bargain effectively at the national level.

In these societies, the context of economic policy making has been one of class compromise, based on a set of understandings between the state and the organized representatives of labor and capital, institutionalized in broad national agreements, and implemented by the participating groups themselves. The formal role of the state in such national agreements has varied considerably. In Austria and Norway, the state has been deeply involved in industrial relations both procedurally, in the creation of a variety of channels for conflict resolution and arbitration, and substantively, as government agencies have actively participated as a third force in national wage-related negotiation (Lehmbruch, 1979, 158–60; Schwerin, 1980). In Sweden, on the other hand, the role of the state has generally been more indirect, although by no means passive. There the major union federations and employer associations traditionally have pursued wage-related bargaining autonomously. The role of the state has generally been to provide the context for that bargaining through social welfare, tax policies, and manpower policies, although governments have been induced to intervene directly when incomes policy bargaining between unions and employers has broken down (Flanagan, Soskice, and Ulman, 1983, ch. 6).

Sources of Neocorporatist Class Compromise

Consensual incomes policy appears to form part of a mutually reinforcing set of factors encompassing (1) the organizational strength of the working class, both in the labor market (strongly entrenched trade unions) and in the state (socialist party participation in government); (2) highly centralized and coherent trade union organization; and (3) a distinctive union strategy, oriented to the political regulation of the labor market rather than piecemeal collective bargaining. Of the fifteen larger societies in Western Europe and North America over the thirty-year period from 1951 to 1980, those societies in which employees are highly organized in trade unions, in which those unions are highly centralized, and in which Socialist or Social Democratic parties have consistently formed or participated in governments have tended to pursue consensual incomes policies, and where this syndrome of factors has been present, unemployment has been lowest, the volume of strikes smallest, and the share of resources distributed by government the largest (Marks, 1983).

As Walter Korpi and Michael Shalev have emphasized in their analysis of class relations in Sweden, the organizational resources available to the working class are especially important: "On the one hand, they provide labour with the ability to grasp control of the government. On the other hand, they also imply an internal discipline which makes possible the implementation of the new strategy of conflict" (Korpi and Shalev, 1979, 180). Durable socialist participation in government provides trade unions with enlarged opportunities for improving the conditions of their members in the labor market by influencing the state, which may both pursue economic policies favoring employment and legislate social welfare and manpower programs (reflected in the large share of government receipts in the gross national product). Internal discipline, or centralization, enables unions to provide the collective restraint in the labor market (reflected in low strike levels), which serves as an implicit exchange for favorable state policies and avoids embarrassing socialist governments with economic disruption.

In terms of organizational structure, the ideal type of "societal corporatism," developed by Philippe Schmitter, may be regarded as highly suitable for consensual incomes policy. Under societal corporatism, interest groups are pyramidlike; they are hierarchical organizations clearly differentiated from neighboring interest group organizations at the base as well as the top (i.e. they are noncompeting) and have single, rather than multiple, peaks (Schmitter, 1979). Such an interest group structure is conducive to policy bargaining at the national level. Interest constituencies are clearly defined and uniquely represented; the interests of each constituency are aggregated within the interest group before, not during, the process of national negotiation; and interest group leaders are secure in their leadership. Any bargains they make will not be undercut by competing interest groups bidding for the support of their own constituency. Moreover, as Mancur Olson has argued, the more encompassing an interest group (which is a function of unitary representation and the scope of interest group coverage), the more likely are interest group leaders to consider the wider social consequences of their own actions since their constituency is a not insignificant part of the entire society (Olson, 1982, 48).

This discussion suggests that neocorporatist state–economy linkages form part of an inclusive set of political relationships. Consensual incomes policy, as a central feature of neocorporatist state–economy linkages, serves political as well as economic purposes. Viewed narrowly, as a means of restraining real wage inflation, this form of incomes policy is usually judged by economists to be irrelevant or a failure. The societies in which consensual incomes policy has been a durable feature of economic policy have no better records on inflation than those societies in which this kind of policy has been absent (Marks, 1983; Schmidt, 1982, 155). But the real economic significance of consensual incomes policy appears to lie elsewhere, in the forging of linkages between the economic decision making of the major functional interest groups and the economic decision making of the state.

Growing Difficulties: The Case of Sweden

In recent years the pursuit of consensual incomes policy has become considerably more difficult than in the two decades following World War II. First, and most obviously, low rates of economic growth in the 1970s and early 1980s meant that economic bargaining between labor and management increasingly became a zero-sum game, the gains for one side translating into losses for the other. In addition, the political bases of neocorporatist state–economy linkages have been eroded by profound changes in the configuration of class forces and interest group formation. Several factors—the emergence of a split within the left, between a traditional wing consisting disproportionately of blue collar unionized workers and a newer wing consisting disproportionately of the educated young in white collar occupations; the increase in electoral volatility as class and party ties become weaker; the mobilization of white collar and professional employees in separate unions—have had the affect of reducing the coherence of labor movements in Western societies (Inglehart, 1977, ch. 10; Lipset, 1981, ch. 14).

These developments are particularly marked in Sweden, where the Social Democratic party (SAP) was displaced from power in 1976, after over forty years of virtually uninterrupted hegemony, in large part because the party was split over the issue of nuclear energy. The relegation of the SAP to opposition from 1976 to 1982 strained relations between the major union federations, the LO and TCO, and the employers' national association, the SAF, and contributed to the eventual breakdown of incomes policy negotiations in the general strike/lockout of May 1980. At the same time the concertability of unions has declined with the sharp growth since the early 1970s of white collar/professional unions, the SACO in the private sector and the PTK in the private sector. The trade-off between the major functional interest groups and the state, involving the formal autonomy of wage negotiations from government control, moderate wage claims, an effort to decrease wage differentials throughout the economy, an extensive welfare state, and a predisposition on all sides to avoid industrial conflict, has been challenged by white collar/professional unions that are determined to preserve traditional income and status differentials between higher white collar and blue collar occupations. Since the early 1970s, these unions of relatively privileged employees, rather than the LO or TCO, have been the most disruptive force in incomes policy bargaining (Flanagan, Soskice, and Ulman, 1983, 336–42; Van Otter, 1975, 205–07).

The indications are that the differentiation of interests among various grades of employees is not a temporary phenomenon. John Goldthorpe has described professional and managerial white collar workers as a "service class," whose economic interests are likely to be distinct from, and even opposed to, those of blue collar workers:

> There would seem little reason to suppose that as the degree of formation of the service class increases, it will become in any way less ready, or less able, to engage in distributional conflict—in which the working class could be reckoned as its major adversary. Indeed, a greater degree of stability and social homogeneity within the service class may be expected to provide a firmer basis for a tendency that is clearly strengthening: that is, for service-class groupings to pursue further their material interests through organization and various forms of "trade-union" action (Goldthorpe, 1982, 181).

The formation of separate white collar/professional union federations has generally proceeded furthest in those societies where neocorporatist state–economy linkages are strongest. Where the major union federation is centrally organized on the principle of industrial unionism, as are the respective LOs in Sweden and Norway, white collar workers are generally represented as a minority within a blue collar–dominated union representing all workers in the industry. If they wish to create their own unions, white collar workers must exit from the central federation. There is an element of competitive mobilization in this development: strong blue collar organization may actually precipitate separate white collar organization, as white collar workers feel that their privileged position is eroding.

In Sweden, the percentage of union members belonging to white collar/professional federations has grown from around 2 percent in 1957–58 to 7 percent in 1977–78, while that of the lower white collar federation, the TCO, has increased from 19 to 32 percent in the same period. The membership of the major blue collar–dominated federation, the LO, has grown in absolute terms, by more than half, but as a result of the dynamic growth of the white collar federations the proportion of total union members encompassed by the LO decreased from 77 to 61 percent. In Norway the picture is similar. In the years from 1957–58 to 1977–78, white collar unions outside the major union federation increased their share of total membership from 16 to 29 percent (Windmuller, 1981, 47).

Ironically, such multiplication of channels of interest representation at the peak or national level is not present where industrial relations are more pluralist. Peak union organization in the United States and in Britain is unitary, not multiple, encompassing the vast majority of union members in a single national federation. In the United States, the proportion of union members encompassed by the AFL-CIO had grown to over 80 percent by 1980, while in Britain that encompassed by the TUC in the same year was 92 percent. In these societies, the variety of union forms and the weakness of central direction have made it relatively easy for white collar workers to create their own organizations while remaining affiliated with the central body.

These considerations indicate that neocorporatist state–economy linkages are being altered from within. The organizational strength and centralization of union organization that is a vital feature of neocorporatist state–economy linkages induce white collar/professional workers to countermobilize, and they do so by creating separate federations, which tend to "crowd" the policy arena (Ruin, 1982, 156). In other words, there is a dynamic contradiction between two important characteristics of "societal corporatism." The conditions that give rise to centralized union federations also give rise to fractionalized, not unitary, union movements. This suggests that societal corporatism cannot be understood as a Weberian ideal type, a syndrome of variables abstracted from a concrete historical situation. In the sphere of industrial relations, societal corporatism seems to provide us with a set of ideal conditions for consensual policy making rather than a composite set of characteristics that "go together" in a given set of societies.

The rise of white collar/professional union federations is part of the mobilization of a variety of previously quiescent constituencies over the last two decades. Established channels of interest representation in many policy areas have been bypassed by groups that, for one reason or another, have felt excluded from them and have demanded some direct means of expression. At the same time, centralized decision making within unions has been challenged both in the name of increased worker participation and because certain strategically placed groups of workers have come to realize that they could get more if they acted outside of the general wage settlements negotiated by union leaders for the union membership as a whole.

Neocorporatist state–economy linkages presuppose a delicate process of interest aggregation and bargaining, a situation in which a limited and predictable range of interests is packaged and parlayed by a coherent set of organizations. Given this, one must be wary of extrapolating the past successes of public economic policy under neocorporatist state–economy linkages into a future of tumultuous interest mobilization and realignment.

Pluralist State–Economy Linkages

Under pluralist state–economy linkages, economic interest groups are politically strong, but unconcertable. They have the might to make it very difficult for the state to force its will on them, yet lack the organizational coherence necessary for consensual policy making and implementation. In the sphere of industrial relations, both the United States and Britain approximate such a condition, although for different reasons.

United States

In the United States, the tendency toward pluralist state–economy linkages derives from basic structural elements of the political system. The power of Congress, the decisive role of the courts, in short, the division of powers among separated political institutions, severely limits the capacity of the executive to act as a central negotiator with functional interest groups on questions of economic policy (Salisbury, 1979). The widespread mobilization of support necessary to overcome the obstacles in the path of economic policy initiatives is extraordinarily difficult to generate once the "honeymoon" period of a new Presidency has passed.

The barriers to concertation on the side of the state are matched by those on the side of interest groups themselves. The organizational structure of the major economic interest groups in the United States is highly decentralized, a reflection of their gradual and unplanned growth, the size and heterogeneity of the society, and the logic of operating within a fragmented political system. Labor unions are represented in a unitary federation, the AFL-CIO, that, according to conventional arguments linking interest group structure to modes of policy making, should be well suited to national bargaining. But the AFL-CIO has very little power over its union constituents. The weight of decision making, especially on questions relating to wages, lies within the individual unions and their shop floor organizations. The peak interest associations formed by employers are equally decentralized and far more fragmented. None of the three major associations—the Chamber of Commerce, the Business Roundtable, or the declining National Association of Manufacturers—has the power to enter into binding negotiations on wage issues or the resources to implement any bargain that might be made there.

By comparison with the societies of central and northwestern Europe, the major functional interest groups in the United States are weak, both in organizational coverage and in internal unity. The levels of unionization and employer associability rank at, or very near, the bottom among Western democracies. Yet what interest groups lack in membership or cohesion they can make up for by exploiting the unparalleled opportunities for influence offered within the political system. As Graham Wilson has summarized, "Federalism, the separation of powers, the fragmentation of power within both Congress and the executive, the absence of a strong system of party discipline combine to create a multiplicity of channels of access for the accepted interest group which it is impossible to control" (G. K. Wilson, 1981, 225).

In this context, the linkages between the state and organized economic groups are likely to be numerous, but incoherent. In the 1950s and 1960s such pluralist state–economy linkages were "managed" through a system of relatively autonomous subgovernments, or "iron triangles," composed of key bureaucrats, interest group representatives, and senior members of congressional subcommittees, which dominated the policy-making process in discrete policy sectors. Over the last decade or so, the autonomy of iron triangles has declined. The growth of state economic intervention, both regulatory and distributive, the increasing role of policy specialists, the intensification of interest group activity on the part of established groups, especially those representing business, and the proliferation of new public interest groups have together opened up, and immensely complicated, policy making (Heclo, 1978; Gais, Peterson, and Walker, 1984, 25).

The consequences of this are evident in the difficulties faced in the 1970s in implementing economic policies designed to coordinate economic activity directly. As Arnold Heidenheimer, Hugh Heclo, and Carolyn Teich Adams have pointed out:

> Rather than straining for analogies, it is well to recognize that the U.S. national government has little capacity to pursue coherent courses of action below the most aggregate levels of economic management. Experience with wage and price controls during the 1970s provides one outstanding example, but there are others. As economic problems mounted later in that decade, some effort was made to use the President's Council on Wage and Price Stability to analyze industrial sectors and their particular problems. But these efforts produced little enduring policy, and by the end of the Carter administration the latter council was abandoned with hardly a murmur of dissent (Heidenheimer, Heclo, and Adams, 1983, 142).

Great Britain

In Britain, the sources of pluralist state–economy linkages are quite different from those in America. The strength of party discipline, the absence of federalism, and the marginal political role played by the courts contrast sharply to the American political system, at least when one party has a majority in the House of Commons. But the concentrations of power that lie outside the central political institutions, in the form of economic interest groups, are far more formidable than in the United States. This is especially true in the sphere of industrial relations, where the factors that have been responsible for the greater salience of class conflict in Britain have also contributed to the greater organizational strength of trade unions.

Trade union organization is highly decentralized in Britain. British trade unions form a unitary peak or national organization, the Trades Union Congress (TUC), but the very breadth of the organization and the diversity of the organizational forms and constituencies represented within it have impeded its capacity to aggregate workers' interests coherently at the national level. The TUC has little power to enforce majority decisions over its constituent unions, short of expulsion. Moreover, many of its constituent unions have to cope with extraordinarily strong and independent organizations on the shop floor. The peak association of employers, the Confederation of British Industry (CBI), is in a similar position. It is charged with the function of national representation but has, according to the authors of a comprehensive study of the organization, "no meaningful sanction to impose on its members" (Grant and Marsh, 1977, 213). Both the TUC and the CBI have gained prestige and moral weight within their respective constituencies in recent years, but their lack of formal authority and financial resources has meant that they continue to lead from behind, on the basis of the lowest common denominator of their memberships.

As in the United States, union decentralization in Britain appears to be an outcome of a deep-seated historical process, in which a large number of relatively autonomous and competing unions emerged in the nineteenth century with little regard for the organizational prerequisites of state coordination of the economy. In both the United States and Britain, economic associations were formed in a haphazard fashion, following much the same unplanned pattern as the process of industrialization itself. In many sectors of the economy, sectional and decentralized interest groups were long established by the end of the nineteenth century. In both societies, later developing forces of interest group centralization—the increase in economic concentration in the decades around the turn of the twentieth century and the growth of state intervention in the economy during World War I—were weakened because they acted on interest groups that were already well entrenched. Thus, the early heterogeneous and unplanned character of economic development in Britain and the United States contributed to interest group decentralization, which, in the present-day context, negates the possibility of concerting interest group demands.

In Britain, the potentially destabilizing consequences of strong but unconcertable unions opposite a centralized state were eased, at least until the 1970s, by what Keith Middlemas has called a "corporate bias," a preference on the part of governments and major functional interest groups to operate in the middle ground between them, to solve political crises, when they occurred, through compromise rather than conflict (Middlemas, 1979, ch. 13). However, the "corporate bias" in relations among government, employers, and unions did not arise as a systematic outcome of group bargaining on the neocorporatist model, but was a tendency implicit in a shared desire for consensus and political stability.

The limitations of this arrangement became increasingly apparent as governments in the 1960s and 1970s attempted to supplement Keynesian fiscal policies by more discriminating intervention at the micro level. The principal form that such intervention took was incomes policy. From the standpoint of rectifying the imbalances of Keynesian fiscal policy this was logical enough. Incomes policy was intended to counteract the spiraling wage settlements that seemed to follow from Keynesian policies sustaining high levels of employment, increasing union membership, and expanding governmental responsibilities—without actually abandoning the commitment to full employment, support for unions, or an extensive state role in the economy. However, in the context of British industrial relations, such a strategy revealed both the difficulties governments had in assuring unions that their short-term sacrifices would result in longer-term gains and the inability of the TUC to guarantee the compliance of the union movement with national bargains. The first problem was acute even under sympathetic Labour governments, partly because the government itself lacked control over the investments that would have to be made by private capital if present wage restraint were to be translated into future economic growth, and partly because under Britain's adversary two-party system, the tenure of a Labour government was always in doubt. For these reasons, even if an incomes policy were launched with the initial support of the TUC, as was the case in 1966–67 and 1975–76, it eventually became a source of fractious dispute among unions. In both cases, the policy ended in wage explosions and demands on the part of most trade union leaders that the Labour government release the TUC and individual unions from the burden of policing their own ranks.

An implication of this experience, when it is compared with that of societies that have neocorporatist state–economy linkages, is that British unions are not sufficiently integrated in economic policy making to accept responsibility for it. Henry Phelps Brown has cogently argued this point of view in his study of trade union power:

> The threat to incomes policy arises when the trade unions have not too much power but too little. When the adversary system keeps them in the role of claimants, not to say assailants, they cannot identify them-

selves with the policy. They will accept the need for a standstill in a national emergency; and when a Labour government imposes the policy they may accept it for a time as a sacrifice they should make for the government's sake; but the policy is still part of the line that is habitually held against them, and sooner or later they will use their power to break through. International comparisons suggest that where they are not kept outside the walls, but take an effective part in the relevant decisions, power brings responsibility (Phelps Brown, 1983, 299).

Compulsory Controls

In the absence of the political conditions for consensual incomes policy, governments in both Britain and the United States have, on occasion, retreated to statutory policy instruments as a substitute. Compulsory incomes policies, formulated unilaterally by the state and implemented by wages and prices agencies with legal powers, have been pursued in Britain most recently under the Wilson government (1966–70) and under the Heath government (1972–74), and in the United States under the Nixon administration (1971–73).

Authoritative intervention in industrial relations may buttress consensual bargains by penalizing "free riders," i.e., workers or employers who seek to gain the benefits of the policy without paying the cost of abiding by the agreement. But as a substitute for consensus in wage regulation, statutory authority is a blunt instrument and may serve to extend wage disputes into deeper conflicts about the legitimacy of the regime, as happened in Britain during the Great Coal Strike of 1973–74. In this case, a wage demand by the National Union of Coalminers in contravention of the Heath government's incomes policy led to a bitter strike that disrupted the British economy and precipitated a General Election in which the Conservative party campaigned on the issue, "Who governs Britain: the unions or the government?"

The limited effectiveness of coercion is made very clear by Arnold Weber in his overview of incomes policies in the United States:

> In a political democracy wage-price policy cannot be effective unless it is accepted, tacitly or otherwise, by the major groups that will be affected by it. Even when the program is based on statutory authority, as in the Nixon administration, its viability must stem from acceptance rather than coercion for the simple reason that in a democracy the economy cannot be managed by throwing union leaders and businessmen in jail. (Weber, 1975, 368)

State influence over the decision making of economic interest groups through incomes policy is very difficult to achieve under pluralist state–economy linkages, as the experiences of the United States and Britain over the past two decades have shown. But incomes policy is only one of a number of strategies that governments may pursue in the sphere of industrial relations. The ineffectiveness of incomes policies in the United States and Britain has led governments of the right in these countries to reject incomes policy altogether in favor of "neo-laissez-faire" policies that are intended to exert indirect influence in the labor market through tighter control of the money supply, a tougher stance against unions in the public sector, and in the case of Britain, the legislation of constraints on a range of union activities (Marks, 1985).

DIRIGIST AND QUASI-CORPORATIST STATE–ECONOMY LINKAGES

Neocorporatist and pluralist state–economy linkages describe contrasting potentials for state influence in the economy under a similar constraint— powerful economic interest groups. In the sphere of industrial relations this means, most importantly, trade unions capable of mounting effective resistance to public policy initiatives concerning questions of wage regulation. Both neocorporatism and pluralism may thus be distinguished from the types of state–economy linkages that presuppose weakly organized economic interests, whether these are concertable or not.

The concertation of interest groups having little influence is typified in the corporatism of the authoritarian regimes that came to power in Italy and Germany between the two world wars. In liberal democracies such a combination is unlikely. However, the case of industrial relations in Switzerland shares some of the features of this type, which, to emphasize the contrast with its authoritarian variant, we shall term quasi-corporatism.

Switzerland

Labor unions and business interests in Switzerland are informally integrated into a coherent "policy network" through which they play an integral role in the formulation and implementation of economic policy. As Peter Katzenstein observes in his overview of the Swiss political economy, "Distinctive of Switzerland's domestic structure is the 'cooperative regulation of conflict' between business and labor, between internationally and nationally oriented segments of business, between industry and finance, and between industry and agriculture" (Katzenstein, 1984, 124).

However, trade unions do not participate in this system as decisively as they do in the Nordic countries. The national representation of workers in Switzerland is deeply fragmented; the major union federation, the SGB, encompasses only about half of all unionized workers, and less than a quarter of potential members. Moreover, the organizational structure of the SGB is decentralized: the sixteen unions that make up the federation bargain autonomously with employers on a variety of levels, from the individual company, to the canton, to the whole industry (Siegenthaler, 1975). These factors, alongside others, including the weakness of the Social Democratic party and the tentative relations between the party and the unions, relegate labor to a subsidiary position in the policy network. The nexus of public power and private power runs mainly through the axis between the government bureaucracy and business, which unlike labor is coherently organized at the national level in the Vorort (peak association of employers).

Thus, the organizational strength of labor is not a precondition of consensual economic policy, as it is under neocorporatist state–economy linkages. In fact, as Katzenstein argues, the reverse seems to be the case. Labor's political standing depends on the benefits of incorporation:

> . . . the power of the unions and the Left in Switzerland's policy network rests heavily on the special delegation of public power, especially in the areas of collective bargaining and social welfare. That delegation strengthens a weak sector of society, the labor movement, in the same way that tariffs protect agriculture and a lenient enforcement of cartel legislation protects domestic business. The strength that all these social sectors derive from the delegation of public power is considerable; but it is a brittle kind of strength which does not compensate for the fundamental asymmetry in power relations in Swiss society (Katzenstein, 1984, 148).

France

In policy sectors where the relevant interest groups are weak and uncon-certable, the state may have great latitude to influence organized decision making directly in a manner that may be described as "dirigist." In an age of organization, and under basic freedoms of association and combination that are common to all liberal democracies, dirigist state–economy linkages are likely to be the exception rather than the rule. In the field of industrial relations, the nearest example appears to be that of France, where trade unions are exceptionally weak and fractionalized and the state bureaucracy is centralized and able, in John Zysman's words, "to initiate policy and direct events rather than simply to react to domestic pressure" (1977, 195). Under the Fifth Republic, government influence has, at least until the Socialist electoral victories of 1981, been exercised through tightly knit policy networks, based on a "state-led symbiosis . . . between the ruling elite, the national organization of businessmen (CNPF) and the largest national organization of farmers (FNSEA)" (Hoffmann, 1982, 9–10).

A necessary though not sufficient factor in the symbiotic relationship between the state and employers seems to be the political and industrial weakness of trade unions. In France this is the outcome of a set of mutually reinforcing conditions. The fractionalization of unions into competing communist (CGT), socialist–syndicalist (CFDT), anticommunist (CGT-FO), and other smaller federations; the low level of union membership (less than 25 percent); the traditional animosity of many employers to unions; the financial poverty of unions; the penchant for ideological dispute rather than collective bargaining—each tends to reinforce the other in a vicious circle of political impotence and ideologization and serves to increase the autonomy of the state from interest group participation in economic policy making (Schain, 1980). Trade unions have tended to place their ideological purity and institutional autonomy ahead of the potential benefits from actively participating in the policy process, and state bureaucrats have justified their autonomy by reference to a concept of the state as separate and superior to the society of organized pressures.

Incomes policy is not a major instrument of economic policy in France. The main avenue of influence over organized economic decision making has been through employers and their organizations, as specified by the extensive state planning apparatus and exercised by the state bureaucracy. To the extent that incomes policies have been adopted, they have followed the same pattern, as Robert Flanagan, David Soskice and Lloyd Ulman have observed:

> With unorganized labor markets, productivity has been safeguarded because businesses have had freedom, within limits, to determine work practices, employment, and type of investment. When governments have been concerned about aggregate wage developments they have been able to pressure companies into containing wage increases, again within limits. With weak unions and strong links between government and industry, incomes policies could be run through industry. (Flanagan, Soskice, and Ulman, 1983, 646)

Under such circumstances, the government's task in making and carrying out economic policy is simplified. Electoral concerns may, as Jonathan Story has argued, constrain and shape the government's choices, but the weakness of labor has allowed the state to approach economic policy in a way more oriented to efficiency, as interpreted by the ruling elite, and less to fairness than is the case in the Anglo-American societies (Story, 1983).

As Michele Salvati argues in his comparative overview of economic policy in France and Italy after 1968, such freedom from interest group pressures may be advantageous: "When consensus and mediation are not politically necessary, and the number of major collective actors (and of divergent interests) who influence decision making can be reduced with-

out grave consequences, decision making is likely to be quite 'effective'"
(Salvati, 1981). However, such effectiveness comes at a high cost in terms
of predictability. The social consequence of dirigist state–economy linkages in an advanced capitalist democracy is a potential for the mobilization of discontent outside of established channels, as the events in France
of 1968 amply illustrate. The same conditions that insulate economic
policy making from organized group pressures reduce the value of economic interest groups as a means for expressing political grievances.

CONCLUSION

The societies that have provided the foci of comparison in this chapter,
Sweden, the United States, Britain, France, and Switzerland, form an
unlikely combination. Yet they serve to map the broadest contrasts in
state–economy linkages to be found among Western advanced industrialized societies in the sphere of industrial relations. As I have tried to
show in this chapter, distinctive types of state–economy linkages seem to
form part of a larger syndrome of interrelated factors, including the political leverage of interest groups, the institutional configuration of the policy-making process, party participation in government, and interest
group structure.

If this analysis is on the right track, the attempt to formulate economic policy as a technical exercise, aided by the appropriate *ceteris
paribus* clauses, will result in frustration. There is, in other words, no
recipe for policies that are the "best," abstracted from the particular
circumstances of the society or policy sector in which that policy is applied. Instead, it seems to make more sense to adopt a less ambitious,
perhaps Aristotelean, approach that seeks to find the most fitting policy
rather than the ideal one.

Such an approach may moderate the claims of economists who argue
that market competition is, a priori, the best solution to the production
and allocation of scarce economic resources and that the benefits of incomes policies are always outweighed by the economic distortions they
produce. At the same time, a contextual approach also calls into question
the opposing view that the practice of incomes policy in societies such as
Sweden, Norway, and Austria provides a model for effective and consensual economic policy that may be adopted elsewhere.

This raises a question not discussed here but worthy of further
thought. If certain modes of economic policy are contextually dependent,
to what extent may the context be altered? Which of the factors analyzed
in this chapter may be influenced within the political process, and how?
For to say that economic policy rests on "structural" conditions begs the

question of whether and how that structure—or institutionalized set of activities—may also be subject to purposeful change.

REFERENCES

Finer, S. E. 1976. "The Political Power of Organised Labour." Reprinted in *Studies in British Politics*, by R. Rose. 3d ed. New York: St. Martin's Press.

Flanagan, R. J., Soskice, W., and Ulman, L. 1983. *Unionism, Economic Stabilization, and Incomes Policies*. Washington, D.C.: Brookings Institution.

Gais, T. C., Peterson, M. A., and Walter, J. L. 1984. "Interest Groups, Iron Triangles and Representative Institutions in American National Government." *British Journal of Political Science* 14 (April): 161–85.

Goldthorpe, J. 1982. "On the Service Class, Its Formation and Future." In *Social Class and the Division of Labour*, ed. A. Giddens and G. Mackenzie. Cambridge: Cambridge University Press.

Grant, W., and Marsh, D. 1977. *The Confederation of British Industry*. London: Hodder and Stoughton.

Heclo, H. 1978. "Issue Networks and the Executive Establishment." In *The New American Political System*, ed. A. King. Washington, D.C.: American Enterprise Institute.

Heidenheimer, A. J., Heclo, H., and Adams, C. T., eds. 1983. *Comparative Public Policy*. Rev. ed. New York: St. Martin's Press.

Hoffmann, S. 1982. *Mitterrand's First Year in Power*. Boston: Harvard University Center for European Studies.

Inglehart, R. 1977. *The Silent Revolution*. Princeton: Princeton University Press.

Katzenstein, P., ed. 1984. *Corporatism and Change*. Ithaca, N.Y.: Cornell University Press.

Korpi, W., and Shalev, M. 1979. "Strikes, Industrial Relations and Class Conflict in Capitalist Societies." *British Journal of Sociology* 30:164–87.

Lange, P. 1981. "Consensual Conditions for Consensual Wage Regulation: An Initial Examination of Some Hypotheses." Paper delivered at the Annual Meeting of the American Political Science Association, New York.

Lehmbruch, G. 1979. "Liberalism, Corporatism, and Party Government." In *Trends Toward Corporatist Intermediation*, ed. P. C. Schmitter and G. Lehmbruch. Beverly Hills, Calif.: Sage.

Lindblom, C. E. 1977. *Politics and Markets*. New York: Basic Books.

Lipset, S. M. 1981. *Political Man*. Baltimore: Johns Hopkins University Press.

Marks, G. (1983). "Neocorporatism, Incomes Policy, and Socialist Participation in Government." Paper delivered at the Annual Meeting of the American Political Science Association, Chicago.

——— 1985. "The Revival of Laissez-Faire: The United States and Britain in Comparative Perspective." In *Politics in Britain and America in Comparative*

Perspective, ed. J. W. Ceasar and R. Hodde-Williams. Durham, N.C.: Duke University Press.

Marsh, D., and Locksley, G. 1983. "Capital in Britain: Its Structural Power and Influence Over Policy." *West European Politics* 6 (April):36–59.

Middlemas, K. 1979. *Politics in Industrial Society.* London: Andre Deutsch.

Offe, C. 1981. "The Attribution of Public Status to Interest Groups: Observations on the West German Case." In *Organizing Interests in Western Europe,* ed. S. Berger. Cambridge: Cambridge University Press.

Olson, M. 1982. *The Rise and Decline of Nations.* New Haven: Yale University Press.

Phelps Brown, H. 1983. *The Origins of Trade Union Power.* Oxford: Clarendon Press.

Pontusson, J. 1984. "Behind and Beyond Social Democracy in Sweden." *New Left Review* 143 (January–February): 69–96.

Ruin, O. 1982. "Sweden in the 1970's: Policy-Making Becomes More Difficult." In *Policy Styles in Western Europe,* ed. J. Richardson. London: Allen and Unwin.

Salisbury, R. H. 1979. "Why No Corporatism in America?" In *Trends Toward Corporatist Intermediation,* ed. P. C. Schmitter and G. Lehmbruch. Beverly Hills, Calif.: Sage.

Salvati, M. 1981. "May 1968 and the Hot Autumn of 1969: The Responses of Two Ruling Classes." In *Organizing Interests in Western Europe,* ed. S. Berger. Cambridge: Cambridge University Press.

Schain, M. 1980. "Corporatism and Industrial Relations in France." In *French Politics and Public Policy,* ed. P. G. Cerny and M. Schain. London: Frances Pinter.

Schmidt, M. G. 1982. "The Role of the Parties in Shaping Macroeconomic Policy." In *The Impact of Parties,* ed. F. G. Castles. Beverly Hills, Calif.: Sage.

Schmitter, P. C. 1979. "Modes of Interest Intermediation and Modes of Societal Change in Western Europe." In P. C. Schmitter and G. Lehmbruch, eds., *Trends Toward Corporatist Intermediation.* Beverly Hills, Calif.: Sage.

————— 1981. "Interest Intermediation and Regime Governability in Contemporary Western Europe and North America." In S. Berger, ed., *Organizing Interests in Western Europe.* Cambridge: Cambridge University Press.

Schmitter, P. C., and Lehmbruch, G., eds. 1979. *Trends Toward Corporatist Intermediation.* Beverly Hills, Calif.: Sage.

Schwerin, D. 1980. "The Limits of Organization as a Response to Wage-Price Problems." In *Challenge to Governance,* ed. R. Rose. Beverly Hills, Calif.: Sage.

Siegenthaler, J. K. 1975. "Current Problems of Trade Union–Party Relations in Switzerland: Reorientation Versus Inertia." *Industrial and Labor Relations Review* 28 (January): 264–81.

Story, J. 1983. "Capital in France: The Changing Pattern of Patrimony." *West European Politics* 6 (April): 87–127.

Van Otter, C. 1975. "Sweden: Labor Reformism Reshapes the System." In *Worker Militancy and Its Consequences,* ed. S. Barkin. New York: Praeger.

Weber, A. R. 1975. "The Continuing Courtship: Wage-Price Policy Through Five Administrations." In *Exhortation and Controls,* ed. C. D. Goodwin. Washington, D.C.: Brookings Institution.

Weber, M. 1978. *Economy and Society.* Edited by G. Roth and C. Wittich. Berkeley: University of California Press.

Wilson, F. L. 1982. "Alternative Models of Interest Intermediation: The Case of France." *British Journal of Political Science* 12 (April): 173–200.

Wilson, G. K. 1981. *Interest Groups in the United States.* Oxford: Clarendon Press.

Windmuller, J. P. 1981. "Concentration Trends in Union Structure: An International Comparison." *Industrial and Labor Relations Review* 35 (October): 43–57.

Zysman, J. 1977. *Political Strategies for Industrial Order.* Berkeley: University of California Press.

4 DEMOCRATIC CAPITALISM AT THE CROSSROADS

Adam Przeworski and Michael Wallerstein

The ideology that orients the current right-wing offensive is in many ways a ghost of the 1920s: antistatist, emphasizing the hegemony of the entrepreneur, portraying popular consumption as inimical to national interests, and based on the belief in the rationality of the market and in the autonomous importance of money. Yet what is new in this ideology is the dominant role played by technical economic theory. In the 1920s, deflationary policies and the principles of the gold standard and of balanced budgets were justified as an accumulated wisdom derived from experience. The only abstract basis for these principles was the quantity theory of money. The ideological appeal was couched in terms of popular values, such as thrift, responsibility, and common sense. The spokesmen for this ideology were typically officials of the Treasury and the bankers. In the 1980s, in contrast, the justification is derived from seemingly technical theories: "monetarism," "*la nouvelle économie*," and "rational expectations" are all being offered as scientific reasons why everyone will be better off if the state withdraws from the economy and capitalists are allowed to accumulate without distributional considerations. Even the most naked program for an upward distribution of income—Reagan's economic policy—is masked as a "supply-side theory," with a concocted Laffer curve as its theoretical mainstay.

It was Keynes who transformed macroeconomics from a frame of mind into a theory: a deductive method for analyzing the determinants of national income and for evaluating alternative policies. His followers constructed mathematical models of capitalist economies and described statistically particular economies in terms of these models. The new theory became the framework within which particular groups presented their interests as universal. It became the vehicle for the articulation of claims to hegemony and the language of economic policy. It is a lasting legacy of the Keynesian revolution that the terrain of ideological conflict has been conquered by technical economic theory.

While many people have subsequently claimed that the central principles of Keynesian economics had been presaged by Marx and some of his followers, in fact Marxist economic theory has never been of economic importance for the left. Marx's theory provided a useful threefold analysis: first, capitalism is based on exploitation (the source of profit is surplus value); second, the private property of the means of production is the source simultaneously of the injustice and the irrationality of capitalism; third, the falling rate of profit is the source of crisis. The theory has been politically useful only as a justification of revolutionary goals, specifically of the program of nationalization of the means of production. Marx's economics, even its most sophisticated version, is not a helpful tool for addressing workers' distributional claims within capitalism, and it is useless as a framework for administering capitalist economies. It is easy to say, "So what?" but the fact is that all mass movements of the left historically have had to face precisely these tasks.

As a result, it has been the understanding of the capitalist economy and the policy recommendations provided by Keynesian economics that the left has embraced. But Keynesian economics is now badly tarnished. Two phenomena that have characterized much of the developed capitalist world since the early 1970s, a gradual increase in the rate of inflation and a gradual decline in the rate of growth, have proved remarkably unresponsive to the traditional interventions prescribed by Keynesian theory. Yet this deeply ingrained tradition perseveres, providing the basis for much of the left's current reaction to the conservative offensive. Many continue to insist that the supply of savings is not problematic, that demand is chronically insufficient, and that a redistribution of income, full-employment policies, and social spending are the only ways to get out of the current crisis. The problem is that such a response is no longer convincing. It represents a reaction of clinging to old ideas and old policies that the right claims, with some justification, have been tried and found wanting. An obstinate defense of policies associated with past failures abdicates the ideological terrain to the right and, we believe, is not necessary.

What, then, are the choices we face? At one level we are discussing a question about an economic project that would constitute a reasonable and appealing alternative both to the policies of demand management and to the current wave of right-wing supply-oriented economics. But economic theories are rationalizations of the political interests of conflicting classes and groups, and should be treated as such. Behind economic alternatives lurk visions of society, models of culture, and thrusts for power. Economic projects entail political and social ones.

The combination of democracy and capitalism constitutes a compromise: those who do not own instruments of production consent to the institution of the private ownership of capital stock while those who own productive instruments consent to political institutions that permit other groups to effectively press their claims to the allocation of resources and the distribution of output. It may be worth recalling that this compromise was deemed unfeasible by Marx, who claimed that the "bourgeois republic" is based on a contradiction that renders it inherently unstable as a form of social organization. A combination of private ownership of the means of production with universal suffrage, Marx argued, must lead either to "social emancipation" of the oppressed classes utilizing their political power or to "political restoration" of the oppressing class utilizing its economic power. Hence, Marx held, capitalist democracy is "only the political form of revolution of bourgeois society and not its conservative form of life," "only a spasmodic, exceptional state of things . . . impossible as the normal form of society."

It was Keynesianism that provided the ideological and political foundations for the compromise of capitalist democracy. Keynesianism held out the prospect that the state could reconcile the private ownership of the means of production with democratic management of the economy. As Keynes himself put it: "It is not the ownership of the instruments of production which it is important for the state to assume. If the state is able to determine the aggregate amount of resources devoted to augmenting the instruments and the basic reward to those who own them, it will have accomplished all that is necessary" (Keynes, 1936, 378). Democratic control over the level of unemployment and the distribution of income became the terms of the compromise that made democratic captialism possible.

The problem of the 1930s was that resources lay fallow: machines stood idle while men were out of work. At no time in history was the irrationality of the capitalist system more blatant. As families starved, food—already produced food—was destroyed. Coffee was burned, pigs were killed, inventories rotted, machines rusted. Unemployment was the central political problem of society.

According to the economic orthodoxy of the time, this state of affairs was simply a given and the only recourse was to cut the costs of production, which meant cutting wages and transfers. Some relief measures to assist the unemployed were obviously urgently required, but whether such measures were advisable from an economic point of view was at best controversial. In Great Britain the Labour government in fact proposed to reduce unemployment compensation: this was the condition for being bailed out by the IMF of the time, where "M" stood for the Morgan Bank. But in Sweden the Social Democratic party, having won the election of 1932, broke the shell of the orthodox monetary policy. As unemployment climbed sharply with the onset of the Great Depression, they stumbled upon an idea that was truly new: instead of assisting the unemployed, the Swedish Social Democrats employed them. It was the beginning of the marriage of the left and Keynesian economics.[1]

Keynesianism provided the foundation for class compromise by supplying those political parties representing workers with a justification for holding office within capitalist societies. And such a justification was desperately needed. Ever since the 1890s, Social Democrats had thought that their irreversible electoral progress would culminate in an electoral majority that would allow them one day to enter into office and legislate their societies into socialism. They were completely unprepared for what ensued: in several countries Social Democratic, Labor, and Socialist parties were invited to form governments by default, without winning the majority that would have been necessary to pursue the program of nationalization but because the bourgeois parties were too divided to continue their traditional coalitions. Indeed, the first elected socialist government in the world was formed by the Swedish Social Democrats in 1920 just as they suffered their first electoral reversal. And once in office, socialists found themselves in the embarrassing situation of not being able to pursue the program of nationalization and not having any other program that would distinguish them from their bourgeois opponents. They could and did pursue ad hoc measures designed to improve conditions for their electoral constituency: the development of public housing, the institution of unemployment relief, the introduction of minimum wages, income and inheritance taxes, and old-age pensions. But such measures did not differ from the tradition of conservative reforms associated with Bismarck, Disraeli, or Giolitti. Socialists behaved like all other parties: some distributional bias toward their own constituency but full of respect for the golden principles of the balanced budget, deflation, gold standard, etc.

Keynesianism suddenly provided working-class political parties with a reason to be in office. It appeared that there was something to be done, that the economy was not moving according to natural laws, that economic crises could be attenuated and the waste of resources and the suffering alleviated if the state pursued anticyclical policies of demand management. If the economy was producing at a level below its capacity, given the existing stock of capital and labor, a proper government policy could increase output until it approached the economy's full potential. The government had the capacity to close the "full-employment gap," to ensure that there would be no unemployment of men and machines. Full employment became a realistic goal that could be pursued at all times.

How was this to be done? Here again Keynesian economics provided a technical justification for class compromise. The answer it provided was to increase consumption. In the Keynesian diagnosis, the cause of unemployment was the insufficiency of demand. Hence any redistribution of income downward to people who consume most of it and any expansion of government spending will stimulate production and reduce unemployment.[2] Given the existing capital stock, the actual output can always be raised by increasing wages, transfers to the poor, and government spending, or by reducing taxes. Since raising output means augmenting the rate of utilization of resources, the same policies will diminish unemployment. Thus the distributional bias of the left toward their electoral constituency found a rationalization in a technical economic theory. As Léon Blum put it, "a better distribution . . . would revive production at the same time that it would satisfy justice."

But more was at stake. In the orthodox thinking, any demands by workers or the unemployed for higher consumption appeared as a particularistic interest, inimical to future national development. To increase wages or social services was to raise costs of production and to divert resources from the investment necessary for growth, accumulation of capital, and improved productivity. The welfare of the poor was a matter of private charity, not of economics. But in the Keynesian framework it is consumption that provides the motor force for production, and suddenly workers and the poor turned out to be the representatives of the universal interest. Their particularistic interest in consumption coincided with the general interest in production. The "people" became the hegemonic force in society. As Bertil Ohlin stated in 1938, "In recent years it has become obvious that . . . many forms of 'consumption'—food, clothing, housing, recreation— . . . represent an investment in the most valuable productive instrument of all, the people itself" (Ohlin, 1938, 5). The terms of discourse became transformed.

Not all "Keynesian" positions are the same. One policy direction—warmly embraced by the radical left—focused on the redistribution of income toward wages and transfers. This is what happened in France in 1936. A more cautious, and more successful, policy consisted of manipulating government spending, taxation, and the money supply. The Swedish policy of 1932 was exclusively an "employment policy": it consisted of productive public employment financed by deficits and increased taxation. Wage rates did not increase in Sweden until 1938, well after the economy was out of the slump. In fact, the simple formal framework of Keynesian economics, as is found in modern macroeconomic textbooks, favors government spending over redistribution of income: the "multiplier" for government spending is greater than unity, while for wages and transfers it is less than unity. Hence, at least in principle, government spending more than pays for itself in increased production, while distribution of income partially hurts other components of demand.

In all of its forms, the Keynesian compromise consisted of a dual program: "full employment and equality," where the first term meant regulation of the level of employment via the management of demand, particularly government spending, and the latter consisted of the net of social services that constituted the "welfare state." The Keynesian compromise, therefore, came to consist of more than an active role for the government in macroeconomic management. As the provider of social services and regulator of the market, the state acted in multiple social realms. Governments developed manpower programs, family policies, housing schemes, income assistance nets, health systems, etc. They attempted to regulate the labor force by mixing incentives and deterrents to participation in the labor market. They sought to alter patterns of racial and regional disparities. The result is that social relations are mediated through democratic political institutions rather than remaining private.

At the same time, the Keynesian compromise became increasingly dependent upon economic concessions granted to groups of people organized as nonmarket actors. Politics turned into an interplay of coalitions among such groups, giving rise to corporatist tendencies of direct negotiation, either between organized groups—particularly labor and capital—under the tutelage of the government or between each group and the government. The allocation of economic resources became increasingly dominated by relations of political forces.

The compromise was tenable as long as it could provide employment and material security. Indeed, by most criteria of economic progress the Keynesian era was a success. Whether or not this was due to the efficacy of Keynesian economic policies or was merely fortuitous is a matter of debate. Nevertheless, output grew, unemployment was low, social services were extended, and social peace reigned. Until the late 1960s, Keynesianism was the established ideology of class compromise, under which different groups could conflict within the confines of a capitalist and democratic system. And, with the possible exception of Karl Rehn's 1951 program in Sweden and the Italian Communist party's short-lived austerity policy of the mid-1970s, Keynesianism provided the only framework for such a compromise. The crisis of Keynesianism is a crisis of democratic capitalism.

Keynesian economics is demand economics. The supply of capital and the supply of labor are assumed to be constant. The supply of savings is determined endogenously: it always equals investment. As demand is stimulated, whether by government policies or exogenous events, production expands to match demand, income increases, and so do savings until a new equilibrium is reached where savings again equal investment at a higher level of capacity utilization. The level of output shifts to maintain the equality of savings and investment. Moreover, since the Keynesian problem is to bring the actual output to the potential level of the already existing capital stock, the accumulation of capital is ignored altogether, to the point where new investment is assumed to be nonnegative at the same time that the total stock of capital is assumed to be constant.

Keynesian economics is the economics of the "short run," where the short run is a situation, rather than a period of time, in which cumulative changes of capital stock can be ignored. Given the Keynesian problem, this assumption is not unreasonable, but the effect is that this framework has nothing to say about the determinants of the potential level of output, about capital accumulation, or about productivity. The problem for Keynesian policies is always to close the gap between actual output and potential output, whatever the potential might happen to be.

Suppose for the moment that this problem has been solved and the economy is producing at its full potential. Since the already installed capital stock is now fully utilized, output cannot be increased without investment, that is, without new additions to the capital stock. In the demand view of the world, no longer Keynes's own but nevertheless very much "Keynesian," demand stimulation will still have the effect of increasing output, this time by "accelerating" investment.[3] Investors are assumed to make their investment decisions in order to increase production to match the expected future aggregate demand. Hence, the same government policies—spending, distribution of income, reduction of taxation—will continue to be effective, since by stimulating demand past the level of potential output the government will stimulate investment and economic growth.

But things look different when the supply of productive inputs is no longer taken to be fixed or passive. Now the question of whether the supply of savings is sufficient becomes problematic. The supply of savings available for investment is what is left from the total output after wages, transfers, and government expenditures have been subtracted. Hence the very measures designed to stimulate demand have the effect of reducing potential savings, that is, the savings that are available when the economy is running at its full potential.

As long as the economy operates below the full potential level, there is no contradiction involved. The output determined by the level of aggregate demand is assumed not to be greater than the level possible given the already existing capital stock, and the supply of savings is not a constraint. Indeed, in such circumstances, savings are too high and the Keynesian remedies all involve a reduction of savings as a proportion of output. But when the economy is close to full employment, the measures meant to increase aggregate demand and therefore to decrease aggregate saving have the effect of limiting the rate of growth of potential output. And since potential output is the ceiling for actual output, short-run demand stimulation turns out to have perverse effects for the long run. When we encounter symptoms of insufficient investment—the stagnation of real wages, the decline of productivity, the obsolescence of plant and equipment—demand management provides no solution. Indeed, the stimulation of demand accentuates the problem when the problem is the shortage of capital.

The supply side is the kingdom of the bourgeoisie. Here the bourgeoisie appears hegemonic: the realization of its interest in profits is a necessary condition for the improvement of the material conditions of everyone. Increased output requires investment, investment is financed by savings, savings are financed by profits. Hence profits are the condition for growth. From the supply side it is savings that provide the motor for accumulation, and, as all studies show, workers do not save much. Increases in wages and transfers as well as "welfare" spending appear, therefore, as hindrances to growth. So does taxation of the wealthy and any form of government intervention that restricts profitability, even if such restrictions reflect social costs and negative externalities.

Clearly, such a rendition of the economic system is not particularly appealing to those who consume most of their incomes. The natural response of the left is to claim that the very problem of the supply of savings is a false one (see, e.g., Perlo, 1976; Sweezy and Magdoff, 1980; or, most recently, Rothschild, 1982). This is a response embedded in the Keynesian framework, in which investment and growth are constrained by insufficient demand, not by available savings. But the response is wrong. The inadequate rate of investment in the United States did not suddenly appear in the recessions of the last ten years. Investment, capital accumulation, and growth of output per worker have been lower in the United States than in any major advanced capitalist economies, except for Great Britain, throughout the postwar period (for a recent study, see Kendrick, 1981). What is fallacious in the claims of right-wing economists is not the assertion that the supply of savings is insufficient to finance the desirable

level of investment, but the argument that savings are insufficient because profits are too low.

True, the mere fact that the level of investment is inadequate does
not imply that savings must be increased—at least if we accept the possibility that most of current investment may be socially wasteful, superflu-
ous, or otherwise undesirable. The aggregate balance always hides
qualitative alternatives. One bomber absorbs as much savings as would a
modern mass transit system for the city of Chicago. If investment is
insufficient, there are many places to look for waste, and nonmilitary
public expenditures would not necessarily be the first place selected by a
rational observer.

But such a qualitative response is not sufficient. Moreover, it is not
synonymous with an indiscriminate cry for a continued expansion of government spending, for supporting obsolete industries, and for an obstinate stimulation of demand. The problem of the supply of savings must be
faced as such.

The historical experience of several countries demonstrates that
growth can be generated without pernicious effects upon the distribution
of income when governments actively influence the rate and the direction
of investment and the supply of labor. The postwar German "miracle," the
rapid growth of Japan, and the apparent success of the Swedish Social
Democrats in combining relatively fast growth of productivity with the
most egalitarian distribution of income in the West demonstrate that
there exists an alternative to demand management as well as to profit-
oriented, right-wing, supply policies.

Although they have been pursued in somewhat different forms in
several countries, these alternative supply-oriented policies have never
been formalized in a theoretical framework. Indeed, the Swedish Social
Democrats seem to have stumbled upon them in 1951 in a manner reminiscent of their discovery of deficit spending in 1932: mainly as a remedy
to the problem of maintaining price stability under conditions of full
employment (Rehn, 1952). Of the German post-1949 policies it is typically said that they were a discovery of bankers who behaved as if Keynes
had never existed. Yet both the Germans and the Swedes, along with a
number of other countries, successfully pursued sustained programs consisting of public control over investment, elimination of inefficient industries, manpower policies designed to reduce structural unemployment,
and expansion of the welfare system.

In order to understand abstractly these investment-oriented supply
strategies, one must note first that in advanced capitalist economies productive investment is financed largely out of profit incomes. This implies
that the rate of accumulation, that is, the ratio of the change in capital
stock over total capital stock, is approximately equal to the product of two

quantities: the rate of saving out of profits and the aftertax rate of profit.[4] For example, a 6 percent rate of growth could be accomplished by a saving rate of 60 percent combined with a rate of profit of 10 percent or, equivalently, by a saving rate of 30 percent combined with a rate of profit of 20 percent.

The crucial question is whether firms can be made to invest when the rate of profit is low. The argument of the right is that this situation is unfeasible, since without sufficient future rewards capitalists will not abstain in the present. Big business and the political forces that represent it always claim that the only way the volume of savings can be increased is by raising the aftertax rate of profit, an increase that is supposed to have two effects. First, given a constant rate of saving out of profits, either directly by firms or by the recipients of profit income, the aggregate volume of savings will rise in proportion to the increase in the aggregate volume of profits. Second, a higher rate of return is promised to induce a higher propensity to save out of profits. Giving more money to "those who save," in the words of the *Wall Street Journal*, will encourage them to save at a higher rate. Indeed, the central tenet of the new economics is that a redistribution of income in favor of profits is a necessary cost the society must bear in order to produce a higher rate of investment and economic growth. The policies of the right, therefore, are designed to increase the effective rate of profit by sharply reducing nominal rates of taxation of incomes derived from property, by cutting down nonmilitary public expenditures, by eliminating all of the profit-constraining regulation, and by limiting the right of workers to organize and strike. They offer in return the promise of increased investment, improvement of productivity, and an acceleration of growth.

Yet there are countries—those mentioned above among them—in which the rate of investment has been relatively high while the aftertax rate of profit has been relatively low. These are the countries in which governments sought to alter the terms of choice of private decision makers between consumption and investment through taxes, credits, and direct subsidies.

Let us concentrate on the use of the tax system. Consider all taxes levied on incomes derived from the ownership of capital. They typically include a personal income tax on earned income ("salaries" of top executives), a personal income tax on property income, a tax on wealth, and a corporate profit tax. Given any mixture of these incomes there exists some average nominal rate of taxation of the aggregate property income. At the same time, all Western countries use the tax system as an instrument for stimulating investment: by a preferential treatment of capital gains, depreciation write-offs, investment credits, and grants. Given a mix of these different manners of investing, there exists again an average rate of investment relief, a rate that depends upon the rate of investment. Hence, the effective tax rate—the rate at which incomes from profits are in fact taxed—will be determined by the difference between the nominal rate of taxation and the rate of investment relief.

Let us now compare different tax systems. When the nominal tax rate on profits is low, the tax system has the effect of keeping the aftertax rate of profit high—independent of the rate of investment. Such a tax system rewards wealth, not investment. It may—although the evidence is at best mixed (New York Stock Exchange, 1981)—provide an incentive to invest, but it provides no assurance. It imposes no penalties on unproductive uses of profits. Hence, lowering the nominal rate of taxation of profits is the program of business. Owners of capital are then free to do whatever they find in their self-interest without any control.

But suppose that the nominal tax rate on profits is high—*very* high— and the marginal rate of investment tax relief is also high, at least for some chosen types of investment.[5] Unproductive uses of profits are now being punished. People and firms that do not invest do not receive tax breaks. The terms of choice facing the owners of capital are altered, presenting the choice of investing in publicly designated directions or paying taxes. It is now in the interest of firms to invest.

Consider, again, the example of two societies that add to their capital stock and output at the rate of 6 percent per year: one with the aftertax rate of profit of 20 percent and the rate of investment of 30 percent, the other with the aftertax rate of profit of 10 percent and the rate of investment out of profits of 60 percent. As is illustrated in Table 4.1, the distributional implications of these alternative patterns of growth are quite staggering. When accumulation is financed by a high rate of investment with a low rate of profit, Case B, the share of wages and government spending is much higher and the rate of consumption out of profit incomes much lower than Case A, where accumulation is financed with a high rate of profit and a low rate of investment. The choice is brutally clear. The same rate of growth can be obtained in different ways. The question is simply who will pay the cost of accumulation: the wage earners and unemployed or the owners of capital.

Hence, the problem of the supply of capital, that is, of investment and productivity, can be addressed without redistributing incomes upward and dismantling government services—if the tax system is used to reward investment and discourage consumption of profit incomes. This kind of tax system satisfies three criteria. First, it delivers investment. Second, it does not place the burden of sacrifice on wage earners and those dependent upon the government for survival. Third, if applied with qualitative criteria, it allows society to choose the directions of investment on the basis of criteria other than private profitability.

TABLE 4.1
Two Hypothetical Patterns of Capital Accumulation
at 6 Percent per Year
(Net incremental capital–output ratio is 2)

	CASE A	CASE B
Rate of growth of output and capital stock	6%	6%
Net investment/output	12%	12%
Rate of profit	20%	10%
Rate of saving out of profits	30%	60%
Share of profits in output	40%	20%
Share of wages and government	60%	80%
Share of consumption out of profits	28%	8%

Investment + Wages and government + Consumption out of profits = 100%

None of the above is intended to suggest, however, that democratic control over investment, exercised through the tax system, is a panacea. Decisions over the allocation of investment involve a number of trade-offs that are painful, as trade-offs are. We do not have consensual criteria by which to evaluate the choices presented by considerations of social effects, environment, health and safety, depletion of natural resources, and profitability. And in the absence of such criteria qualitative control over investment could lead to whimsical rule by government bureaucrats responding to political pressures. The exercise of discretion in investment policy makes it possible for firms (private and public) to succeed on the basis of influence within government bureaucracies rather than on the strict merits of their undertakings. And as long as market rationality remains the international criterion of efficiency in the allocation of resources, market criteria tend ultimately to prevail under the pressure of international competition.

Moreover, the goals of economic growth and increased productivity are in conflict with the goal of protecting existing jobs. A policy that encourages labor-saving innovations, that refuses subsidies to inefficient producers or protection to obsolete industries, must be coupled with Swedish-style manpower programs of job retraining and subsidies for labor mobility. But as the Swedes discovered, such manpower policies are socially costly and may be politically intolerable.[6] Measures designed to make people move according to the shifting patterns of industry imply that families are uprooted, social ties are fractured, and even entire communities may die when deserted by the breadwinners.

Yet a comprehensive, consistent system of public control over investment and income distribution opens the possibility for the realization of the original goal of the socialist movement, the goal that has been abandoned and perverted in its history, namely, reduction of the necessary labor time. It is ironic that, since the 1930s, full employment has been the predominant concern of the left. What in the middle of the nineteenth century used to be called "wage slavery" became the condition to be made universal. The working class has traveled a long road from seeking to abolish the wage relation to attempting to ensure that none are excluded from it. As Rosa Luxemburg observed in 1906, workers had become an obstacle to technical change that would make possible their own liberation. Defense of obsolete plants and inefficient industries for the sake of maintaining jobs has been an almost irresistible stance to the left, with inevitable detrimental effects for economic welfare. The maintenance of full employment has turned into a major barrier to investment that would improve productivity, increase output, raise wages, and/or reduce working time.

The priority that the left has given to the creation of jobs is inevitable as long as a decent standard of living is contingent upon being employed. Only when a sufficient minimum income is guaranteed to all will the maintenance of full employment no longer be a necessary object of economic policy. A substantial degree of equality, then, is a precondition for a working class–supported macroeconomic policy that would allow jobs to be lost for the sake of productivity growth that would not protect technologically backward plants and industries and that would encourage rather than block labor-saving innovations. But consider the rewards. At an annual rate of productivity growth of less than 3 percent, output per worker doubles in twenty-five years: within one generation we could reduce labor time by one-half. Whether people would opt to use productivity gains to increase consumption or free time we do not know. But once the maintenance of full employment ceases to be a fetish, once decent life conditions are assured for everyone, this choice will be open.

In any society some decisions have a public impact while others have a private, or limited, effect. And in any society some decisions are made by the public while others are restricted to the private realm. Investment decisions—decisions to withhold a part of society's resources from current consumption and to allocate them to replace or augment the instruments of production—have an impact that is both general and long-lasting, that is, public. Yet the very institution of private property implies that they are a private prerogative. Control over investment is the central political issue under capitalism precisely because no other privately made decisions have such a profound public impact.

The program of the right is to let the type and quality of investment be determined by the market. The market, after all, is an institution that coordinates private decisions and aggregates preferences. If the market is undistorted by monopolies, externalities, etc., and consumers are sovereign, the market aggregates private decisions in a way that corresponds to preferences of individuals as consumers. The decisions made by profit-maximizing investors will respond to the preferences of consumers concerning the atemporal and intertemporal allocation of resources. But the preferences to which the market responds are weighted by the amount of resources each individual controls. That an idealized "perfect" market matches aggregated consumer preferences for private goods efficiently is the first lesson of welfare economics. That aggregated consumer preferences reflect the distribution of income and wealth is an often neglected corollary.

A democratic political system constitutes another mechanism by which individual preferences are aggregated. If political competition is free of coercion and if voters are sovereign, then government policies will reflect the aggregated preferences of individuals as citizens. But as citizens individuals are weighted equally. Hence, the same set of individual preferences, for private as well as public goods, will normally yield a demand for a different allocation of resources when they are aggregated by political institutions rather than by the market.

Further, the market provides no guarantee that those whose consumption is most restrained in the present will reap the rewards of investment in the future. In any society some part of the current output must be withheld from consumption if production is to continue and consumption is to increase. What distinguishes capitalism is that investment is financed mostly out of profits, the part of the product withheld from wage earners. It is upon profits that the renewal and enlargement of the capital stock depend. Hence, under capitalism, the presence of profits is a necessary condition for the improvement of material conditions of any group within the society. But it is not sufficient. Profits may be hoarded, consumed, exported, or invested badly. Even if capitalists are abstemious, efficient, and prescient, their market relation with workers ends as the cycle of production is completed and the wages are paid, and there is nothing in the structure of the capitalist system of production that would guarantee that wage earners would be the ones to benefit from the fact that a part of the product is currently withheld from them as profit.

Any class compromise must, therefore, have at least two aspects: one concerning the distribution of income and the second concerning investment. If those who do not own capital are to consent voluntarily to the private property of the instruments of production, they must have a reasonable certainty that their material conditions will improve in the future as the result of current appropriation of profit by capitalists. Until recently, this compromise was rarely stated explicitly, for it is basically institutional: workers consent to the institution of private property of the instruments of production and owners of these instruments consent to political institutions through which other groups can effectively process their demands. Today, as trust in the compromise is eroding, workers are demanding more explicit commitments. As a recent report commissioned by the European Trade Union Confederation declared: "To accept the level of profits required for investments and to give companies a sound financial basis, workers will increasingly demand a say in decisions about investments and a fairer share of the income they generate" (Köpke, 1979, iv).

The current period, however, is the first moment since the 1920s in which owners of capital have openly rejected a compromise that involves public influence over investment and the distribution of income. For the first time in several decades, the right has an historical project of its own: to free accumulation from all the fetters imposed upon it by democracy. For the bourgeoisie never completed its revolution.

Just as it freed accumulation from the restraint of the feudal order, the bourgeoisie was forced to subject it to the constraint of popular control exercised through universal suffrage. The combination of private property of the means of production with universal suffrage is a compromise, and this compromise implies that the logic of accumulation is not exclusively the logic of private actors.

What is involved in the current offensive of the right is not simply a question of taxes, government spending, or even the distribution of income. The plans for relaxing taxation of profits, abolishing environmental controls, eliminating welfare programs, removing government control over product safety and conditions of work, and weakening the labor unions add up to more than a reorientation of the economic policy. They constitute a project for a new society, a bourgeois revolution.

It is thus necessary to consider the following question: What kind of a society would it be in which accumulation would be free from any form of political control, free from constraints of income distribution, from considerations of employment, environment, health of workers, and safety of consumers? Such hypothetical questions have no ready-made answers, but let us speculate.

It would be a society composed of households and firms related to each other exclusively through the market. Social relations would become coextensive with market relations, and the role of the political authority would be reduced to defending the market from attempts by any group organized as nonmarket actors (i.e. other than households and firms) to alter the rationality of market allocations. Since social and political relations would be depoliticized, demands by nonmarket actors would find no audience. The tension between accumulation and legitimation would be overcome: accumulation would be self-legitimizing for those who benefit from it, and no other legitimacy would be sought. As it has been said, "The government does not owe anybody anything."

Household income would depend solely upon the market value of the labor performed. Reproduction of the labor force would be reprivatized, and the traditional division of labor within the household—between earners and nurturers—would be restored. Persons excluded from participation in gainful activities would have no institutional guarantee of survival. They might be isolated on "reservations," whether inner cities or depressed regions, where they could be forgotten or ignored.

Workers would be disorganized as a class. If wage bargaining is decentralized by law to the level of the firm (as it is now in Chile) and if the process of internationalization of production continues, the monopoly power of unions would be effectively broken. Workers would be controlled by a combination of decentralized co-optation by some firms, by repression oriented against monopoly power, and—most importantly—by the threat of unemployment.

All of these changes would represent a reversal of trends that we are accustomed to see as irreversible. Indeed, the picture we drew can be easily obtained by combining the trends of contemporary capitalism described by, say, E. H. Carr (1961) or Jurgen Habermas (1975), and reversing them. Economic relations would be depoliticized. Government economic planning would be abandoned. Legitimation would be left to the market. The "economic whip" would be reinstated as the central mechanism of political control.

Is such a society feasible? The Chilean experience demonstrates that it is feasible when accompanied by brutal repression, the destruction of democratic institutions, the liquidation of all forms of politics. At least in Chile—most observers agree—such a restructuring of the society could not have succeeded under democratic conditions, without the military dictatorship. But is it feasible without destroying formal democracy, without a "Chileanization" of capitalist democracies?

Where electoral participation has traditionally been high, where working-class parties enjoy electoral support, and where access to the electoral system is relatively open—in most Western European countries—the project of the right seems doomed to failure under democratic conditions. But in the United States, where about 40 percent of adults never vote, where parties of notables have a duopolistic control over the electoral system, and where the barriers to entry are prohibitive, one must be less sanguine about the prospects. For suppose that the project is economically successful, even if for purely fortuitous reasons, and beneficial for a sizable part of the electorate, that the right captures both parties, and the offensive enjoys the support of the mass media. . . . Such a prospect is not totally farfetched.

NOTES

1. In fact, whether the Swedish policies were an application of the ideas of Keynes or were developed autonomously, from Marx via Wicksell, continues to evoke controversy (see Gustafsson, 1973).

2. In theory there is another Keynesian instrument: increasing investment expenditures—and thus aggregate demand—by lowering interest rates. But the effect of nominal interest rates upon the level of investment proved empirically to be the weakest link of the Keynesian approach, a conclusion reached by Tinbergen in 1939. Therefore monetary policy was used in practice mainly to accommodate fiscal policy, that is, to prevent government deficits from driving up interest rates or to control inflation, but not to stimulate demand, at least not intentionally.

3. This theory of investment was first suggested by J. Maurice Clark (1917). Its modern form is Hollis Chenery (1952).

4. Formally, $\Delta K/K = sP/K$, where K is the capital stock and ΔK its change, s is the rate of saving out of profit, P is the volume of profits, and P/K is the rate of profit.

5. As Andrew Shonfield put it, referring to Germany, "To make the trick work, tax rates had to be high. They were" (Shonfield, 1969, 282).

6. For discussions of the problems encountered by the Swedish Social Democrats in the most ambitious attempt to date in a capitalist economy to shape the supply of both labor and privately owned capital through government policies, see Ohlin, 1977; Heilbroner, 1980.

REFERENCES

Carr, E. H. 1961. *The New Society*. London: Oxford University Press.

Chenery, H. 1952. "Overcapacity and the Acceleration Principle." *Econometrica* 20: 1–28.

Clark, J. M. 1917. "Business Acceleration and the Law of Demand: A Technical Factor in Economic Cycles." *Journal of Political Economy* 25: 217–35.

Gustafsson, B. 1973. "A Perennial of Doctrinal History: Keynes and the 'Stockholm School.'" *Economy and History* 17: 114–28.

Habermas, J. 1975. *Legitimation Crisis*. Boston: Beacon Press.

Heilbroner, R. 1980. "Swedish Promise." *New York Review of Books* (December 4): 33–36.

Kendrick, J. 1981. "Sources of Growth in Real Product and Productivity in Eight Countries, 1960–1978." Paper prepared for the Office of Economic Research, the New York Stock Exchange, New York.

Keynes, J. M. 1936. *The General Theory of Employment, Interest, and Money*. 1964 ed. New York: Harcourt Brace Jovanovich.

Köpke, G. 1979. *Keynes Plus: A Participatory Economy*. Brussels: European Trade Union Institute.

New York Stock Exchange. 1981. *U.S. Economic Performance in a Global Perspective.* New York: New York Stock Exchange.

Ohlin, B. 1938. "Economic Progress in Sweden." *Annals of the American Academy of Political and Social Science* 197.

Ohlin, G. 1977. "The Changing Role of Private Enterprise in Sweden." In *Scandinavia at the Polls,* ed. K. Cerny. Washington, D.C.: American Enterprise Institute.

Perlo, V. 1976. "The New Propaganda on Declining Profit Shares and Inadequate Investment." *Review of Radical Economics* (Fall).

Rehn, G. 1952. "The Problem of Stability: An Analysis and Some Policy Proposals." In *Wages Policy Under Full Employment,* ed. R. Turvey. London: William Hodge.

Rothschild, E. 1982. "The Philosophy of Reaganism." *New York Review of Books* (April 15): 19–26.

Shonfield, A. 1969. *Modern Capitalism.* London: Oxford University Press.

Sweezy, P., and Magdoff, H. 1980. "Are Low Savings Ruining the U.S. Economy?" *Monthly Review* 7:1–12.

THE CRISIS OF THE WELFARE STATE

The growth and management of the welfare state has become a major political battleground in the past decade. From the 1950s to the 1970s economic growth permitted rapid expansion of social welfare programs without undue budgetary strain. But the economic adversity of the 1970s produced a fiscal crisis as tax revenues fell behind expenditures. Controversy now surrounds the ethical basis of welfare policies, the efficacy of particular programs, and the impact of public spending on economic performance. The following chapters analyze these issues from different perspectives.

In Chapter 5, B. Guy Peters breaks down the question, How much welfare spending is too much? into a series of definitional problems and shows that the answer is dependent on the criteria one employs. He presents four possible standards for evaluating the welfare state: public opinion, economic efficiency, ethical values, and policy analysis. How might these criteria, singly or in combination, best be employed in appraising welfare policies? A recurrent theme in Peters's essay is that capitalist welfare states may be "victims of their own success" in meeting popular needs. To what extent is this the case? What are the implications for democratic politics?

Why has welfare spending grown so rapidly? And what have the consequences been for social equality? What might appear to be a relatively straightforward problem of overgrown government becomes far more complex when the determinants of public sector growth and the effects of welfare programs are analyzed empirically and cross-nationally. Duane Swank and Alexander Hicks present the results of an eighteen-nation study covering the period 1960–80 in Chapter 6. Their analysis is particularly interesting because it measures the effects of a broad range of "state-centered" and "society-centered" variables on welfare spending and shows that a different mix of factors shaped welfare policy after the 1973 crisis than before. Their research also indicates that welfare programs have had a significant impact on social inequality. What factors are likely to determine the level of welfare spending in the future? What are the consequences for social justice? How important is economic growth to these programs?

Manfred Schmidt concludes this section, in Chapter 7, with a wide-ranging empirical survey of how the governments of twenty-one advanced industrial nations have coped with the welfare state crisis since 1973. He finds that most "muddled through" this period with various mixes of policies that reflected a fundamental trade-off between either restrictive fiscal and monetary measures to encourage long-term capital accumulation or additional social welfare expenditures, which increased public debt. What factors account for different resolutions of this dilemma in different countries? Schmidt reaches some interesting conclusions about the relevance of alternative hypotheses for explaining political responses to economic crisis.

The complexity of the empirical and theoretical issues is reflected in the variety of methodologies illustrated in these chapters. Peters demonstrates the importance of conceptual frameworks, while Swank and Hicks and Schmidt utilize multiple regression analysis to measure empirical relationships and test alternative explanatory theories. All three selections highlight the linkages among the political, economic, and ethical dimensions of the welfare state crisis.

5 THE LIMITS OF THE WELFARE STATE

B. Guy Peters

How much welfare spending is too much? This is a complex question, despite its apparent simplicity, and before attempting to answer it the question should be "unpacked," the assumptions and implications involved explicated, and possible alternative definitions of key terms explored. In fact, attempting to provide any definitive answer to this question may be a fool's errand. There are a sufficient number of differences across time and political systems to make any attempt to provide an unwavering answer to the question rather fruitless. This has not, however, prevented others from attempting to provide answers. The economist Colin Clark (1945) argued that a capitalist society could not survive with public expenditure greater than 25 percent of gross national product. After that figure had been surpassed and even doubled in a number of countries, Milton Friedman (1976) argued that freedom would be threatened in a country in which public expenditures were greater than 60 percent of gross national product. Roy Jenkins, formerly Labour Chancellor of the Exchequer in Britain, called the same 60 percent a "frontier of social democracy" (1976). In retrospect, with public expenditures accounting for some 65 percent of GNP in Sweden and over 60 percent in the Netherlands and Luxembourg, and with those countries appearing to revel in their freedom, the selection of any magic threshold figure for government being "too large" seems fruitless.

Welfare-state expenditures did not grow to such levels overnight, but were the product of a long historical development. When these programs began—the first social insurance program was initiated by Otto von Bismark in Germany in 1883—they covered only a small segment of the population and provided very meager benefits. The history of social programs has been their extension to cover more social problems, more people, and a greater level of benefits. The first social programs covered sickness and industrial injuries, and the system was then extended to cover old-age pensions, unemployment, and family allowances. The first programs tended to cover only industrial workers but later ones have been extended to cover virtually the entire population. Finally, with political pressures and indexing the benefit levels have tended to rise.

But why should this question of how much welfare expenditure is too much be raised at this time? What aspects of contemporary government and economy would lead anyone to question whether welfare spending— or total government spending, with which it is closely associated—had become too large? The most obvious answer is that whether or not government spending for social programs is *too* large, it is certainly large. In the great majority of industrialized democratic countries, government spending is more than one-third of gross national product; the mean percentage in 1981 was 46 percent of GNP (see Table 5.1). Thus, government in these countries now takes almost one dollar, pound, or franc in every two earned in the country to use for its (and the public's) purposes.

TABLE 5.1
*Public Expenditure as a Percentage
of Gross National Product, 1981*

COUNTRY	PERCENTAGE OF GNP
Australia	34.4
Austria	50.0
Belgium	56.1
Canada	41.4
Denmark	59.0
Finland	39.2
France	48.9
West Germany	49.3
Ireland	54.5
Italy	50.8
Japan	34.0
Luxembourg	60.1
Netherlands	61.5
New Zealand	35.2
Norway	48.1
Sweden	65.3
Switzerland	28.1
United Kingdom	47.3
United States	35.4

Note: Total public expenditure; GNP at market prices.

Source: OECD, 1983.

TABLE 5.2
Social Expenditures as a Percentage of
Total Expenditures, 1981

COUNTRY	PERCENTAGE OF TOTAL EXPENDITURES
Australia	59
Austria	54
Belgium	58
Canada	56
Denmark	52
Finland	60
France	62
West Germany	55
Ireland	41
Italy	56
Japan	46
Luxembourg	53
Netherlands	57
New Zealand	68
Norway	54
Sweden	61
Switzerland	64
United Kingdom	52
United States	56

Note: It is difficult to differentiate social expenditures clearly from other expenditure. Therefore, these must be regarded as estimates.

Not only is government spending very large, but so is the social component of public expenditure. In the nineteen most industrialized countries in the Western world, an average of 56 percent of total public expenditure is for health, education, and income maintenance.[1] Even removing educational expenditure from that total, an average of 49 percent of total public expentiture goes for social purposes (see Table 5.2). Thus, for the majority of democratic, industrialized countries, half of every monetary unit collected as taxes (or borrowed) must be spent for social purposes. Many citizens regard this as a very large—and perhaps a too large—burden for the taxpayers.

In addition to their absolute size, the costs of government social programs have been increasing. This increase has been perhaps the most dramatic in the United States, where public expenditures for social programs increased during the postwar period from a relatively meager 26 percent of public expenditures (all levels of government expenditures included) to over half of public expenditures. As we will point out below, the United States has not been a leader in the provision of social services to its population, but even it is now committed to spending very large sums of money (over $500 billion in 1983) for social services.

Another problem with social expenditures is that they are often perceived as being "out of control." This perception is to some degree fostered by the use of terms such as "uncontrollable" to describe large segments of public expenditure. In 1983, 77 percent of the federal budget was classified as uncontrollable. The majority of these uncontrollable expenditures (58 percent by my count) were social programs. Of course, the language that surrounds these expenditures may be more uncontrollable than the expenditures themselves (Peters and Hogwood, forthcoming). The majority of these expenditures could be controlled or curtailed in any budget year—all that is lacking is the political will. This may be another way of saying that, despite all the rhetoric of the political right, the majority of social programs are quite popular and are supported by both broad popular opinion and well-organized interests of both providers and clients.

Another factor that must be considered in the apparent concern over the size of welfare budgets in democratic countries is that these expenditures must be funded. This appears quite obvious, but at times it would appear that many practicing politicians forget what even the most naive householder must remember: revenue must equal expenditure. Most politicians love to participate in the joy of spending but are eager to avoid the pain of taxation. Citizens, on the other hand, cannot escape most taxation, and they see the effects of public expenditures reflected in their tax bills. These tax bills have increased almost as fast as the expenditure totals in Table 5.1, the major difference being a more than doubling in the proportion of public expenditure financed by borrowing (OECD, 1983). In addition, while high rates of taxation were once the sole concern of the wealthy, the expansion of the public sector has meant that a larger share of the population has to bear the costs of government. Otherwise, there simply is not enough money. For example, those earning $500,000 and more in the United States account for only 1.0 percent of the total income earned by the state; those earning over $100,000 account for only 5.7 percent.[2] If government is to pay for its current programs, those in the middle and even lower income brackets will have to pay a considerable share of the costs. Thus, the average worker in the Organisation for Economic and Co-operative Development (OECD) countries must now pay an average of 26 percent of his or her income (single worker; those with families pay slightly less) as income and social security taxes. Even a worker (single) who earns only two-thirds of the average industrial wage must pay 21 percent of his or her income in those two taxes (OECD, 1983). These figures totally ignore the impact of consumption taxes (both general consumption and specific excises on goods such as alcohol, tobacco, and gasoline) as well as the impact of property taxes and the indirect effects of taxes on employers. Thus, high taxes are now a concern of almost the entire population, and therefore it is understandable that there would be concern over how this tax money is spent.

The final reason that welfare expenditures may be perceived as a problem in contemporary societies is that they are perceived as being wasted, or being received by the wrong people for the wrong reasons. Cries of "welfare fraud," "scrounger," and a host of other, less polite phrases have punctuated the discourse concerning the role of government in providing social services to its population (Goulding and Middleton, 1983). This has been true even in societies such as the Scandinavian countries with well-developed systems of social welfare and ideologies generally supportive of welfare state programs. These views have been encouraged by the political leaders of some countries. For example, in the United States, one presidential counselor has said that those standing in line for free food are not hungry but simply too lazy to work to buy their own food. Similarly, in the United Kingdom, Mrs. Thatcher and her followers have campaigned vigorously against the "nanny state," with the implication that those who choose to, or must, depend upon state welfare benefits are less than fully developed members of society. Interestingly, the complaints against welfare abuse are much more strident than complaints against the members of the middle class who fiddle on their taxes—this is regarded as a necessity, not a crime (Lewis, 1979). Similarly, it is not noted that providers are apparently as guilty of abuse as are recipients of public benefits, e.g., the abuse of the Medicaid and Medicare systems by physicians in the United States.

Thus, there are a number of reasons why there has been concern over the size of public expenditure, and especially public social expenditures, during the past decade. Some of these reasons are quite real and compelling, whereas others are perhaps the product of the activities of the press and some political leaders. Regardless of the legitimacy of the complaints, in political terms a perceived problem is a real problem and must be addressed by government.

PROBLEMS OF DEFINITION

For anyone sufficiently foolhardy to answer my question about welfare spending, the first thing to do is to ask just what constitutes each of the major terms in the question: "welfare," "spending," and most importantly, "too much." We will now examine each of these terms in sequence.

Welfare

This term has very different meanings in the United States and in Western Europe. In the United States the term is pejorative and generally is applied to Aid to Families with Dependent Children (AFDC), which is the principal program of direct relief to the poor. It is targeted for women with dependent children and with no male income earner in the household. The program is means-tested, so that a woman must prove indigence in order to be eligible for benefits. Associated with AFDC are a number of other means-tested programs such as Medicaid, providing medical care, and food stamps, providing subsidies for food for the poor. The phrase "welfare mothers" has become a shibboleth for conservatives arguing that the system of social welfare encourages idleness, illegitimate children, and general social malaise.

In contrast, for most Western Europeans, welfare and the welfare state are positive images. In these societies the development of the welfare state has been associated with the supplanting of programs of direct relief, such as "welfare" in the United States, with comprehensive programs of social insurance including old-age pensions, unemployment insurance, sickness benefits, health insurance, and a number of other social programs. The majority of these social programs are universal, as opposed to means-tested, and citizens receive them (assuming that they qualify on other criteria) regardless of their level of income. Thus, the concept of the welfare state has been to create universality rather than separate classes of citizens. T. H. Marshall (1965), one of the major theorists of the welfare state, discussed this in terms of citizenship, with the welfare state conferring upon its citizens the same access to social rights as political citizenship conferred for voting rights.

In fairness, however, the United States has adopted many of the welfare state programs mentioned above, such as social security for old age and disability and unemployment insurance. However, these programs were adopted much later than in the majority of European countries and in some instances have been only partially adopted. For example, Medicare provides only partial coverage for the medical expenses of one segment of the population, albeit the segment in the greatest medical need. The United States still has a long way to go, both in programs and in attitudes, if it wishes to emulate the welfare states of Western Europe.

At a somewhat less abstract level, it must be remembered that not all spending affecting the welfare of the less affluent is labeled "welfare" or "social" as it passes through the governmental process. In fact, perhaps some of the most efficient means of achieving welfare goals may be through programs that do not appear to be "welfare." For example, Crouch (1977) has argued that the best way for government to address the needs of the working classes is to maintain full employment. If a government were to attempt to do that (or be successful) it may be that the programs would be labeled "industrial" policy as likely as "social welfare."

Or "regional" policy. Or possibly even "defense" policy. Of course, the objective analyst can see that a great deal of industrial policy is in fact disguised welfare policy, but politically they may be treated very differently. Similarly, the nutritional needs of the less affluent may be addressed through policies nominally labeled "agricultural" rather than through a "welfare" program.

In addition to the definitional and attitudinal questions surrounding welfare, there are other empirical questions. First of all, why are payments intended to support the income of some groups, e.g., AFDC recipients or pensioners, considered welfare, whereas payments intended as income supports for other segments are not considered "welfare" but rather the rightful claims of those groups? One such group that comes to mind first is farmers, not only in the United States but also in the majority of industrialized countries. A large amount of the spending for agricultural programs by these industrialized countries and by the European Economic Community provides income support for farmers. In economic terms, these are much the same as the transfers made to the welfare mother, although neither legislators nor the farmers would like them to be regarded in that way.

Much the same can be said of other social programs that tend to be provided in kind rather than in cash. We know that the middle classes are the major beneficiaries of educational expenditures, especially for higher education. They rarely receive any cash directly but instead are able to receive a service at a lower cost. The major exception to that generalization would be student loans (see below). In a like manner, expenditure for public mass transit tends to benefit those who ride the services and pay a fare that is below the actual cost of producing the service. This ridership is by no means composed entirely of the poor. In short, when thinking about government provision of income supports it is easy to overlook supports that go indirectly to the individual through the direct provision of the service. One study in Sweden, for example, estimated that those families in the lowest income class received benefits of 9,345 SKr (approximately US $1,000) from government purchases of goods and services (leaving aside health and personal social services), while those in the highest income class received benefits of 15,486 SKr (approximately $1,750). Under a less conservative set of assumptions, the differences were 6,801 SKr ($740) for the lowest income class as compared to 32,116 SKr ($3,750) for the highest.

At a more theoretical level, neo-Marxist scholars have attempted to distinguish various sorts of "welfare" expenditures. James O'Connor (1973), for example, distinguished between two broad forms of welfare expenditure. The first was "social capital expenditures," which are intended to make the capitalist system more profitable for the entrepreneur. Social capital expenditures are in turn divided into two types. The first of these are social investment expenditures, which increase the value of a single unit of labor. Educational expenditures are the best example of this type of expenditure. The other category of social capital expenditures are social consumption expenditures, which "lower the reproduction costs of labor," i.e., make individuals more willing to join the labor force. Social insurance expenditures that guarantee the worker a reasonable level of existence at retirement would be an example of these types of expenditures.

The second major category of "welfare" expenditures is "social expenses." These expenditures are intended to maintain social harmony and fulfill the legitimation needs of the state. These expenditures are directed primarily at the lower end of the income distribution, including programs such as AFDC, food stamps, and Medicaid. In O'Connor's analysis these expenditures are necessary to paper over the wide (and, in his analysis, widening) gap between classes in advanced capitalist societies.

One must also ask the question, Welfare for whom? There is a tendency to assume that the massive amounts of money spent for social programs, even in the rather poorly developed welfare state in the United States, will produce significant changes in the distribution of incomes. In fact, this has not been the case (Page, 1983). The welfare state is more successful in redistributing income across time than across individuals, and much of its purpose appears to be to preserve the income streams of individuals rather than to create sufficient new streams of income. This is especially evident when pension schemes are to some degree income related—either the main scheme or a supplemental state scheme—so that individuals who have earned more during their working lives will receive more pension benefits after they retire. In fairness, most public pension programs tend to have higher replacement ratios for lower-income workers (the lower-paid receive a higher proportion of their former earnings in a pension than do the more highly paid), but the more highly paid receive (and have contributed) more.

Finally, some of the major beneficiaries of the welfare state are not the nominal clients of the programs but those who administer the programs. Some welfare state programs, e.g., pensions, can be administered with relatively few people and a large computer linked to a check-writing machine. Other programs, e.g., medical programs and AFDC, require large numbers of individuals to administer. It is perhaps especially interesting that the medical profession in the United States, which fought so long and hard against "socialized medicine" in the form of Medicare and Medicaid, has become one of the major beneficiaries of the programs. Almost all physicians now receive payments from these two programs, and these payments comprised approximately 30 percent of the income of the medical profession in 1982. The constellation of forces around social welfare programs—both clients and providers—makes the program very difficult to change or certainly very difficult to terminate.

The term *welfare* is complex and multifaceted. Any attempt to deal with the provision of welfare and related services by the modern state defies the simple slogans so often used in political discourse. Further, the political forces that surround the welfare state are also complex, and any attempt to engage in a simple class analysis of those politics would be fruitless. In fact, the political success of the welfare state may ultimately be its undoing. By becoming a cornucopia available to everyone, the welfare state has lost its ability to redistribute income without imposing massive tax costs onto the members of society. Thus, if the welfare state is not to be seen as ineffective, it must be very costly.

Spending

A second definition problem is what constitutes spending. This may appear a simple enough problem, but in reality several questions should be addressed when considering what is meant by welfare expenditures.

First, in economic terms, there are a number of different types of expenditures, which may have different economic effects. The most fundamental distinction is between consumption and transfer expenditures. Transfer expenditures take money from one person and give it to another, the actual recipient of the money deciding how to spend it. Pensions are transfer expenditures, as are AFDC payments and payments of debt interest to the holders of government bonds. Consumption expenditures, on the other hand, involve the government deciding how the money is to be spent. Consumption expenditures are also referred to as "exhaustive expenditures" for they exhaust the stock of real goods and services in the society. Examples of consumption expenditures are hiring personnel, purchasing food for hospital patients, and building a new hospital.

In general, economists favor providing a service through transfer programs rather than directly providing, which involves exhaustive expenditures. This choice preserves consumer sovereignty and thus, it is hypothesized, the maximum utility will be created in the economy. So, for example, the needs of the elderly could be met by paying them a pension such as social security or by building large apartment buildings and providing for all their needs directly. If the option of providing a cash pension is accepted, then the elderly recipients are free to do what they want with the money; instead of spending it for food or housing, they could gamble it away or buy food for their pets. Thus, the direct delivery of a service ensures that the service is provided, but it also removes the element of citizen and consumer choice. A choice therefore must be made between ensuring that a service is delivered (with the state then acting *in loco parentis* and reducing consumer sovereignty) and allowing citizens to make their own choices.

In most welfare states the proportion of expenditure devoted to consumption expenditures has been decreasing, while the amount spent on transfers has been increasing (see Table 5.3). This represents in part conscious policy choice, but more importantly, it reflects changes in the population receiving social payments from government. The major increases in social programs have been in the programs for the elderly as the populations of all industrialized countries have continued to age. Thus, although taxation may be increasing along with levels of expenditure, in some ways the welfare state may be becoming less intrusive. Certainly it is less likely to produce economic distortions in the production of goods and services since consumers will be making an increasing proportion of the decisions about how that money is to be spent.

Another important thing to remember about welfare "spending" is that many things that may have the same effect as an expenditure are not accounted as public expenditures in most systems of public finance. One of the most important of these is "tax expenditures," which are subsidies coming to various sorts of activities through the tax system rather than through direct government expenditure (Surrey, 1967; Willis and Hardwick, 1978). For example, the tax system of the United States allows a citizen to deduct the interest paid on the mortgage for buying a home. This is, in effect, the same as providing a subsidy for the purchase of that home; the major difference is that the "tax expenditure" will not appear in any table showing public expenditures. The major difference between revenue forgone because of a certain type of expenditure and direct public expenditures for the same purpose is accounting. Another differ-

TABLE 5.3
Consumption Expenditures as a Percentage of
Total Public Expenditures

COUNTRY	1965	1970	1980
United States	67	63	54
Canada	59	59	52
France	39	38	35
W. Germany	50	50	49
Italy	49	46	39
Japan	58	53	41
Sweden	59	58	51
United Kingdom	55	53	51

Source: OECD, *National Accounts of OECD Member Nations* (Paris: OECD, annual)

ence is political, in that it is generally easier to introduce a "loophole" into a tax law than it is to include a subsidy in an expenditure program. Tax policy making is generally less visible to the public and is perceived as technical and complex even by those involved in government. Thus, the scrutiny over these policies may not be as stringent as over the more readily comprehended expenditure programs.

Although a large number of individuals in a society may benefit from tax expenditures, the major beneficiaries are in the middle classes. Thus, although the expenditures of government are not by any means radically redistributive to the working classes, the net effect of government activity in redistribution is lessened by the impact of the tax systems. If one is to look at the nominal rates of taxation, especially income taxation, in most industrialized countries, we might expect that a great deal of redistribution would occur; the availability of tax expenditures makes the systems much less redistributive. Further, as the middle classes are in general more effective politically, they continue to be able to have loopholes written into tax legislation even in countries that are nominally committed to more egaliatarian income distributions.

Finally, there are a host of other instruments that government can employ to produce benefits for the members of the society that do not involve the direct expenditure of funds (Peters and Heisler, 1983). These include insurance programs, loans (which are usually not counted as an expenditure as they will be repaid), and loan guarantee programs. As with tax expenditures, these programs do create real benefits for individuals and facilitate some forms of economic activity. Also, like tax expenditures, their benefits accrue primarily to the middle and upper classes and hence constitute a disguised welfare system of sorts for those segments of the society.

Too Much?

The final term in the topic question for this chapter is "too much?" This is obviously a value-laden term, and also obviously one about which reasonable people could disagree. It is also a term about which too little systematic thought, and too much rhetoric, has been developed. From the perspective of the policy sciences, at least four sets of criteria could be applied when attempting to decide how much welfare spending is too much: politics, economics, ethics, and general policy analysis. We should not, however, take great comfort from the availability of these alternatives, for few if any provide unambiguous answers about the appropriate size of government or of the welfare activities of government.

Politics
How much welfare spending would be too much can be determined by

applying political criteria, in the sense of mass political democracy, with the assumption that governments should not spend more money than their populations wish them to. Some have gone further, using the "median voter model," to assume that governments could not, in fact, spend more than desired by the median voter; if they did a political coalition could be formed to defeat the big spenders (Downs, 1957; Gramlich, 1982). Unfortunately for the practical application of the political criterion, however, the demands expressed by the populations of most industrialized countries are ambiguous and somewhat contradictory. The most general pattern of public opinion with respect to public expenditure is that the public wishes to reduce expenditure (or perhaps more precisely, taxation) but does not wish to have programs cut. They certainly do not want to have the programs that benefit them directly terminated or reduced, and frequently they do not want to have *any* programs reduced. For example, voters leaving the voting booths after having voted for Proposition 13 in California wanted only one program—public welfare—reduced as a result of their actions. They wanted other programs—including some that benefited the less affluent differentially—to continue as before and even to increase in expenditure (Sears and Citrin, 1982, 43).

Free and Cantril (1968, 32) argued that Americans were "ideological conservatives" and "operational liberals." Similarly, Sears and Citrin argue that citizens respond differently to very general symbols ("big government") and more specific symbols (individual programs). Thus, Americans are in general hostile to the idea of a big government and the welfare state, but tend to evaluate the impacts of individual programs positively. Only public welfare among all the programs mentioned was regarded sufficiently poor value for money to be cut, and even then there was a bare majority in favor of cutting the program.

This inconsistency in evaluating government and its programs is not confined to the United States. In a 1977 survey of Danish voters, 77 percent agreed that government was being too lavish with the taxpayers' money. On the other hand, the same respondents had a majority for cutting only one of thirteen government services, defense, and that was by a majority of 51 percent. For the remaining twelve services, including primarily social welfare services, an average of 12.5 percent of the respondents wanted expenditures reduced (Hibbs and Madsen, 1981). In a related piece of research, Taylor-Gooby (1982) found that although an overwhelming majority of British respondents supported state provision of services such as health care, education, and old-age pensions, majorities also would like the opportunity to have private supplements or replacements for those services.

How much, then, is too much social expenditure in political terms? The answer is far from clear and depends upon how the question is phrased. It also depends upon the manner in which the decisions about social expenditures are made. In general, decision making in government tends to maximize the pressures for expenditure. Both institutionally and temporally different types of expenditure are considered separately, allowing those who favor a particular expenditure to mobilize supporters who make it appear that "public opinion" strongly supports the program. Frequently, the total sum of public expenditure is then determined after individual decisions are made. This is the familiar politics of concentrated benefits and dispersed costs (Wilson, 1980). Recipients of concentrated benefits mobilize to gain their desires, while those who must bear the dispersed costs—the taxpayers—are rarely well organized. In addition, individual legislators who have concentrated benefits to gain from the passage of certain legislation—namely reelection—are frequently willing to engage in logrolling in order to gain the passage of their program, even if they have to vote for other expenditure programs to which they are indifferent or even mildly opposed. Thus, it may be that the institutions of government produce solutions that are, indeed, "too much" given the preferences of the majority of citizens for an aggregate outcome. We must remember, however, that the aggregate is composed of a large number of parts, and the same citizens who abhor the size of the aggregate would be equally dismayed by the termination or reduction of the services from which they benefit, or even the services that they believe to benefit society as a whole.

Economics

A second of the policy sciences that may offer an answer to the question of how much is too much is economics. Actually, two sets of answers for this question may come from economics. The first would be the macroeconomic answer, with the question being at what level of public expenditure—especially expenditures for social welfare—are macroeconomic problems (such as slowed growth and increased inflation) encountered? In other words, does public social expenditure, as fiscal conservatives have commonly argued, slow the rate of economic growth, reduce capital investment, and thereby over time reduce levels of employment and promote inflation? The belief that "big government" does produce such outcomes is the principal justification for the economic programs of fiscal conservatives such as President Reagan and Prime Minister Thatcher.

The evidence on the effects of public expenditure on macroeconomic outcomes is more mixed than the rhetoric on the subject from the conservative camp. Cameron (1982) found a moderately strong correlation (-0.58) between the *rate of growth* of public expenditure and macroeconomic growth. However, the *impact* of spending growth was very slight on economic growth as well as on other macroeconomic aggregates such as inflation and unemployment. There does not appear to be much evidence that a large public sector affects economic performance to any significant extent. The acceptance of the null hypothesis that the size of public expenditure makes little difference places into some doubt both the conservative and the liberal/Keynesian approaches to economic management. As noted, conservatives have assumed that if government is "taken off the backs" of the private sector then improved performance will result. On the other hand, liberals have argued that without government intervention in the economy, there might not be sufficient demand to sustain high levels of employment. Since we can find countries with large public sectors that have performed well economically (Austria) as well as performed poorly economically (Britain), and find countries with small public sectors that have performed well (Japan) and poorly (Australia), then perhaps we may have to explain macroeconomic outcomes by something other than simply the size of the government budget.

As mentioned above, public expenditures are not an undifferentiated whole, but can be disaggregated into a number of categories, most importantly transfer and consumption expenditures. Social expenditures are largely transfer expenditures (except for most education, the direct provision of health care, and the hiring of other personnel), so they may be expected to have somewhat less impact on economic performance than would programs, e.g., defense, that require more consumption expenditure. If we reexamine the relationship between the size of the public sector and economic performance using only transfer expenditures, what emerges is *no* pattern; there is a correlation of only 0.06 between the size of transfers as a percentage of gross national product and economic growth between 1975 and 1980. On the other hand, if consumption expenditures are used as a measure of the size of the public sector, there is a rather strong correlation ($r = -0.41$) between spending and economic growth. This corresponds to an earlier finding that an increase of 1 percent in public consumption expenditures produced a 0.2 percent decrease in economic performance (Smith, 1975). This does not imply, however, that government consumption expenditures are wrong, or too much; it merely implies that they do have some costs in economic growth. The question remains whether what is being funded in the public sector is more desirable than the growth forgone.

The effects of generous systems of social welfare benefits on economic growth are assumed to operate in part through a reduction in the incentives for people to work. It is assumed that a more generous welfare system will make it as "profitable" to remain at home as to go out and work. Whether that assumption would be valid if welfare systems were extremely generous can be debated. We do know, however, that the existing welfare systems of Western societies are not yet at a point of such generosity. For example, Kahn and Kamerman (1984) found that in eight industrialized democracies a single woman with two children (the stereo-typical "welfare mother") is an average 46 percent better off working at half the average national factory wage than in relying on social benefits. Even in the most generous system surveyed—Sweden—that woman would be 31 percent better off working, while in the least generous system—the United States—she would be 70 percent better off working.[3] Thus, although social welfare programs certainly do cost a great deal of money, they cannot even compete with half the average industrial wage as a means of support for a family, and it would appear that anyone with marketable skills would be substantially better off in the job market than in the dole line.

Another means of looking at the macroeconomic question of alloca-tion is to use an economic analog of the political criterion of voting. In politics, each citizen presumably has a single vote; in economics citizens have multiples of dollars, lira, or whatever. Thus, they vote with their money, and government spending too much would imply that govern-ment is spending more than citizens would collectively buy of the goods and services provided by government (Musgrave, 1983). Citizens may be coerced into making these purchases because of the government's power to levy taxes. Any number of problems arise in attempting to employ this criterion practically. Many of the products of government are collective goods, which, once produced, are difficult to exclude all citizens from consuming; therefore, citizens have an incentive to disguise their own preferences for such goods and thereby to lower their own contributions. Similarly, citizens may underestimate their benefits from certain types of public expenditures (Downs, 1960), or underestimate the amount of tax they are paying, and hence make faulty judgments about how they would like their money spent. If such a solution could be implemented, how-ever, it would provide an approach to the size of government emphasizing consumer (as opposed to voter) sovereignty.

The other economic question to be asked concerns the microeconom-ics of each individual government project. This form of evaluation, through techniques such as cost–benefit analysis and risk–benefit analy-sis, has become a standard component of policy making in most indus-trialized societies. The underlying assumption of this analysis is that if a proposed government project will create a net economic benefit for the society, then it is worth doing. A project that does not create such a net benefit should not be undertaken. Thus, in this form of reasoning, gov-ernment would be spending too much if it decided to spend money for projects that, although they may be desired by the population and be ethically justifiable, produce a net economic loss.

Some important objections have been raised to the economic criteria used to assess the value of public programs, including the fundamental question of why, given that the public and not the private sector is undertaking the project in question, private sector (market) values should be placed upon the outcome? There are also questions concerning the valuation assigned to some commodities rarely if ever traded in the marketplace, e.g., human life (Graham and Vaupel, 1983) and the choice of social discount rates (Flemming, 1977). Finally, there are questions concerning ethical factors such as the absence of any explicit distributional criteria in evaluating the outcomes of the projects; it does not appear to matter who receives the output of the project as long as that output is produced. Thus, any reliance on the single microeconomic criterion is likely to produce a result relatively similar to the choices made in the market, which therefore may conform neither to political demands nor to ethical standards for distribution. These considerations are, of course, especially important for "welfare" expenditures, which may produce little if any direct economic benefit or may produce only benefits that are extremely difficult to value in a market.

The microeconomic approach does have the advantage of being able to generate an answer in more or less "hard" numbers, although as many commentators have pointed out, the firmness is frequently illusory (Self, 1975; Graham and Vaupel, 1983). What this approach may not do, however, is to produce an answer acceptable to others than firm believers in the methodology.

Ethical Standards
Another means of justifying the size of government and of welfare expenditures is ethical. This would involve developing standards against which to compare the real world and then proposing changes in the status quo that do not conform to the generalized standards. The development of ethical standards should be thought of as going beyond utilitarian standards, as those are largely embodied in the economic standards discussed above. These standards could be developed in either a "liberal" or a "conservative" fashion. The liberal argument would call for greater government intervention in the economy to rectify the distributional injustices created by the marketplace, or to guarantee each individual in the society a minimum standard of existence. The argument would be that each individual, by virtue of citizenship or membership in the human race, deserves the right to survive and to participate in the affairs of the community. Further, the state has the obligation, acting *in loco parentis,* to maintain the life and well-being of its citizens. There is, of course, a very big question as to how far the rights of individuals—and the obligations of government—extend. Government may be obligated to provide food and health care to its citizens, but is the food only surplus cheese or does it also include steak? Is the right to health care good only for life-

threatening, acute treatment, or does it also extend to plastic surgery? Simply stating that citizens have rights and governments have obligations does not fully define the degree to which government should intervene and consequently may not say a great deal about how much spending is too much or too little.

The "conservative" approach, on the other hand, might argue that individual rights and property are important and should be preserved by government. Hence, any intervention by the state to limit the freedom of an individual or to remove some of his or her property by taxation is suspect. This argument is based not upon economic efficiency, as is the macroeconomic argument above, but rather upon the rights of individuals to get and retain as much property as they are able to in the marketplace (Nozick, 1974). Even conservative thinkers, however, ascribe some role to government—typically that of the "nightwatchman state," providing security and the enforcement of contracts—and there may again be questions as to where the line can and should be drawn in defining how much is "too much."

One means of getting around the need to provide definite measurements of the appropriate levels of expenditure is to apply what Rawls (1971) called the "veil of ignorance." The concept is that if individuals were to choose a distribution of goods and services in their society ignorant of their own placement in that distribution, they would tend to pick a more equal distribution than exists in most industrialized societies. This, in turn, would mean that they would opt for a more extensive role for government taxation and expenditure to generate that greater equality. Thus, if we did not know in advance if we were to be rich or poor, out of self-interest we would attempt to eliminate the possibility of being very poor. Of course, we would also eliminate the possibility of being very rich. In the real world, individuals do know their economic circumstances and cannot make such unbiased choices. However, this form of choice may serve as an ethical standard against which to judge outcomes in the real world: is this what people would have chosen if they did not know how they would fare?

Naturally, there have been a number of critiques of Rawls, led by Robert Nozick, who has concentrated upon the role of procedural rights in determining a just distribution of rewards in the society. The argument here is that any property that has been acquired by accepted procedures is rightfully held, and any attempt to remove it is therefore wrong. Thus, individuals acquire rights to income and other benefits not as a function of their citizenship or their humanness; desert comes through earning and action, primarily in the marketplace. Attempts at the redistribution of income are therefore illegitimate.

Thus, using different ethical standards and different concepts, two very disparate answers can be given as to how much government spending and how much welfare spending is too much. As with the other approaches we have already mentioned, there is little clear guidance as to how much government should spend.

Policy Analysis

The final set of criteria for assessing how much welfare expenditure is too much might be termed the policy-analytic set of answers. Although policy analysis involves all the criteria already discussed, some particular concerns about policy and its characteristics should be emphasized. In the first place, policy analysis should force its practitioners to look beyond narrow organizational and functional categories and to adopt a long-term perspective on the effects of policy choices rather than the short-term perspective that seems especially to afflict political analysis. Thus, answers to how much spending is too much may be different from this perspective than if only a single program is being evaluated along a single dimension over a short period of time.

Two particular policy-analytic concerns arise here with respect to government social expenditure. If we adopt a long-term perspective of social expenditures as investments in underdeveloped human capital—an approach common in discussing educational expenditures but less so for other types of social expenditures—then what may appear as "too much" in the short term may be "not enough" in the long term. We start with the knowledge that the majority of social welfare programs, especially in the United States, have been failures at their stated purpose of providing short-term relief so that recipients can return to the marketplace and the "mainstream of American life." Rather, the programs have become constant facts of life for generation after generation; a large proportion of the current recipients of AFDC had parents who received the same or similar benefits. Poverty and dependence are inherited just like eye color. This is true in part because of the social and cultural aspects of receiving AFDC payments, but it may also be physical. Children born of poorly nourished mothers and who are themselves poorly nourished have been shown to have more learning disabilities, to be less healthy, and to be more likely to fall into poverty (or not get out) than children from more affluent homes. Thus, spending money for social programs in the short run may reduce long-term costs for the same programs. These costs are certainly borne by the individuals involved, but they are also borne to some degree by the economy and society as a whole. Unfortunately, it has been the practice to budget social programs in a manner that has them spend the least money, regardless of the long-term costs.

The second policy-analytic point is that no policy exists in isolation from all other policy areas and that apparent savings in one area may impose costs in others. For example, in the case of social welfare expenditures, a number of other programs are affected by the failure of the programs to provide adequately for the needs of citizens. Poor nutrition and housing produce more demand for expenditures on health care and perhaps money wasted in education. The most obvious impact of failures in the social welfare system is manifested in the criminal justice system, which is bursting at its seams. Some portion of the blame for the massive increases in crime in the United States must be borne by the continuation of poverty for a large segment of the population and the meager sums paid as benefits by many public programs. Of course, even the most lavish welfare states have not eliminated poverty or crime, but they appear to have reduced crime by eliminating some of the need for theft and some of the frustration that would engender crimes of violence. Leaving aside the humane elements of this argument, in simple policy terms it may mean that money spent for welfare in the present may reduce the total costs of government by reducing the amount of money spent for prisons, policing, etc. For example, it is estimated that the average annual cost to incarcerate one criminal in New York state is $48,000. This is much greater than the average family income in the United States (approximate median family income was $21,000 in 1983). It is very much greater than the average social benefit paid under AFDC ($3,500 nationwide; $4,500 in New York) or Supplemental Security Income ($2,100). The fundamental point here is that failure to examine the amount spent for social programs in light of other programs and their costs, and the interactions of the programs, may lead to the faulty conclusion that welfare expenditures are excessive and that the general welfare of the society can be enhanced by spending less. We do not expect more spending for social purposes necessarily to create domestic peace and harmony overnight, but neither should the opponents of these programs be so confident that the money spent for social programs could be better spent elsewhere or better yet retained by the private sector.

We should also point out here that the size of the public sector can be measured by the number of policy areas with which it is concerned or the number of organizations that function under its umbrella, as well as by the amount of money it collects and spends. It may be that although the size of welfare expenditures makes little difference in terms of the effectiveness of the economy or of government itself—some large expenditure programs are actually quite efficient check-writing operations—the complexity of government and its interorganizational politics may create a great drain on the effectiveness of government (Rose, 1981; Peters, 1984). This is true in terms of the problems of bureaucratic politics and organizational politics, but it may also be true in terms of the possibly contradictory and confusing dictates of different programs and organizations

(Peters, 1982). Thus, the analysis of "big government" should not be concerned entirely with just how much money is spent but should also include some attention to the organizational network created to spend the money. Also, there may be some feedbacks, as more organizations are created to spend money—each with its own conception of the public interest and each with its own clientele—producing a proliferation of demands for expenditure. This need not result from the nefariousness of bureaucrats, as is often assumed, but even if it results from good intentions and noble ideals, it is still money spent.

BIG GOVERNMENT AND THE CRISIS OF THE STATE

The preceding attempt to unravel the question of how much welfare spending is too much has been more than an exercise in semantics and sophistry. There are many alternative ways of understanding the question, and the interpretation chosen will have a definite impact on the possible answers. But now let us return to the question and try to determine the impact of large welfare expenditures on the state of governments and economies in the penultimate decade of the twentieth century. We can argue about definitions of terms and advance alternative ethical positions, but soon the real world of politics intrudes on the exercise and we must try to understand why there is an apparent crisis—be it called "overload," "bankruptcy," or whatever (Rose and Peters, 1978).

As argued above, many of the problems of the modern industrial state arise not so much from the absolute amount of public expenditure as from the number of policy areas and the number of different programs devised to meet the needs of those policy areas. In essence, governments have not learned how to say no to groups that press demands upon them, although in fairness there may be as many "pressured groups" as pressure groups, and government itself rather than society may be the source of many policy initiatives. By attempting to cope with all the problems of society, government has constructed a massive level of internal contradiction, redundancy, and coordination problems. Some of these problems—the poverty trap in the United Kingdom and the conflict between the control of smoking and tobacco crop supports in the United States—are very well known, but such problems are more a part of the everyday life of bureaus and programs than usually understood. This "satrapic competition," to use a Weberian term (Page, forthcoming), may produce higher levels of expenditure than might otherwise be needed for at least two reasons. First, government may spend money for programs that have a net effect of zero: their effects cancel each other out, or in even a worse case the programs may interact negatively requiring a third program to correct the harm produced. Second, more resources may be required to produce an output simply because of the problems of coordination and potential conflict; internal politics may dominate over output goals. And the apparent incoherence of government activity and the absence of clear priorities—as in *Alice in Wonderland* we have all won and we must all have prizes— gives citizens the impression that no one is really in charge. Government is doing more but we are enjoying it less.

Going along with the above may be a problem of satiation. There are relatively few new frontiers for government to explore. As three students of policy put it: "The frontiers of policy development no longer stretch towards the horizon allowing unimpeded expansion with cheap resources; they are now the internal frontiers of integration, harmonization and trade-offs" (Heidenheimer, Heclo, and Adams, 1975, 220). As important as these internal changes are, and as often as they occur (Hogwood and Peters, 1983), they are not very exciting and there may be a feeling among the public that government has stopped producing the string of benefits it appeared to be producing at least during the postwar period and even before. Unfortunately, even if the public may have forgotten the continuation of old programs and may have become so accustomed to receiving those benefits that they have little perceived value, the accountants have not forgotten and old benefits must be paid for as much—or more—than new ones. Again, government is doing more but the public may be enjoying it less—and therefore rating the performance of the public sector lower.

It may be that governments in industrialized societies have become accustomed to satisfying demands for a certain type of "good" that it can readily supply, while an increasing source of demands in the society are for goods that are more difficult or impossible to supply in greater quantities. Governments learned that they could be successful by providing an increased quantity of material goods such as social welfare, education, health, and recreational services, and they were quite successful as long as these were the things people wanted from government. With the end of industrial politics and the advent of postindustrial politics (Benjamin, 1980), however, there are increasing demands for values such as justice and equality, which are more difficult for governments to supply in a demonstrable fashion. Governments will have to continue to supply all the material benefits they have always provided, but no amount of these benefits can satisfy the malaise felt by some citizens. Further, as Hirsch (1976) points out, there are a limited number of "positional goods" in a society—only one person can be prime minister at a time—and government can do nothing to rectify any perceived status deprivations resulting from that simple fact. Thus, having gone a long way in satisfying the material demands of their citizens, governments are faced with attempting to satisfy more vague and perhaps insatiable demands.

Is government too large? As we have seen, there is no definite answer. What we can say is that government is now frequently perceived as too big and further is perceived as too costly for the benefits produced. Politics is a game played with images and symbols, and as long as the perception of government as large, clumsy, and ineffective persists there will be a "crisis" in public expenditure and public management.

NOTES

1. It is difficult to separate "social" or "welfare" expenditures from the complex programs in a national budget. Thus, any figures given must be taken as best estimates of the magnitude of social spending.

2. These figures are based upon tax returns rather than an income survey. Therefore, there may be some slight bias in these figures, almost certainly in the direction of showing the wealthier to have a higher share of incomes.

3. The U.S. figures are an average for two states—New York and Pennsylvania—both of which have generous welfare programs by American standards. The inclusion of less generous programs (e.g. Mississippi's average welfare payments are 24 percent of New York's) would make the advantage of being employed even greater.

REFERENCES

Benjamin, R. 1980. *The Limits of Politics.* Chicago: University of Chicago Press.

Cameron, D. 1982. "On the Limits of the Public Economy." *Annals* 459: 46–62.

Clark, C. 1945. "Public Finance and Changes in the Value of Money." *Economic Journal* 45: 371–89.

Crouch, C. 1977. *Class Conflict and the Industrial Relations Crisis.* London: Heinemann.

Downs, A. 1957. *An Economic Theory of Democracy.* New York: Harper & Row.

———. 1960. "Why the Government Budget is Too Small in a Democracy." *World Politics* 12: 541–63.

Flemming, J. S. 1977. "What Discount Rate for Public Expenditure?" In *Public Expenditure,* ed. M. V. Posner. Cambridge: Cambridge University Press.

Free, L., and Cantril, H. 1968. *The Political Beliefs of Americans.* New York: Simon and Schuster.

Friedman, M. 1976. "The Line We Dare Not Cross: The Fragility of Freedom at 60%." *Encounter* 47 (November): 8–14.

Goulding, P., and Middleton, S. 1983. *Images of Welfare*. Oxford: Martin Robertson.

Graham, J. D., and Vaupel, J. W. 1983. "The Value of Life: What Difference Does It Make?" in *What Role for Government?* ed. R. J. Zeckhauser and D. Leebart. Durham, N.C.: Duke University Press.

Gramlich, E. M. 1982. "Models of Excessive Government Spending: Do the Facts Support the Theories?" In *Public Finance and Public Employment*, ed. R. H. Haveman. Detroit: Wayne State University Press.

Heidenheimer, A. J., Heclo, H., and Adams, C. T. 1975. *Comparative Public Policy: The Politics of Social Choice in Europe and America*. New York: St. Martin's Press.

Hibbs, D. A., and Madsen, H. J. 1981. "Public Reactions to the Growth of Taxation and Government Expenditure." *World Politics* 33: 413–35.

Hirsch, F. 1976. *Social Limits to Growth*. Cambridge: Harvard University Press.

Hogwood, B. W., and Peters, B. G. 1983. *Policy Dynamics*. New York: St. Martin's Press.

Jenkins, R. 1976. Speech to the Anglesey Constituency Labour Party, January 23.

Kahn, A. J., and Kamerman, S. B. 1984. *Income Transfers for Families with Children: An Eight Country Study*. Philadelphia: Temple University Press.

Lewis, A. 1979. "An Empirical Assessment of Tax Mentality." *Public Finance* 32: 245–57.

Marshall, T. H. 1965. *Class, Citizenship and Social Development*. New York: Anchor.

Musgrave, R. A. 1983. "When Is the Public Sector Too Large?" In *Why Governments Grow*, ed. C. L. Taylor. Beverly Hills, Calif.: Sage, 50–58.

Nozick, R. 1974. *Anarchy, State and Utopia*. Oxford: Basil Blackwell.

OECD. 1982. *The Tax/Benefit Position of Selected Income Groups*. Paris: OECD.

———. 1983. *Economic Outlook* (July).

O'Connor, J. 1973. *The Fiscal Crisis of the State*. New York: St. Martin's Press.

Page, B. 1983. *Who Gets What from Government*. Berkeley: University of California Press.

Page, E. C. Forthcoming. *A Comparative Study of Bureaucracy*. Brighton, Sussex: Wheatsheaf.

Peters, B. G. 1982. "The Problem of Bureaucratic Government." *Journal of Politics* 43: 56–82.

———. 1984. *The Politics of Bureaucracy*. 2nd ed. New York: Longmans.

Peters, B. G., and Heisler, M. O. 1983. "Thinking About Public Sector Growth: Conceptual, Operational, Theoretical and Policy Considerations." In *Why Governments Grow*, ed. C. L. Taylor, Beverly Hills, Calif.: Sage.

Peters, B. G., and Hogwood, B. W. Forthcoming. *The Pathology of Policy*. New York: Oxford University Press.

Rawls, J. 1971. *A Theory of Justice*. Cambridge: Harvard University Press.

Rose, R. 1981. "What if Anything Is Wrong with Big Government." *Journal of Public Policy* 1: 5–36.

Rose, R., and Peters, B. G. 1978. *Can Government Go Bankrupt?* New York: Basic Books.

Sears, D. O., and Citrin, J. 1982. *Tax Revolt: Something for Nothing in California.* Cambridge: Harvard University Press.

Self, P. 1975. *Econocrats and the Policy Process.* London: Macmillan.

Smith, D. 1975. "Public Consumption and Economic Performance." *National Westminster Bank Review* (November): 17–30.

Surrey, S. 1967. *Pathways to Tax Reform.* Cambridge: Harvard University Press.

Taylor-Gooby, P. 1982. "Two Cheers for the Welfare State." *Journal of Public Policy* 2: 319–46.

Willis, J. R. M., and Hardwick, P. J. W. 1978. *Tax Expenditures in the United Kingdom.* London: Heinemann.

Wilson, J. Q. 1980. *The Politics of Regulation.* New York: Basic Books.

6   THE DETERMINANTS AND REDISTRIBUTIVE IMPACTS OF STATE WELFARE SPENDING IN THE ADVANCED CAPITALIST DEMOCRACIES, 1960–1980

Duane H. Swank and Alexander Hicks

The precipitous growth of state welfare spending since World War II is now widely recognized as one of the most notable characteristics of the postwar development of the advanced capitalist democracies. The share of national economic product allocated by the state for welfare purposes (i.e. income maintenance and redistribution) increased more rapidly between the mid-1950s and mid-1970s than in any other period (OECD, 1978). Cash transfer payments to individuals (pension benefits, unemployment compensation, poor relief, and so forth) made under the core programs of the welfare state rose from 6.8 to 15.3 percent of the gross domestic product (GDP) between 1950 and 1975 in the advanced capitalist democracies (Swank, 1984). As Jurgen Kohl (1981) and others have shown, this increase accounts for over 50 percent of the growth in governmental expenditures during the post–World War II era.

As Table 6.1 illustrates, the average growth rate of income transfer spending as a percentage of GDP was 89 percent over the last two decades. Japan, the Netherlands, Ireland, Sweden, and Denmark led all countries with growth rates significantly in excess of 100 percent. While transfer payments grew slowly in a few nations (15 percent in New Zea-

Thanks are offered to Ted R. Gurr, Valerie Bunce, Kenneth Janda, and many others for comments on work contributing to this essay.

land and 20 percent in West Germany, for example), no nation experienced a decline in the relative share of national economic product devoted to income transfer spending between 1960 and 1980.

What has caused the dramatic postwar expansion of welfare expenditures? What are the impacts of welfare expenditures on income inequality in the advanced capitalist democracies? These questions have been among the most widely debated topics in the fields of political science, economics, and sociology in recent years and constitute the subject of this chapter. As we shall demonstrate below, the expansion of welfare spending in the postwar era has been linked to a wide variety of factors, including levels and rates of economic growth, increases in need for state assistance, the expansion of the institutions of political democracy, the

TABLE 6.1
The Growth of Income Transfer Spending as a Percentage of GDP in 18 Advanced Capitalist Democracies, 1960–1980

	INCOME TRANSFER SPENDING AS A PERCENTAGE OF GDP			
COUNTRY	1960	1973	1980	Percentage Change 1960–1980
Australia	5.7	6.4	8.9	56
Austria	9.9	15.4	19.2	94
Belgium	11.5	15.7	21.1	83
Canada	8.0	9.0	10.2	28
Denmark	8.4	12.4	17.8	112
Finland	5.7	8.7	10.0	75
France	13.2	17.5	23.2	76
West Germany	12.3	13.2	15.9	29
Ireland	6.2	11.9	14.4	132
Italy	11.6	14.0	19.8	71
Japan	3.6	5.3	10.6	194
Netherlands	10.1	20.4	27.2	169
New Zealand	7.8	5.7	9.0	15
Norway	8.2	13.9	14.7	79
Sweden	8.2	13.0	18.8	129
Switzerland	5.7	8.1	10.3	81
United Kingdom	6.9	9.7	12.4	80
United States	5.6	9.0	11.3	102
Average	8.2	11.6	15.3	89

Note: Income transfer spending includes expenditures for pensions, unemployment compensation, injury and sickness benefits, family allowances, poor relief, and related categories.

political power of labor and business, and the accumulation and legitimation needs of advanced democratic capitalist political-economic systems (e.g. Flora and Heidenheimer, 1981; and Hicks and Swank, 1984). As we have noted elsewhere (Hicks and Swank, 1984), the theoretical and empirical literature on the determination of welfare policies is varied and unintegrated.

With respect to the impact of welfare expenditures on income inequality, substantial evidence now exists to support the view that governmental expenditures under the principal income maintenance programs of the modern welfare state, coupled with progressive tax policies, appear to reduce notably the inequality in primary income (i.e. income before the effects of government taxes and transfers are accounted for) (e.g., van Arnhem and Schotsman, 1982; Hicks and Swank, in press).

We will attempt to provide some insight and evidence on the basic factors that facilitate and constrain the growth of welfare spending. We will also attempt to pinpoint the impacts of welfare expenditure on inequality of income in the advanced capitalist democracies. While several possible definitions of welfare spending are possible, we choose to focus upon direct income transfer payments as our indicator of welfare expenditure. As noted above, direct cash transfers represent spending under the core programs of the modern welfare state—pension, unemployment compensation, sickness and injury, family allowances, and poor relief programs—and are responsible for over 50 percent of the growth in all governmental expenditures in the postwar era. Our focus is on cash transfers in the eighteen affluent democracies with populations of at least three million in 1975.[1] Given that relevant social, economic, and political data are not available for many of these nations prior to 1960 and not yet published for the last several years, we will confine our attention to the years 1960–80.

Within the advanced capitalist democracies, the first portion of our focal period—from 1960 to the early 1970s—can be characterized as a period of strong economic performance and at least a modicum of political compromise concerning the basic parameters of economic and social policy. In contrast, the years following the OPEC (Organization of Petroleum Exporting Countries) "oil shock" of 1973 can be distinguished as a period of economic stagnation and crisis and of the dissolution of political consensus. With respect to welfare spending, these two periods constitute relatively distinct economic and political contexts for welfare expenditure growth. Consequently, we will examine the validity of the various explanations of changes in welfare spending during the two periods separately. Clearly, our confidence in any explanation of welfare expansion can be greatly enhanced if support is obtained in both periods.

DETERMINANTS OF STATE WELFARE SPENDING, 1960–1980

Explanations for state policies may focus on state-centered or society-centered factors. In the former, specific policy decisions or variations in public policies across time and political units are outcomes of the self-interested or ideological behavior of state policy makers (elected officials, their appointees at the highest levels of government, and bureaucrats) or, less directly, of government structures, such as the degree of state centralization. In the latter, policy decisions can be viewed as significantly influenced by aspects of social and economic structures and processes (changes in need for state assistance, levels and rates of economic growth, and so forth) and the political capacities of policy-relevant groups and classes in society. We will utilize the distinction between state- and society-centered factors to organize our discussions of welfare spending.

State-Centered Determinants

Individual Level Determinants

In recent years it has become quite clear that the self-interested actions of elected officials and their appointees in the highest positions in state bureaucracies—actions defined in terms of monetary, careerist, prestige-related, and power-related objectives of these decision makers—have played a substantial role in macroeconomic and social policy making. One popular form of this argument has become known as the "political- or electoral-business cycle" thesis. Politicians as well as the high-level state managers dependent upon them are viewed as vote seekers, enacting various policies that improve employment levels and stimulate the income of voters immediately before elections (e.g. Tufte, 1978; and on the original, somewhat different formulation of the thesis, Kalecki, 1943).

Tufte and others have provided evidence indicating the existence of the electoral-business cycle in the postwar United States and several other advanced industrial democracies. Although not all advanced capitalist democracies evince this tendency, the implications for social expenditure growth are clear for those that do. As Cameron (1978) has noted with respect to the growth of the public sector as a whole, the existence of frequent elections in which politicians pursue popular policies to enhance their reelection prospects may well lead to an overall expansion of state expenditure. Tufte, Cameron, and others have noted that incumbent administrations typically may use pre-election transfer payment increases (in combination with other policies) to stimulate voter income and, hence, voter approval. On the basis of this theorizing and evidence, we will examine whether rates of welfare expansion are greater in the presence of electorally motivated fiscal behavior (i.e. election-year economic stimulus) than in its absence.

The magnitude of change in social spending may also be determined in part by another type of policy-maker behavior: the self-interested actions and related organizational behaviors of bureaucrats. This argument has two different forms, each of which is relevant to our inquiry into the sources of welfare spending change. The most commonly held view is that bureaucrats strive to expand the budgets of their agencies in a quest for career advancement prestige, power, and so on (e.g. Rose and Peters, 1978). As a result, state expenditures are said to follow a steady upward trend over time, reflecting bureaucratic success in mobilizing program constituencies and obtaining periodic legislative acquiescence to larger budgets. With respect to welfare spending, Wilensky (1975) and others have provided evidence that a substantial degree of program momentum, as a manifestation of bureaucratic aggrandizement, exists with respect to the core programs of the welfare state.

It has also been observed that bureaucrats may not necessarily seek *large-scale* increases in program benefits; they will tend to act incrementally. Incrementalist theory holds that changes in policy expenditures will generally consist of marginal shifts from past levels of expenditures (e.g. Wildavsky, 1975). Accordingly, we will examine the following propositions: (1) 1960–80 growth in welfare spending was determined by the program momentum of bureaucratic aggrandizement; and (2) 1960–80 welfare spending changes can be characterized by incremental adjustments to past spending levels.

In addition to actions that revolve around the pursuit of career objectives, prestige, power, and the like, policy makers act upon their ideological preferences concerning the substance and direction of public policies. These preferences are primarily shaped by membership in a political party. Ideological preferences and pursuant policy and program decisions reflect party norms and traditions, general policy orientations of parties, and the interests and preferences of the parties' constituencies.

With regard to the determination of social welfare policy, the ideological dispositions of the political party in control of government have been central to past inquiries. Social democratic, labor-oriented, and most smaller left-wing parties are regarded as favoring the expansion of social welfare spending. The major conservative parties and smaller parties of the right are generally regarded as opposing most forms of social spending expansion.

David Cameron (1978) and others have supplied empirical evidence that government control by left-wing parties does indeed lead to larger social welfare budgets, while Francis Castles (1982) has provided empirical support for the hypothesis that the strength of right-wing parties has served as a principal impediment to welfare state expansion. On the basis of these observations, we will examine the propositions that (1) government control by left-wing parties facilitates welfare spending growth and (2) government control by right-wing parties inhibits it.

An additional explanation of welfare spending patterns—a factor related to both the self-interests of policy makers and their ideological dispositions—is the familiar notion that increases (decreases) in military expenditures result in decreases (increases) in welfare spending. This "welfare–warfare" trade-off is said to exist because of the budget limitations imposed on policy makers by finite economic resources and by the political and economic costs placed on policy makers by deficit financing and tax increases, measures necessary to finance the simultaneous expansion of military and social welfare spending (e.g. Russett, 1970). Consequently, we will examine the proposition that military and welfare spending inhibit each other.

State Structure as a Determinant of Welfare Spending Patterns

More supraindividual, structural factors, in particular the mode of tax collection and the degree of government centralization, have also been argued to affect welfare expansion. Scholars have noted that indirect taxes such as sales and value-added taxes may obscure the extent of tax levies, facilitating taxing and spending increases in turn (Cameron, 1978). In addition, scholars have argued that various aspects of governmental centralization may, by facilitating nationwide collective action by governments, tend to augment spending (e.g. Castles, 1982). They have also noted that state *de*centralization, by shifting spending decisions to subnational political jurisdictions that are more accessible to "have-not" demands than national governments may increase welfare spending (e.g. Piven and Cloward, 1981). In response to these arguments, we hypothesize positive impacts of relatively indirect tax extraction upon welfare spending and we examine centralization–welfare relationships for either positive or negative tendencies.

Society-Centered Determinants

Up to this point we have considered arguments to the effect that changes in state expenditure can be understood as consequences of the pursuit of self-interest and ideological preferences by state policy makers as well as of the impacts of certain aspects of governmental structure on policy makers' choices. However, those choices may also be influenced by pressures exerted on them from the state's environment. First, policy makers may be influenced by actions of various groups within society who attempt to mobilize resources (e.g. money, votes, and regime support) to win enactment of policies and programs favorable to their members. Second, policy makers may respond to pressure exerted by social and economic change, such as increased need for welfare assistance created by economic downturn and increased availability of economic resources necessary to finance social spending increases. We will discuss two sets of "society-centered" factors frequently cited as important determinants of welfare spending: the policy-related actions of class-based actors, principally labor and business; and various aspects of social and economic change, primarily changes in need for welfare assistance and economic growth.

The Role of Class-Based Actors

It is widely recognized that lower- and working-class groups, particularly labor unions and business, constitute the most salient nongovernmental actors in the determination of welfare policy within the advanced capitalist democracies. As Gough (1979) and Hicks and Swank (1984) note, labor unions, business firms, and the interest associations representing them (union confederations and employers' associations) frequently engage in a wide range of political action in an effort to influence the direction and scope of welfare policy.

In general, unions tend to favor strongly most forms of income transfer programs and other social policies providing benefits to lower- and working-class groups (e.g. Hicks and Swank, 1984). Unions favor increases in welfare payments, which maintain the living standards of their members, improve the long-term (i.e. retirement) income of their members, and shift upward the pay range left to collective bargaining, given that employers cannot offer less pay and benefits than members could achieve through state assistance. They also will commonly favor increases in forms of poor relief that do not necessarily benefit union members, given that such welfare support is often crucial for union-oriented parties' efforts to secure the electoral support of low-income groups and egalitarian electoral allies.

What are the various interests of business with respect to welfare spending? There are two distinct views on this question. "Corporate liberalism" views social expenditures as serving the accumulation and legitimation needs of business, particularly larger firms in the monopoly sector (e.g. O'Connor, 1973; Gough, 1979). Certain forms of income transfers such as poor relief and social services targeted at low-income groups are seen to socialize the costs of maintaining the legitimacy of social and economic arrangements favorable to business. Pensions and other forms of income maintenance spending are viewed to moderate strike activity and to socialize the costs of maintaining a cheap supply of reserve labor that may be used to depress wages and absorb merely cyclical demands for labor. Most other forms of welfare spending such as health expenditures are also regarded as essential to capital accumulation; they enhance the quality of the work force, improve labor productivity, and, in general, facilitate profitability.

A second body of literature suggests that larger corporations and the employer associations they dominate will, for several reasons, generally oppose increases in welfare spending. First, business firms have an interest in maintaining a low wage floor, or "reservation wage." The reservation wage, or the income a worker may receive when separated from a firm, is substantially affected by welfare spending (unemployment compensation, family allowances, and so forth). In general, social spending increases reduce the availability of low-wage labor and shift upward the base wage of unionized workers and the pay range left to collective bargaining. In addition, business firms are said to be opposed to most increases in welfare spending because they must help finance them and because they have interests against uninvited governmental incursions into the private sector. (For a detailed review of these arguments, see Hicks and Swank, 1984.)

Conventional Political Resources. Both business firms and unions have a number of conventional political resources for influencing state policy decisions concerning changes in welfare spending. Business organizations, particularly large firms in monopoly sector industries, possess numerous resources for affecting the substance and direction of state policies. Specifically, these groups possess the ability to fund and coordinate extensive public relations, lobbying, and electoral campaign activities; monopolies over information and expertise valuable to state policy makers; and control over valued private sector positions and social prestige that can be transferred to state policy makers. They also possess the capacity to control, to some extent, investment levels, production levels, and, in general, levels of prosperity upon which governments depend for financial (tax revenues) and electoral support. As Charles Lindblom (1977) and others have observed, business's discretionary control over the economic environment confers upon business a degree of "structural" power with respect to state decision making. Overall, these resources are likely to increase with the scale and concentration of business organization; increasing scale and concentration are likely to facilitate the development of relatively inclusive and coordinated employers' confederations (e.g. Causer, 1978). Thus, we will explore the hypothesis that the presence of large monopoly-sector firms within an economy significantly affects welfare spending patterns. The "corporate liberal" theorists would have us believe that greater presence of monopoly-sector firms will be associated with larger rates of increase in welfare spending, while other scholars suggest just the opposite.

Unions also possess several resources to influence welfare policy decisions: the ability to fund lobbying and campaign activities; the possession of a variety of selective incentives for mobilizing the votes of their members; and the ability to stimulate collective identification and solidaristic sentiments behind social policy initiatives. The capacities of unions to engage in effective policy action also involve the ability to manipulate production (and consequently the economic environment) through work slowdowns and strikes. This is so given the costs of work slowdowns and strikes for productivity, output, jobs, profits and hence, incumbent politicians held accountable for national economic performance.

These observations suggest that higher levels of unionization of a nation's work force are associated with greater increases in welfare spending. However, John Stephens (1980) has argued that it is not only unionization itself that is important for the expansion of state social expenditure but the degree of organization of the union movement. Stephens argues (1980, 99–103) that highly centralized unions incorporated in structures of economywide wage bargaining have been able to gain a large number of welfare-related concessions from the state in return for wage restraint. Given the relationship (real and perceived) between wage increases and inflation, policy makers concerned with negative political ramifications of accelerating inflation appear to have been willing to concede to a variety of demands of labor for increased income maintenance spending. Cameron (1978), Gough (1979), and other scholars have also stressed the importance for welfare expansion of "neocorporatist" arrangements, specifically, systems of economywide bargaining among highly centralized union confederations, employers' associations, and the state. Taken together, these observations suggest that the presence of highly unionized work forces coordinated through centralized union confederations may have significantly influenced the expansion of welfare spending in the postwar period, through lobbying, campaigning, and production-related activities and through their participation in economywide bargaining with employers and government.

Unconventional Political Resources. The organizations of business and labor—large firms and unions, employees' and employers' associations—can realize their welfare policy-related interests by influencing the choices of state policy makers through the mobilization of resources in institutionally sanctioned ways (i.e. lobbying, campaigning, and bargaining). However, groups may also influence the choices of state policy makers through forms of collective political action that are not sanctioned by the institutions and norms of democratic political systems. As Francis Fox Piven and Richard Cloward (1971; 1977) and others have noted, groups—particularly lower-class groups—may influence policy makers through the use of disruptive political action, primarily politically motivated strikes, demonstrations, and, occasionally, violent activity such as riots. Protest activity can (1) mobilize public support for certain policy actions through the dramatization of the plight of particular disadvantaged groups, (2) force various social and economic elites through disruption to apply pressure to state policy makers, (3) threaten the breakdown of the general level of social and economic order viewed as necessary for system legitimacy, and (4) signal the decline of electoral support for state elites.

Historical studies of working-class mobilization have revealed that the use of political protest and/or violence has played an important role in securing working-class objectives and concessions from upper-class groups and the state (e.g. Tilton, 1974). Studies of contemporary social policy development in all advanced capitalist democracies (e.g. Swank, 1983; Hicks and Swank, 1984) and the postwar United States (e.g. Hicks and Swank, 1983) have found support for the proposition that lower-class economic protest is associated with changes in income transfer spending. Given these findings, we will consider the hypothesis that 1960–80 changes in welfare spending were influenced by the magnitude of economic and welfare-related lower-class protest.

With respect to business and upper-class groups more generally, the use of disruptive protest is much less prominent in the political histories of the advanced capitalist democracies. However, recent tax-welfare backlash movements involving upper- and middle-class groups in the United States, Denmark, and other nations have entailed substantial levels of protest activity (e.g. Gough, 1979). In nations such as France, the role of protest demonstrations by associations of small shopkeepers and other petit bourgeois groups have been salient for welfare and economic policy throughout the postwar era. Consequently, we will examine the proposition that the magnitude of protest by middle- and upper-class groups will be associated negatively with rates of expansion in welfare expenditure.

The Role of Economic Performance and Need

The level of economic development and its social and demographic correlates have been widely cited as central determinants of welfare state development (e.g. Wilensky, 1975). The relationship between economic development and state social spending can be understood in terms of the impact of economic development on resources available for financing extensions of welfare spending and in terms of citizen and policy-maker willingness to fund expansions of welfare programs. As the nineteenth-century economist Adolf Wagner (1883) argued, increasing levels of affluence tend to generate a willingness among taxpayers to devote larger portions of their income to the provision of social goods and services. In addition, other observers (e.g. Hicks and Swank, 1984) have pointed out that economic growth rates may constrain the magnitude of changes in public expenditure in the short term primarily through their effects on revenue pools available for financing increases in spending. In general, the level of economic development can be regarded as an indicator of the overall level of affluence and expenditure-related attitudes associated with affluence. The rate of economic growth can be thought of as a central indicator of increases in potential resource pools and short-term changes in attitudes toward public expenditure. Accordingly, we will investigate the relationships between levels of economic development and rates of economic growth on the one hand and patterns of welfare spending on the other.

In addition to the welfare-spending impacts of levels and rates of economic growth, the need for increased state assistance may also result in changes in welfare expenditure. Changes in need for state welfare assistance may affect welfare spending in three ways. Demographic shifts in a nation's population (particularly in the number of elderly) and changes in economic conditions (and therefore unemployment rates) will result in certain automatic increases in relevant state expenditures (pension benefits and unemployment compensation) because of program entitlement provisions that qualify all individuals in a particular group to program benefits. Second, changes in need may lead to increased demands for the expansion of state assistance as needy groups and their political allies engage in collective political action. Third, state policy makers may advocate the real or perceived needs of various groups in efforts to bolster their own popularity. Given these observations, we will examine the claims that changes in need for welfare programs, specifically fluctuations in the sizes of the elderly and unemployed population, are related to patterns of welfare expenditure.

The Determinants of Welfare Expansion, 1960–1980

The hypothesized sources of 1960–80 changes in welfare spending—operationalized in terms of cash transfers as percentages of GDP—are summarized in the first column of Table 6.2. The nature of the relationship between the hypothesized determinant of welfare spending and changes in welfare expenditure is represented by the symbols P (positive relationship), N (negative relationship), and ND (no direction hypothesized). Thus, the greater the control of government by left-wing parties, the greater the increase in transfer payments; the greater the control of government by right-wing parties, the smaller the increase in transfer expenditures; and so forth. The hypotheses were tested utilizing a multiple regression framework that is discussed at length by Hicks and Swank (1984) and Swank (1984).[2] The measurement of all variables is briefly detailed in the appendix to this chapter. Measurement procedures and data sources are fully described in Swank (1984) and, for most variables, in Hicks and Swank (1984).

The third and fourth columns of Table 6.2 report the results of the multiple regression analyses for the 1960–73 and 1973–80 periods. We conclude that strong support exists for a hypothesized explanation of patterns of welfare spending if the regression coefficient of the factor representing the hypothesis is statistically significant at the .05 level or below (represented by " + +" and " + + +" in the table). Weak support

TABLE 6.2
Determinants of Cash Transfer Payments Expansion,
1960–1980

| | | FINDINGS | |
VARIABLE	HYPOTHESIS	1960–73	1973–80
State-centered			
Election-year fiscal			
stimulus	P	+ + +	
Government control			
Left	P	+ +	
Right	N	+ + +	
Incrementalism	ND		
Program momentum	P		+ +
Military spending	N	+ +	
State centralization	P/N		+ + + (N)
Fiscal illusion	P		
Society-centered			
Labor organization	P	+ + +	+ + +
Monopoly capital	P/N	+ + +	+ + +
Lower-class protest	P	+ + +	+ + +
Upper-class protest	N		
Economic development	P	+	
Economic growth	P		+ + +
Elderly	P		
Unemployment	P		+ + +
Dependent population	P		

P = positive effect hypothesized
N = negative effect hypothesized
P/N = both positive and negative effects hypothesized
ND = nondirectional hypothesis
+ = statistically significant at .10 level
+ + = significant at .05 level
+ + + = significant at .01 level

for a hypothesis is concluded if the corresponding regression coefficient is significant only at the .10 level (denoted by " + " in the table).

Determinants of Welfare Expansion, 1960–1973

The results of the analyses of 1960–73 changes in income transfer spending are displayed in the third column in Table 6.2. The analyses reveal a fairly clear pattern of findings with respect to the causes of welfare spending change between 1960 and 1973. The self-interested behavior and ideological dispositions of state policy makers did indeed affect changes in welfare spending during this period. Those nations in which incumbent governments engaged in frequent election-year economic stimulus experienced a larger long-term increase in income transfer spending than those nations where little evidence of election-year stimulus exists. Similarly, governments controlled by left-wing political parties expanded income transfer payments, while governments controlled by right-wing political parties constrained the growth of welfare spending. However, analyses also revealed that government control by center and nonconservative Christian democratic parties have positive effects on transfer spending increases similar in magnitude to the positive effect of left-wing parties. This indicates that the relevant distinction to be made is a right-vs.-nonright one as opposed to a right-vs.-left one when discussing party effects on welfare spending.

There is little evidence that income transfer spending grew as a result of bureaucratic momentum or in an incremental fashion. In fact, analyses reveal that, net of the influences of other factors, nations that had a relatively low level of transfer expenditure in 1960 increased their commitment to the core income maintenance programs at very rapid rates. For example, as Table 6.1 illustrates, nations such as Japan, Finland, and Ireland spent relatively low proportions of national economic product for income transfers in 1960 (3.6, 5.7, and 6.2 percent of GDP, respectively). However, between 1960 and 1973 alone, Japan, Finland, and Ireland increased expenditure at a much faster rate than the average (42 percent) for all advanced capitalist democracies (47, 53, and 92 percent increases, respectively).

Of the remaining state-centered explanations for welfare spending growth, only one factor—changes in military spending—had a significant effect upon 1960–73 changes in income transfer spending. In nations that experienced higher rates of growth in military spending, transfer payment increases were lower. This finding adds support to the notion that a basic trade-off exists between the commitment of societal resources to military spending and to social welfare expenditure. Our analysis produced no support for the hypothesis that welfare spending changes were affected by the level of state centralization or the degree of reliance on indirect (or hidden) taxes.

With respect to society-centered explanations, our analyses reveal that changes in income transfer spending during the 1960–73 period were significantly affected by the political strength and collective political action of policy-relevant groups, particularly labor and business. Countries that have relatively high levels of union organization (indexed in terms of unionization and union centralization) experienced higher rates of transfer spending growth during the 1960s and early 1970s. Consistent with the "corporate-liberal" thesis, the presence of politically powerful monopoly sector firms is associated with more rapid welfare growth. The magnitude of lower- and working-class protest over economic and welfare-related issues is also associated positively with rapid rates of change in transfer payment outlays. However, there is no observable relationship between magnitudes of upper-class protest (i.e. tax-welfare backlash protest) and rates of change in income transfer spending.

As Table 6.2 illustrates, there is little or no support for the propositions that rates of change in welfare spending were affected by levels of economic development and rates of economic growth or changes in need for state assistance during the 1960–73 period. The only evidence of significant economic or need effects is the moderate to weak relationship between the level of economic development and transfer payment changes. That is, 1960–73 rates of change in transfer outlays may have been moderately affected by the levels of societal affluence during the period. In sum, changes in income transfer spending during the 1960s and early 1970s can best be understood in terms of the electorally motivated behavior and ideological dispositions of incumbent politicians and the collective political action of lower- and working-class groups and large monopoly-sector firms.

The Determinants of Welfare Spending Change, 1973–1980

The fourth column of Table 6.2 displays the results of our analyses of 1973–80 changes in income transfer spending. Again, the results produce a clear pattern of findings concerning the determinants of 1973–80 transfer spending changes. Unlike the 1960–73 analyses, the 1973–80 findings indicate that electorally motivated behavior and ideological dispositions of incumbent governments had no impact on changes in transfer spending during the 1973–80 period (we discuss this difference below). With respect to the other state-centered explanations of welfare policy change, only the program momentum and state centralization hypotheses receive support. Our analyses reveal that, net of other influences on transfer spending, expenditure growth conformed to the pattern of bureaucratic momentum; expenditures grew more rapidly in nations characterized by large, well-developed bureaucracies at the beginning of the period. Second, our analyses show that the hypothesis indicating that public expenditures grow more rapidly in decentralized systems is accurate for the 1973–80 period. Specifically, we find that 1973–80 changes in income transfer spending were larger where the growth in the revenue share of subnational governments was larger. That is, increases in transfer spending are associated with growing decentralization. This finding is consistent with the bureaucratic momentum hypothesis. As David Cameron (1978) and others have noted, decentralized governmental structure is characterized by a proliferation of bureaucratic entities across and within levels of government that, in the absence of centralized fiscal control, may lead to substantial expansion in state taxing and spending.

With respect to the society-centered explanations of welfare expansion, our findings reveal both similarities and differences among 1960–73 and 1973–80 determinants of transfer spending change. As in the 1960–73 period, the political capacities and collective political action of policy-relevant groups were quite important for welfare spending patterns in the mid- and late 1970s. The degree of union organization and the presence of politically powerful, monopolistic corporations positively affected the expansion of transfer outlays in our eighteen advanced capitalist democracies. Again, our findings indicate that, contrary to some theory and research introduced and reviewed above, the presence of large monopoly-sector corporations sufficiently connotes enough corporate support for the social wage or diminution of small business opposition to it to contribute to transfer spending growth. In addition to the conventional forms of collective political action, our results indicate that lower- and working-class protest over economic and welfare-related matters led to transfer spending increases during the period 1973–80. The magnitude of protest by upper-class groups showed no visible relationship to transfer spending change.

The main divergence between the 1960–73 and 1973–80 analyses involves the impacts of economic growth and need. Unlike the earlier period, the rate of economic growth and changes in unemployment had significant effects on changes in transfer spending. These findings suggest that nations that escaped economic stagnation during the mid- and late 1970s continued to expand transfer payments as the tax base continued to expand and as policy-maker confidence in future affluence was bolstered by high rates of economic growth. However, economic stagnation, to the extent that it produced upward shifts in unemployment, also contributed to the expansion of transfer spending as the unemployed swelled the pool of people eligible for a wide range of social assistance. Levels of economic development and shifts in the size of the elderly population had no discernable effects on transfer spending patterns.

The Determination of Welfare Expansion

The most consistent findings to emerge from our analyses are those that pertain to the political strength of class-based actors, principally labor and business. In both the 1960–73 and 1973–80 periods, the change in income transfer spending was significantly influenced by the extent of union organization. Highly unionized work forces coordinated through centralized union confederations in nations such as Sweden, Norway, and Austria were apparently able to exert a variety of pressures on the state for continued expansion of pension programs; unemployment, sickness, and injury compensation; family allowances; poor relief; and other forms of state assistance directly and indirectly benefiting lower- and working-class groups. The rate of change in income transfer outlays was also significantly influenced in both periods by the presence of large monopolistic corporations. While we have no direct evidence concerning the policy-related behavior of these enterprises, both theorizing by scholars adopting the "corporate-liberal" perspective and our findings suggest that monopoly-sector corporations exerted pressures for transfer spending growth. As noted above, such spending helps to socialize many work force–related costs faced by large corporations, facilitates industrial peace, and generally helps to legitimize social and economic arrangements conducive to capital accumulation.[3]

Finally, our analyses reveal that the magnitude of lower- and working-class economic and welfare-related protests positively affected income transfer payment growth in both the 1960s and 1970s. Reinforcing cross-national findings in previous research, the present findings indicate that state policy makers did respond at least occasionally to economically based protest demonstrations, political strikes, and other types of unconventional political action with concessions. That is, our findings suggest that in an effort to restore social and economic stability and, in general, system legitimacy, policy elites frequently increased various forms of income transfer spending in response to economic grievances of lower-income groups.

Our analyses also suggest two notable differences between the determination of welfare spending during the 1960–73 and 1973–80 periods. During the 1960s and early 1970s, state policy makers apparently made policy decisions on the scope and direction of welfare policy in part on the basis of electoral and ideological goals. In many nations, incumbent governments utilized transfer payments in efforts to bolster reelection prospects. Transfer payments increased more rapidly in nations whose politicians engaged in net fiscal stimulus, presumably because welfare spending substantially underlay many fiscal stimuli. In addition, policy makers of both left and right ideological persuasions appeared to pursue ideological goals; governments controlled by left-wing political parties facilitated the growth of transfer spending, whereas governments controlled by right-wing parties impeded transfer outlay expansion. However, during the mid- and late 1970s, electoral and ideological factors had no impact upon the scope and direction of income transfer spending. In addition to the influence of class-based actors, rates of economic growth and changes in unemployment seem to have been quite consequential for transfer spending changes. How can we account for these differences?

As noted above, most advanced capitalist democracies were characterized by relatively high rates of economic growth, low unemployment, and low inflation during the 1960s. This relatively strong economic performance provided a climate in which policy makers could pursue self-interested and ideological objectives. Affluence and economic growth not only provided resources to fund welfare expansion and to enhance citizen willingness to support increases in welfare spending but bolstered the confidence of policy makers and citizens in continued economic growth necessary to sustain long-term welfare expansion. However, in the economic climate of the 1970s, particularly after 1973, slow rates of growth in investment, productivity, and national economic output as well as high rates of unemployment and inflation severely constrained policy makers. That is, policy decisions concerning the scope and direction of welfare spending were strongly influenced in a direct fashion by declining resource pools, fears of inflationary impacts of increased social spending, and elite and mass resistance to tax increases necessary to finance extensive growth in welfare programs. On the other hand, policy makers also had to balance these concerns with rising needs and demands for state assistance from the unemployed and displaced.

WELFARE STATES AND INCOME REDISTRIBUTION

What impact do income transfers have upon income inequality in the advanced capitalist democracies? More specifically, what is the magnitude of the redistributive impact of transfer spending and its relative impact in comparison to other types of redistributive policies? These are the questions to which we now turn.

In general, governments in the advanced capitalist democracies affect the distribution of income in several ways. They may do it *fiscally*, that is, by means of expenditure and tax policies. Second, they may do it *normatively*, that is, by means of regulatory policies. Third, they may affect the distribution of income *directly*, that is, by means of the immediate, direct impacts of tax, spending, and regulatory policies upon individual income. And they may do it *indirectly*, that is, by policies (fiscal and normative) that affect income distribution through relatively long-term and multistage processes. Based on this fourfold classification, Table 6.3 displays the typology of principal ways in which governments in advanced capitalist democracies may alter the distribution of income.

Evidence of some redistributive effects of governments' taxing and spending policies, or direct fiscal distribution, is now ample (e.g. van Arnhem and Schotsman, 1982). These studies all indicate that the immediate direct impact of government taxing and spending policies is to lessen income inequality, primarily distributing income downward toward households below the median income. Although the long-term, indirect effects of these policies may negate some of this redistribution (through compensatory wage policies, erosion of work incentives of the working poor, shifting labor demand, and so on), those studies that have attempted to examine the departure of long-term effects of fiscal policies from their direct redistributive impacts indicate that such departures are not great (e.g., Golliday and Haveman, 1973; and Devarajan et al., 1980).

In order to estimate the effects of income transfer spending (and tax policies) on income inequality, we collected data (circa 1970) on the size and distribution of income in thirteen of the eighteen advanced capitalist democracies discussed above. Unfortunately, comparable income distribution data on all eighteen countries are not available. The nations included are Australia, Canada, Finland, France, West Germany, Ireland, Italy, Japan, the Netherlands, Norway, Sweden, the United Kingdom, and the United States. The data include information on the distribution of primary, posttransfer, and postdirect tax income across deciles of households for each nation (i.e. the percent of total income received by each decile of households).[4] The postindirect tax distribution (the distribution that takes into account the effect of sales, value-added, and other indirect taxes) was estimated utilizing procedures outlined in Hicks and Swank (in press). The extent of income inequality for each nation was summarized using the familiar GINI index of inequality. Despite deficiencies in this index, it provides a succinct summary indication of the degree of inequal-

TABLE 6.3
Principal Types of Government Redistribution

	FISCAL	NORMATIVE
Direct	*Direct fiscal policies:* e.g., transfer payments, progressive taxes	*Direct normative policies:* e.g., affirmative action
Indirect	*Indirect fiscal policies:* e.g., high-employment policies	*Indirect normative policies:* e.g., property rights

ity present in a nation. (A GINI score of 0.00 would indicate perfect equality of income; a GINI approaching 1.00 would indicate severe inequality of income.) By examining the change in the GINI index after the impact of each element of direct fiscal redistribution is accounted for, we can ascertain the importance of transfer payments and other direct forms of fiscal redistribution for income inequality.

Table 6.4 displays the GINI scores for each country with respect to each of the four income distributions—primary, posttransfer, posttransfer and direct tax, and posttransfer and total taxes. Column V displays the total direct fiscal distribution that occurs in each of the thirteen nations. Total direct fiscal redistribution is simply the extent to which taxing and spending policies reduce the GINI index of primary income inequality. Column VI lists the percentage change in income inequality due to direct fiscal redistribution. As Column I illustrates, inequality in the distribution of primary income—the distribution before taxes and spending of government are accounted for—is greatest in Sweden, France, the United States, and Finland. The distribution of primary income is the most equal in Japan, Australia, West Germany, and Norway.

As Table 6.4 reveals, transfer payments and direct taxes result in notable reductions in inequality in most nations. However, indirect taxation exhibits a different effect. In general, indirect taxes such as sales and value-added taxes fall disproportionately on lower-income households. As a result, GINI indexes increase marginally after direct taxes are taken into account. Net fiscal redistribution is greatest in Sweden, the Netherlands, and Finland. These countries reduced income inequality by 36, 34, and 26 percent, respectively, through tax and spending policies. Direct fiscal policies had the smallest effects on income inequality in West Germany, Italy, and France. Inequality declined only 4, 7, and 9 percent, respectively, in these nations. Examining the final income distributions (Column IV), the Netherlands, Sweden, Australia, Norway, and Japan are the most equal nations. Income inequality is greatest in France, Italy, West Germany, and the United States.

With respect to income transfer spending, Column II indicates that transfer spending accounted for sizable reductions in income inequality in a majority of nations. On the average, transfer spending reduced income inequality by 14.3 percent. This downward shift in income inequality accounted for, on the average, 77.4 percent of all reductions of inequality that did occur as a result of direct fiscal redistribution. As a comparison of Columns I and II indicates, nations such as Sweden, the Netherlands, and Norway, which spent relatively large percentages of national economic product on transfer programs, experienced substantial reductions in primary income inequality as a result of transfer spending. Apparently,

TABLE 6.4
The Impact of Cash Transfers and Other Fiscal Policy Instruments on Income Inequality

COUNTRY	I		II		III		IV		V		VI	
Australia	.396	(12)*	.313	(13)	.312	(10)	.316	(11)	.080	(6)	20.3	(6)
Canada	.430	(8)	.383	(5)	.354	(6)	.360	(6)	.070	(7)	16.3	(7)
Finland	.438	(4)	.334	(11)	.321	(7)	.321	(8)	.117	(3)	26.0	(3)
France	.462	(2)	.416	(1)	.414	(1)	.422	(1)	.040	(11)	8.8	(11)
West Germany	.404	(11)	.396	(4)	.389	(3)	.389	(3)	.015	(13)	3.7	(13)
Ireland	.437	(6)	.380	(6)	.363	(5)	.369	(5)	.068	(8)	15.5	(8)
Italy	.434	(7)*	.403	(3)*	.398	(2)	.404	(2)	.030	(12)	6.9	(12)
Japan	.365	(13)*	.333	(12)	.316	(9)	.318	(10)	.048	(10)	13.0	(10)
Netherlands	.437	(5)	.355	(8)	.292	(13)	.293	(13)	.148	(2)	33.9	(2)
Norway	.415	(10)	.355	(8)	.309	(11)	.318	(10)	.097	(4)	23.3	(4)
Sweden	.471	(1)	.344	(9)	.302	(12)	.303	(12)	.172	(1)	36.4	(1)
United Kingdom	.418	(9)	.343	(10)	.319	(8)	.324	(7)	.094	(5)	22.6	(5)
United States	.446	(3)	.406	(2)	.380	(4)	.383	(4)	.063	(9)	14.1	(9)

Note: Income inequality is measured using the GINI index of inequality.

I. Pretax, pretransfer income.

II. Pretax, posttransfer income.

III. Postdirect, posttransfer income.

IV. Post-total tax, posttransfer income.

V. Direct fiscal distribution.

VI. Percentage change in GINI, Column I to Column IV.

*Values estimated despite lack of direct information on appropriate size distribution of income.

the impact of transfer policies was substantial in a large majority of our thirteen nations and was much more important for total direct fiscal redistribution than that of taxation policies.

WELFARE SPENDING AND INCOME INEQUALITY

Income transfer spending relative to national economic product increased dramatically in the post–World War II period. By the early 1970s, transfer spending was, on the average, roughly equivalent to 12 percent of GDP; by 1980, it typically accounted for roughly 15 percent of GDP. We have argued that income transfer spending growth in the 1960s and 1970s could be partially understood as the result of the electorally and ideologically motivated choices of incumbent governments, and we found evidence for this in the 1960s. We also argued that the growth in transfer spending during these decades was substantially a result of responses to the collective political action of lower- and working-class groups and monopolistic corporations. Our analyses revealed that changes in transfer expenditure in both the 1960s and the 1970s did largely result from these factors. In the 1973–80 period, economic growth and unemployment replaced the self-interested and ideological behavior of policy makers as central determinants of transfer spending patterns. Whether or not continued economic stagnation and the political pressures it generates for welfare state retrenchment will continue to play a role in the determination of welfare policies in the 1980s remains to be seen. However, our analyses do suggest that the political actions of highly centralized labor confederations, monopoly corporations, and lower-class protesters in all likelihood will continue to influence the overall determination of transfer spending policies in the future. Governments faced by demands from highly unionized and well-organized work forces and from other lower-class actors for the maintenance or expansion of the "social wage" are likely to be unable to engage in significant reductions in income transfer spending. Thus nations such as Sweden, where labor is highly organized via an encompassing centralized union confederation, are much less likely than the United States and the United Kingdom, where the labor movements are relatively fragmented, to experience substantial welfare state retrenchment.

The second question addressed above concerns the impact of transfer policies on income inequality. Did the relatively large expenditures made by most governments by the early 1970s for income maintenance and assistance substantially reduce inequality of incomes? The answer suggested by our analysis is clear. Income transfer spending on the average reduced inequality in primary income by about 14 percent. Of the total direct fiscal distribution that did take place in the thirteen advanced capitalist democracies, roughly 77 percent was accomplished through transfer expenditures. We may therefore conclude by noting that the extent to which income inequality will increase in the 1980s will in all likelihood be notably determined by the extent of cutbacks in welfare programs. Our analyses suggest that such retrenchment and subsequent income distribution effects will not only occur in nations under conservative governments (e.g. Reagan's United States and Thatcher's United Kingdom). It is also likely in nations that continue to suffer from slow economic growth. In the slowest growers, however, shifts toward more stringent programs seem likely to be at least partially offset by the entitlement pressures of higher unemployment. Thus, in nations such as the United States and the United Kingdom, the presence of conservative governments and slow economic growth on the one hand and the presence of high levels of unemployment and concomitant welfare need on the other may work at cross-purposes with regard to welfare spending growth. The mobilization of unions, nonunion welfare beneficiaries, and other extragovernmental actors may well shift the balance toward either retrenchment, maintenance of current levels, or, perhaps, further expansion.

NOTES

1. The eighteen nations are Australia, Austria, Belgium, Canada, Denmark, Finland, France, West Germany, Ireland, Italy, Japan, the Netherlands, New Zealand, Norway, Sweden, Switzerland, the United Kingdom, and the United States.

2. Several precautions were taken to evaluate fully the results of the regression analyses for problems that appear when the number of variables is relatively large and the number of cases relatively small. These procedures are presented in Hicks and Swank (1984).

3. It is also important to note that large monopoly-sector firms may also be able to divert the costs of financing welfare spending increases through foreign tax write-offs, transfer pricing, and so forth. Smaller, competitive sector firms may not be able to do this.

4. Information on primary income distributions in Australia, Italy, and Japan was unavailable. These distributions were estimated using procedures described in Hicks and Swank (in press).

APPENDIX: MEASUREMENT PROCEDURES

1. *Changes in Income Transfer Spending, 1960–1973/1973–1980.* For statistical reasons, changes in income transfer spending were operationalized by taking

the difference of the natural logarithm of the ratio of income transfer expenditure to GDP in 1960 (1973) from the same ratio in 1973 (1980).

2. *Presence of Electorally Motivated Fiscal Behavior.* The degree incumbent governments engaged in election-year fiscal stimulus was operationalized by computing "net fiscal stimulus" for each election year, where net fiscal stimulus is defined as $[E_t - E_{t-1}] - [R_t - R_{t-1}]$ and E and R equal governmental expenditures and revenues for all levels of government, respectively. The actual measure is equal to: $\sum_{i=1}^{N} NFS_i > 0$, where i through N are years between 1960 and 1973 (1973–1980) in which elections occurred and in which the change in GDP was positive.

3. *Program Momentum and Incrementalism.* Program momentum effects and incrementalism hypotheses were tested by examining the relationship of transfer spending levels at the beginning of the period to changes in transfer expenditure. For a detailed discussion of this procedure, see Swank, 1984.

4. *Ideological Dispositions of Incumbent Governments.* Left and right government control was computed according to the following algorithm:

$$(\sum_{i=1}^{N} G_i P_i \times 100)/14,$$

where i to N delineates the years 1960 to 1973 (or 1973 to 1980); G is 1.00 if the relevant type of party is participating in government, 0.00 if it is not; and P is the number of legislative seats controlled by the relevant type of party as a proportion of seats held by all parties participating in government.

5. *Military Spending.* Changes in military spending were computed as percentage and raw changes in military spending as a proportion of GDP between 1960 and 1973 (and 1973 to 1980).

6. *The Fiscal Illusion and State Centralization.* The reliance on hidden or indirect taxes was operationalized as the percentage of all government revenues accounted for by indirect taxes (i.e., sales, value-added taxes). State centralization was measured in two ways. First, unitary political systems were coded 1.00 while federal systems were coded 0.00. Second, the percentage of total government revenue collected by the central government in 1960, 1973, and 1980 was calculated. Levels and changes of indirect tax and central government tax measures were both evaluated.

7. *Labor Organization.* The degree of labor organization was measured by computing the percentage of the civilian labor force unionized circa 1960 and 1970 and the level of centralization of the labor movement in the late 1960s. Union centralization is measured in terms of the control of union confederations over local unions. The two measures were multiplied together to form the measure of union organization strength.

8. *Presence of Monopoly Sector Firms.* For each nation, the presence of large, monopoly-sector corporations was indexed by computing the total assets of the world's largest 450 industrial enterprises headquartered in a particular nation in 1962, 1966, and 1970 (and 1974, 1976, and 1978), dividing these assets by GDP for each year, and averaging the resulting proportions for the relevant period.

9. *Lower- and Upper-Class Protest.* The magnitudes of upper- and lower-

class protest are expressed as the 1960–73 (1973–80) average of annual mandays (protest participants multiplied by the duration of protest events) of protest (per 100,000 population) involving the relevant types of groups, directed toward political targets, and motivated by economic issues.

10. *Levels of Economic Development and Rates of Economic Growth.* The level of economic development is operationalized as the 1960–73 (and 1973–80) average gross national product per capita and, alternatively, as the average amount of energy consumption per capita. Economic growth was measured by calculating the 1960–73 (and 1973–80) average annual rate of change in real GDP per capita.

11. *Welfare Need.* The average number of persons over age sixty-five expressed as a proportion of the total population was computed for the period 1960–73 (and 1973–80). The percentage change in the total population over sixty-five was also computed. Similarly, levels and changes in the percent of the civilian labor force unemployed were computed. An additive index combining both the elderly and unemployed population was also computed. See Swank (1984) for a detailed discussion of need measures.

REFERENCES

Arnhem, J. C. van, and G. Schotsman. 1982. "Do Parties Affect the Distribution of Income?" In *The Impact of Parties,* ed. Francis Castles. Beverly Hills, Calif: Sage.

Cameron, D. R. 1978. "The Expansion of the Public Economy." *American Political Science Review* 72: 1243–61.

Castles, F. G. 1982. "The Impact of Parties on Public Expenditures." In *The Impact of Parties,* ed. Francis Castles. Beverly Hills, Calif.: Sage.

Causer, G. 1978. "Private Capital and the State in Western Europe." In *Contemporary Europe: Social Structures and Cultural Patterns,* ed. S. Giner and M. Archer. London: Routledge and Kegan Paul.

Devarajan, S., Fullerton, D., and Musgrave, R. 1980. "Estimating the Distribution of Tax Burdens: A Comparison of Different Approaches." *Journal of Public Economics* 13: 155–82.

Flora, P., and Heidenheimer, A., eds. 1981. *The Development of Welfare States in Europe and America.* New Brunswick, N.J.: Transaction.

Golliday, F., and Haveman, R. 1973. "Efficiency and Equity Effects of Income Transfers: A Simulation Analysis." Discussion Paper. Madison: Institute of Research on Poverty, University of Wisconsin.

Gough, I. 1979. *The Political Economy of the Welfare State.* London: Macmillan.

Hicks, A., and Swank, D. 1983. "Civil Disorders, Relief Mobilization, and AFDC Caseloads: A Reexamination of the Piven and Cloward Thesis." *American Journal of Political Science* 27: 697–716.

———. 1984. "On the Political Economy of Welfare Expansion: A Comparative

Analysis of 18 Advanced Capitalist Democracies, 1960–1971." *Comparative Political Studies* 17.

————. In press. "Redistribution in Rich Capitalist Democracies." *Policy Studies Journal.*

Kalecki, M. 1943. "Political Aspects of Full Employment." *Political Quarterly* 14: 302–31.

Kohl, J. 1981. "Trends and Problems in Postwar Public Expenditure Development in Western Europe and North America." In *The Development of Welfare States in Europe and America,* ed. P. Flora and A. Heidenheimer. New Brunswick, N.J.: Transaction.

Lindblom, C. 1977. *Politics and Markets.* New York: Basic Books.

O'Connor, J. 1973. *The Fiscal Crisis of the State.* New York: St. Martin's Press.

Organization of Economic Cooperation and Development. 1978. *OECD Studies in Resource Allocation: Public Expenditure Trends.* Paris: OECD.

Piven, F. F., and Cloward, R. 1971. *Regulating the Poor.* New York: Vintage.

————. 1977. *Poor People's Movements: Why They Succeed, How They Fail.* New York: Pantheon.

————. 1981. *The New Class War.* New York: Pantheon.

Rose, R., and Peters, B. G. 1978. *Can Governments Go Bankrupt?* New York: Basic Books.

Russett, B. M. 1970. *What Price Vigilance?* New Haven: Yale University Press.

Stephens, J. D. 1980. *The Transition from Capitalism to Socialism.* Atlantic Highlands, N.J.: Humanities Press.

Swank, D. H. 1983. "Between Incrementalism and Revolution: Protest Groups and the Growth of the Welfare State." *American Behavioral Scientist* 26: 291–310.

————. 1984. "Ascent and Crisis of the Welfare State: A Comparative Analysis of 18 Advanced Capitalist Democracies." Ph.D. Thesis. Northwestern University, Evanston, Illinois.

Tilton, T. 1974. "The Social Origins of Liberal Democracy: The Swedish Case." *American Political Science Review* 68: 561–71.

Tufte, E. 1978. *Political Control of the Economy.* Princeton: Princeton University Press.

Wagner, A. 1883. "The Nature of the Fiscal Economy." In *Classics in the Study of Public Finance,* ed. R. A. Musgrave and A. R. Peacock. London: Macmillan, 1958.

Wildavsky, A. 1975. *Budgeting: A Comparative Theory of the Budgetary Process.* Boston: Little, Brown.

Wilensky, H. 1975. *The Welfare State and Equality.* Berkeley: University of California Press.

7 THE WELFARE STATE AND THE ECONOMY IN PERIODS OF ECONOMIC CRISIS: A COMPARATIVE STUDY OF TWENTY-THREE OECD NATIONS

Manfred G. Schmidt

POLICY MAKING IN PERIODS OF ECONOMIC CRISIS

When the history of the second half of the twentieth century comes to be written, no doubt the achievements of high growth rates, full employment, low rates of inflation, and the expansion of the welfare state in the 1950s and the 1960s will be seen as the hallmark of a successful partnership between economic and social policies in the industrialized countries with managed capitalist economies. In the 1970s the setback to economic growth, rising rates of unemployment and inflation and the increase in postmaterialist demands, and the fiscal crisis of the welfare state have produced difficult problems for the reconciliation of a managed market economy and the maintenance of a developed welfare state.

The political science literature is packed with descriptive and explanatory accounts of a deep crisis. According to a widely shared view, the stage was set for longstanding ungovernability problems (Lehner, 1979; Offe, 1979; Rose, 1979; Dror, 1981); policy makers were confronted with self-produced overload (Luhmann, 1981); the Social Democratic consensus (Dahrendorf, 1979, 147–66) and the Keynesian class compromise (Alt-

Reprinted with permission from *European Journal of Political Research* 2 (1983): 1–26. Copyright © 1983 Elsevier Science Publishers B.V.

vater, 1981) were tending to break down; and the redistributive welfare state had overburdened the market economy (Wittmann, 1981; OECD, 1981; OECD Economic Surveys: Sweden, 1981; Stephens, 1981)—not only in the leading welfare states in Scandinavia, but also under bourgeois rule (Dahrendorf, 1981).

The economic and labor market crisis from 1973 to 1974 onward was the result of five interrelated developments which tended to undermine the successful partnership of a managed capitalist economy and a welfare state which had emerged in the 1950s and 1960s. These were: the wage policy of organized labor; the strong expansion of nonwage labor costs; the emergence of newly industrialized nations which challenged the competitiveness of old industrial branches in the developed nations; the increase in raw material prices; and the instability inherent in a market economy. All these factors contributed to a decline in capital return rates. The outcome resembles the "political business cycle" which Michael Kalecki (1943) had described. Entrepreneurs responded to the profit squeeze with lower investment rates, export of capital, and investment in labor-saving new technology. As a result, the number of unemployed increased, rates of economic growth and revenues declined, and the public authorities were sooner or later confronted with a fiscal crisis of the state and with requirements of a restrictive policy stance and a decremental budgetary process. They had thus to face a new challenge which could not any longer be managed within the old model of incremental and distributive policy formation (Dror, 1981). The response to economic crisis has not been uniform across the capitalist democracies. All advanced industrial democracies were hit by the economic constraints of the mid-1970s, but there was a wide range of variation in both political initiatives and policy outcomes.

In which way have the governments of the economically developed democratic OECD nations reacted to the unprecedented challenge? Which policy stance did they choose? To what extent have they been successful in maintaining and expanding welfare state provisions and in fulfilling the growth requirements of a market economy? How is the observable variation in policy efforts, outputs, and outcomes to be explained? To what extent is the political composition of government a variable which accounts both statistically and substantively for the variation? Under which conditions were the public authorities punished or rewarded by the electorate? Can we still assume that the notion of a constant and positive relationship between the degree of policy effectiveness and the degree of political support is a valid formula for the 1970s and early 1980s? These are the questions to which we will now turn.

We focus our study on twenty-three OECD nations which are economically more or less advanced and which have a democratic order with competitive regular and general elections in the majority of the years under study.[1] The period under investigation is from the beginning of the worldwide recession in 1973–74 to the opening of the 1980s. The policy indicators we have chosen are basically quantitative in character. The first indicator measures the economic performance—judged by "bourgeois economic common sense." This indicator was taken from the Euromoney study on "The End of the OPEC Era" (Euromoney, 1981).[2] A second class of indicators measures the extent to which governments have been capable of solving problems which are associated with class conflicts and demands made by organized labor. Measures of the rate of unemployment and the trend in civilian employment indicate the extent to which demands for employment security have been met.[3] Third, our focus will be on the changes in social security expenditures between 1973 and 1979–80. This indicator measures the extent to which demands made by the clientele of the welfare state have been met.[4] Fourth, we will study the extent to which governments have based their policies on an increase of public debt. This indicator reveals the extent to which contemporary policy making is short-sighted in character and operates at the expense of the future.[5]

Further, the thrust of our investigation will be on the extent to which the results of comparative studies on public policy in periods of economic prosperity are also valid explanations for policy making in periods of economic crisis. Basically, our focus will be on variables which are political, sociological, and cultural in character (Hibbs, 1977; Cameron, 1978; Tufte, 1978; Stephens, 1980; Castles, 1982a, 1982b; Schmidt, 1980, 1982a, 1982c). It is not our intention to direct the focus of our study on explanations which have been advanced by Keynesian and neoclassical schools of thought. Generally speaking, economic explanations, by themselves, do not adequately account for the observable variations in policy outcomes. The major reason seems to be that variables, which can be broadly grouped together under the "institutionalist" and "sociological" labels (Goldthorpe, 1978; Andrain, 1980; Scharpf, 1981)—for example, the importance of cultural and legal norms, organizational structures, political interests and strategies beyond the reach of the economic calculus—tend to be neglected in explanations advanced by economists.

For example, within the context of an "institutionalist" paradigm, scholars have frequently argued that the political composition of governments and the distribution of power in the party system are variables which account for a wide range of variation in policy outputs and outcomes. According to this school of thought, the reward structure, the laws of motion, and the imbalances of a capitalist economy and a democratic political order are basically amenable to political control. They can be changed, provided that governments, and especially socialist governments, are willing and politically strong enough to overcome the resistance of entrenched business interests. The underlying assumption in this school of thought is that different political structures have a differential impact on the course, content, and consequences of public policies.

According to another school of thought it is class politics which makes a difference. Authors who write in terms of a class politics paradigm argue that conflicts between social classes, the growth and strength of the labor movement and of business power, the mode of regulating the class conflict, the strength and cohesiveness of bourgeois and left-wing tendencies, and strategies of social demand anticipation on the part of governments have determined public policies within the scope of the relative autonomy of the state. In this view, it is not party politics that matters but rather the balance of competing forces in the society as a whole (see, for example, Stephens, 1979; Korpi, 1980; Schmidt, 1982a, 1982c; Madsen, 1981; Wilensky, 1981).

Finally, according to a third view which is typically taken by authors who write in terms of structural functionalism, it is the socioeconomic imperatives and constraints inherent in a capitalist economy and a democratic political order which are primarily responsible for shaping the actions of governments. The problems of capital—such as business cycles, waste of resources, and environmental pollution—combined with the structures of a "tax state" (Schumpeter) and with the need for legitimation have created the agenda for the modern state's activities, largely irrespective of which political tendency is in power (see, for example, Offe, 1972; and, as an example of older versions of this theory, Bauer, 1928).

It is our intention to put the competing explanations to the test. The key concepts of the various hypotheses were translated into the language of quantitative and qualitative indicators (see Appendix; and for a more detailed discussion, Castles, 1982b; Schmidt, 1982a, 1982c). The inference presented in our study is based on a wide range of one-country and comparative studies in policy making and on a statistical analysis of available comparable data (see Appendix).[6]

THE DISTRIBUTION OF POWER IN POLITICAL SUPERSTRUCTURE AND POLITICAL SUBSTRUCTURE

We will begin our investigation with a brief look at the distribution of political power between the "bourgeois" (conservative, Christian democratic, and center parties) and the "socialist" (social democratic and communist) tendencies. We classify the democratic industrial countries by the strength and duration of bourgeois and socialist tendencies: the extent to which they have participated in governments.[7]

The political composition of national governments in the OECD area between 1974 and 1980 is strongly skewed toward the dominance and hegemony of the bourgeois tendency (see Figure 7.1). No more than three countries—Sweden, Luxembourg, and Finland—are characterized by a "balanced" complexion of government. In Denmark, the United Kingdom, and the Federal Republic of Germany, Social Democratic parties were the leading governing parties, whereas a Social Democratic hegemony in this period was the exception (Norway and Austria) rather than the rule.

However, the distribution of power is not fully characterized by the political complexion of governments. For example, there is a large difference between a bourgeois government confronted with both a strong and powerful trade union movement and a strong and united socialist opposition, and one which is supported by a dominance of bourgeois tendencies in the party system and industrial relations. Further, the degree of ideological and organizational cohesiveness of the bourgeois and the socialist tendencies is a crucial variable which influences the overall distribution of power.

The typical pattern in the OECD nations is that of a differential disharmony between the power distribution in the "political superstructure" (measured by the political composition of governments) and that in the "political substructure" (defined by the power relationship within the party system and industrial relations and measured by the number of conditions which are favorable to "bourgeois policies").[8] Frequently, governments in the OECD area are confronted with adverse power relationships in the political substructure, and thus their room to maneuver is typically far more limited than might be expected on the basis of their political complexion (see Figure 7.2).

Figure 7.1
Political Composition of National Governments, 1974–1980

Source: Schmidt, 1982a, *Keesing's Archiv der Gegenwart*.
For the definition of the categories see note 7.

POLICY MAKING, ECONOMIC PERFORMANCE, AND THE WELFARE STATE

The governments of the industrial democracies reacted to the challenge of the economic crisis in the mid-1970s in a way which differed strongly from the policy stance which governments generally had taken in the depression years of the 1930s.[9] In the 1970s the public authorities were generally more inclined to contain the setback to economic growth, to expand the scope of state-financed programmes, and to expand labor market policies and social security expenditures. It is true that the overall policy stance was in general not more than moderately expansive, and it is also true that governments met the second oil price shock of 1979–1980 with a tightening of aggregate demand policies. Nevertheless, there was no real parallel to the strongly restrictive policy making which had featured so prominently in the late 1920s and early 1930s. The restrictive policy stance taken by the Reagan administration and the Thatcher government was the exception.

Variation in the Politics of Crisis Management: Muddling Through and Successful Political Control of the Economy

The response to the economic crisis has not been uniform among the democratic OECD nations. A wide range of variation in policy efforts, outputs, and outcomes was observable in the industrialized Western world (see Table 7.1). At the bottom we find nations whose economies and policy making are characterized by a pattern which may be described as "unsuccessful muddling through." Great Britain, Ireland, Italy, and Spain belong to this category. In these countries the economic performance was unstable, with low growth rates and high rates of inflation, declining competitiveness, high rates of unemployment, and low growth rates in social expenditures. Moreover, in Ireland and Italy the public debt increased to an enormous extent. Norway, Austria, and Japan are the nations which rank at the top, with growth rates being on the whole relatively high, comparatively low rates of inflation, stable or increasing competitiveness, low unemployment figures, and, in the Japanese case, high growth rates in social expenditures (whereas the Norwegian and Austrian authorities expanded their social security program at a slower pace). It was in these countries that the increase in the public debt seems to have been successfully used for the promotion of stable economic growth with low unemployment and an expansive welfare state. However, it is obvious that the Japanese authorities operated on a quite different basis from the Norwegian and Austrian governments. Whereas in the latter cases efforts to control the economy politically took place on the basis of a developed welfare state, in Japan economic growth and the

Figure 7.2
Disharmony Between Power Relationships in the Political Superstructure and the Political Substructure, 1974–1979/80

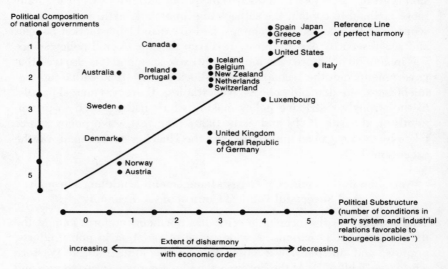

expansion of social security expenditures started from the baseline of an underdeveloped welfare state.

The majority of the OECD nations rank in between these extremities of "unsuccessful muddling through" on the one hand and successful economic and welfare state management on the other. In these nations, governments were in general only successful in one or two areas and unsuccessful in others. It was in these countries that the requirements of balanced economic growth or the demands for full employment and/or the demands for social security expenditures were not met. However, different strategies and policy results can be observed also in this group of countries. The first strategy is characterized by the primacy of economic accumulation and inflation control. Low or moderate rates of inflation and low rates of increase in the public debt were achieved, but this was done at the expense of full employment and social security efforts. The United States, Canada, and the United Kingdom under the Thatcher government belong to this group. The overall policy stance taken by the authorities in Sweden, Denmark, and Luxembourg is completely different. A primacy of welfare state policies—at the expense of balanced economic growth and competitiveness—is typical for these cases. Luxembourg, Denmark, and Sweden are nations in which the relative political weight

TABLE 7.1
Economic Performance and Policy Outcomes
in 23 OECD Nations, 1974–1980

Nation	Rank-order of economic performance 1974–80[a]	Labor market performance and rates of unemployment 1973–80[b]	Growth of social security expenditure in percentage points of GDP 1973–79[c]	Public debt as % of GDP 1973 and 1979[d]	
Australia	8	average (4.5)	2.6	—	
Belgium	10	bad (6.8)	5.7	53	61
Federal Republic of Germany	4	bad (3.2)	2.7	18	29
Denmark	15	average (6.0)[e]	4.7	16	36
Finland	12	average (4.6)	1.6	6	15
France	11	bad (4.8)	4.9	13	16
Greece	14	good (1.9)	2.1	—	
United Kingdom	17	bad (5.4)	2.5	73	62[f]
Ireland	13	bad (7.0)[e]	2.1	60	91
Iceland	22	good (0.5)	−1.5	—	
Italy	18	bad (6.7)	0.3	33	69
Japan	1	good (1.9)	5.8	13	36
Canada	6	average (7.2)	0.8	—	
Luxembourg	—	good (0.5)[e]	7.5	28	25
New Zealand	19	good (1.9)	—	—	
Netherlands	9	average (4.1)	7.1	43	44
Norway	3	good (1.8)	1.6	33	53
Austria	5	good (1.8)	2.7	17	31
Portugal	21	bad (7.0)[e]	5.4	—	
Sweden	16	good (1.9)	5.7	36	50
Switzerland	7	average (0.5)	2.5	25	30
Spain	20	bad (6.1)	2.5	—	
USA	2	average (6.7)	1.6	49	45

[a] Based on Euromoney, 1981 (rank 1 = best performance, rank 22 = worst performance). See note 2.

[b] Data in parentheses are rates of unemployment (average 1974 to 1980). "Bad" means a rate of unemployment which is greater than 2 percent and a decline in the level of employment between 1973 and 1980. "Good" means a low rate of unemployment (less than 2 percent) and an increase in the level of employment. "Average" means either a low rate of unemployment and a decrease in the level of employment (for example, the Swiss case) or a high rate of unemployment and an increase in the level of employment (for example, the United States). Source: see note 3.

[c] See note 4.

[d] See note 5.

[e] Estimate.

[f] Relative decrease between 1974 and 1979 (see Ridley, 1979, 100–6).

of the welfare state bureaucracy and the welfare state clientele is relatively strong. Hence, it is not too surprising that the course and the content of policy making in periods of economic crisis were strongly influenced by the entrenched interest of the "welfare state class." On the other hand, a strong welfare state class does not automatically produce an expansive social security policy process at the cost of the accumulation process. For example, in other developed welfare states (the Netherlands, West Germany, and Finland) the policy stance chosen by the public authorities was quite different from the Swedish one. The main thrust was on the modernization of the economy and a modest growth of the welfare state, with a moderate expansion of the public debt. The overall costs of this strategy were clearly visible in the labor market: the rates of unemployment increased very strongly. Rising unemployment was alleviated to some extent by relatively generous unemployment insurance funds. However, the absolute number of unemployed and the fiscal crisis of the state tended to undermine the monetary base of the unemployment insurance funds. Frequently, and to an increasing extent, the provision of unemployment benefits was applied much more restrictively and with an increase in social control.

The Swiss case stands apart from the other states insofar as the good economic performance and the extremely low rate of unemployment hide an enormously strong reduction in the labor force, which took place at the expense of foreign workers. Portugal experienced a strong increase in social security expenditures and a bad economic record with low growth, high rates of inflation, and high rates of unemployment. Elsewhere, it has been pointed out that the expansion of social security programs was the combined result of the consequences of the revolution, immigration from the former colonies, and the economic depression (OECD Economic Surveys: Portugal, 1981).

The Political Composition of Governments Does Not Make a Difference

These data provoke a host of questions: Why do the nations vary so widely in the way they responded to the setback to economic growth in the mid-1970s? How can we account for the difference between the "muddling through" nations and those states which were more or less successful in their efforts to control the economy politically? And to what extent is the political composition of government a variable which explains observable differences in policy outputs and outcomes?

Contrary to what many political scientists and politicians believe, and contrary to many findings in studies on policy making in the 1960s and early 1970s, there is no clear-cut relationship between the partisan composition of government and our indicators of social and economic performance. In other words, there is not much support for the view that countries under social democratic rule produced policies that were consistently different from those with bourgeois governments (see Figure 7.3).[10] Nor is there much evidence for the view that the size and unity of the "parties of the right" (Castles, 1982b) produce clear-cut policy differences.

This is not to say that the political complexion of governments does not matter for policy formation processes. The crucial points are, however, first that the political composition of governments produces different policies if, and only if, some additional conditions are fulfilled, and, second that governments with ideologically widely divergent parties in power produce equifunctional policy outputs and outcomes if, and only if, additional conditions are met. Of these additional conditions, it is the structure of class politics arrangements, the structure of the political culture, the economic strength, and levels of economic productivity in the period before the crisis which make a difference—largely, though not exclusively, irrespective of which party is in power.

Economic Performance After the First Oil Shock: Levels of Productivity Prior to the Crisis and Extraparliamentary Distributions of Power Make a Difference

The economic performance of the industrialized democracies after the first oil shock is largely independent of the size and the growth rates of the public economy and the welfare state.[11] There is not much evidence for the view held by the new fiscal orthodoxy according to which the economic miseries were the product of government, in particular the rapid expansion and the excessive levels of government spending (see additionally Cameron, 1982). Nor is there much evidence for the view that the blame for market failure ungovernability problems can be laid at the door of either left-wing or right-wing governments.

The explanation for the differential performance of the capitalist democracies has to be sought elsewhere. It is to be found in a number of economic, sociocultural, and political variables that our empirical analysis demonstrates to be of substantial importance in determining the performance of the economies. The most successful economies were those which were economically powerful and economically highly productive before the worldwide recession began and in which the dominance of the bourgeois tendency in the sphere of production was in harmony with the power distribution in the party system and in industrial arenas *or* in which powerful but ideologically moderate trade unions, whose strength was institutionalized in a corporatist mode of class conflict regulation,

Figure 7.3
Policy Outcomes and the Political Composition of Governments, 1974–1979/80

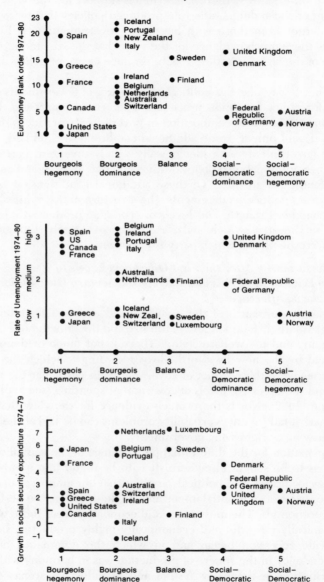

Figure 7.3 (continued)

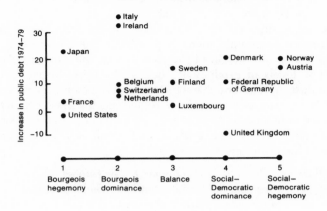

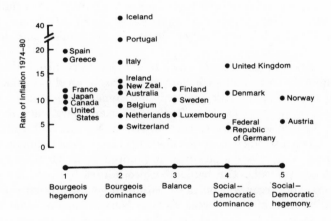

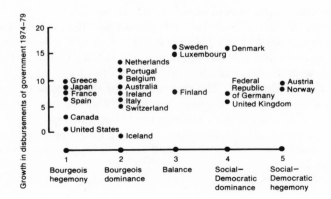

pursued moderate wage policies which were compatible with accumulation requirements on the part of capital.[12]

On the other side, states with an economy haunted by low growth rates, high rates of unemployment, and inflation have, in general, been characterized by a low weight of the economy on the world market and relatively low levels of productivity before the crisis began and by a system of industrial relations characterized by a fragmented structure, an authoritarian or competitive mode of regulating the class conflict, and frequent labor conflicts. In these states, the economic resource base was too weak to allow a peaceful, gradual, and economically successful restructuring of the economy.

Labor Markets and Rates of Unemployment: The Impact of Productivity, Corporatism, Solidaristic, and Paternalistic Values

The performance of the labor market, the content of labor market policy, and the rates of unemployment are also the result of the combined influence of a strong and productive economy in the period before the crisis began, a more or less corporatist regulation of class conflict, and, additionally, a set of solidaristic values shared by the public and the authorities.[13]

Labor market developments which tend to favor organized labor (low rates of unemployment and a constant or increasing level of civilian employment) were characteristic of Japan and some of the smaller states (Sweden, Norway, Austria, New Zealand, Luxembourg, and Iceland, and—if the figures do not lie—Greece). Sweden, Norway, and Austria are nations in which a strong corporatist mode of class conflict regulation with powerful trade unions and a powerful and united Social Democratic left-wing tendency prevails. The bargaining procedures between the state, labor unions, and organized business within the context of an extraparliamentary balance of class forces and (in Norway and Austria) under Social Democratic rule resulted in active demand management policies and a labor market policy committed to full employment.

Although the strength of the trade unions and the degree to which they are incorporated in the policy-making structure are lower in New Zealand, Luxembourg, and Iceland than in the nations mentioned above, the governments in these small states were more or less strongly committed to full employment. The explanation for these cases has to take sociocultural and political concomitants of small states into account. A high density of communication between the élites, a strongly interlocking network of decision-making structures, and a political culture in which solidaristic values are deeply embedded seem to be important explanatory variables.

In the Japanese case, the patterns of a paternalistic capitalism held the rate of unemployment below the average level in the OECD area. The extremely low unemployment figures in Switzerland hide the dramatic decrease in civilian employment between 1973 and 1980, which took place at the cost of the foreign labor force and the discouraged female workers and elder workers covered by early retirement schemes.

Spain, Portugal, Ireland, Belgium, France, Great Britain, and West Germany were strongly hit by the labor market crisis. Rates of unemployment went up, and the level of civilian employment declined or stagnated. The efforts to modernize the economy through a mixture of supply-side and demand-oriented crisis management were in these countries strongly facilitated by the weakness of the trade unions and/or by the unions' moderate behavior (whose constituencies were not yet affected by the labor market crisis in the same way as were the marginal groups on the labor market; see, for example, Armingeon, 1981) and by the peacekeeping functions of the unemployment insurance system.

Determinants of Social Security Expenditure Growth in Periods of Economic Crisis: Built-in Stabilizers, Dominant Parties, Corporatism, Openness of the Economy, and the Clientele of the Welfare State

When we come to examine the determinants of the change in social security expenditure between 1973 and 1979 (the latest year for which comparable data were available), we are confronted with the problem that a substantial part of welfare state measures automatically increases whenever the economy is depressed. This is because in periods of economic crisis, unemployment insurance, social assistance, and early retirement schemes expand the costs of social security, both in absolute terms and relative to GDP. Thus, it is hardly surprising that, overall, nations with low levels of economic growth tended to expand social security expenditures at a faster pace than nations with a more resilient economy.[14] However, an examination of the residuals suggests additional insights into the policy processes that characterized the crisis period. Once we have accounted for the proportion of the variance that is explained by economic growth, there remain important political factors at work. The expansion of social security expenditures was, overall, markedly overproportionate in nations in which the Social Democratic party was the center of gravitation of the party system (and thus in a position where it could strongly influence and constrain the room to maneuver by its bourgeois opponents); in which the regulation of the class conflict was corporatist in nature (and thus increased the probability of equal-exchange-bargaining procedures among the state, the unions, and organized business); in which the age structure of the population had established a numerically and politically important stratum of old-age pensioners to whose demands governments were forced—or more or less automatically willing—to respond in their social security policies; and in which the domestic repercussions of an "open economy" required an active social security policy stance on the part of the government (Pearson's r with imports and exports as a percentage of GDP is .37 in 1972 and .43 in 1979).

Among the OECD nations two different strategies for the expansion of social security expenditures were observable: first, the politics of welfare state expansion on the basis of a highly developed welfare state (Belgium, the Netherlands, Sweden, Denmark, and Luxembourg are the most notable examples); and second, a strategy of expansion which may aptly be described as the "catching-up phenomenon." Japan and Portugal are the most important examples for this developmental path. The reasons are idiosyncratic in character. The major reason in the Japanese case seems to be the fact that the worldwide recession had undermined the privately organized welfare provision schemes and that the period of rapid economic growth in the 1960s had produced high and politically dangerous social costs. The Liberal government sought to restrain the consequences of the crisis through the expansion of state activities in environmental pollution control, in labor market schemes, and in social security efforts (Lörcher, 1981; Foljanty-Jost, 1978; Ike, 1978). The expansion of social security provisions in Portugal was also related to a catching-up phenomenon. The major background factors in the Portuguese case were clearly the consequences of the regime change in the mid-1970s, the requirement to integrate the immigrants from the former colonies, and the effect of the economic depression, which tended to inflate the expenditures on social security programs.

Determinants of Economic and Political Performance in the Industrial Democracies

Our empirical analysis lends support to the view that the following conditions are favorable to a pattern of balanced economic development, a relatively good labor market record with low unemployment, and a further expansion of the welfare state—even under restrictive circumstances:

—a distribution of power in industrial relations which comes close to a "balance of class forces." Under this condition no class is strong enough to dominate its opponent, and thus the probability of equal-exchange bargaining between capital and labor increases;

—highly organized, ideologically united, and moderate trade unions whose power is institutionalized in corporatist arrangements;

—a set of sociocultural values which stresses the importance of solidaristic (re)distribution;

—an economy which had the privilege of entering the period of economic crisis with productivity levels above the average;

—a small state—not primarily because of the sheer "impact of size" but primarily because of the solidaristic values embedded in the political culture and the most densely integrated communication network between the elites.

On the other hand our empirical analysis would lead us to argue that economic and political performances tend to be worse (that is, low economic growth, high inflation, high levels of unemployment, and a low rate of welfare state expansion) if the following conditions are met:

—an authoritarian or competitive mode of regulating the class conflict (within this context distributional conflicts between labor and capital occur more frequently and intensely and inhibit both the successful restructuring of the economy and the expansion of a welfare state);

—a dominant position of the bourgeois tendency both in industrial relations and in the party system;

—a political culture which is strongly influenced by competition and possessive individualism;

—an economy which entered the period of economic crisis with comparatively low productivity levels;

—a large state with a low degree of interlocking communication and decision-making structures.

These factors shape the content and the impact of public policies to a large extent, though not exclusively, irrespective of which party is in power.

THE IMPACT OF POLICY ON ELECTION OUTCOMES: PARADOXES OF MUDDLING THROUGH AND SUCCESSFUL CRISIS-MANAGEMENT POLICIES

It is a well-established fact that governments are far from being altruistic providers of public goods. The content and the timing of governmental policy making are quite frequently shaped by the electoral calendar and the effort to increase the probability of reelection. The literature on governability and legitimation problems in late capitalist societies has been guided by the assumption that a government with a "successful" and "favorable" record in its social and economic policies would be politically rewarded. Conversely, a "bad" record would fuel social conflicts and gradually undermine political support for the governing parties. We will argue that this assumption is not compatible with what we empirically observe in Western nations.

Our contention is that the relationship between the degree of policy effectiveness on the one hand, and political support and social peace on the other, should be treated as a variable. Our contention is based on two interrelated empirical observations. First, we can observe across the industrial democracies that political reactions to high and increasing rates of unemployment and decreasing margins for redistribution of resources have been less sharp than expected. Undoubtedly, this is mainly due to higher levels of income protection and to the fact that long-term unemployment is falling to a large extent on weak and unorganized groups in society. But it may also be the case that to some extent attitudes to work, leisure, and employment are changing, so that less employment security in the formal economy is accepted by some in return for greater leisure or for work in the informal economy.

Second, the "reward–punishment hypothesis" is called into question by the results of a recent study conducted by the author on the impact of the electoral calendar on economic policies and economic outcomes, and on the extent to which the state of the economy determines the fate of governing and opposition parties in elections (Schmidt, 1983). For example, governing parties which were, by and large, successful in steering the economy and generous in welfare spending efforts were quite often "punished." The proportion of the vote they mobilized declined below a threshold which was critical for reelection. And more often than not, governing parties which had an unfavorable record successfully survived an election. One can thus argue that four different combinations of policy effectiveness and reward–punishment outcomes are to be observed among Western nations, as seen in Figure 7.4.

The most interesting cases are in the upper righthand cell ("paradox of a successful welfare state") and in the lower lefthand cell ("paradox of muddling through"). The elections in Sweden in 1976 and Norway in 1981 might be taken as examples of the "paradox of a successful welfare state." The active labor market and welfare state policy stance taken by the Social Democratic governments in these countries was—judged by the aggregate outcome of the vote—"punished." One can plausibly attribute this result to the impact of long-term partisan forces and short-term nonpartisan variables, with postmaterialistic demands being on the whole conducive to a punishment effect. The elections in Italy in 1979 and West Germany in 1980 might be taken as examples of the "paradox of muddling through": the policy records of the governments were, in balance and in general, unfavorable for reelection prospects, and much worse than the

FIGURE 7.4
Policy Performance, Reward, and Punishment.

ELECTION RESULTS

	Reward[a]	Punishment[b]
High policy effectiveness[c]	Japan 1979 Austria 1975, 1979	Sweden 1976 Norway 1981
Low policy effectiveness[d]	Federal Republic of Germany 1980 Italy 1979	United Kingdom 1979 USA 1980

[a] Reelection.
[b] Turnover in political composition of governments.
[c] Successful political control of the economy (measured by our indicators for economic performance, labor market developments, and social security policy).
[d] Partially successful or unsuccessful political control of the economy.

records of previous governments, yet the governing parties were nevertheless reelected. As far as the West German election of 1980 is concerned, it seems as if the candidate of the Christian-Democratic party (Franz Josef Strauss) polarized the electorate to such an extent that even those voters who were very critical of, and disappointed with, the Social Democrat/Free Democrat coalition government still voted for one of the government parties (for example, a large proportion of Green party voters).

It is not our intention to investigate fully the determinants of voting behavior in the Western nations.[15] Our focus is on the aggregate outcome of the vote. In this respect we are confronted with a politically highly explosive paradox. The governments of the Western nations are to an increasing extent faced with a dilemma: the probability of reelection and the probability of gaining or losing votes is some 50 percent, largely regardless of the economic performance, and largely irrespective of a good or bad record of economic and social policy making. We are thus inclined to argue that governments which take this equation into account content themselves with "muddling-through" policies.

CONCLUSION: THE STATE OF THE ART REVISITED

In the introduction to this chapter we outlined some of the competing explanations that feature in the literature on public policy in advanced industrial democracies. To conclude our presentation we shall summarize briefly what our analysis contributes to our understanding of the validity of these explanations.

One general position in the literature is that increasing state intervention has created the basis for successful political control of the economy (for example, Stephens, 1979). This view has been opposed by Marxist writers who have taken the position that the policies adopted in industrial democracies were unable to cope with the structurally given instabilities of the capitalist order (for example, Kirchheimer, 1981; Offe, 1972; Ronge, 1977). Our analysis does not confirm either of these extreme positions. Rather, the evidence seems to point to what may be described as a "partial political control" hypothesis. The imbalance of capitalist economies is amenable to varying strategies of more or less successful political control in certain areas—in particular, interventions to expand the size of the tax and welfare state and to limit labor market fluctuations. However, the success of intervention in one area does not usually spill over into all other aspects of policy. Indeed, in the majority of the OECD nations there seems to be an empirically identifiable tendency for there to be a trade-off by which success in one area limits successful control elsewhere. Because the autonomy of the capitalist economy remains considerable in all these nations, governments must necessarily order their priorities in the field of macroeconomic policy.

However, the order of the priorities varies widely among the OECD nations. For example, Sweden might be taken as an example of the primacy of a welfare state and a commitment to full employment at the expense of a sound capitalist accumulation process. Norway and Austria are examples of a political stalemate between bourgeois and socialist forces both in the industrial and the party system's arenas of power, with the socialist governments being on the whole quite successful in reconciling the requirements of a capitalist economy with demands for full employment and the delivery of more or less generous welfare provisions. Japan is unique insofar as a bourgeois hegemony in both the political superstructure and the political substructure produced a sound economic development, low unemployment levels, and a remarkable expansion in social security expenditure. However, these nations will probably have to face increasing difficulties in maintaining low levels of unemployment over the long run. It is very likely that the tightening of demand management in the other major OECD economies and, in particular, the increasing availability of extremely productive, cheap, and laborsaving new technologies will strongly, and to an increasing extent, undermine the efforts to keep the rate of unemployment down.

Another position, frequently adduced in the literature, is that the political composition of governments will be the decisive factor in determining the priorities of governmental policy making. In our analysis the evidence for this "party control does matter" hypothesis is weak. There is no clear-cut dividing line between the policies adopted by Social Democratic and bourgeois governments. This is not to say that party control of the reins of power is irrelevant for social and economic policy and policy outcomes. Rather, our analysis repeatedly demonstrated that party control was of importance if other conditions are met, as in the pronounced tendency for a strong combination of a balance of class forces in the industrial arena and strong Social Democratic government to lead to active labor market policy. The real issue is not whether party control matters but rather to what extent and, in particular, in what circumstances it matters.

On the whole, those explanations which rest on the primacy of economic factors are to some extent compatible with the data. However, the crucial point that emerges is that in many capitalist democracies the links between the economy and public policy are, to a varying extent and in a variety of ways, mediated by intervening societal and political factors. For example, the setback to economic growth in the mid-1970s, by itself, does not account for the differential performance of the OECD nations in the late 1970s and early 1980s, although we frequently had the opportunity to demonstrate that the level of economic productivity in the period before the crisis began crucially influenced the choices open to governments.

Perhaps the most interesting and important finding is the degree to which those variables that intervene between the economy and public policy are of the kind suggested by the class politics paradigm. The view that extraparliamentary politics is an important determinant of policy is supported by our analysis. The strength of trade unions relative to the strength of organized business, the mode of regulating the class conflict, the degree of harmony between the political superstructure and the political substructure in both party system and industrial arenas, and the degree to which "solidaristic" values characterize the political culture seem to be vital factors, taken in conjunction with economic variables, in determining the success or failure of political control of the economy.

The hypothesis of ungovernability in democratic states is generally not confirmed by our analysis. Up to the present a clear tendency toward ungovernability seems to be the exception rather than the rule. It is only in those nations where a set of other conditions is met (for example, an economy which was weak before the crisis began; a fragmented system of industrial relations; weak trade unions) that the probability of governability problems increases dramatically. On the other hand, there is some evidence for the result of Phillippe Schmitters's empirical contribution to the study of governability problems (Schmitter, 1981). It seems as if nations under Social Democratic rule and, additionally and probably more important, nations with a balance of class force in the industrial and party-system arenas are more governable than their bourgeois-dominated counterparts.

Our "partial political control hypothesis" indicates that governments which are supported by a stalemate in class conflict arenas (and, in addition, governments which act within the context of a paternalistic capitalism) were, up to the present, able to handle the problems associated with the instability inherent in a capitalist order. This is not to say that these governments will in the future automatically be able to continue the policy stance they adopted in the mid-1970s. Indeed, there is some evidence for the view that the low unemployment nations (Austria and Sweden might be taken as examples) have reached the upper limits of successful political control of the economy, with unemployment rates in the early 1980s being on the whole on the increase. This is a not too surprising observation, since the monetary and fiscal policy stance of the major OECD nations has tended to be more restrictive in character after the second oil shock than it was before, and since laborsaving new technology is on the advance.

Our analysis would, however, lead us to believe that "old issues," that is, issues associated with the nature of a capitalist economy and the dynamics of latent and manifest conflicts between labor, capital, and the welfare state clientele, can in principle be solved. However, the most important barriers which strongly restrict the room to maneuver for this policy are not only economic and technological but also political in character, with the paradox of the successful welfare state and the paradox of muddling through being on the whole one of the major impediments.

Our study would lead us to argue that the future of policy making, policy outputs, and outcomes is dismal in character. Paradoxical dynamics of party competition and election outcomes, the long-term consequences of a strong expansion of the welfare state, and the policy process inertia, combined with the momentum of a capitalist order and, in particular, the laborsaving consequences of new technology, have, unintentionally, undermined the foundations on which the policy process of the 1950s and 1960s was based.

NOTES

1. This paper summarizes some of the results of an ongoing study on determinants and consequences of policy responses to "old" and "new" issues in industrial democracies. This research project is a follow-up to the author's studies on comparative partisan differences in public policy (Schmidt, 1980, 1982a, 1982b, 1982c), and it is associated with the Future of Party Government project at the European University Institute.

2. Euromoney, 1981. The summary of economic performance is based on five measures over the period 1974 to early 1981: the rate of real growth, the rate of consumer price inflation, the strength of the currency in terms of Special Drawing Rights, the average size of the current account relative to GNP, and the strength of the export sector. The strength of the export sector was measured by whether exports have grown faster than GDP. The statistical method used to combine each country's five scores into one overall score was a principal component analysis. The overall index combines all the information on each country. It works by giving a weight to each measure. A good growth score is given a weight of 0.45. A poor inflation score is given a weight of -0.55. A strong exchange rate has a weight of 0.52, a good export performance has a weight of 0.49, and a current account surplus has a small weight of 0.05.

3. The data were taken from the OECD Economic Outlook and the OECD Labor Market Statistics series.

4. *OECD National Accounts 1960–1979* (Paris: OECD, 1981), table 9, rows 17–20. The data include social security benefits, social assistance grants, current transfers to private nonprofit institutions serving households, and unfunded employee welfare benefits as a percentage of GDP. Comparable data which include government final consumption expenditures for welfare purposes were not yet available for all nations under investigation. The data on social security expenditure correlate strongly with the data on disbursements of general government (data base: *OECD Economic Outlook* 31 [1981]), which were separately analyzed (see the results of the statistical analysis in Appendix 7.3).

5. Data were taken from the *Statistische Jahrbuch der Bundesrepublik Deutschland*, edited by the Statistische Bundesamt in Wiesbaden (West Germany). The data are preliminary.

6. In general, the data on economic and socioeconomic variables were taken from OECD publications (in particular, *OECD Economic Outlook, OECD National Accounts, Main Economic Indicators, Labour Force Statistics,* and *OECD Economic Surveys*). Political data were based on Schmidt, 1982a, and *Keesing's Archiv der Gegenwart.*

7. The classification is based on the left-wing parties' and the bourgeois parties' share of cabinet seats within a given period on a monthly base. The original values were converted into a rank-order scale. The scale runs from "bourgeois hegemony" (the bourgeois parties' share of cabinet seats equals 100 percent) through "bourgeois dominance" (their share ranges from greater than two-thirds to less than 100 percent), "balance" (the bourgeois parties' share and the left-wing parties' share are larger than one-third and equal to or less than two-thirds of the total of cabinet seats), "Social Democratic dominance" (analogous to "bourgeois dominance"), to "Social Democratic hegemony" (the share of cabinet seats for the left-wing parties is equal to 100 percent).

8. The selection of the variables is based on their explanatory power in a cross-national study of twenty-one capitalist democracies (Schmidt, 1982a). Five indicators were supposed to represent conditions which are favorable to "bourgeois policies": a proportion of the vote for bourgeois parties which is greater than 50 percent; a left-wing tendency which is organizationally and ideologically split (i.e. whenever non-Social-Democratic left-wing parties score more than 10

APPENDIX 7.1
Data (Selection)

Nation	Case-N	Euromoney indicator of economic performance V013	Rates of inflation 1974–80 V026	Rates of unemployment 1974–80 (1 = 0 to 2.0%, 2 = 2.0 to 5.0%, 3 = > 5%) V029	Labor market performance* V033	Public debt (% GDP) 1973 (General government) V046	Public debt (% GDP) 1973 (Central government) V048
Australia	1	8.00	11.90	2.00	1.00	—	—
Belgium	2	10.00	8.20	3.00	0.00	53.00	43.00
Federal Republic of Germany	3	4.00	4.80	2.00	0.00	18.00	7.00
Denmark	4	15.00	11.00	3.00	1.00	16.00	5.00
Finland	5	12.00	12.60	2.00	0.00	6.00	4.00
France	6	11.00	11.10	3.00	0.00	13.00	8.00
Greece	7	14.00	17.50	1.00	2.00	—	—
United Kingdom	8	17.00	16.00	3.00	0.00	73.00	54.00
Ireland	9	13.00	15.50	3.00	0.00	60.00	60.00
Iceland	10	22.00	43.10	1.00	3.00	—	5.00
Italy	11	18.00	17.10	3.00	0.00	33.00	32.00
Japan	12	1.00	9.90	1.00	2.00	13.00	12.00
Canada	13	6.00	9.30	3.00	1.00	—	—
Luxembourg	14	—	7.20	1.00	2.00	28.00	23.00
New Zealand	15	19.00	14.30	1.00	2.00	—	—
Netherlands	16	9.00	7.10	2.00	1.00	43.00	23.00
Norway	17	3.00	9.00	1.00	2.00	33.00	25.00
Austria	18	5.00	6.30	1.00	2.00	17.00	10.00
Portugal	19	21.00	22.70	3.00	0.00	—	—
Sweden	20	16.00	10.30	1.00	3.00	36.00	41.00
Switzerland	21	7.00	4.00	1.00	2.00	25.00	5.00
Spain	22	20.00	17.90	3.00	0.00	—	—
USA	23	2.00	9.30	3.00	1.00	49.00	37.00

*3 = three targets are met (low rate of unemployment, no increase in rate of unemployment, and upward trend in level of total employment)

2 = two out of three targets are met

1 = one out of three targets is met

0 = none of the targets is met

Social security expenditure growth 1974–1979 (in percentage points of GDP)	Political composition of governments 1974–80 (1 = bourgeois hegemony, 5 = Social Democratic hegemony)	Union density (−1 = > 50%, 1 = ≤ 50%)	Split in trade union movement (1 = split, −1 = else)	Cohesiveness of left-wing tendency (−1 = strong, 1 = weak)	Cohesiveness of bourgeois tendency (−1 = weak, 1 = strong)	GNP 1973 ($U.S.)	Population 1973 (1.000)	Corporatism (1 = weak, 2 = medium, 3 = strong)
V057	V002	V006	V007	V008	V009	V036	V037	V040
2.60	2.00	−1.00	−1.00	−1.00	−1.00	65.65	13379.00	2.00
5.70	2.00	−1.00	1.00	1.00	−1.00	45.51	9742.00	2.00
2.70	4.00	1.00	−1.00	−1.00	1.00	347.31	61976.00	2.00
4.70	4.00	−1.00	−1.00	−1.00	−1.00	27.30	5922.00	2.00
1.60	3.00	−1.00	1.00	1.00	−1.00	17.44	4666.00	2.00
4.90	1.00	1.00	1.00	1.00	−1.00	248.93	52118.00	1.00
2.10	1.00	1.00	1.00	1.00	−1.00	16.17	8929.00	1.00
2.50	4.00	1.00	−1.00	−1.00	1.00	175.81	56000.00	1.00
2.10	2.00	1.00	−1.00	−1.00	−1.00	6.61	3051.00	1.00
−1.50	2.00	−1.00	1.00	1.00	−1.00	1.06	212.00	2.00
0.30	2.00	1.00	1.00	1.00	1.00	140.90	54913.00	1.00
5.80	1.00	1.00	1.00	1.00	1.00	407.92	108702.00	3.00
0.80	1.00	1.00	−1.00	−1.00	−1.00	123.49	22072.00	1.00
7.50	3.00	−1.00	1.00	1.00	−1.00	1.82	353.00	2.00
—	2.00	1.00	−1.00	−1.00	1.00	11.90	2970.00	2.00
7.10	2.00	1.00	1.00	−1.00	−1.00	60.14	13439.00	2.00
1.60	5.00	−1.00	−1.00	−1.00	−1.00	19.32	3961.00	3.00
2.70	5.00	−1.00	−1.00	−1.00	1.00	27.24	7525.00	3.00
5.40	2.00	−1.00	1.00	1.00	−1.00	11.37	8978.00	1.00
5.70	3.00	−1.00	−1.00	−1.00	−1.00	50.42	8136.00	3.00
2.50	2.00	1.00	1.00	−1.00	−1.00	41.07	6431.00	3.00
2.50	1.00	1.00	1.00	1.00	−1.00	70.91	34976.00	1.00
1.60	1.00	1.00	1.00	1.00	−1.00	1302.14	210410.00	1.00

APPENDIX 7.2
Correlations Between Major Dependent and Independent Variables

Variable	Euromoney[a]	Labor market performance[a]	Social security[b] expenditure growth	Public debt[c] increase	Unemployment 1974–1980	Inflation 1974–1980	Government political complex[a]	Party[a]	Cohesiveness	Left vote
Euromoney	1.0									
Labor market		1.0								
Social security			1.0							
Public debt				1.0						
Unemployment 1974–80		−.85			1.0					
Inflation 1974–80	.81	−.48				1.0				
Government						−.30	1.0			
Party		−.29			.31	.33		1.0		
Cohesiveness						.39	−.50	.48	1.0	
Left vote			.45				.61	−.77		1.0
Corporatism	−.40	.63	.34		−.74	−.58	.50	−.54	.35	.34
GDP 1973	−.48	−.32			.38					−.63
Population 1973	−.35	−.45			.47		−.39	.34	.30	−.54
Productivity 1973	−.45	.41		−.47		−.38		−.41	−.32	.43
Growth I				−.29	.43			.34		
Growth II							−.30			
Unemployment 1973		−.54			.65		−.31	.33		
Social security 1973						−.34	.37			
Public debt 1973				−.23	.34	.37		.40		−.50
Disbursements 1973							−.30	.45	−.32	−.50
Inflation 1966–73				−.32	.34	.85				
Elder				.32			−.36	.59	−.44	.31
Demography					.30		−.79	.56	.41	−.60
Import and export 1972				.37				.51	−.30	

Variable Definitions:

Euromoney   Euromoney indicator of economic performance 1974–1980/81, after the first oil price shock (see note 2).

Labor market   Labor market performance 1974–80 (see note to Table 7.1).

Social security   Growth in social security expenditure as a percentage of GDP between 1973 and 1979 (first differences) (see note 4).

Public debt   Change in public debt as a percentage of GDP between 1973 and 1979 (first differences).

Unemployed   Average rate of unemployment 1974–80 (percentage of total labor force).

Inflation   Consumer Price Index (average 1974–80).

Government   Political composition of national government (average 1974–80). (see note 7).

Party   Dominant party in party system (1 means a bourgeois party is dominant, i.e. it is stronger than the major left-wing party by at least 5 percent of the popular vote in the majority of elections from 1974 to 1980 (including the latest election before 1974); 0 means "balance" or "nondominant party," i.e. the criteria stipulated for rank 1 and rank 3 are not met; 3 means that a left-wing party is dominant (classified in the same way as rank 1).

Cohesiveness   Cohesiveness of the left-wing tendency 1974–80 (see note 8).

Left vote   Average of left vote in national elections between 1974 and 1980 and the latest election before 1974.

(Footnotes at bottom of next page)

Corporatism[a]	GNP 1973	Population 1973	Productivity 1973	Growth 1974–79	Growth 1974–80	Unemployment 1973[a]	Social security 1973	Public debt 1973	Disbursements 1973	Inflation 1966–1973	Elder	Demography	Import and export 1972
1.0													
	1.0												
	.97	1.0											
	.32		1.0										
			−.35	1.0									
			−.37		1.0								
−.52						1.0							
.39				−.37		−.31	1.0						
−.36						.50	.32	1.0					
			.37			.31	.84	.38	1.0				
										1.0			
							.53		.57	−.34	1.0		
−.44	.86	.90				.48	.33		−.34		−.42	1.0	
.36	−.46	−.53		−.37	−.37		.44	.30			.29	−.36	1.0

Corporatism Corporatist mode of regulating the class conflict (see note 12).

GNP 1973 Gross National product 1973 ($U.S. and current exchange rates).

Population 1973 Population 1973 (in 1000s).

Productivity Level of productivity (GNP 1973/Population 1973).

Growth I Growth rates of GDP (real terms, average 1974–79).

Growth II Growth rates of GDP (real terms, average 1974–80).

Unemployed 1973 Rate of unemployment in 1973 (as a percentage of labor force).

Public debt 1973 Public debt (general government) as a percentage of GDP 1973.

Disbursements Growth of disbursements of general government as a percentage of GDP between 1973 and 1979 (first difference). Disbursements mainly consist of government final consumption expenditure, subsidies, social security transfers to households, and interest on public debt.

Inflation 1966–73 Consumer Price Index, average 1967–73.

Elder Population at age 65 and above as a percentage of total population in 1973.

Demography Change in population at age 65 and above between 1973 and 1979 (first differences).

(Footnotes for Appendix 7.2—page 164)

[a] Spearman's rank-order correlation coefficient r_s. The major reason for the selection of this coefficient was pragmatic in character: first, one can easily understand the logic of this coefficient, and second, its values can more easily be compared with Pearson's r. All other coefficients are Pearson's r.

[b] Number of cases: 22 (comparable data for New Zealand were not available).

[c] N = 16 (comparable data were not available for Australia, Greece, Iceland, Canada, New Zealand, Portugal and Spain).

The table includes only those correlation coefficients which are larger than 0.3 (significance level with 23 cases at some 0.09).

percent in the majority of the elections within a given period and the latest election before this period); a bourgeois tendency which is organizationally and ideologically cohesive (i.e., if not more than one bourgeois party scores 10 percent of the vote in the majority of the elections within a given period, inclusive of the latest election before this period); a union density score which is less than 50 percent; and a trade union movement which is politically split along religious, ethnic, and political cleavages.

9. See *OECD Economic Outlook* (Paris: OECD, biannually).

10. See the results of the statistical analysis in Appendix 7.2. The data confirm a hypothesis which von Beyme (1981) has recently advanced (and contradict the inference which Cameron, 1982, has drawn from his study of comparative economic policy making in the 1970s).

11. The interpretation is based on the *OECD Economic Surveys* and on a statistical analysis of the data (see Appendix 7.3).

12. A *corporatist* mode of regulating the class conflict is the label for those nations in which trade unions, employers associations, and the state are committed to a social partnership ideology and collaborate in the policy-formation process in some policy areas. Empirical correlates of a corporatist mode are: very low strike volume; typically, though not exclusively, the absence of an authoritarian incomes policy enacted from above; and an ideologically and organizationally united trade union movement. An *authoritarian* mode of regulating the class conflict is characterized by cooperation between the state and the entrepreneurs against the trade unions. A *competitive* mode is characterized by a low degree of interference in industrial relations on the part of the state. In this study we content ourselves with a corporatism indicator which runs from "strong" to "medium" and "weak." For the meaning of "strong corporatism" see above: "weak" corresponds to a varying mixture of authoritarian and competitive modes of conflict regulation, while "medium" is a residual category.

13. This interpretation is based on a wide range of more detailed one-country studies (for example, Dahrendorf, 1981; Scharpf, 1981; the *OECD Economic Surveys*) and the results of a statistical analysis (see Appendix 7.3).

14. Data base: see Appendixes 7.1 and 7.3. If one were to analyze the expansion of the total state expenditures between 1973 and 1979, the results would basically be identical. A minor difference should be pointed out: the growth rates of disbursements of government correlate weakly with an additional variable—the union density measure ($r = -.35$).

15. A fascinating account has recently been advanced by Budge and Farlie (1982).

APPENDIX 7.3

Correlations Between the Political Composition of Governments and Indicators of Economic Performance and Policy Outcome

Variable	Spearman's Rank Order Correlation Coefficient (r_s)
Euromoney indicator of economic performance[a]	$-.01$[b]
Labor market performance 1974–80[c]	$.09$
Rates of unemployment 1974–80	$-.25$
Change in rate of unemployment 1973–80	$-.06$
Trend in levels of employment 1973–80 (1 = increase, 0 = else)	$.00$
Rate of inflation 1974–80	$-.30$
Change in rate of inflation between 1960–73 and 1974–80[d]	$-.34$
Growth of disbursements of government 1974–79[d]	$.24$[b]
Growth of government final consumption expenditure 1974–80[d]	$.28$[b]
Growth in social security expenditure 1974–79[e]	$.11$
Increase in public debt (general government) 1974–79[d]	$.11$[f]
Increase in public debt (central government only) 1974–79[d]	$.08$[f]

[a] See note 2.
[b] $N = 22$.
[c] See note 3 to Table 7.1.
[d] First difference.
[e] See note 4.
[f] $N = 16$.

REFERENCES

Altvater, E. 1981. "Der gar nicht diskrete Charme der neoliberalen Konterrevolution." *Prokla* 11.

Andrain, C. F. 1980. *Politics and Economic Policy in Western Democracies.* North Scituate, Mass.: Duxbury Press.

Armingeon, K. 1981. "La Confédération des syndicats allemands (DGB) face à la crise." In *Les Syndicats européennes et la crise,* by Klaus Armingeon et al. Grenoble: Presses Universitaires de Grenoble.

———. 1982. "Socialist Governments and Trade Unions—The Impact on Wages and Policy." In *The Impact of Political Parties,* ed. F. G. Castles. Beverly Hills, Calif.: Sage.

Arrighi, G. 1981. "Der Klassenkampf in Westeuropa im 20. Jahrhundert." In *Krisen in der kapitalistischen Weltökonomie,* by F. Fröbel, J. Heinrichs, and O. Kreye. Reinbek bei Hamburg: Rowohlt.

Bauer, O. 1928. "Kapitalsherrschaft in der Demokratie." *Der Kampf Sozialdemokratische Monatsschrift* 21.

————. 1970. "Das Gleichgewicht der Klassenkräfte." In *Austromarxismus,* ed. Hans-Joerg Sandkuhler and Rafael de la Vega. Frankfurt: EVA.

Berger, J. 1981. "Wandlungen von Krisenursachen im Wohlfahrtsstaatlichen Kapitalismus." In *Monetäre Restriktionen: Die Inflationsbekämpfung.* Argument Sonderband AS 68. Berlin: Argument-Verlag.

Beyme, K. von, 1981. "Do Parties Matter?" *Politische Vierteljahresschrift* 22.

Budge, I., and Farlie, D. J. 1982. "Explaining and Predicting Elections: Issue Effects and Party Strategies in 23 Democracies." Mimeo. University of Essex.

Cameron, D. R. 1982. "On the Limits of the Public Economy." *Annals of the American Academy of Political and Social Science,* no. 459.

Castles, F. G., ed. 1982a. *The Impact of Political Parties.* Beverly Hills, Calif.: Sage.

————. 1982b. "Politics, Public Expenditure and Welfare." In *The Impact of Political Parties,* ed. F. G. Castles. Beverly Hills, Calif.: Sage.

Dahrendorf, R. 1979. *Lebenschancen. Anläufe zur sozialen und politischen Theorie.* Frankfurt: Suhrkamp.

————, ed. 1981. *Trendwende. Europas Wirtschaft in der Krise.* Vienna: Verlag Fritz Molden.

Dror, Y. 1981. "Social Policy in a Period of Decrement: A Perspective of Governments." In OECD, *The Welfare State in Crisis: An Account of the Conference on Social Policies in the 1980s.* Paris: OECD.

Essert, J. 1983. *Gewerkschaften in der Krise. Die Anpassung der deutschen Gewerkschaften an neue Weltmarktbedingungen.* Frankfurt: Suhrkamp.

Euromoney. 1981. "The End of the OEPC Era." In *Euromoney,* October 1981. London: Euromoney.

Flora, P. 1979. "Krisenbewältigung oder Krisenerzeugung? Der Wohlfahrtsstaat in historischer Perspektive." In *Sozialer Wandel in Westeuropa. Verhandlungen des Soziologentages in Berlin,* ed. J. Matthes. Frankfurt: Campus.

Foljanty-Jost, G., Park, S.-J., and Seifert, W., eds. 1981. *Japans Sozial- und Wirtschaftsentwicklung im internationalen Kontext.* Frankfurt: Campus.

Fröbel, F., Heinrichs, J., and Kreye, O. 1981. *Krisen in der kapitalistischen Weltökonomie.* Reinbek bei Hamburg: Rowohlt.

Giersch, H., ed. 1981. *Macroeconomic Policy for Growth and Stability: A European Perspective.* Tübingen: J. C. B. Mohr (Siebeck).

Goldthorpe, J. T. 1978. "The Current Inflation: Towards a Sociological Account." In *The Political Economy of Inflation,* ed. F. Hirsch and J. T. Goldthorpe. Cambridge: Harvard University Press.

Gould, A. 1981. "The Salarized Middle Class in the Corporatist Welfare State." *Policy and Politics* 9.

Hibbs, Jr., D. A., and Fassbender, H., with the assistance of Rivers, R. D., eds. 1981. *Contemporary Political Economy.* Amsterdam: North-Holland.

Ike, N. 1978. *A Theory of Japanese Democracy.* Boulder, Colo.: Westview Press.

Kalecki, M. 1943. "Political Aspects of Full Employment." *Political Quarterly* 14.

Kirchheimer, O. 1981. "Weimar—und was dann? Analyse einer Verfassung." In *Politik und Verfassung*, by O. Kirchheimer. Frankfurt: Suhrkamp.

Korpi, W. 1980. "Social Policy and Distributional Conflict in the Capitalist Democracies: A Preliminary Comparative Framework." *West European Politics* 3.

Lehmbruch, G., and Schmitter, P. C., eds., 1982. *Patterns of Corporatist Policy-Making.* Beverly Hills, Calif.: Sage.

Lehner, F. 1979. *Grenzen des Regierens. Eine Studie Zur Regierungsproblematik hochindustrialisierter Demokratien.* Königstein, Ts.: Athenäum.

Leibfritz, W. 1980. "Die Staatsverschuldung im internationalen Vergleich—einige Aspekte der empirischen Entwicklung." In *Probleme der Staatsverschuldung, Beihefte zur Konjunkturpolitik*, no. 27. Berlin: Duncker und Humblot.

Lörcher, S. 1981. "Japans Sozialkapital im internationalen Vergleich." In *Japans Sozial- und Wirtschaftsentwicklung im internationalen Kontext*, ed. G. Foljanty-Jost, S.-J. Park, and W. Seifert. Frankfurt: Campus.

Luhmann, N. 1981. *Politische Theorie im Wohlfahrtsstaat.* Munich: Günter Olzog Verlag.

Madsen, H. J. 1981. "Partisanship and Macroeconomic Outcomes: A Reconsideration." In *Contemporary Political Economy*, ed. D. A. Hibbs, Jr., and H. Fassbender. Amsterdam: North-Holland.

Malecki, E. S. 1981. "The Capitalist State—Structural Variation and Its Implication for Radical Change." *Western Political Quarterly* 34.

OECD. 1980. Main Economic Indicators—Historical Statistics 1960–1979. Paris: OECD.

———. 1981a. *National Accounts of OECD Member Countries.* Paris: OECD.

———. 1981b. *The Welfare State in Crisis: An Account of the Conference on Social Policies in the 1980s. OECD, Paris, 10–12 October 1980.* Paris: OECD.

OECD: Economic Outlook. Paris: OECD, biannually.

OECD: Economic Surveys. Paris: OECD, annually.

OECD: Labour Force Statistics. Paris: OECD, annually.

Offe, D. 1972. *Strukturprobleme des kapitalistischen Staates.* Frankfurt: Suhrkamp.

———. 1979. "'Unregierbarkeit,' Zur Renaissance konservativer Krisentheorien." In *Stichworte zur 'Geistigen Situation der Zeit,'* ed. J. Habermas. Vol. 1: *Nation und Republik.* Frankfurt: Suhrkamp.

Ridley, A. 1979. "Die öffentlichen Ausgaben in Grossbritannien—Die grösste aller Krisen?" In *Wachsende Staatshaushalte*, ed. H. Rühle and H. J. Veen. Stuttgart: Bonn Aktuell.

Ronge, V. 1977. *Forschungspolitik als Strukturpolitik.* Munich: Piper.

Rose, R., ed. 1980. *Challenge to Governance.* Beverly Hills, Calif.: Sage.

Sachs, J. D. 1979. "Wages, Profits and Macroeconomic Adjustment: A Comparative Study." *Brookings Papers on Economic Activity* 2.

Scharpf, F. W. 1981. *The Political Economy of Inflation and Unemployment in Western Europe: An Outline.* Discussion Papers IIM/LMP 81-21. Berlin: Wissenschaftszentrum.

Schmidt, M. G. 1980. *CDU und SPD an der Regierung. Ein Vergleich ihrer Politik in den Ländern.* Frankfurt: Campus.

———. 1982a. "Die Politik der CDU/CSU und der SPD-Regierungen." In *Bürger und Parteien,* ed. J. Raschke. Bonn: Bundeszentrale für politische Bildung.

———. 1982b. "The Role of the Parties in Shaping Macroeconomic Policy." In *The Impact of Political Parties,* ed. F. G. Castles. Beverly Hills, Calif.: Sage.

———. 1982c. *Wohlfahrtsstaatliche Politik unter bürgerlichen und sozialdemokratischen Regierungen. Ein internationaler Vergleich.* Frankfurt: Campus.

———. 1983. "Politische Konjunkturzyklen. Ein internationaler Vergleich." In *Wahlen und politisches System,* ed. M. Kaase and H. D. Klingemann. Opladen: Westdeutscher Verlag.

Schmitter, P. C. 1981. "Interest Intermediation and Regime Governability in Contemporary Western Europe and North America." In *Organizing Interests in Western Europe: Pluralism, Corporatism and the Transformation of Politics,* ed. S. Berger. Cambridge: Harvard University Press.

Schmitter, P. C., and Lehmbruch, G., eds. 1980. *Trends Toward Corporatist Intermediation.* Beverly Hills, Calif.: Sage.

Statistisches Bundesamt. 1973ff. *Statistisches Jahrbuch der Bundesrepublik Deutschland.* Stuttgart: Kohlhammer.

Stephens, J. D. 1979. *The Transition to Socialism.* London: Macmillan.

———. 1981. "Impasse and Breakthrough—in Sweden." *Dissent* (Summer).

Tufte, E. R. 1978. *Political Control of the Economy.* Princeton: Princeton University Press.

Wilensky, H. L. 1981. "Democratic Corporatism, Consensus and Social Policy: Reflections on Changing Values and the 'Crisis' of the Welfare State." In OECD, *The Welfare State in Crisis.* Paris: OECD.

Wittmann, W. 1981. "Der Steuerstaat am Wendepunkt." *Frankfurte Allgemeine Zeitung,* no. 229 (October 3).

COMPARATIVE MACROECONOMIC POLICIES

The economic crises of the 1970s and early 1980s produced a high rate of political turnover among the governments of Western democratic nations. Governing parties of both the left and the right were defeated by opposition parties that promised new remedies for inflation and industrial decline. In the United States and Britain the electorate turned to radically conservative leaders, in France two decades of center-right government gave way to a new socialist regime, and in West Germany the Social Democratic coalition shifted to one dominated by the more conservative Christian Democrats. This section examines these transitions and their economic consequences.

Steven Schier and Norman Vig demonstrate in Chapter 8 that both Prime Minister Thatcher and President Reagan assumed that a permanent rollback in the size and economic functions of the state and restrictive monetary policies to control inflation were necessary preconditions for economic recovery. Both rejected the tradition of Keynesian counter-cyclical demand management in favor of new market-oriented approaches. Although Thatcher's restrictive monetary and fiscal policies produced record unemployment, Reagan's unorthodox "supply-side" tax cuts promoted economic expansion at the expense of huge budget deficits. The ultimate success of these attempts to "revive capitalism" seems questionable. What is the theoretical reasoning behind each? Have the economic benefits of disinflation been worth the costs? What economic legacy is left for successor governments in each country?

France attempted a very different, expansionary course under President Mitterrand. In Chapter 9, William Safran notes that, despite early visionary rhetoric, the initial socialist policies relied on Keynesian techniques accompanied by increased nationalization and direct planning. As these efforts were

171

vitiated by inflation and world recession, the government has been forced to adopt unpopular austerity measures and forgo some objectives. Yet Safran argues that the government has had considerable success in implementing what is essentially a social democratic program. What does he feel has been accomplished? What economic and political constraints has the socialist experiment encountered? Was the government's remarkable change of course necessary?

West German economic policy since 1973 has often been labeled a Social Democratic success story, although in recent years unemployment and inflation have reached dangerous levels there as well. Jeremiah Riemer notes in Chapter 10 that, although a wide range of policy options has been discussed in Germany since 1973, economic crisis management has been very cautious in practice. Keynesian attempts at expansion were carefully coordinated with monetary control, reflecting a political consensus favoring macroeconomic management by monetary and fiscal policies while leaving microeconomic behavior relatively unregulated. Attempts to implement "industrial policies" have been much less extensive than is often thought. The current conservative government of Helmut Kohl seems intent on retreating from even these efforts, and Riemer suggests that an economic policy "vacuum" is now evident. Why was the Social Democratic government so successful in the 1970s? Has the institutional consensus on West German economic policy broken down?

Overall, the governments of Western Europe and North America had adopted more "neoliberal" or market-oriented economic policies by the mid–1980s. Why has economic crisis produced this shift to the right rather than a turn toward the left as occurred in the 1930s? Have governments been able to limit the economic role of the state, or are they only managing their economies somewhat differently? Is any basis emerging for a new "post–Keynesian" consensus?

8   REVIVING CAPITALISM:
MACROECONOMIC POLICIES IN BRITAIN
AND THE UNITED STATES

Steven E. Schier and Norman J. Vig

The election of Margaret Thatcher in 1979 and Ronald Reagan in 1980 marked a crucial turning point in political economy. For the first time since World War II, ideological conservatives came to power determined to revive capitalism by drastically restricting the economic role of the state. Although they have not yet succeeded in this larger purpose, Prime Minister Thatcher and President Reagan have radically altered the conduct of macroeconomic policy. They have abandoned the Keynesian approach to macroeconomic management that facilitated political compromise in the postwar era (see Chapter 4 by Przeworski and Wallerstein), turning instead to monetarist and "supply-side" doctrines that promised relief from the "stagflation" that had emerged in the 1970s.

The Thatcher and Reagan administrations obviously have much in common. They share a free market philosophy rooted in the classical liberalism of the nineteenth century and in the recent writings of such economists as Hayek and Friedman (see Chapters 1 and 2). They are attempting to devolve governmental functions to the private sector and to reverse the growth of public spending. They have both cut income taxes and provided numerous other incentives for private saving and investment. And they have both given top priority to disinflation, even at the cost of high unemployment and recession.

Nevertheless, it would be a mistake to view the macroeconomic policies of Thatcher and Reagan either as identical to each other or as total departures from the actions of previous governments. There are several major differences in the strategies of the two regimes that reflect underlying differences in the British and American economies, in the economic theories of the governments, and in national political structures and processes.

This chapter presents a comparative analysis of "Thatcherism" and "Reaganomics," stressing national continuities and differences as well as the many common elements in what have been labeled "hypercapitalist" regimes (Amott and Krieger, 1982). In the next section we briefly discuss the economic problems and policies that gave rise to these governments and some of the political differences between the two countries that continue to influence their macroeconomic policies. We then examine the British and American cases in more detail and attempt to draw some comparative conclusions about the goals and performance of these new conservative governments.

BACKGROUND: ECONOMIC PROBLEMS AND POLICY CHANGE

Economic Performance

The Thatcher and Reagan governments were responses to the relatively poor economic performance of the British and American economies in the 1970s and, particularly, to the increasing economic uncertainty caused by inflation in the second half of the decade. In fact, both countries had achieved lower economic growth rates than their competitors throughout the postwar period. Table 8.1 shows comparative growth rates during the two decades prior to 1979 and during selected subperiods. The British economy clearly fared worst, but the United States also lagged well behind the average for OECD countries. After 1973 all of the industrial economies stagnated, but the drop in Britain was particularly severe (to an average of barely 1 percent annually). Between 1967 and 1978, British per capita national income fell from 86 percent of the OECD average to 72 percent. Tables 8.2 and 8.3 present some more detailed economic data for the 1970s. These figures indicate that Britain suffered higher rates of inflation than most countries (averaging 13 percent annually during the period 1970–79), while unemployment showed a secular upward trend from under 3 percent in 1970 to 6 percent at the end of the decade. On the other hand, the United States had among the highest unemployment rates (averaging 6 percent throughout the decade) but below average inflation *until 1979 and 1980*, when it averaged 12.4 percent.

The most troublesome symptoms of the "British disease" were persistently lagging rates of productivity growth (Table 8.4) and rapidly increas-

TABLE 8.1

Average Annual Growth Rates of Gross National Product for the United Kingdom, 4 Other Industrial Countries, and OECD Countries as a Whole, Selected Periods, 1957–1978

(percent)

COUNTRY	MAIN PERIODS		SUBPERIODS	
	1957–1967	1967–1978	1967–1973	1973–1978
United Kingdom	3.1	2.3	3.4	1.1
United States	4.1	3.0	3.5	2.4
Japan	10.4	7.2	10.2	3.7
France	5.6	4.4	5.6	2.9
West Germany	5.5	3.8	5.3	2.0
All OECD countries	4.8[a]	3.8[b]	4.8[b]	2.5[b]

[a] Based on 1970 GNP weights and exchange rates.
[b] Based on 1977 GNP weights and exchange rates.

Source: Caves and Krause, 1980, 3.

TABLE 8.2

Standardized Unemployment Rates in 7 Countries, 1970–1980

COUNTRY	1970	1971	1972	1973	1974	1975	1976	1977	1978	1979	1980
United States	4.8	5.7	5.4	4.7	5.4	8.3	7.5	6.9	5.9	5.7	7.0
Japan	1.1	1.2	1.4	1.3	1.4	1.9	2.0	2.0	2.2	2.1	2.0
Germany	0.8*	0.9*	0.8*	0.9*	1.6*	3.7*	3.7*	3.7*	3.5*	3.2*	3.1*
France	2.4	2.6	2.7	2.6	2.8	4.1	4.4	4.7	5.2	5.9	6.3
United Kingdom	3.1*	3.7*	4.1*	3.0*	2.9*	3.9*	5.5*	6.2*	6.1*	5.7*	7.4*
Italy	5.3	5.3	6.3	6.2	5.3	5.8	6.6	7.0	7.1	7.5	7.4
Canada	5.6	6.1	6.2	5.5	5.3	6.9	7.1	8.0	8.3	7.4	7.5
Seven major countries	3.2*	3.7*	3.8*	3.4*	3.7*	5.4*	5.4*	5.4*	5.1*	4.9*	5.6*

*Adjusted by OECD.

Source: *OECD Economic Outlook* (July 1981): 142.

ing unit labor costs compared to other countries. The consequence was a steady decline in Britain's ability to compete in international trade and a precipitous decline in the manufacturing sector during the 1970s—often referred to as "deindustrialization" (Blackaby, 1979). Employment in British manufacturing industry declined by 20 percent between the mid-1950s and the mid-1970s, and the U.K. share of world manufacturing exports fell from 20.5 percent (1951–55) to 9.1 percent (1973–77). The underlying causes have been debated extensively but with little agreement; indeed, Britain's relative decline goes back a century or more and

TABLE 8.3

Consumer Prices in 7 Countries, 1970–1980

(percentage changes from previous year)

COUNTRY	1970	1971	1972	1973	1974	1975	1976	1977	1978	1979	1980
United States	5.9	4.3	3.3	6.2	11.0	9.1	5.8	6.5	7.7	11.3	13.5
Japan	7.7	6.1	4.5	11.7	24.5	11.8	9.3	8.1	3.8	3.6	8.0
Germany	3.4	5.3	5.5	6.9	7.0	6.0	4.5	3.7	2.7	4.1	5.5
France	5.2	5.5	6.2	7.3	13.7	11.8	9.6	9.4	9.1	10.8	13.6
United Kingdom	6.4	9.4	7.1	9.2	16.0	24.2	16.5	15.8	8.3	13.4	18.0
Italy	5.0	4.8	5.7	10.8	19.1	17.0	16.8	18.4	12.1	14.8	21.2
Canada	3.3	2.9	4.8	7.6	10.8	10.8	7.5	8.0	9.0	9.1	10.1
Total of above countries	5.7	5.0	4.3	7.5	13.3	10.9	7.9	8.1	7.0	9.3	12.2

Source: *OECD Economic Outlook* (July 1981): 140.

TABLE 8.4

Productivity Growth Rates for the European Community as a Whole and Selected Member Countries, 1960–1977

(percent a year)

COUNTRY	1960–1965	1965–1970	1970–1975	1976	1977
West Germany	4.5	4.7	2.7	6.5	4.6
France	5.0	4.9	3.2	5.7	3.8
Italy	6.1	5.9	2.1	4.9	2.6
EC countries	4.3	4.5	2.6	5.1	3.0
United Kingdom	2.4	2.7	1.8	2.6	1.1

Source: Caves and Krause, 1980, 49.

appears deeply rooted in its social system and culture as well as its peculiar imperial role (see, e.g., Caves and Krause, 1980; Gamble, 1981; Shonfield, 1958).

The decline in the international position of the American economy was not as precipitous as that of Britain, but similar problems were evident in the 1970s. Increasing unit labor costs and lagging productivity growth caused certain core sectors—such as automobiles and steel—to suffer in competition with foreign, particularly Japanese, producers (Reich, 1983). By 1980 America's living standard had fallen below that of several of her industrial competitors. Employment growth was most evident in low-skill service occupations; high-tech industries in computers and electronics have not proven to be labor-intensive avenues of economic growth (Bluestone and Harrison, 1982). The sense of economic malaise was almost as pervasive in the United States as in Britain by the end of the decade.

Economic Policy Making and Change

Governments became increasingly more preoccupied with these economic problems but progressively less capable of managing them. Britain was a case in point. Both Labour and Conservative governments followed what came to be known as "stop-go" policies in an effort to maintain financial stability (symbolized by the exchange value of the pound sterling). The first Labour administration of Harold Wilson (1964–70) sacrificed most of its economic development plans in vain attempts to avoid devaluation and control inflation. The Conservative government of Edward Heath responded to growing unemployment by reflating the economy in 1972, only to slam the brakes on the next year when prices began rising. A burst of spending by the second Wilson government stimulated the economy again in 1974–75—just as the impact of the first OPEC oil price rise was also felt, contributing to record inflation (24 percent) in 1975, another economic downturn, and a balance of payments and currency crisis that required emergency support from the International Monetary Fund (IMF) in late 1976. In the last three years of the Labour government under James Callaghan (1976–79), stringent monetary and fiscal controls were imposed by the Chancellor of the Exchequer, Denis Healey.

The overall result of short-term Keynesian demand management in Britain was thus repeated economic deflation rather than expansion. As it became clear that aggregate controls of this kind could not solve Britain's underlying structural problems, governments resorted to increasing intervention in the microeconomy. Beginning with the Conservative government of Harold Macmillan in the early 1960s, governments attempted to encourage sectoral economic planning through the National Economic Development Council, modeled after the Economic Planning Commission in France. But "Neddy" and the sectoral and regional planning committees it spawned ("little Neddies") had little impact on industrial growth. Efforts by the Wilson and Heath governments to encourage the amalgamation and modernization of declining sectors such as steel, shipbuilding, and automobiles degenerated into subsidy and bail-out programs for the most part (see Grant, 1982; Beer, 1982). All governments from the early 1960s on also attempted to control inflation through wage-price controls or "incomes policies" (some twenty different attempts were made between 1965 and 1975 alone, ranging from voluntary guidelines to statutory freezes). None of these policies succeeded in holding wages in check very long, and all were followed by even higher demands and settlements. Thus, although numerous attempts were made to control costs and encourage modernization and rationalization in British industry, these "supply-side" efforts did nothing to halt Britain's secular decline (Maunder, 1980; Whitely, 1983).

The economic policy shifts of the 1960s and 1970s more often occurred during the life of a government than between governments (see Rose, 1980). These "U-turns" did not help to create a stable economic climate conducive to investment and growth and alienated many party supporters who saw their leaders adopt the opposition's tactics. Interest groups repeatedly stymied government policies; most notably, attempts to control wages and prices and to reform the industrial relations system foundered on political opposition from the trade unions. Wilson, Heath, and Callaghan all fell victim to strikes and the collapse of government incomes policies. These experiences, particularly Heath's defeat in 1974 following a miners' strike that brought the economy to a virtual halt, convinced Margaret Thatcher that the power of the trade unions must be broken and that only a truly conservative government willing to stick to monetarist principles over an extended period of time could save Britain from accelerating inflation and economic collapse (see Behrens, 1980).

American administrations attempted to control both inflation and unemployment through a variety of policies that resulted in an American version of "stop-go" in the 1970s. Efforts to reduce inflation resulted in higher unemployment and vice versa; expansionary and restrictive monetary and fiscal policies varied as alternatively prices or joblessness reached politically unacceptable levels. Overall, the macroeconomic policies of Presidents Nixon, Ford, and Carter (in 1979 and 1980) tended to give top priority to fighting inflation, viewed by them as the more pressing problem. Methods of accomplishing this varied over the decade. Nixon's initially austere fiscal and monetary policies gave way to an expansionary 1971 budget ("Now I am a Keynesian," the president proclaimed). Rising prices by late 1971 led the president to commence a two-year sequence of wage and price controls, employing special powers granted him by Congress but never before used in peacetime. These anti-inflation efforts were contradicted by the expansionary monetary policies of the Federal Reserve Board (FRB) in 1971 and 1972. When controls were abandoned by the president in late 1973, inflation shot upward again. Expansionary fiscal and monetary policies of previous years combined with OPEC price shocks to move the Consumer Price Index up 8.8 percent in 1973 and 12.2 percent in 1974.* The failure of compulsory controls caused subsequent administrations to eschew any attempt at mandatory incomes policies.

*Data on the U.S. in this section are from the *Economic Report of the President* (annual), and differ somewhat from the OECD figures in Tables 8.2 and 8.3.

By 1974, Nixon had reverted to the "old-time religion" of Republican economics, namely, efforts at fiscal and monetary restraint in order to bring down the rate of inflation at the expense of employment, long urged by monetarist economists (Stein, 1984). Gerald Ford initially sought to continue these efforts, but accepted a mildly stimulative tax cut in 1975, when unemployment had reached 9.1 percent. The FRB accommodated this with monetary expansion. In 1976, inflation and, to a lesser extent, unemployment moderated to 4.8 and 7.7 percent, respectively.

The persistence of relatively high unemployment contributed to Jimmy Carter's election in 1976 (Miller, 1978). His administration immediately adopted policies which assumed unemployment to be the "privileged problem" in the economy. It was believed that because of underutilization of capacity in the economy, fiscal and monetary stimulus could reduce unemployment to between 5 and 5.5 percent without inflationary effects (Heineman and Hessler, 1980). Increased domestic expenditure and deficits were coupled with sizable increases in the money supply in 1977 and 1978. This strategy produced some decline in unemployment as real GNP rose 5.5 percent in 1977 and 4.8 percent in 1978, but at the cost of higher inflation (9 percent in 1978, 13.3 percent in 1979) and weakness in the exchange value of the dollar.

These results forced a series of policy "U-turns" on Carter, resulting in a new array of policies aimed at reducing inflation as the primary goal. In October 1979, FRB chair Paul Volcker announced a policy of targeting money supply and allowing interest rates to move freely upward in order to check inflation. The administration's fiscal year 1980 budget proposal was withdrawn and resubmitted with further budget cuts to reduce the anticipated deficit. Implementation of these policies encouraged a recession which arrived in early 1980, but did not reduce inflation in that year (12.4 percent), in part because of the doubling of world oil prices in late 1979. Carter's conversion to the "old-time religion" did not save him in the November election.

The oscillation between expansionary and restrictive policies over the 1970s produced scant economic success and considerable political difficulties. As in Britain, this inconstancy engendered economic uncertainty and alienated activists in each administration's party who sought policies more consistent with party ideology. The serious challenges to incumbent presidents seeking renomination by Ronald Reagan in 1976 and Edward Kennedy in 1980 reflected this dissatisfaction. A successful policy would have to reduce both inflation and unemployment through consistent means acceptable to the public and party activists. Reagan proposed what seemed to be such a policy throughout the 1980 campaign. He adopted "supply-side economics," which promised lower inflation, higher employment, and reduction in the size of government, all at the same time (Bartlett, 1982).

We will explore these and other aspects of the Thatcher and Reagan programs in the sections which follow. Before doing so we need to point out some of the factors that may account for differences in the British and American approaches to capitalist revival.

Some Underlying Differences

As a relatively small, open economy with a large foreign trade and banking sector, Britain is considerably more vulnerable to international financial pressures than the United States. Hence British governments have repeatedly adopted negative internal policies to protect financial interests and improve Britain's competitive position, whereas the size and strength of the American domestic economy have traditionally encouraged policy makers to ignore external complications. The United States can try to "go it alone," but the British cannot. This disparity explains some of the variance between Thatcher's emphasis on monetary discipline to restore competitiveness and Reagan's riskier "supply-side" strategy.

Another source of differences lies in the structure of the labor movement and the relationship of trade unions to the state. The union movement has a much longer tradition in Britain than in the United States and is much more closely tied to the Labour party and its socialist doctrines (see, e.g., Taylor, 1980). More recently, unionization has proceeded rapidly among public sector and white collar employees as economic pressures have increased. By the end of the 1970s about 55 percent of the total labor force was unionized (compared to barely 20 percent in the United States). The Heath and Wilson governments attempted to establish a neocorporatist bargaining structure for controlling wage demands in return for government subsidies and social benefits. But Margaret Thatcher and her supporters came to see the unions and their socialist allies in the Labour party as a direct threat to the survival of capitalism and freedom. Thus to a greater extent than in the United States, Thatcher used the authority of the state to create legal and market conditions that would undermine the economic and political power of the unions.

Third, political-institutional differences are also significant. Authority is much more highly concentrated in the executive in the British parliamentary system than in the United States. The prime minister and chancellor of the exchequer (occupying No. 10 and No. 11 Downing Street, respectively) are responsible for the formulation of economic policy, and parliament has little influence over its passage and implementation. Conflicts may develop in cabinet between different ministries and departments, but once a policy is adopted it is usually carried out. By contrast, in the United States power is dispersed among different branches and levels of government. The president proposes a budget but the Congress disposes of both tax and appropriation legislation, while monetary policy is separately controlled by the Federal Reserve Board. Thus it is more difficult for an American administration to implement a coherent macroeconomic policy.

In addition, the greater frequency of elections in the United States puts pressure on the incumbent leaders to seek quick results. In Britain a government is normally secure for four to five years and can choose the most propitious date for reelection, but the electoral calendar in the United States encourages economic expansion during all congressional and presidential election years (Tufte, 1978). Thus a British government has greater political leeway in carrying out a macroeconomic strategy that may be unpopular in the short run than has an American president (see Chapter 11).

To summarize, factors such as relative dependence on foreign trade, labor organization and structure, and the nature of policy-making institutions and electoral processes affect the general policy options available to the respective governments and account for some of the key differences between the Reagan and Thatcher programs. But the president and the prime minister have also had exceptional personal influence on policy development. They have both imposed their conservative economic doctrines on the policy-making apparatus and engineered major changes of direction. We can now compare their records in more detail.

MACROECONOMIC STRATEGIES AND IMPLEMENTATION

Macroeconomic policies are not simply a set of technical instruments wielded by economists to meet certain targets. They are rather a mix of political and economic judgments about what has gone wrong in the past, whose interests have been and ought to be served, what principles should guide future economic and social development, and how these goals can be achieved. The formulation and implementation of macroeconomic policies is thus an intensely political process. We will compare three aspects of policy making under Thatcher and Reagan: (1) the *rationale,* or how the macroeconomic problem was interpreted and defined, including diagnosis of past failures, application of new principles, and choice of policy instruments to be used; (2) political and economic *constraints*— what opposition and difficulties the governments encountered as they attempted to carry out their strategies; and (3) the *outcomes* or results, in terms of major economic indicators of current performance and potential longer-term consequences.

Thatcherism: The Monetarist Experiment

The ideological perspectives and economic doctrines of the Thatcher government were developed in opposition following the disastrous electoral defeats of 1974. Sir Keith Joseph, Margaret Thatcher, and some other members of the Heath government attributed its collapse to a failure of willpower and a mistaken turn toward the "collectivist" and "corporate-state" policies of the left. Mrs. Thatcher underwent "conversion" to Milton Friedman's monetarist philosophy in the winter of 1974–75, this coinciding with a general mood of disillusionment that enabled her to defeat Mr. Heath for the Conservative party leadership in early 1975. In the next four years she presided over a broad reappraisal of party policy that elevated monetarism to a central place in the party's platform—even though the majority of her shadow cabinet still represented the Heath wing and never fully accepted the monetarist approach (Riddell, 1983). In the 1979 election campaign the Conservative manifesto promised tax reductions, monetary discipline, and a crackdown on the trade unions (Särlvik and Crewe, 1983). But it was only after the 1979 election that it became clear that the prime minister and her chancellor, Sir Geoffrey Howe, would design their entire macroeconomic strategy around monetary control.

The monetarist thesis holds that inflation is caused by (and only by) an excessive rate of growth in the money supply—i.e., by growth in the money stock at a rate that exceeds the real growth of production. Although money itself only affects the general price level and not real supply and demand in the long run, inflation can periodically become a source of uncertainty and business fluctuations if nominal price changes are misinterpreted as real ones. Most importantly, Keynesian attempts to stimulate the economy or to maintain full employment by raising aggregate demand are bound to fail: changes in nominal demand may temporarily encourage economic activity, but over time they will only raise prices. In contrast to Keynesian assumptions, there is no lasting trade-off between inflation and employment. Milton Friedman (1968) coupled this principle to the concept of a "natural rate of unemployment" determined by technology and market structures. Efforts to hold unemployment below this level artificially would inevitably be inflationary, whereas higher levels of unemployment were "voluntary."

The monetarist analysis was based on the neoclassical model of free market equilibrium, i.e., the idea that economies perform best if left to themselves, provided that a minimal set of conditions or "rules" is enforced by the state. Monetarists such as Milton Friedman advocated a fixed (or constitutional) rule limiting expansion of the money supply to something like the long-term rate of productivity growth. In the absence of such a fixed rule governments must have a credible plan for gradually ratcheting down the rate of monetary growth (Fellner, 1976).

The problem in Britain from this point of view was excess monetary growth created by high public spending to maintain "full employment" and high nominal wage increases, the trade unions being the chief culprit behind both tendencies. The expansion of public spending after 1970 was especially marked and was financed in part by public borrowing. The deficit or "public sector borrowing requirement" (PSBR) grew rapidly and threatened to "crowd out" private sector investment (Bacon and Eltis, 1976). But the most important factor to the monetarists was that the money supply had been relaxed to accommodate fiscal policies. In 1972 and 1973, for example, the monetary aggregate sterling M3 increased by about 25 percent annually, causing the runaway inflation of 1974–75.[1] The attempt to control inflation by incomes policies (which temporarily held wage increases in check) was pointless because workers would always try to compensate later even though nominal increases were eroded away by inflation. The results were said to be spiraling inflationary expectations, growing financial uncertainty, and declining competitiveness as the price of British goods increased.

Three conclusions were drawn by the Thatcherites. (1) The top priority of a Conservative government must be to get inflation down—the essential precondition for any lasting recovery. (2) This could be done only through a new, long-range financial strategy for controlling monetary growth. (3) Fiscal policy (spending and taxation) must henceforth accommodate monetary policy rather than vice versa. The third point meant that public expenditure must be cut substantially in order to reduce and eventually eliminate the PSBR; otherwise the strategy would not be "credible."

This rationale for public expenditure cuts dovetailed neatly with the argument of the new Conservative right that the public sector was growing out of control and that taxes must be cut to revive private incentives. The party manifesto emphasized the need "to restore incentives so that hard work pays, success is rewarded and genuine new jobs are created in an expanding economy." Although the "supply-side" arguments of economists such as Arthur Laffer were never fully accepted in Britain, high priority was given to reducing marginal income tax rates. The Thatcherites also saw an opportunity to roll back the public sector by "privatization," or turning some of the nationalized industries and unnecessary public functions over to private enterprise.[2]

Monetarism also provided a strategy for dealing with the trade unions. Instead of confronting the unions directly over incomes policy, the government would leave wage determination to private bargaining; however, it would be made clear that if wage increases were unreasonably high, the unions would have to take the blame for layoffs, plant closures, and unemployment, since easy money and credit would no longer be available to finance inflationary settlements. One flaw in this strategy was that as the largest employer in Britain the government could not avoid extensive bargaining with the public sector unions, which would eventually lead to confrontation.

It was assumed that the economy would have to go through a difficult transition period before "sound money" was firmly established. To her credit, Mrs. Thatcher warned that it might be painful. Chancellor Geoffrey Howe stated, "It is not possible to reduce inflation without some early loss in employment and output," but these "transitory" losses need not "have a permanently adverse effect on growth potential" (Treasury and Civil Service Committee, 1981, I:xxxi).

If these were the basic ideas behind Thatcherism, how were they implemented? Sir Geoffrey Howe's first budget in June 1979 lowered income taxes (the standard rate from 33 to 30 percent, the top rate from 83 to 60 percent) but raised indirect taxes (notably the value added tax, from 8 to 15 percent). In November the government raised the minimum lending rate (which determined interest rates) to a record high of 17 percent and announced substantial cuts in planned public expenditure. It was not until March 1980 that the monetarist program was introduced in the form of the Medium-Term Financial Strategy (MTFS), which accompanied the new budget and public expenditure white paper. The MTFS called for a phased reduction in money supply (sterling M3) growth from 7–11 percent in 1980–81 to 4–8 percent in 1983–84; at the same time the white paper projected a similar decline in real public spending of about 1 percent a year, with the object of reducing the PSBR by two-thirds by 1983–84.

These targets were published in order to convey a clear signal to the unions and the business community that the government was determined to control monetary growth over an extended period of years. At the same time, by refusing to set any targets for output and employment, and by eliminating controls over wages, prices, dividends, and foreign exchange, the government indicated that it would stick to its monetary policies whatever the other consequences for the economy. In this sense it was intended to be a "credible threat" strategy (Buiter and Miller, 1981).

In fact, the Thatcher government has never come close to meeting most of these targets (for details, see, e.g., Buiter and Miller, 1981, 1983; Riddell, 1983). Monetary growth exploded in 1980 (sterling M3 increased by 17.5 percent) and continued to overshoot; subsequently in 1982 the government redefined and deemphasized such targets. Real public expenditure *increased* 7 percent by 1983–84 rather than falling by 4 percent, and the public sector actually grew from 40.5 to 44 percent of the national economy. Taxes and social security contributions also increased substantially in line with expenditures (from 34 percent of GDP in 1978–79 to nearly 40 percent by 1982–83). Thus, in contrast to the United States, the deficit or PSBR was cut from 5.7 percent of GDP in 1980–81 to 3.25 percent in 1983–84.[3]

What accounts for the departures from the intended monetary and fiscal policies? Commentators have pointed to a large number of political and economic constraints and mistakes on the part of the government. On the political side, Mrs. Thatcher had committed herself to honoring the findings of a commission on public sector wages (the Clegg Commission) rather than taking on the unions at the outset of her administration. The result was a round of public sector pay increases averaging 20–25 percent in 1979–80, adding to inflation and requiring the government to overshoot both its spending and monetary targets. The value-added tax increase also caused a one-time jump of 4 percent in the inflation rate.

The principal economic constraints resulted from the world recession which began in late 1979 and which contributed to the rapid increase in British unemployment during 1980–81 (it is estimated that at least half of this increase was due to external factors). With unemployment rising rapidly, the "wets" or moderates in the cabinet were able to fend off budget cuts, and government spending on unemployment benefits and other social programs rose automatically. The government pumped additional money into the nationalized industries as their revenues fell and introduced a variety of other programs to prevent employment from falling even more rapidly than it did (see below). Mrs. Thatcher apparently did not gain full control of her cabinet until after several members were replaced in the fall of 1981 (*Economist*, 1983).

Nevertheless, it is not true that the Thatcher government allowed easy credit or that its fiscal policies were expansionary. In order to control appreciation of the pound (which rose dramatically in 1979–80, making it more difficult to export British goods), interest rates were not allowed to rise to free market levels. But they were at historically high levels (in the 14–17 percent range) during 1979–82, and analyses of a variety of monetary aggregates and credit measures indicated that money and credit had been much tighter than the sterling M3 figures suggested (leading the government to abandon its M3 target for a broader range of indicators in 1982). Moreover, despite spending growth resulting from the recession and from planned program increases (e.g., for defense and the police), overall fiscal policy was tighter than in any country in Europe. In fact, if one adjusts for the effects of higher interest rates and cyclically induced spending, the Thatcher government actually ran a budget *surplus* equal to 7 percent of GDP during the period 1980–83 (Buiter and Miller, 1983, 327). Some commentators see a close parallel in this to the Treasury orthodoxy of 1925–31, when industrial growth was sacrificed in a vain attempt to restore the prewar value of the pound (Nevin, 1983, 119–23).

The short-term economic results of Thatcher's first term are summarized in Table 8.5. Whatever the causes, it was a dismal performance—the worst since the Great Depression of the 1930s. Between the fourth quarter of 1979 and mid-1981, national output fell about 5 percent, industrial production 12 percent, manufacturing 15 percent, and construction nearly 20 percent. Caught in a severe profits squeeze, firms cut production, laid off workers, and engaged in massive destocking to maintain liquidity. Bankruptices reached record levels, manufacturing investment

TABLE 8.5
United Kingdom, Selected Economic Indicators, 1979–1984
(percent)

INDICATOR	1979	1980	1981	1982	1983	1984[h]
GDP/GNP[a]	2.1	−4.8	1.9	1.4	3.5	2.6
Industrial production[b]	2.7	−11.6	2.3	0.2	3.4	−1.8
Unemployment[c]	5.1	6.4	10.0	11.7	12.4	12.9
Inflation[d]	13.4	18.0	11.9	8.6	4.6	5.0
Money supply[e]	12.9	17.5	12.9	9.0	10.0	8.2
Public expenditure (% GDP)[f]	40.5	42.5	44.0	43.5	43.0	42.0
Deficit (PSBR) (% GDP)[g]	5.0	5.7	3.5	3.3	3.25	NA

[a] Gross Domestic Product at factor cost, average estimate, at 1980 prices, fourth quarter over one year earlier (1984 = GNP). Source: *Economic Trends* (May 1984), table 6.

[b] Real output of all industries, percentage change in fourth quarter over one year earlier. Calculated from *Economic Trends* (May 1984), table 26.

[c] Unemployment rate excluding school leavers. Source: *Economic Trends* (May 1984), table 36.

[d] General index of retail prices. Source: *Economic Trends* (May 1984), table 42.

[e] Sterling M3, excluding public sector deposits, percentage change for four quarters. Source: *Economic Trends* (May 1984), table 52.

[f] Total government expenditure as percentage of GDP at market prices (1984 = estimate). Source: H.M. Treasury, *The Government's Expenditure Plans 1984–85 to 1986–87* (Cmnd 9143-I), chart 1.8.

[g] Public sector borrowing requirement as percentage of GDP. Figures approximate. Source: *The Economist* (March 10, 1984):14–15.

[h] Figures for 1984 from *The Economist* (Dec. 1, 1984):121–22, unless otherwise indicated.

plunged by 30 percent, and unemployment more than doubled from 5.3 percent to 11.5 percent (excluding school leavers). Inflation also got worse before getting better: the retail price index rose from 10.6 percent in the second quarter of 1979 to 21.5 percent a year later, before gradually declining to 11.9 percent in 1981, 8.6 percent in 1982, and about 5 percent in 1983. Since 1981 the economy has gradually recovered, with real growth averaging 2.4 percent annually. However, unemployment stood at 12.9 percent at the end of 1984, and there was little hope that it would improve since joblessness is concentrated in the declining manufacturing sector.

The government nevertheless claimed that Britain had "turned the corner" and had been put on a new, more disciplined, and efficient foundation for long-term growth. It claimed large productivity increases in the manufacturing sector, and managers were said to be "taking charge" again. However, critics argued that the productivity increases were merely a temporary consequence of shedding labor and the closure of less efficient plants during 1980–81. The only unequivocal achievement that Thatcherism could claim was the dramatic reduction in the inflation rate.

This was of course the government's top priority. Can the monetarist strategy then be judged a success, at least in terms of its own goals? Critics point to two major flaws in the argument. First, it is claimed that inflation was "controlled" not by the government's monetary policy— which was never effectively implemented—but by the severity of the recession and unemployment that the government's policies induced. Whatever "credibility" the policy had in terms of lowering inflationary expectations stemmed from the government's willingness to accept a doubling of the unemployment rate, not from its ill-fated monetary targets. Second, even though inflation has fallen to the lowest level in fifteen years, there is no reason to believe that it has been more than temporarily subdued or that the costs of achieving it (in terms of lost output, productive capacity, and employment) will be worth the benefits. In particular, the 20 percent drop in manufacturing employment between 1979 and 1982 reduced capacity and accelerated deindustrialization. Some studies suggest that prospects for growth in the British economy are now considerably less favorable than in the 1930s (Buiter and Miller, 1983). But even sympathetic critics conclude that "no lasting improvement in the performance of British industry has been confirmed" (Riddell, 1983, 243).

The social and political consequences are potentially far-reaching. It appears that Thatcher's policies have resulted in an upward redistribution of income. Data indicate that only the wealthiest 20 percent of households gained in real disposable income between 1978–79 and 1981–82, while the poorest 20 percent suffered a real income decline of 9.7 percent (Alt, 1984). The government has since ceased publication of such data, but the record unemployment, shift to consumption taxes, and public expenditure cuts have probably continued the trend.

If one of the government's purposes was to discipline the unions by allowing unemployment to rise to a level that threatened their authority and bargaining power, it had some success in the early years. As manufacturing employment plummeted after 1979, union membership fell by two million members and, as in the United States, many workers were forced to accept wage concessions or face layoffs. The government has also weakened institutions other than trade unions in which the labor movement has its greatest strength: e.g., local government authorities, the nationalized industries, the civil service generally, and council house estates (Hall and Jacques, 1983). The policies have hit the older cities of the Midlands and the north and Scotland much more severely than the southern parts of England in which new industry is concentrated. Finally, in 1984 the government was embroiled in the longest and most violent strike (by the coal miners) since 1926, the outcome of which could affect labor relations for many years to come.

Reaganomics: The Supply-Side Experiment

Ronald Reagan described his administration's view of the causes of American economic difficulties in his inaugural address:

> In this present crisis, government is not the solution to our problem; government is the problem. . . . It is time to awaken this industrial giant, to get government back within its means and to lighten our punitive tax burden. And these will be our first priorities, and on these principles there will be no compromise (Dallek, 1984, 63–64).

This statement reflected many of Reagan's longstanding beliefs: that the national government through an absence of fiscal and monetary discipline over the years was primarily responsible for stagflation, and the era of useless federal programs, chronic deficits, and easy money had to end. These beliefs echoed the traditional Republican critique of economic policy, which for decades had served to justify a prescription of fiscal and monetary austerity to combat inflation. Reagan himself had espoused this approach as a presidential candidate in 1976. By 1980 that had changed. His prescription now included "supply-side economics."

Congressman Jack Kemp of New York successfully led an effort to convince congressional Republicans to adopt this alternative fiscal strategy in the late 1970s. Kemp was aided in his efforts by economists Paul Craig Roberts and Norman Ture as well as by Jude Wanniski, an associate editor of the *Wall Street Journal* (Roberts, 1984; Bartlett, 1982). They argued that large cuts in personal income tax rates would stimulate capital investment and labor productivity such that the resultant high economic growth would produce additional tax revenues offsetting most if not all of the revenue lost through the tax cuts. This supply-side approach contradicted the traditional Republican orthodoxy that spending cuts and budget balance must precede any tax cuts. Instead, it was argued that tax cuts could promote employment and budget balance *without* causing inflation, if growth in the money supply remained moderate and consistent as the tax cuts took effect (Ture, 1982). In short, increasing microeconomic incentives would produce noninflationary economic growth.

Supply-side economics diverges from Keynesian and monetarist approaches in assuming that government cannot directly alter the level of national income by manipulating either monetary or fiscal aggregates. Instead, the impact of government is largely through the effect of tax rates upon relative prices. Income taxes act as a "wedge" that lowers the relative price paid for supplying effort and capital that contribute to production. Although all economists believe that extremely high tax rates diminish personal incentives, supply-siders hold that these incentive effects are large and direct at all economic levels. Thus, people will vary their amount of work, saving, and investment in direct response to marginal tax rates, and the most significant thing that government can do is to lower income taxes. Orthodox Keynesian and monetarist economists disputed these claims, arguing that lower taxes would not necessarily induce substitution of greater effort for leisure, saving for consumption, etc., and that large government deficits would result from the policy (Tobin, 1981; Thurow, 1984; Stein, 1984).

Whatever its theoretical defects, the supply-side strategy provided Republicans with a much more electorally palatable alternative than the old cure of monetary and fiscal constraint, which entailed fighting inflation by deliberately encouraging recession. Its simplicity was part of its popular appeal. As one Reagan administration official confided, it was "a simple idea that could be grasped by Joe Sixpack" (Broder, 1984). It was also consistent with Reagan's "strong belief that big government and high taxes have destroyed the incentive to work, save and invest, and that the diminution of incentives lies at the root of our economic malaise" (Bartlett, 1982, 222).

During the 1980 nomination campaign, Reagan endorsed the Kemp-Roth tax bill, which called for a 30 percent cut in personal income tax rates, even though his opponent George Bush referred to this approach as "voodoo economics." Reagan later tempered his stance by agreeing to support restricted money supply growth and deep federal budget cuts to be enacted simultaneously with the tax cuts (Silk, 1980). Nevertheless, the basic principles of supply-side economics were retained. The result-

ing approach, labeled "Reaganomics," became the policy of the administration. Herbert Stein, a former head of Nixon's Council of Economic
Advisers, summarized its assumptions:

1. There is no necessary connection between inflation and unemployment, even in the short run, and inflation can be reduced without a
transitional period of increased unemployment.
2. Reduction of tax rates will not prevent balancing the budget but
will actually contribute to balance, because reducing tax rates will raise
national income enough to increase revenues.
3. Government expenditures can be reduced significantly without
injuring anyone except government bureaucrats, because the budget is
full of waste, fraud, and counterproductive programs. (Stein, 1984, 236)

Four specific policies would be pursued in accordance with these
assumptions: (1) a large cut in marginal tax rates—25 percent over three
years, and reduction in taxes on income from business investment; (2) a
large reduction in nondefense spending; (3) slower and steadier monetary
growth; and (4) a substantial reduction in government regulation. Two
other administration goals also would have to be accommodated: (5) a
large increase in defense spending; and (6) achieving federal budget balance in a few years (Silk, 1980).

A distinguishing characteristic of Reaganomics was the assertion that
reducing inflation and unemployment and cutting taxes and spending
could all be done concurrently. In contrast to Margaret Thatcher, who
"recognized the costs of the objectives" and was willing to pay them,
Ronald Reagan denied that "the objectives being pursued had any costs"
(Stein, 1984, 236).

The absence of perceived costs partly explains Reagan's resounding
success in getting his fiscal program through Congress in 1981. In a series
of hard-fought and dramatic votes, Congress approved almost 80 percent
of the cuts in 1982 nondefense outlays proposed by the administration
($27.1 of $34.8 billion). Although practically every category of spending
was cut substantially from the base of the Carter administration's proposals (with the exception of defense), most cuts fell upon discretionary
domestic programs and entitlement programs such as Aid to Families
with Dependent Children, Medicaid, food stamps, and school lunches. In
late July Congress agreed to most major provisions of the administration's
Economic Recovery Tax Act of 1981. In accordance with supply-side principles, the bill provided for a 23 percent reduction in personal income
taxes over three years, a reduction in the top marginal tax rate for individuals from 70 to 50 percent, and indexing the tax code to inflation
beginning in 1985. The act also included a number of breaks for business

not requested by the administration. These prompted some commentators to label the bill "not a Christmas tree, but a Christmas forest." Reagan and his advisers nevertheless embraced the bill. Treasury Secretary Donald Regan boasted that the administration had received "95 percent" of what it had sought.

This success marks a turning point in Reagan administration policy. The Federal Reserve Board in the meantime had maintained a rate of growth in the money supply within its 1981 target range of 4–6.5 percent, consistent with the expressed desire of the administration. The monetary and fiscal components seemed in place to assure a noninflationary boom. Yet this did not transpire. By October, with nominal interest rates still over 15 percent and real interest rates at 7 percent, stock and bond markets remained sluggish and economic indicators suggested a recession was in the offing. Stern monetary policy seemed to override any positive expectational effects of budget and tax cuts, resulting in a slowing of the moderate growth experienced during the first half of 1981. Recession portended huge federal deficits due to the recent passage of the largest tax cut in American history. By December both the Congressional Budget Office and Office of Management and Budget predicted that annual federal deficits would total over $100 billion a year in each of the next three fiscal years, increasing each year.

This crisis revealed a major political constraint upon the successful implementation of Reaganomics in that the administration was sharply divided internally over how to respond to these conditions. A battle ensued between more "mainstream" and "radical" supply-side advisers, each group seeking the support of the president (Willet and McClure, 1983; Roberts, 1984). This heated and at times public dispute concerned two issues: the macroeconomic impact of the deficits; and the desirability of tax increases to offset them. More radical advisers Paul Craig Roberts and Norman Ture argued that tax cuts came too little and too late to prevent a recession and that the size of deficits would diminish once the personal tax cuts took effect in subsequent years. Budget Director David Stockman and Council of Economic Advisers Chairman Murray Weidenbaum urged tax increases in order to limit the "crowding out" of private borrowers from credit markets by the government, which they thought could substantially prolong the recession. After months of resistance, the president in July 1982 "swallowed hard" and accepted major tax increases, which he termed not a tax hike but "revenue enhancements." Ture and Roberts had by this time resigned.

The state of the deficit and macroeconomy steadily worsened (see Table 8.6). From January to December unemployment increased from 8.5 to 10.7 percent; GNP shrank by 3 percent from the third quarter of 1981 to the end of 1982. This was accompanied by a marked decline in the

TABLE 8.6
United States, Selected Economic Indicators, 1979–1984
(percent)

INDICATOR	1979	1980	1981	1982	1983	1984[h]
GNP[a]	2.8	−0.3	2.6	−1.9	3.3	6.8
Manufacturing output[b]	3.4	−4.5	2.5	−8.5	7.7	11.0
Unemployment[c]	5.1	7.1	7.6	9.7	9.6	7.4
Inflation[d]	13.3	12.4	8.9	3.9	3.2	4.3
Money supply[e]	7.1	6.5	6.4	8.5	9.0	5.2
Public expenditure (% GNP)[f]	31.1	33.0	33.3	35.4	35.4	36.3
Federal deficit (% GNP)[g]	1.1	2.3	2.0	3.6	5.9	4.7

[a] Gross national product in 1972 prices, fourth quarter over one year earlier. Source: *Economic Report of the President* (1984), table B-2.

[b] Industrial production index in manufacturing in 1967 prices. Source: *Economic Report of the President* (1984), table B-42.

[c] Unemployed as percent of civilian labor force. Source: *Economic Report of the President* (1984), table B-33.

[d] Change in the consumer price index over one year earlier. Source: *Economic Report of the President* (1984), table B-55.

[e] Percent change in M1 from one year earlier. Source: *Economic Report of the President* (1984), table B-61.

[f] Public expenditure at all levels of government as a percentage of GNP. Calculated from *Economic Report of the President* (1984), tables B-8 and B-75.

[g] Annual federal deficit as a percentage of GNP. Calculated from *Economic Report of the President* (1984), tables B-8, B-76.

[h] 1984 estimates from Data Resources Inc., November 1984.

inflation rate from 8.9 percent in 1981 to 3.8 percent in 1983. As a result of looser monetary policy and greatly expansionary budgets (the FY 1982 deficit was $112.2 billion, 3.9 percent of GNP, and the FY 1983 deficit $185.7 billion, 5.6 percent of GNP), a gradual but strong economic recovery began in early 1983. In 1984, inflation was estimated at 4.3 percent and unemployment at 7.4 percent. Both liberal and conservative economists, including Martin Feldstein, head of Reagan's Council of Economic Advisers in 1983–84, viewed this as a result of Keynesian style short-term expansion of aggregate consumption at variance with Reaganomics (Thurow, 1983; Barry, 1984). It should also be noted that personal savings rates—a key indicator of supply-side effects—have remained nearly constant since 1981.

The onset of deficit problems also underscored the potential problems a president encounters in attempting to implement economic policy when authority is dispersed. From 1979 to 1982 the FRB pursued a highly restrictive monetary policy, which encouraged the deep recession throughout 1982. The FRB gradually responded with more expansionary policies after this, but did so autonomously. In this instance presidential persuasion was successful only because of similar congressional and Wall Street complaints and the onset of the worst economic downturn since the 1930s.

The administration found Congress a severe constraint on its fiscal policy goals in 1982, 1983, and 1984. Presidential advisers initially hoped that the impending deficits would pressure Congress into accepting further spending cuts. However, the president's budget proposals received little serious attention in these years, as deficit projections produced skepticism about defense spending increases and a desire for additional revenues. The electoral calendar also worked against the administration when mid-term congressional elections occurred in the midst of the recession. The Republicans lost twenty-six House seats, and as a result the administration could no longer forge a majority coalition of Republicans and conservative Democrats on budget and tax votes. Reagan was forced to accept smaller tax increases in 1983 and 1984, although he managed to preserve both tax indexing and the personal income tax cuts.

The economic events of the years 1982–84 have discredited some assumptions of Reaganomics, which explains the growth of political constraints to administration policy implementation. The recession of 1981–82 produced a surprisingly fast disinflation (Cagan and Fellner, 1984), but at the cost of unemployment levels unprecedented in the postwar era. Cuts in program expenditure did not merely exorcise "waste, fraud, and abuse" from various programs, but imposed hardships upon the poor and working poor (Haveman et al., 1982). The assumption of supply-side fiscal effects has never been fully tested. The tax cuts of 1981 did not provide the full incentives intended as they were countered by subsequent tax increases (in social security and excise taxes, for example) and bracket creep, which left personal tax burdens virtually unchanged (Stein, 1984). Although administration tax policies have failed to pursue supply-side goals consistently, huge deficits resulted from defense spending increases, cuts in business taxes, and congressional resistance to further deep cuts in domestic spending. As a result, the administration has failed in its attempt to reduce the national budget's share of the GNP.

The distributional impacts of fiscal policies also belie the administration's claims to "fairness." Impartial studies indicate that while the top 40 percent of income earners gained substantially in real personal disposable income from 1980 to 1984, the real disposable incomes of the lowest 40 percent declined (the poorest 20 percent by 7.6 percent) (Palmer and Sawhill, 1984, 321).

A new term—*structural deficit*—has entered the economic lexicon in recent years. This is the deficit remaining when the cyclical effects of less than full employment are removed from a given year's budget. The Congressional Budget Office estimated that this deficit totaled $104 billion, or 46 percent of the total deficit, in FY 1983 and will be $218 billion or 88 percent of the estimated deficit by 1988 (Mills and Palmer, 1983). This has led even conservative commentators and economists to claim that we are "undertaxed" (Will, 1983; Stein, 1984).

Aware and concerned about this problem, David Stockman and CEA Chair Martin Feldstein in 1983 and 1984 urged slowdowns in defense spending and tax increases, but met with presidential reluctance. In 1984 the president proposed a slowdown in growth of defense spending (from 18 to 12 percent), some small tax increases, and large additional cuts in domestic spending. Congress responded midyear by producing a package of tax increases and expenditure cuts totaling $60 billion over three years, which the president signed into law.

Walter Mondale attempted with little success to make the deficit a major campaign issue in 1984. President Reagan minimized the problem and stated in a nationally televised debate that economic growth would eliminate the deficit, thus reaffirming the supply-side orthodoxy. But shortly after the election it was revealed that the federal shortfall would rise to at least $210 billion for FY 1985. Deficits remained the administration's central economic and political frustration. Economically, the unprecedented government borrowing kept interest rates high, which in turn raised federal debt service costs and threatened to choke off growth. Politically, deficits confronted the administration with the vexing task of drastically cutting back programs that benefit the middle class as well as the poor. This painful choice between politically costly action and economically costly inaction promised to dominate Reagan's second term.

CONCLUSION

The Thatcher and Reagan governments both changed the rules by which macroeconomic policy had been made since World War II. Inspired by new conservative ideologies, they rejected the "managed capitalism" of the Keynesian era in favor of a rejuvenated market capitalism driven by a liberated private sector. But despite many similarities in their visions of capitalist restoration, they have followed different macroeconomic strategies in their attempts to stabilize prices and restore growth.

Thatcherism grew out of monetarism, the "new orthodoxy" that came to the fore with the unprecedented inflation of the mid-1970s—although monetarist theory had a long and respected tradition among conservative economists. Reaganomics, on the other hand, drew its inspiration from supply-side ideas that surfaced at the end of the decade but had little support among professional economists. Their operational strategies differed accordingly: Thatcher's called for a long and painful period of adjustment to bring wage expectations into line with productivity and eliminate inefficient practices; Reagan's promised a "quick fix" in the form of rapid, noninflationary growth that would solve all problems (what Herbert Stein calls "the economics of joy"). Although initially the monetary policies of the two governments were relatively similar—both were restrictive, bringing record interest rates—their fiscal components were dramatically different. To establish "fiscal rectitude," Thatcher's government refused to reflate the British economy (despite some counter-cyclical spending); in fact, the deficit was cut during the worst recession in fifty years. By contrast, Reagan's gamble on a massive tax cut produced the largest budget deficits in peacetime history and, ironically, created a new "fiscal crisis of the state."

Both monetarism and supply-side economics represented radical attempts to break the pattern of stagflation that characterized advanced capitalism in the 1970s by manipulating a narrower range of macroeconomic instruments than previous governments had used: in Britain the sterling M3 monetary aggregate and PSBR, in the United States tax rates and monetary growth. It was believed that if new "rules" were established in these areas and the state refused to accommodate other interests and pressures, the private economy would adjust to a new, more efficient, and competitive footing. The implication is that the resulting economic growth and market distribution of gains will strengthen the long-term prospects for capitalist democracy.

The results thus far provide little assurance that this will be the case. Monetary disinflation has involved severe costs to output and employment, has produced high real interest rates that inhibit investment, and has made government finance immensely more difficult. In Britain the government has explicitly abandoned the goal of full employment that all governments had honored since World War II. Continued adherence to restrictive monetary and fiscal principles will severely limit policy options for reducing the massive unemployment and class tensions which now exist. Britain may have returned for the moment to her traditionally low growth path, but without greater flexibility it is doubtful that this government can long weather the political divisions it has created. In America Reagan's growth strategy has been more successful and popular in the short run (see Chapter 11). But even more than in Britain, the use of macroeconomic policy instruments to handle future crises will be severely circumscribed, in this case by enormous structural deficits. The means as well as the ends of macroeconomic policy making have been changed.

These conservative regimes have not yet succeeded in their larger goal of permanently reducing the size and scope of the state. Although the public sector is growing at a slower rate, it now consumes a larger share of national income than when Mrs. Thatcher and Mr. Reagan took office (this could, of course, change if economic growth continues). As in the past, economic interest groups and other political constituencies have thus far been able to resist cuts in the large subsidy and entitlement programs that primarily benefit the middle class. Despite much general antigovernment feeling, there is no evidence that popular majorities will support the large program cuts needed to approach budget balance.

Finally, although beyond the scope of this study, the international implications may be most serious of all. High interest rates in the United States have attracted a flood of foreign capital (estimated at $117 billion in 1984) that has partially offset government borrowing and raised the value of the dollar by 70 percent against European currencies. But this appreciation of the dollar has in turn priced American goods out of world markets, creating a record United States trade deficit of $123 billion for 1984 alone. This deficit has shifted an estimated 1.5 million jobs abroad and has turned the United States into a net debtor nation. Together with the enormous foreign debts of other countries such as Mexico, Argentina, and Brazil, these imbalances place greater strain on the international financial system than at any time since World War II. In sum, attempts to control one set of problems may have created far bigger ones for the future.

NOTES

1. Sterling M3 is a broad monetary aggregate which includes currency in circulation, sterling checking accounts, and time deposits owned by the U.K. private sector, and sterling deposits by the U.K. public sector. For detailed discussions of monetary policy in Britain, see the Treasury and Civil Service Committee's 1981 report, *Monetary Policy;* a report by the Joint Economic Committee of the U.S. Congress, 1981; Meyer, 1982; and Nevin, 1983. Nevin argues that the growth rate of the money supply in Britain has been lower than average for the Western world since 1952 and that the great expansion of credit in the early 1970s was due to private bank lending and not the PSBR (pp. 103–05).

2. Privatization, or sale of government-owned assets to private buyers, was relatively limited during Thatcher's first term, but has increased about fivefold since 1983. The case for privatization is examined in Shackleton, 1984.

3. Sale of government property, including shares in several large public corporations, such as British Petroleum and Cable and Wireless, has contributed

to reduction in the PSBR. In late 1984 the government began sales of $4.7 billion of British Telecom shares, the largest single stock offering in history and equivalent to half the annual PSBR. Whether such transactions should be considered as "reducing" the public deficit or simply "financing" it is open to dispute. See Brittan, 1984, for details.

REFERENCES

Alt, J. E. 1984. "Pound's Up! Your Money or Your Oil? An Evaluation of the Political Economy of Thatcher's Britain." Paper presented to the Conference Group on Political Economy, Washington, D.C.

Amott, T., and Krieger, J. 1982. "Thatcher and Reagan: State Theory and the 'Hyper-Capitalist' Regime." *New Political Science* 8 (Spring): 9–37.

Bacon, R., and Eltis, W. A. 1976. *Britain's Economic Problem: Too Few Producers.* London: Macmillan.

Barry, J. M. 1984. "A Final Bow from the Man Who Made the White House Boo." *Washington Post National Weekly Edition* (June 23): 20–21.

Bartlett, B. 1982. *Reaganomics: Supply Side Economics in Action.* New York: Quill.

Beer, S. H. 1982. *Britain Against Itself: The Political Contradictions of Collectivism.* New York: Norton.

Behrens, R. 1980. *The Conservative Party from Heath to Thatcher.* Farnborough, Hants.: Saxon House.

Blackaby, F., ed. 1979. *De-Industrialisation.* London: Heinemann.

Bluestone, B., and Harrison, B. 1982. *The Deindustrialization of America.* New York: Basic Books.

Brittan, S. 1984. "The Politics and Economics of Privatisation." *Political Quarterly* 55 (April–June):109–28.

Broder, D. 1984. "Let Reagan Be Reagan Again." *Washington Post National Weekly Edition* (June 23): 4.

Buiter, W. H., and Miller, M. H. 1981. "The Thatcher Experiment: The First Two Years." *Brookings Papers on Economic Activity,* no. 2, 315–79.

——. 1983. "Changing the Rules: Economic Consequences of the Thatcher Regime." *Brookings Papers on Economic Activity,* no. 2, 305–65.

Cagan, P., and Fellner, W. 1984. "The Cost of Disinflation, Credibility and the Deceleration of Wages 1982–1983." In *Essays in Contemporary Economic Problems: Disinflation,* ed. W. Fellner. Washington, D.C.: American Enterprise Institute.

Caves, R. E., and Krause, L. B. 1980. *Britain's Economic Performance.* Washington, D.C.: Brookings Institution.

Dallek, R. 1984. *Ronald Reagan: The Politics of Symbolism.* Cambridge: Harvard University Press.

Economist. 1983. "The Thatcher Style: The Trials and Triumphs of a Party Ideologue," *Economist* (May 21): 21–28.

Fellner, W. 1976. *Towards a Reconstruction of Economics.* Washington, D.C.: American Enterprise Institute.

Friedman, M. 1968. "The Role of Monetary Policy." *American Economic Review* 58 (March): 1–17.

Gamble, A. 1981. *Britain in Decline.* London: Macmillan.

Grant, W. 1982. *The Political Economy of Industrial Policy.* London: Butterworth.

Hall, S., and Jacques, M., eds. 1983. *The Politics of Thatcherism.* London: Lawrence and Wishart.

Haveman, J., et al. 1982. "Sharing the Wealth." *National Journal* 14:1788–1807.

Heineman, B. W., Jr., and Hessler, C. A. 1980. *Memorandum for the President: A Strategic Approach to Domestic Affairs in the 1980s.* New York: Random House.

House of Commons. Treasury and Civil Service Committee. 1981. *Monetary Policy.* Third Report (H.C. 163-I). 3 vols. London: Her Majesty's Stationery Office.

Maunder, W. P. J., ed. 1980. *The British Economy in the 1970s.* London: Heinemann.

McClure, J. H., and Willett, T. D. 1983. "Understanding the Supply Siders." In *Reaganomics: A Midterm Report,* ed. W. C. Stubblebine and T. D. Willett. San Francisco: Institute for Contemporary Studies.

Meyer, S. A. 1982. "Margaret Thatcher's Economic Experiment: Are There Lessons for the Reagan Administration?" *Business Review* (Federal Reserve Bank of Philadelphia) (May–June).

Miller, A. 1978. "Partisanship Reinstated? A Comparison of the 1972 and 1976 Presidential Elections." *British Journal of Political Science* 8:129–52.

Mills, G. B., and Palmer, J. L. 1983. *The Deficit Dilemma: Budget Policy in the Reagan Era.* Washington, D.C.: Urban Institute Press.

Nevin, M. 1983. *The Age of Illusions: The Political Economy of Britain 1968–1982.* London: Victor Gollancz.

Palmer, J. L., and Sawhill, I. V., eds. 1984. *The Reagan Record.* Cambridge: Ballinger.

Reich, R. B. 1983. *The Next American Frontier.* New York: Penguin Books.

Riddell, P. 1983. *The Thatcher Government.* Oxford: Martin Robertson.

Roberts, P. C. 1984. *The Supply-Side Revolution.* Cambridge: Harvard University Press.

Rose, R. 1980. *Do Parties Make a Difference?* Chatham, N.J.: Chatham House.

Särlvik, B., and Crewe, I. 1983. *Decade of Dealignment: The Conservative Victory of 1979 and Electoral Trends in the 1970s.* Cambridge: Cambridge University Press.

Shacklteton, J. R. 1984. "Privatisation: the Case Examined." *National Westminster Bank Quarterly Review* (May): 59–73.

Shonfield, A. 1958. *British Economic Policy Since the War*. Harmondsworth: Penguin Books.

Silk, L. 1980. "On the Supply Side." In *Reagan the Man, the President*, by H. Smith et al. New York: Macmillan.

Stein, H. 1984. *Presidential Economics*. New York: Simon and Schuster.

Taylor, R. 1980. *The Fifth Estate: Britain's Unions in the Modern World*. London: Pan Books.

Thurow, L. 1984. "The Ultimate Keynesian." *Newsweek* (January 23): 86.

Tobin, J. 1981. "Supply Side Economics: What Is It? Will It Work?" *Economic Outlook USA* 8: 51–53.

Tufte, E. 1978. *Political Control of the Economy*. Princeton: Princeton University Press.

Ture, N. 1982. "Supply Side Economics and Public Policy." In *Essays in Supply Side Economics*, ed. D. G. Raboy. Washington, D.C.: Institute for Research on the Economics of Taxation.

U.S. Congress. Joint Economic Committee. 1981. *Monetary Policy, Selective Credit Policy, and Industrial Policy in France, Britain, West Germany, and Sweden*. Washington, D.C.: Government Printing Office.

Whitely, P. 1983. *The Labour Party in Crisis*. London: Methuen.

Will, G. 1983. "On Revenues and Ronald Reagan." *Newsweek* (July 18): 80.

9   THE SOCIALIST ALTERNATIVE IN FRANCE: MITTERRAND'S ECONOMIC POLICIES

William Safran

The year 1981 was a turning point for France. Not only did it bring a Socialist government to power for the first time since the establishment (in 1958) of the Fifth Republic, it also brought the Assembly, the popular house of Parliament, under solid Socialist control for the first time in half a century. The political system that the Socialists inherited—a system tailor-made for General de Gaulle and once vigorously opposed by most of the left—represents a hybrid of the classic parliamentary regimes found in Britain, West Germany, and elsewhere in Western Europe and of the presidential system of the United States. The 1958 constitution distinguishes between the president, who is chief of state, and the government, which is headed by a prime minister. The government functions as long as it enjoys the confidence of the Assembly, which may oust the premier and his cabinet colleagues by a vote of no confidence. But the premier and the rest of the ministers, who are charged with the day-to-day tasks of running France, are, in fact, appointed by the president; they do his bidding, promote the policies desired by him, and resign when their continuance in office is no longer convenient for the president. While ministers may not formally belong to Parliament, they effectively control its legislative agenda and dominate its deliberations. The relative weakness of Parliament—reflected *inter alia* in the limitation of ordinary sessions to five and a half months each year—is aggravated by the fact that the president has the power to dissolve the Assembly and thus to force new elections before the expiration of the normal five-year term of that chamber. The Senate, the other chamber, is the product not of direct popular elections but of the votes of municipal and regional politicians; it has even less power than the Assembly, since the Assembly can ultimately override the Senate's objections to bills.

Another significant element of the Fifth Republic is the electoral system. Based on single-member constituencies and providing for "second rounds," or run-off contests among the highest vote-getters, this system has been one of the factors contributing to the simplification (and "bipolarization") of the party system. From about six important parties in Fourth Republic Parliaments—the Communists and Socialists on the left, the Christian Democrats and Radical-Socialists in the center, and the Gaullists and miscellaneous conservatives on the right—the number of political parties or "camps" was gradually reduced to four: the Socialists and Communists, and the Gaullists and the Union for French Democracy (UDF). The UDF or "Giscardist" group was set up in 1978 as an electoral federation of right and center parties opposing both charismatic and ultranationalist Gaullism and leftist "collectivism" and supporting the presidency of Valéry Giscard d'Estaing (see Safran, 1985, esp. chap. 3).

While the French learned that an institutional arrangement set up for Gaullists could also serve Socialists, the pursuit of economic policies since 1981 has provided an even more interesting variety of lessons to numerous observers. For many leftists, the initial optimism about the possibilities of an economic policy that would be genuinely socialist rather than social democratic has been replaced by a sense of disappointment; for many Gaullists, Giscardists, and other "moderates," there is an "I told you so" feeling, based on the conviction that a policy of realism cannot be socialist and that a genuinely socialist policy cannot be realistic.

In dealing with the French socioeconomic policies under the Mitterrand presidency, this essay will make the following points, *inter alia:* (1) that Socialist policy tried initially to be consistent with the party's program *and* with what party politicians perceived to be the electorate's expectations from the new government, particularly in the area of redistribution; (2) that many of the initial Socialist programs were foreshadowed by, and hence logical developments from, Gaullist–Giscardist policies; (3) that the shift to an austerity policy after 1982 did not constitute a wholesale abandonment of socialist principles and an embrace of "right-wing" policies; and (4) that not all the failures of the French economy from 1981 to 1983 should in fairness be attributed to either lack of foresight on the part of the present government or the intrinsic shortcomings of socialism.

PRE-ELECTORAL EXPECTATIONS AND IDEOLOGICAL UNDERPINNINGS

The Socialist takeover of the government, for the first time since the establishment of the Fifth Republic, was accompanied by a seemingly endless outpouring of commentary about the socioeconomic programs that could now be expected. According to most analyses, the new government was assuming power with a clear commitment to solve the most pressing problems—unemployment, high inflation rates, and persistent economic inequalities—in an original French fashion that would be different from the standard social democratic policies of Western Europe. While the West German, British, and Scandinavian social democratic governments merely wished to "humanize" a capitalist system by piecemeal reforms from within—and ended up consorting with businessmen and bankers and stressing productivity—the French Socialists would pursue a set of policies that would radically transform, if not destroy, the capitalist system. It would do this by means of the nationalization of major industries, a tax on the wealthy and the corporations, an active full-employment policy, and a gearing up of the French productive machinery by a demand-side economic policy.

To what extent the economic program envisaged by the government was inspired by Marxist, Keynesian, or traditional French (Colbertian) dirigist reasoning—or, for that matter, by the tactical exigencies of the electoral alliance with the Communists—is a matter of controversy. *Changer la vie*, the Socialist party program of 1972, makes numerous critical references to capitalism and outlines specific measures that would help to undermine it, including the nationalization of banks and crucial sectors of industry, the extension of trade union rights, and stiff taxes on private corporations, but most of the concrete policy proposals are in fact standard social democratic ones: a reduction of the work week; an increase in minimum wages; a lowered retirement age; and greater social security for farmers, artisans, shopkeepers, and other disadvantaged social categories. Mitterrand himself, in a preface to this work, while asserting that "capitalist growth enchains the daily life of the worker in its rhythms," does not advocate the abolition of capitalism, private initiative, or the profit motive. On the contrary, he affirms that "a vast private sector will freely pursue its activities, and will develop itself [further]" (*Changer la vie*, 1972, 12–18). "Collective appropriation" is envisaged only for the "major means of production" (*les grandes moyens de production*) and only in the context of an economic plan and of social needs. In 1974, Mitterrand had said: "The debate that opposes the right to the left is based on a misunderstanding: that the one speaks of [the total economic] structure, while the other speaks of business cycles" (Manceron and Pingaud, 1981, 91–92).

It is true that Mitterrand, as leader of the opposition, had articulated visions going well beyond social democracy. On several occasions between 1977 and 1981 he had asserted that France had not yet broken decisively with capitalism and insisted that a major problem in his country was the division of its society into the two hostile camps of the propertied and the wage earners (Rémond, 1982). The Common Program, to which the Socialist party subscribed, had perhaps gone further in attacking capitalism and advocating nationalization than the Socialists had wanted. Nevertheless, the economic realism (or unrealism) of the Common Program was clearly less important than the overriding consideration of political tactics. These tactics were aimed at "plucking the Communist chicken"—more specifically, as Mitterrand put it, at "reshaping a great Socialist party on the terrain occupied by the Communist party . . . in order to show that, out of five million Communist voters, three million can vote Socialist . . . and in order that the left can escape being led by the Communists" (quoted in Giesbert, 1977, 267).

The *Projet socialiste pour la France des années 80* (1980) contains the semi-obligatory references to the class struggle as well as several critiques of "the deification of the market by the new economists" (112, 184) and demands "an end to the discretion of the chief of an enterprise with regard to employment" (227). Elsewhere, however, it makes reference to "the industrial imperative" (which would presumably call for consolidation) and to the fostering of "a spirit of enterprise and innovation" in the private sector, in particular the small and medium-sized enterprises (191). Beyond this double talk, there is the standard theme of equality and solidarity and the stress on full employment and the growth of production, both of which would be promoted by a combined policy of state intervention, selective takeovers, the creation of public service jobs, the strengthening of the purchasing power of the masses, the revival of economic planning on a more democratic basis, and the granting of greater worker responsibility in the management of the plant (172–97).

As the presidential election approached, many of these orientations assumed more specific shape. Mitterrand's own pronouncements came to echo some of the more concrete proposals contained in the *Manifeste du Parti socialiste* of January 24, 1981, concerning the reduction of the work week, the raising of minimum wages, the enlargement of the public service sector, the encouragement of savings by an indexing of interest rates, and miscellaneous tax reforms.[1] Just before the election, Mitterrand spelled out his "different kind of policy" *(autre politique)* in even greater detail, when he advocated a "recharging" *(relance)* of the economy by an infusion of money into the hands of the lowest wage earners, the retired, and the handicapped by means of social transfers, and when he called for the creation of 200,000 new jobs—of which 150,000 would be in the public service sector, with many of the remaining in housing and other construction and in the newly-to-be-created or expanded local politico-administrative bodies. Mitterrand also suggested that the survival of small enterprises could be fostered by a reduction of their social security obligations and that the unemployment problem might be reduced by a distribution of employment opportunities through early retirements and a reduction of the work week. However, the Socialist government would not necessarily pass a law to accomplish this; rather, it would "incite the employers and the unions to open . . . negotiations about a phased reduction of the work week [so that it will be possible] by means of agreements that are decentralized and adapted to the situation of each branch and each enterprise, to give some more time to survive, and others, employment" (Manceron and Pingaud, 1981, 92–93). This approach, in stressing autonomous bargaining, came close to being a "neoliberal" adaptation of socialism.[2]

LOOKING BACK AT GISCARDISM

When they took over the government, the Socialists wished not only to operationalize a set of abstract socialist principles but to rectify the alleged failures of the Gaullist and Giscardist regimes with respect to redistribution and social justice and to solve the immediate problem of unemployment. In 1974, when Giscard d'Estaing became president, 500,000 (or under 3 percent of the work force) were out of work; by the spring of 1981, this figure had risen to 1.7 million (or nearly 9 percent). The inflation rate was 12.8 percent, and the balance of trade deficit was over 60 billion francs (about $15 billion at the exchange rate then prevailing). The unemployment figures reflected the fact that, during the Giscard presidency, nearly 700,000 industrial jobs had been lost and had not been replaced; this was, in turn, partly a reflection of the failure of both the private sector and the government to think seriously enough, or to act with sufficient determination, about industrial expansion and structural modernization. The Giscard regime, particularly under the premiership of Raymond Barre, had oscillated between a policy of tight monetarism (accompanied by a refusal to devalue the franc) and austerity (as in 1979–80), which brought the economy close to a positive trade balance and a balanced budget (as in 1980),[3] on the one hand, and a policy of actively promoting the expansion of selected "winner" industries (*industries de pointe*), i.e., those likely to compete globally and earn hard currency, by means of tax concessions and subsidies, on the other. But the balanced budget (and the growth of monetary reserves) had rested in part on an overvalued franc, which had the effect of reducing the cost of imported oil. In any case, the austerity policy was quickly nullified or falsified by the government's pre-election gifts, which took the form of raising the minimum wage (the SMIC), encouraging the reduction of the work week,[4] temporarily rescinding planned increases in social security deductions, a reduction of value-added taxes on selected foodstuffs, and delaying rises in prices of gasoline and railroad tickets. Moreover, much of the "industrial modernization" policy remained a matter of rhetoric and exhortation—since the government did not make enough investment capital available to the "winner" industries.[5]

The tight money policies, the predilection of Giscard, his family, and his friends for personal enrichment, and the occasional maladroit remarks of Barre, some of which were reminiscent of Marie Antoinette[5]—all these convinced the Socialists and Communists that Giscard's policies were grossly unjust. Yet during the Giscard years, the overall level of consumption grew by 25 percent—despite the oil crisis—and the disposable income of most categories of workers (taking into account taxes, social security deductions, and social benefits) increased. During these years, payments to farmers, too, increased, as did the use of government credit, especially for the production of public products and the expansion of such nationalized sectors as the railroads. As the number of unemployed increased, so did the governmental infusion of money to make up shortfalls in the social security funds (in 1980 alone about 56 billion francs were spent on unemployment payments, of which a large proportion came from the Treasury). Moreover, despite the "Orleanism" of the Giscard–Barre entourage, business was left with steadily smaller profits: in 1972, these were 14.4 percent; in 1980, 10.3 percent; and in 1981 (before the elections), 7.8 percent; while the share of salaries rose from 64 percent to 70.9 percent (*Le Monde,* September 29, 1982).

To Raymond Aron this proved that, despite its official commitment to a market orientation, "the government of the right governed in a social democratic fashion" (*Express,* May 27, 1983, 39); to most of the left, the motivation behind these policies, irrespective of their concrete aspects, *had* to be reactionary, given the pronouncements about liberalism, and given the composition of the Union pour la démocratie française (UDF), the Giscardist electoral conglomeration: the Republicans with their closeness to business, the Radicals with their history of protectionist policies, and the Centre des démocrates sociaux (CDS—the Christian Democrats) with its social Catholicism. In short, whatever progressive policies emerged *had* to be inspired by short-term electoral considerations and hence were considered insincere.

REFORMS, TRANSFUSIONS, AND REALLOCATIONS

In 1981 there was no doubt about the direction and motivation of Socialist government policy. This is evident from a recapitulation of the most important socioeconomic reforms undertaken within a year following the presidential elections. Minimum wages were raised by 10 percent, retire-

ment pensions by 20 percent, and subsidies to families with children
(*allocations familiales*) by 25 percent. Social charges on most businesses
were increased, but payroll taxes on firms employing unskilled workers
were reduced. A fifth week of paid vacations, already in effect for some
workers, was extended to all. Bills were passed (the Auroux laws) to
strengthen the presence of trade unions in factories and to oblige unions
and management to negotiate annually about wages and work place democracy. In order to stimulate investment and reduce unemployment,
Parliament, in July 1981, passed a budget bill authorizing the expenditure
of 6 billion francs for several specific measures: (1) the creation of 50,000
public service jobs (at a cost of 1 billion francs) immediately, with additional jobs—in teaching, construction, housing, etc., up to 200,000—to
be created subsequently; (2) low interest loans to business (3.6 billion
francs); and (3) the continuation of agreements with employers (made
annually since 1978) to repay 80 percent of the first six months of wages
paid by them for employing people under twenty-five.

The money to pay for these and other measures, amounting to 7.7
billion francs, was to come from a variety of sources: supplementary taxes
on individuals; surtaxes on businesses; supplementary taxes on oil companies and banks; increases in value-added taxes on luxury hotels; and
surtaxes on pleasure boats, gasoline, and corporate airplanes. Despite the
additional revenue these measures would bring in, the 1981 budget
deficit was still estimated in July 1981 at between 55 and 60 billion
francs—an estimate updated in September to 75 billion, i.e., 2.5 percent
of the GNP. This did not include the shortfall of between 10 and 12 billion
francs anticipated for 1982 in the unemployment and social security system, a shortfall that might raise the total governmental deficit to well over
100 billion francs, unless checked.

Perhaps the most controversial measure was the enactment, in February 1982, of legislation to nationalize about a dozen industrial groups
(among them steel, chemical, aeronautical, electronics, engineering, and
textile firms) as well as thirty-six banks.

These measures' had been inspired by the belief in the efficacy of a
pump-priming approach: a policy of stimulating economic expansion by
means of enhancing the purchasing power of the masses through wage
supplements and transfer payments. This policy had been reaffirmed at
the last pre-election congress of the Socialist party, which took place in
the spring of 1981. The appropriation of funds necessitated by these
measures, and the resulting deficits, would, of course, increase inflation.
But for Socialists (as for many non-Socialist politicians), who in this respect reflected the sentiment of the masses, inflation was not considered
nearly as bad as unemployment and was accepted as a fair price to pay for
growth. The French (like the Swedes) had been spoiled by the dramatic

industrial growth of the "Thirty Glorious Years"—the period from the mid-1940s to the mid-1970s—when a high cumulative inflation rate was more than counterbalanced by an annual average growth rate of 5–6 percent, which translated into a reduction of the work week, an increase in longevity, an expansion of housing space, higher education levels, and more than a threefold increase in real income (Fourastié, 1979, 36, 171, *passim*). The compensations for inflation had been so institutionalized, under both left- and right-of-center governments, by regular adjustments of the minimum wage, price subsidization of staple foods, and other redistributive interventions, that they had become part of the habit background (system of expectations) of French citizens.

The considerations that inspired the nationalization policy were somewhat different. First and foremost, the transfer of certain crucial economic sectors from private to public hands was intended to balance "the logic of profit" with that of "the general interest" ("Nationalisations," 1982, 31–32). This was particularly applicable to the banks. Whereas—so the assumption went—private banks too often made credit available to undertakings that would bring them quick returns, nationalized credit institutions would give priority to investments in innovative and globally competitive industries *as well as* "active and dynamic small businesses" whose operations are riskier but serve a larger socioeconomic purpose. Furthermore, nationalized industries were to serve as pacesetters for the private sector in the areas of industrial democracy, working conditions, and wages; make it easier to promote consolidation, and hence efficiency; and, finally, strengthen the government's hand as it attempted to revive national economic planning.

It would be a mistake to take nationalization as the major distinguishing feature of Mitterrand's economic policies of 1981–82. In 1973, Mitterrand had noted the following:

> Since Roosevelt launched his New Deal in the United States, there has not been a modern industrial state in which the government did not have its say, its authority to exercise in one way or another, in economic matters. . . . Even big business, whose angry campaigns against dirigism have not been forgotten, has adapted to the new situation. After fearing a loss of free choice in matters of investment, and fighting against all forms of planning, it took into account the fact that as long as it [business] continued to control the government and manipulate political power, it had nothing to fear, but on the contrary that [governmental economic policy] if used properly, would furnish for it an instrument for utilizing public funds for its private interests (quoted in Manceron and Pingaud, 1981, 98–101).

Mitterrand reminded his listeners that nationalization had been pursued in earnest in 1945, by a government that was not exactly socialist; but that while at that time the nationalized sectors were crucial for reconstruction, the sectors now to be nationalized would be not only those that tend to monopoly but those that are "the locomotives of the economy"—the banks and industries that have a potential for big global markets. Moreover, some of the firms slated for nationalization—e.g., aeronautics—already did most of their business with the government, so that they were in a state of virtual dependence on it.

Behind these "old" (and more or less transpartisan) reasons there was the tactical political consideration that nationalization, perhaps more than other government measures, would serve to keep the left united; there was also the ideologically derived conviction that many if not all the firms about to be nationalized had great wealth and made great profits and that once the ownership of these firms was transferred to the government it would use these profits not for consumption or speculation but for plant modernization and other public purposes ("Nationalisations," 27ff.).

READJUSTMENTS AND SECOND THOUGHTS

Within about a year after the Socialist party's victories, it had become clear that the government's hopes for an improvement of the French economic situation were not about to be realized; on the contrary, the crisis had deepened. By the fall of 1982, the number of unemployed had risen again—despite the deliberate creation of jobs—from 7.5 percent to 9 percent of the work force and was approaching 2 million and, with about 20,000 businesses declaring bankruptcy, threatened to go even higher. The inflation rate had gone up to 14 percent, and the deficits on the balance of trade and the national budget had risen steeply. The increased purchasing power made possible by the initial wage increases had encouraged a rise of imports, which by April 1982 had reached 59.6 billion francs (a rise of 8 percent in one month alone), while exports had diminished (in the same period) by 2.4 percent to 49.5 billion. The monetary pressures thus created forced the government to spend about $1 billion—i.e., more than 15 percent of its foreign currency reserves—to shore up the value of the franc. Most embarrassing of all, the economic growth rate was near zero, and, as a result, a stagnation, and even a decline, of the workers' purchasing power could be anticipated. In June 1982 the government responded with a number of stabilization measures aimed at holding the line on inflation to 10 percent, containing the deficit to about $21 billion, or 3 percent of the GNP, and, if possible, diminishing the social security deficit of $2 billion. The measures included the following:

—the limitation of public sector jobs to under 100,000;

—the devaluation of the franc by 5.75 percent—the second since Mitterrand's election;

—a delay in the implementation of the reduction of the work week from
1982 to 1985, and an immediate, largely symbolic, reduction to thirty-
nine instead of the promised thirty-five hours;

—a delay in the implementation of the promised lowering of the retirement age to sixty years;

—permitting social security deductions to go up—without a corresponding improvement in entitlements—in order to pay the costs of retirement and unemployment benefits;

—a slowing of the pace of increases of the minimum wage so that it would
be somewhat lower than the pace of inflation; and, after employers and
unions had failed to heed a government call for a voluntary approach to
price and wage restraint, a temporary freeze on prices and wages;

—stretching out the payment of compensation to the private stockholders
of firms in process of nationalization;

—encouraging foreign workers, by means of payment of separation "lump
sums," to vacate their jobs to native French workers and to return to
their countries of origin.

These measures proved to be little more than "bandaid" solutions:
they failed to arrest both the inflationary climb and the growth of unemployment. Specifically, by the first quarter of 1983, overall unemployment was still about 9 percent. Between May 1981 and the end of March
1983, the loss of jobs in industry was 200,000, and in construction,
99,000. These losses were not compensated by gains in the "postindustrial" (i.e., tertiary) sector, for the number of people employed in trade and
commerce had shrunk by 137,000. These statistics were partly modified
by the creation of new public service jobs in 1981–82; but at the end of
1982, 15,000 civil servants were pensioned off and not replaced. It is clear
that the increase in purchasing power,[7] instead of spurring production,[8]
merely continued to spur imports, so that the balance-of-trade deficit
showed a rise from 62 billion francs in 1980 to 93.3 billion francs (or $13.3
billion) in 1982 and 23.7 billion francs in the first quarter of 1983. The
balance-of-payments figures were equally disturbing: they indicated a
change from a 1.2 billion franc surplus in the second quarter of 1981 to a
deficit of 11.4 billion francs in the fourth quarter of 1982. The rate of
inflation had been reduced slightly—in part due to the price and wage
freeze—from 14 percent in 1981 to 9.7 percent in 1982. But the growth of

the GNP remained unimpressive,[9] while the government deficit had gone up from 29.4 billion francs in 1981 to 95.5 billion francs (or 2.6 percent of the GNP) and was estimated at nearly 118 billion francs for 1983 (OECD, 1983, 38–40; French Embassy, 1983b; and Aron, 1983, 38–39).

These outcomes could be attributed to a variety of failings and miscalculations. The Gaullists and Giscardists argued that demand-side economics had been wrong from the start and had to be attributed to the Socialists' failure to liberate themselves from utopian thinking and from the rhetoric of their years in opposition; conversely, the Communists and left-wing Socialists asserted that demand-side economics had been halfhearted and the provision of increased purchasing power insufficient. The trade unions blamed business for its lack of cooperation—specifically, for its failure to invest its profits and its tendency to send its money to foreign banks, where it would at once earn higher rates of interest and escape the clutches of the French tax collector. Business, for its part, contended that it was unable to invest in job-creating industries because it was saddled with excessively burdensome wage structures and social security charges.[10]

A most serious miscalculation had to do with nationalized industry. In the first place, the deficit for the entire nationalized sector in 1982 came to the high figure of 36.5 billion francs; moreover, the deficit for the sector nationalized since 1981 grew from 2.6 billion francs in 1980 (when it was still in private hands) to 15 billion francs in 1982. This jump can be explained in two ways. First, the amount of money the government would be obliged to pay out to the expropriated shareholders had originally been estimated at $6.7 billion (spread over fifteen to twenty years), but this sum had to be increased to $10 billion as a result of a ruling by the Constitutional Council (whose members had been appointed by the previous government and who argued that the original offer constituted an underpayment and hence an unconstitutional deprivation of property). In addition, several of the nationalized companies turned out to be close to bankruptcy, and the government was forced to pay an unexpectedly large sum of money ($2.5 billion in 1983) to keep these companies afloat—lest the rolls of the unemployed be increased further. And the money needed to keep this "row of lemons"[11] alive was taken in part from the banks that had been nationalized during previous regimes and in part from the Treasury, thus leaving fewer funds available for social or investment purposes.

Some Socialists suggested that many economic policy failures could be directly attributed to the machinations of a frustrated opposition; not only was the Constitutional Council's "interference" in the nationalization process viewed as an example of nefarious behavior, there were also charges that many government measures were scuttled by unfriendly

Gaullist and Giscardist holdovers in various ministries. (Such a charge was difficult to prove, especially since there were a number of leftist officials, including adherents of Michel Rocard's faction, among the holdovers.) Other Frenchmen put the blame on outsiders, i.e., "the right-wing policies adopted by France's principal trading partners,"[12] for ruining the calculations of a 3 percent annual growth rate. There were the Japanese, who pursued a particularly aggressive marketing policy in France; the Germans and British, who by putting stumbling blocks in the way of French produce and by demanding a revamping of the Common Agricultural Policy made it difficult for the French agricultural industries to export or to plan for expansion; and the Americans, who, with their unreasonable monetarism and high interest rates, contributed to the illegal outflow of francs. More generally, there was a degree of nervousness in the international market, which created heavy pressure on the franc. This nervousness could in part be attributed to the overinterpretation, by foreign businessmen, of the economic implications of a leftist control of the government—an overinterpretation encouraged by the rather aggressively ideological rhetoric of some Socialist party officials.

A major problem concerning the Mitterrand policies of the years 1981–83 had been the fact that parts of them had been based on questionable assumptions. One of the assumptions long held by the Socialists had been that an increase in worker responsibility—and specifically, an elaboration of factory democracy—would make the workers more productive, or would at least provide a form of "qualitative" payment in compensation for a reduced rate of growth of real wages. Although the evidence about this is not conclusive, there are indications that productivity growth is dependent upon many different factors and that unions have not generally accepted worker participation (in limited management decisions) as a substitute for concrete payoffs. This perhaps explains why *autogestion* (worker "self-management"), once the great rallying cry of the Socialist party, has not been mentioned too often since 1982.

The Socialist policies before 1983—as, indeed, those of Giscard—were faulted for being piecemeal and electorally oriented, rather than multiannual policies aimed at profound structural change. This critique is not entirely justified, for the Socialist party had committed itself to a restoration of multiannual planning; it had put an important politician, Michel Rocard, in charge of it and (as was pointed out) had strengthened its arsenal of planning weapons by enlarging the nationalized sector. The problem was that while the Socialists recognized the need for planning, they did not yet fully recognize that the kind of democratic planning that they favored—one that involved a meaningful participation of unions, consumers, and other sectors—might, because of its pluralist-incrementalist nature, be inflationary and not most suitable for long-term structural change. Nor did the Socialists recognize that national planning could not be easily combined with the administrative decentralization that was an important part of their reform agenda.[13] On the one hand, increased subnational autonomy brings government closer to the people; on the other hand, it tends to fragment policy making and may interfere with productive efficiency and competitiveness, insofar as these depend on consolidation, economies of size, and national coordination. At this point, it is difficult to relate decentralization measures precisely to economic policy, particularly since the attribution of taxing and spending powers to subnational units has not yet been precisely determined. But it is likely that decentralization, if pursued meaningfully, will add to the cost of the French economy: the inevitable politicization of local administration will lead not only to an increase in administrative staff but also to the duplication of economic activities necessary to satisfy the collective egos of local communities. This American kind of pork barrel can in fact already be seen in the government's research and development (R&D) policies, which call for geographic dispersal.

Perhaps it is just as well that the planning process is undermined (or transmogrified) by localization and buck passing, since national planning, necessary as it is, may also be *less possible* in today's globally dependent industrial economies than in an ideal world, simply because planners can no longer produce reliable statistical scenarios in view of unforeseen political and "exogenous" factors. During a discussion of the Ninth Plan (1984–88) in the Assembly in the spring of 1983, both opposition and Socialist deputies criticized this document for its "absence of quantified objectives," that is, a lack of reliable statistical projections regarding growth, investment, balance of payments, and inflation (*Le Monde*, May 28, 1983). Since the late 1960s, national plans have often been ruined by precipitous rises in oil costs, the fluctuation of exchange rates, domestic riots, or dissension within trading blocs. All this accounts for the fact that while the Ninth Plan, whose basic *document d'orientation* dates to September 1982, was put through its formal paces—discussion in various ad hoc committees, deliberations in the Social and Economic Council, and acceptance by Parliament and the Cabinet—it was accompanied, and modified, by a succession of emergency policies (see *"Le 9e plan 1984– 1988,"* 1984).

A POLICY OF RIGOR

One such emergency policy, and the most widely discussed, was the *"politique de rigueur"* introduced on March 25, 1983, by Jacques Delors, minister of economics and finance. This was a ten-point plan aimed at restoring the balance of trade, improving the balance of payments, containing inflation, and reducing the government deficit by 20 billion francs and total spending by 65 billion francs (or 2 percent of the GNP). The *plan de rigueur*, which represented an escalation of the austerity policies inaugurated earlier, contained specific measures designed to curb domestic consumption, reduce imports, and encourage savings, investments, and exports. These measures included the reduction of public sector spending by 11 billion francs—any shortfall to be made up by increased rates, e.g., for gas, electricity, and railroads; a reduction of the social security deficit by a saving of 4 billion francs, through a paring down of benefits and a rise of 1 percent in social security deductions from employees; a levy of 1 percent on all incomes; a forced loan, extracted from wage earners by the imposition, for a period of three years, of a sum equivalent to 10 percent of total income taxes for all who had paid at least 5,000 francs in income taxes in 1982; a surtax on wealth; supplemental taxes on alcohol and tobacco; an increase in cost sharing by patients for each day's stay in a hospital (to the amount of 20 francs per day); a limit of the amount of money a citizen traveling abroad could take out of the country (2,000 francs, about $300); reductions in the amount of loans extended to local communities; and a decision not to pass on to the consumer the savings on imported oil, whose price had been falling.

The reactions of the various sectors of the French public were predictable. The trade unions, while for the most part aware that the measures were unavoidable, feared that too much of the burden might be carried by the industrial worker, whose hard-won gains in real wages would be relinquished. Business welcomed the austerity measures but felt they did not go far enough in controlling and reducing welfare state expenditures. For the Communists and the left-wing factions of the Socialist party (e.g., CERES), the major fear was that the unemployment problem might grow worse; and to the opposition, the policy constituted a belated imitation of the (sometimes ill-fated) attempts of Giscard and Barre at fiscal responsibility (*Le Monde*, March 27–28, 1983).

The policies of rigor were accompanied by a number of collateral efforts aimed at a "reindustrialization" of France. These efforts were outlined in the Ninth Plan; more exactly, concrete ways of pursuing these efforts were gradually introduced into the plan, as it moved from the initial discussion to the later "elaboration" phases (*Le Monde*, April 22, 1983). The plan called not merely for the containment of inflation and the reduction of domestic consumption in the short run; it called for a "mutation of the productive apparatus," which would ultimately ensure employment and prosperity for all. Such a mutation would require an annual rate of investment of 10 percent for the remainder of the 1980s and an increase of expenditure for R&D, which would reach 2.5 percent of the GNP. Part of the cost would be borne by private industry, but a large part would entail a budgetary commitment by the government. Under the *programmes prioritaires d'exécution* the government would spend some 60 billion francs in 1984 and 350 billion francs for the entire planning period (1984–88); well over half of this sum would be earmarked for projects relating more or less directly to industrial modernization, e.g., the quest for new technologies, educational reform with an emphasis on technical-vocational curricula, a reduction of energy dependence, and the development of aggressive sales techniques (*"vendre mieux en France et à l'étranger"*) (see *Loi no. 83-1180 du 24 decembre 1983*).

One of the parallel measures aimed at making the plan work (or, as some critics insisted, confounding it), was the so-called Code VI: a government bill (put into effect in October 1983) to create an "industrial development account" (a variant of the Swedish counter-cyclical fund), into which industrial firms would put their profits. Industrial firms would, in effect, be forgiven the corporate tax; the accounts, which would yield a tax-free interest of 7.5 percent, could be drawn on as needed. It was hoped that in this way a sum of 70 billion francs would accumulate and that about half of that would be used for plant investment. Each account would be limited to 10,000 francs. Code VI generated considerable controversy. It was criticized because it would (1) lead to a banalization of business tax advantages—and in effect be a way of legitimating tax evasion, (2) discourage genuine savings and a genuine reduction of consumption levels, and hence contribute little to the fight against inflation, (3) be insufficient for significant job creation efforts, and (4) deprive the Treasury of needed revenue (*Le Monde,* February 7, 1984), especially in view of the astronomic direct expenditures to which the government had committed itself.[14]

By the end of 1983, the austerity program was showing certain positive results. Although imports had risen somewhat, the rise in exports more than made up for this;[15] consequently, the balance-of-trade deficit had been reduced (from 93 billion francs in 1982 to about 45 billion in 1983). The balance-of-payments deficit had been cut (from 80 to 35 billion francs),[16] and the franc had begun to stabilize. The overall cost to French households had been bearable: with all the increases in taxes and social security deductions, their real income had decreased by less than 1 percent.

Despite the fact that wage increases were held to a relatively modest level,[17] inflation, at 9.2 percent, was still considerable, having gone far above the hoped-for 7 percent, but in the spring of 1984 there were indications that it would be brought below 5 percent. The great price that had to be paid for these achievements was in the increasing number of jobless. To a large extent, the growth of unemployment had become a constituent part of the government's industrial modernization policy, which called for a phasing out of redundant workers, in particular in such relatively antiquated and insufficiently competitive sectors as steel, automobiles, shipbuilding, and mining. Since the Socialists came to power, some 400,000 jobs had been lost; it was estimated that by the end of the 1980s, 500,000 additional jobs would have to be eliminated, 20,000–25,000 (out of 90,000) in the steel industry alone as it rationalized its methods of production. In view of this, the unemployment rate anticipated for 1984—and for the three or four years following—would be over 9 percent (Lewis, 1984; *France*, January–February 1984).

While the government could adopt a relatively cavalier attitude toward small and medium-sized businesses, more than 18,000 of which failed in 1983, it had to be more circumspect when it came to the closing of large factories. When the shipbuilding industry threatened to dismiss several thousand workers, the government refused to grant an import license to a firm that was about to buy foreign ships, pressured the firm to buy more expensive French-made ships, and undertook to pay the difference (which amounted to several hundred million francs). When the privately owned Talbot automobile plant in Poissy (near Paris) decided to lay off 3,000 workers and threatened·to close down altogether after a confrontation between strikers and the remaining workers, the government convinced the managers to keep the plant open by granting it an emergency subsidy—despite the government's acknowledgment that there was an excess of at least 10,000 workers at the plant.[18] Such stopgap measures were responses to the major industrial unions which, as Henri Krasucki, the chief of the CGT, put it, wanted "modernization without unemployment," and which tried to outshout one another with radical rhetoric. In order to keep such rhetoric, and the strikes that would accompany it, from interfering with the government's long-range policies in the future, it was necessary to enlist the active collaboration of the unions more systematically. By early 1984, the policy of *"restructurations industrielles"* was entering the *concertation* phase, as Premier Mauroy held discussions successively with the leaders of five trade unions and the two major business associations (*Le Monde*, February 7, 1984).

The "collective effort toward disinflation" involved a three-pronged process: (1) a stress on the responsibility of the "social partners"—the employers and trade union leaders—who were encouraged to show solidarity with the government, and with each other, by engaging in a dialog and coming up with *contrats de progrès* calling for voluntary wage restraints and commitments to retain (and if necessary retrain) workers (Bérégovoy, 1983); (2) specific governmental commitments to finance the "social" measures needed to help redundant workers; and (3) an attempt at selective delegation (buck passing?) to regional and local authorities.

The "social" measures included (in addition to generous separation pay and unemployment benefits) provisions for early retirement and long leaves of absence to workers so that they could be retrained, with the government paying 70 percent of their salaries for a period of up to two years (see Mitterrand's April 4, 1984, speech on the steel industry). As for the regional approach to economic problems, in 1983, the government had marked out certain areas of the country—*la France fragile*—that were to be favored with grants. There was a national budget allocation of over a billion francs for the creation of 40,000 new jobs to begin with, and more later. A certain amont of money, between 35,000 and 40,000 francs, was to be allocated per employee; this money was to be spent by the regions via DATARs.[19] For investments in smaller firms, the DATARs were to follow the advice of the regional councils, while for larger enterprises—i.e., those with a turnover of more than 500 million francs, or requiring expenditures of more than 25 million francs—DATARs were to make their decisions directly. One interesting instance of the desire by the government to share the onus for unpleasant economic decisions with subnational units was the meeting, in January 1984, of three cabinet ministers with the commissioners of the Republic (the former prefects), at which the latter were directed "to help in the effort at disinflation" and presumably by persuading general councils to cut local expenditures on wages and equipment, to promote efficiency, and to draft regional development plans for creating employment.[20]

In particularly important or politically sensitive cases, decisions on the allocation of investment funds would, of course, continue to be made by the Cabinet: for instance the steel industry would be granted about 30 billion francs between 1984 and 1987 in order to modernize itself,[21] so that it would ultimately be able to operate at a profit, and of this sum, 7 billion francs were earmarked for Lorraine, because the political pressure from that province was especially fierce and because four Socialist deputies from there had resigned from the party in protest against government policy. Similarly, the government continued to subsidize the automobile industry (which was not in the worst shape) in order to moderate the dissatisfactions of the CGT and its patron, the Communist party (*Le Monde*, February 9, 1984).

The sudden restructuring of the Cabinet in July 1984 produced little change in the direction of French economic policy. On the contrary, the replacement of Mauroy by Laurent Fabius as premier and of Delors by Pierre Bérégovoy as minister of economics and finance amounted to a reconfirmation of the austerity policies. As minister for the budget under Delors, Fabius had promoted steep tax increases on wealth as well as measures against currency smuggling, but as minister of industry he toughened his position, stressing profitable private enterprise and cutting

back on subventions to obsolescent industries. As minister of social affairs, Bérégovoy had projected the image of a moderate, intent upon
shoring up the social security system by raising deductions and skimping
on benefits. Among the initial measures undertaken by the new government was the *lowering* of taxes and social security deductions by an
average of 8 percent (effective in 1985). These measures, which were
designed to benefit above all the average and lower wage earners,
reflected not so much "supply-side socialism" (Vinocur, 1984b) as the
recognition that inflation was being controlled and that the social security
funds' deficit had been turned into a surplus.

CONCLUSIONS, EVALUATIONS, AND IMPLICATIONS

The foregoing delineation of France's economic policy, from the postelec-
toral euphoria of 1981 to the sullenness of 1983–84, suggests that this
policy has not followed clear-cut logical or ideological imperatives. Instead, it has represented a succession of adaptive measures that reflect an
eclectic combination of interventionist and market-liberal orientations,
modified by pressures and, as one commentator put it, coming to be
"totally immersed in the immediate" (Delaunay, 1984). This realization
has been disconcerting to those—and they are numerous—who had convinced themselves that the French Socialists, having been rather categor-
ical in their critiques of capitalist-bourgeois society, would be unable to
promote anything other than an anticapitalist policy. While the Socialist
party was out of power, most of its leaders emphatically rejected the social
democratic approaches of Sweden, West Germany, and Britain. Capitalism had to be dealt a mortal blow; the profit motive had to be abandoned;
criteria of productivity had to be replaced by criteria of equity.

Fanciful Socialist prescriptions always have been fun to spin out in
the abstract; since in the past two generations France (before 1981) had
only three Socialist governments of very short duration—in 1924, 1936,
and the mid-1950s—that had little time to put socialist programs fully into
effect, these programs could not be tested against reality.

In an interview with a newspaperman,[22] Mitterrand is reported to
have admitted that much of the policy of reform of 1981 resulted from the
fact that "we dreamed a little"; that he favored a policy of austerity as early
as the spring of 1982, but that he had been dissuaded both by his advisers
(among them Mauroy *and* Delors) and by his perception of the electorate.

> The French like to hear people of the right (Barre, Reagan, Thatcher)
> speak of rigor, but whenever we propose such a policy we are no longer
> credible. Léon Blum launched great reforms . . . but [he was] unable to

> manage things afterward. But I have the time . . . I have always said that
> there would be three difficult years. . . . We will get out of this crisis, but
> then we will have to propose something different for 1985–1986, because
> socialism is not only financial orthodoxy. (*Témoignage chrétien*, July 11,
> 1983)

Mitterrand and his close advisers are not modeled after the forbidding
prototypes evoked by Keynes in his *General Theory:* "madmen in authority, who hear voices in the air . . . distilling their frenzy from some
academic scribbler of a few years back." The turn to realism by the
Mitterrand regime—after a quick learning experience—and the complexity of programs flowing therefrom have represented such a dramatic departure from socialist orthodoxy that a bewildering variety of labels have
been attached to them: bourgeois-centrist (Rosa, 1981, 6), neoliberal,
state capitalist, and even Thatcherist and Reaganite (Will 1983; Vinocur
1984a; Ross and Jensen, 1983).

It is clear that the Socialist party, at least since coming to power, has
been more consistently Keynesian than Marxist in its stress on stimulating aggregate demand, spending on public works, and the importance of
economic planning; its initial refusal to pay too much attention to the
international economic system; and finally, its belief that the capitalist
system, *grosso modo*, should be maintained. It has been a Keynesianism
modified by old-fashioned dirigism, which has manifested itself, under
the Socialists as under preceding conservative regimes, in the government's control and use of a large credit machinery. At the same time, it
has been socialist in its insistence on nationalization, its early redistributive impulses, and its tax policies. But this socialism soon came to be
overlaid with glosses from neoclassical liberal economics, e.g., the refusal
to disengage the franc from the European and world currency systems
and the toleration of high unemployment.

To be sure, some of Mitterrand's post-1982 policies can be found in
various non-socialist industrial democracies as well. In addition to the
measures that have been pointed out—encouraging growth and exports,
increasing social security deductions for workers, imposing an across-the-
board income tax, etc.—the "turn to the right" was manifested above all
in permitting, and even encouraging, the layoff of tens of thousands of
workers and in tax and social security allowances and subventions to
business in order to "stabilize their overhead costs."[23] Finally, the "turn to
the right" appeared in the prolific use of slogans about incentives, investments, personal responsibility, the virtues of the market, and the utility of
profits.

Such measures represent "a sell-out" of socialist principles only if
these are thought of in terms of idealized expectations. When asked at a

recent television interview whether he favored the accumulation of wealth, Mitterrand said yes, but under certain conditions.

> If it is through speculation . . . then no; if it is through inheritance, then it's too easy. The right way to wealth . . . through initiative, individual effort . . . this right to individual accumulation of wealth must absolutely be recognized. . . . I am not an enemy of profit, as long as that profit is fairly distributed (*News and Comments from France*, September 23, 1983).

Mitterrand's economic policy may be considered democratic-leftist, rather than neocapitalist, because the officially articulated motivation behind the policy is not (unlike Roosevelt's New Deal) the salvaging of capitalism for its own sake but rather the utilization of certain market processes associated with capitalism for the purpose of creating a healthier economy, so that social justice can be pursued from a position of strength. It is, of course, true that sometimes politicians become so habituated to a process that it assumes the shape of a policy, i.e., the means become the end.

However, even after the inauguration of the austerity policy, many of its individual measures bear little relationship to the austerity measures of Thatcher and Reagan. The fiscal burden in France appears to be more equitably distributed than it is in the United States: while most of the deficit under Reagan would ultimately be paid for by the middle and lower classes rather than the well-to-do (who could be expected to benefit from the debt repayment at high interest rates), in France *all* social sectors have made sacrifices. The industrial workers have lost a minuscule amount of purchasing power, while the medical profession has been pressured into accepting small fee rises under social security. Under the "Budget of Courage," the line is held not only on workers' wages, but also on dividends, leases, rents, and the distribution of profits (*News and Comments from France*, June 23, 1983). While, in the United States, Reagan's tax concessions on individual incomes have benefited the wealthy, and corporate tax concessions, having no strings attached, have encouraged speculation, vertical acquisitions, and mergers, in France such concessions are designed expressly to lead to the creation of jobs. The surtaxes on high incomes and the wealth tax that were instituted in 1981 have been extended and maintained—with income tax rates going as high as 76 percent—while wage increases have been permitted to go up almost, if not quite, in line with price and productivity increases. Although deductions have been increased, the social benefits have been maintained at the customary levels. The costs to the consumer for certain public products (e.g., railroads and postal rates) will not be permitted to go up more than the general level of price increases (except for gas and electricity); in other words, the government will monitor prices selectively and will continue to spend significant amounts of money on public transport. (Under Reagan, there is no price containment, no profit control, and no meaningful increase in spending on public products other than defense.) Moreover, while in the United States unions have been pressured into accepting wage reductions and have occasionally been "decertified," union rights in France have been strengthened at the plant level, and union representation on social security boards has been increased. These early reforms of Mitterrand have been retained, and others as well: while in the United States, access to higher education has been effectively impeded by a reduction of federal low interest loans, French higher education remains tuition-free, and access to secondary education—which ultimately affects upward mobility—has been made more flexible and democratic.

There is no doubt that the Socialist policy makers have been attempting to learn some lessons from other industrial democracies that appear to be more successful in facing economic challenges. Recently, Delors suggested that "it is necessary . . . to take the longest time possible—at least two years—on the German model, so that growth is based on investments and exports, and not consumption."[24] However, it is doubtful whether Delors in the 1980s could have played the role Ludwig Erhard played in the 1950s and 1960s. France today does not have the advantages West Germany possessed twenty or thirty years ago: an ethic of hard work; a relatively monolithic trade union confederation whose leadership was interested in the strengthening of the republican system and kept wage demands modest; a political climate in which left-wing extremism had been discredited, and an insignificant (and, in fact, illegal between 1956 and 1968) Communist party; an absence of global military commitments and, therefore, no large defense expenditures; and many bombed out plants that simply *had* to be rebuilt on a modern basis. Moreover, German industrial modernization took place in the context of cheap energy supplies. Nor can the United States, with its plentiful supply of energy, its huge internal market, its well-behaved unions, and its underdeveloped working-class radicalism, be useful as a model for France.

If France has been less able than the United States to face the economic crisis, this is also due to a number of structural constraints:

First, the mobility of labor, although somewhat loosened by the influx of foreign workers, is inhibited by the rigidity of the relative wage structure; this rigidity, a consequence of a nationwide, and more or less centralized, pattern of collective bargaining as well as semi-automatic adjustments of the minimum wage, has made it difficult for employers in expanding industries to bid up wages and for employers in declining industries to bid down wages (Marris, 1984, 116). Although the nationalized sector is large in France and the state controls a high proportion (about 38 percent) of the salaries, that sector cannot be expected to function as a role model of efficiency and productivity—that is, set the pattern for modest wages—because of the radicalism of the unions to which many of the workers in that sector belong and because of the radicalizing impact of interunion competition. [25]

Second, there are built-in social transfer payments—paid vacations, medical coverage, family subsidies, etc.—which have become a part of the system of expectations that cannot be easily dismantled.

Finally, despite the recent argument of a well-known commentator that "such firmly left-wing values as universalism, community fellowship, and the concern for equality suddenly look old-fashioned (André Laurens, in *Le Monde*, March 8, 1984), there are the still-important ideological constraints of socialism, the history of general strikes and other anomic mass action, and the (actual or potential) pressures of rival parties on the left, all of which continue to moderate the imperative of structural change with the pursuit of social justice.

THE ELECTORAL DIMENSION

These points inevitably raise the question of whether the economic policies under the Mitterrand presidency correspond to the "political business cycle," i.e., fluctuate according to the evolution of the electorate and the timing of elections (Monroe, 1980). It cannot be denied that the policies pursued after the election constitute in large measure the fulfillment of pre-election promises. At the same time, it is possible to argue any of the following: that after a lapse of two years the Socialists felt that they had been released from their electoral burden and had acquired a freer hand; that the realities of the situation were such that the Socialists had to act as they did, even at the risk of subsequent electoral punishment; and finally, that the electorate was not completely unsympathetic to Mitterrand's policies.

The "electoral rationality" argument is problematic with respect to the Socialists' behavior since 1981; for the heavy thrust of their socioeconomic reforms—including their policies of increasing the money supply and distributing benefits—occurred immediately *after* the parliamentary elections, while their policies became progressively (or rather, regressively) austere midway in the Assembly term, as France moved closer to the next parliamentary elections (1986), and if these policies bear fruit at all, they are unlikely to do so before those elections. Since, according to many assessments, there is no realistic hope that the Socialists would maintain their parliamentary control after the legislative elections, the Assembly deputies might as well be fatalistic and do what is unavoidable. As for the president, he may gradually disengage himself from the Assembly, try to pursue a policy of rapprochement with the center (thereby making it more difficult for Jacques Chirac, the mayor of Paris, to achieve the presidency in 1988), and, if these calculations fail, worry about his place in history (see *"La Conjoncture politique,"* 1983, 478–79).

There are, however, several counter-arguments. The electoral prospects of the Socialists may not look so bad after all. It has been argued that the modification of the approach to employment has been politically easier for the Socialist party in the 1980s than such a policy might have been in the past, because the number and political weight of those who have suffered most from unemployment—the industrial working class— have been steadily declining in favor of the *salariat* (the white collar and tertiary sectors). Moreover, the political risks to the Socialist party are minimized by the fact that the poorest and most unskilled native workers have been voting Communist anyway, and the foreign workers do not vote at all. The contention that the Socialist government no longer worries much about the Communist party (PC) gains some substance if one considers the steady losses of that party in recent elections, the decline in the number of militants in it, and the growing interest on the part of parliamentary politicians of the Socialist party, too, in replacing the "unity of the left" tactic with a left-center approach.[26]

For three years, Communist politicians, while stepping up their attacks on government policy, yet supported the government for the sake of retaining a share of power. Although PC leader Georges Marchais asserted that "President Mitterrand is unfaithful to candidate Mitterrand" (*Le Monde,* January 22–23, 1984), he affirmed that "it is excluded that we would quit the government." This attitude of *participation-contestation* (a French variant of the *Bereichsopposition* that prevailed in Austria until the mid-1960s, under which the parties belonging to the coalition government felt free to criticize some of its policies) was apparent in the Assembly as recently as April 1984, when the PC, while continuing to reprove the government for its policies, obediently joined the Socialists in supporting it in a confidence vote. *Participation-contestation* was not completely reversed even when the PC decided to keep its ministers out of the new government constituted in July 1984. For the sake of programmatic consistency, the PC found it difficult to support as premier one who had developed a reputation as a budget-cutting pragmatist. The continuing decline of its electoral support—reaffirmed in the elections of the European Parliament in June 1984, when the PC, with 11.3 percent of the popular vote and 6 percent of that of young people, put in its worst performance in sixty years—perhaps made the party realize that its formal share of power had paid little dividend and caused some of its leaders to look for a way to combine an image of responsibility with a modicum of left-wing ideological respectability. The result of this ambivalence was that the PC, on the one hand, affirmed that it continued to remain part of the parliamentary majority and, on the other, abstained in the investiture vote in the Assembly that followed the appointment of the new premier.

There is some criticism *within* the Socialist party, particularly in the left-wing CERES faction, which has called upon the government to avoid "sliding toward the [political] center" and to abandon its deflationary policies in favor of a *redressement national* (without, however, clearly spelling out the details of such a move).[27] But CERES represents no more than 15 percent of Socialist party activists; in any case, its leader, Chevènement, had been ousted from the Cabinet in a reshuffle preceding the announcement of the policy of rigor. (In mid-1984, however, CERES was mollified when Chevènement was reappointed to a Cabinet position, albeit one having little to do with economic policy.) The Socialist deputies belonging to the other factions, while differing slightly from one another, have supported Mitterrand, not only because of a feeling that they had been elected on the presidential coattails but also because they have little choice.[28]

It must be assumed that many of those who supported the Socialists in the last presidential and parliamentary elections will *not* switch to the opposition. The Gaullist–Giscardist critique of the "socialo-communist" character of the government sounds hollow; moreover, voters know that, especially since 1983, the Socialist government has been attempting to do what Giscard and Barre had promised to do but failed, owing to internal opposition and electoral pressures, and that the opposition has not produced a credible alternative policy. That is perhaps why the opposition's critiques have concentrated on the government's *noneconomic* policies: its attack on private schools, its attempt to regulate the ownership of newspapers, its foreign and defense policies, and aspects of administrative decentralization.

Finally, what moderates the electoral fears of the Socialists is the possibility that the public at large is aware that "a great historic period [of affluence] has ended" and that it is prepared for a certain degree of austerity ("*La Conjoncture économique*," 1983, 481–82). A series of public opinion polls recently conducted revealed that, although a large majority of respondents judged joblessness to be a major problem, many believed that letting unemployment grow averts even more serious crises and that respondents had a higher opinion of Delors, the chief architect of austerity (45 percent favorable) than of Mitterrand (40 percent), Mauroy (33 percent), or Marchais (16 percent).[29] In summary, the Mitterrand government is given a relatively free hand because (1) right-of-center voters are not too unhappy; (2) the average supporters of Mitterrand may have voted for him not because they wanted a "socialist" program but because they simply wanted the incumbent replaced; (3) left-oriented voters have nowhere else to go; (4) the trade unions are too divided, and too powerless individually, to mount an effective fight against the government; and (5) the French citizen's view of parties and politicians may be more expressive than it is instrumental.

Even if one were to minimize or discount the electoral dimension *and* to admit that the various policy measures chosen by the government were eminently sensible, it is still not certain whether the Socialist party is ideally equipped to preside over the kinds of actions required for industrial modernization. The majority of Socialist politicians, in Parliament and now in executive positions as well, have been intellectuals trained in the humanist rather than technicist tradition, who have tended to see the world of ideas as separate from the world of action, and culture as separate from the marketplace. As humanists, they must find it difficult to promote the "technicization" and commercialization of the educational curriculum, without which economic restructuring would be difficult to achieve, and to promote "champion" industries in a global environment that is pervaded by the odor of plutocracy. In view of this, it may be argued that in order for Socialist policies to succeed, their implementation may have to be delegated to those who are more concerned with techniques than with concepts—bureaucrats and technocrats who are nonpolitical and whose accountability to elected leaders may be weak, or—worse—politicians who are close to the world of business and whose Socialist credentials may be questioned. If the policies of rigor are stretched out over several years, as they must be (*Express*, March 30, 1984, 42–44), the resulting streamlining of the French economy will bring in its train a transformation of the political system as well.

NOTES

1. Adopted by the Socialist party congress at Créteil, cited in "L'Election presidentielle 26 avril–10 mai 1981: la victoire de Mitterrand," *Le Monde: supplément aux dossiers et documents* (May 1981):67, 78–79.

2. *Cartes sur table,* television program, March 16, 1981, cited in Manceron and Pingaud, 1981, 92–93. "Neoliberalism" refers to a selective rediscovery of the virtues of free enterprise.

3. By the end of 1980, however, the balance-of-trade deficit appeared to be rising steeply again. For a variety of (sometimes conflicting) data, cf. *Le Monde,* October 29, 1980, and November 6, 1980; and French Embassy, New York, Press and Information Division, "A Social and Economic Survey," *Bulletin* 80/52.

4. The reduction of the *normal* work week was from 46.3 hours in 1974 to

42.2 at the end of 1979 in the construction industry, and from 42.2 in 1974 to 40.8 at the end of 1979 for the rest of the labor force. This development was not so much the direct consequence of deliberate government policy as the result of the decision of many industries to spread the work and thus to avoid supplementary overtime payments (which since 1976 have been mandated at 20 percent for a work week beyond 42 hours). Further, it should be noted that the *maximum* work week permitted by law was lowered from 57 (since 1971) to 52 (since 1979). At any rate, in 1974 only 21.7 percent of the work force worked 40 hours or less; in 1978; 46 percent. See *La Révalorisation du travail manuel; 1980*. SMIC—*salaire minimum interprofessionnel de croissance,* a minimum-wage system in effect since 1970. It is determined annually by government decree, with the intent of bringing minimum wages in line with the evolution of prices and productivity growth.

5. See Salais, 1978, 312–26. The Eighth Plan, unveiled in October 1980, envisaged the investment of $25 billion of public funds in high-technology industries over a five-year period. At the same time, the appropriations for nationalized industries grew from 30 billion francs ($6.5 billion) in 1978 to more than 40 billion francs ($10 billion) in 1979.

6. For example, early in 1980 Barre suggested that the unemployed start their own enterprises instead of drawing monthly unemployment checks.

7. Purchasing power rose 14.3 percent in 1981, and 12.6 percent in 1982. The SMIC raise of 11.5 percent between 1981 and 1982 was subsequently "chilled" by the imposition of a wage freeze.

8. The index of industrial production was 129 in the first quarter of 1981 and 128 in the first quarter of 1983.

9. From 3.1 trillion francs in 1981 to 3.5 trillion francs in 1982, i.e., near stagnation, if one accounts for the inflationary factor.

10. The actual burden imposed upon business remained a matter of contention. According to the major employers' association, the CNPF, the charges amounted to 44 billion francs in 1982 and 62 billion francs in 1983; according to the government, the figures were 21 billion francs and 27 billion francs, respectively. See "Charges des entreprises," 1983, 23ff., and Groupe de travail CNPF–Administration, 1983.

11. Lewis, 1983. This writer suggests that if only the Socialists had waited a while, many of the industries could have been had for a song.

12. Interview with Pierre Mauroy, *Express,* April 8, 1983.

13. See Commission de réforme de la planification, 1982. This utopian report, submitted to Rocard and to Parliament, was written by a study committee composed of deputies, civil servants, academics, businessmen, party leaders, and local politicians. It recommended greater regional involvement in planning and a more "social" orientation of the plan.

14. For 1983 alone, the total anticipated expenditure for industrial investments was 180 billion francs. A major share of this would come from the government, that is, would be disbursed by a plethora of (sometimes competing) agencies, e.g., the Industrial Modernization Fund of the Ministry of Industry, saving banks and other credit agencies controlled by the Ministry of Economics, *sociétés de développement régional.*

15. In 1983, imports rose 5.7 percent; exports, 14.6 percent.

16. These figures are bound to look much less hopeful at the end of 1984 and in 1985, since the interest payments on the existing foreign debts will be growing considerably.

17. Wage increases in 1983 had been 9.5 percent, compared to 12.6 percent in 1982 and 14.3 percent in 1981. See Vernholes, 1984; and French Embassy, 1984b, 4.

18. There were similar "cave-ins" to pressure from agriculture. In 1983–84, when hog farmers protested a decline in hog prices (and sacked a prefecture in Brittany), the government imposed import restrictions on foreign meat.

19. The Délégation à l'aménagement du térritoire et l'action régionale (DATAR) was composed of civil servants working closely with local politicians and interest group representatives but operating under the close supervision of the national Cabinet.

20. "Le premier ministre assigne aux prefets [sic] 'une obligation de résultats'" (Le Monde, January 26, 1984). The three cabinet members were Premier Mauroy, Economics Minister Delors, and Gaston Defferre, minister of decentralization and interior.

21. Part of that money was intended as an operational subsidy, a measure that required special permission from the Common Market authorities (which was granted under the "emergency" provision [article 58] of the Coal and Steel Treaty).

22. Philippe Bauchard, in Témoignage chrétien, July 11, 1983. Although the confidential remarks were not for attribution, Mitterrand did not disavow their substance.

23. This is the expression of Laurent Fabius, the minister of industry. See Economist (July 16, 1983): 86.

24. French Embassy, France (January–February 1984), 4. Delors's admiration for the structural modernization policies pursued in Germany is also evident in his "France: Between Reform and Counter-Reform," in Dahrendorf, 1982.

25. Note: One sector in which inefficiency has been institutionally protected—that of agriculture under the Common Agricultural Policy—now seems less protected, in view of Mitterrand's expressed willingness (over the protest of farmers) to listen to the requests of his Common Market partners to renegotiate the CAP (Wall Street Journal, March 14, 1984).

26. A manifestation of this was the proposal made by Louis Mermaz, the speaker of the Assembly, that Jacques Delors be put at the head of the Socialist list for the elections to the European Parliament scheduled for June 1984, and that this list include not only Socialists, PSU personalities, and Left Radicals, but also "nonpartisan personalities" (Le Monde, January 17, 1984).

27. Cf. "Congrès de Bourg-en-Bresse, 28, 29, et 30 octobre 1983: contributions au débat," Le Poing et la rose (June 1983).

28. The Mitterrandistes (courant A) affirmed the policies of rigor without qualification and affirmed as well the authority of the state about what measures to take; the Mauroy faction (courant B), while rejecting "excessive statism" and "mere productivism," also rejected protectionism; and the Rocardiens (courant C)

accompanied their firm support of Mitterrand's policy with remarks about *autogestion.*

29. SOFRES polls, cited in *Libération* (February 10, 1984) and *Figaro-Magazine* (July 2, 1983):56–58.

REFERENCES

Aron, Raymond. 1983. "Bilan Provisoire." *Express* (May 27).

Bérégovoy, Pierre. 1983. "Emploi, solidarité, dialogue social: un projet pour l'avenir," *Le Monde* (December 14).

Cerny, Philip, and Schain, Martin, eds. 1980. *French Politics and Public Policy.* New York: St. Martin's Press.

Changer la vie: Programme de gouvernement du Parti socialiste. 1972. Paris: Flammarion.

"Charges des entreprises: ce qu'elles paient en plus depuis mai–juin 1981." 1983. *Regards sur l'actualité,* no. 95.

Commission de réforme de la planification. 1982. *Rapport au ministre du plan et de l'aménagement du térritoire.* Paris: Documentation française.

"La Conjoncture economique." 1983. *Tocqueville Review* 5, no. 2.

"La Conjoncture politique." 1983. *Tocqueville Review* 5, no. 2.

Dahrendorf, Ralf, ed. 1982. *Europe's Economy in Crisis.* New York: Holmes & Meier.

Delaunay, Jean-Claude. 1984. "Sur quelques difficultés de la politique socialiste de l'emploi." *Temps modernes* (February).

Delors, Jacques. 1982. "France: Between Reform and Counter-Reform." In *Europe's Economy in Crisis,* ed. Ralf Dahrendorf. New York: Holmes & Meier.

Fourastié, Jean. 1979. *Les Trente glorieuses: ou la révolution invisible de 1946 à 1975.* Paris: Fayard.

French Embassy. Press and Information Service. 1983a, 1984a. *France.* New York.

———. 1983b. *France in 1983: A Social and Economic Survey.*

———. 1983c, 1984b. *News and Comments from France.*

Giesbert, Franz-Olivier. 1977. *François Mitterrand ou la tentation de l'histoire.* Paris: France-Loisirs.

Groupe de travail CNPF–administration. 1983. *Les charges des entreprises françaises: rapport au premier ministre.* Paris: Documentation française.

Lewis, Paul. 1983. "French Socialism Stubs Its Toe." *New York Times* (July 31).

———. 1984. "France: Left Behind by Upturn." *New York Times* (January 1).

Manceron, Claude, and Pingaud, Bernard, eds. 1981. *François Mitterrand: L'Homme, les idées, le programme.* Paris: Flammarion.

Marris, Stephen. 1984. "Why European Recovery Is Lagging Behind." *Europe* (March–April).

Monroe, Kristen R. 1980, "A French Political Business Cycle?" In *French Politics and Public Policy,* ed. Philip Cerny and Martin Schain. New York: St. Martin's Press.

"Nationalisations". 1982. *Regards sur l'actualité,* special no. 79.

"Le 9e Plan 1984–1988." 1984. *Regards sur l'actualité, no. 98.*

OECD. 1983. Etudes économiques 1982–83. Paris: OECD.

Projet socialiste pour la France des années 80. 1980. Paris: Club socialiste du livre.

Rémond, René. 1982. "Politique 2 de François Mitterrand." *Le Monde* (January 21).

La révalorisation du travail manuel: bilan d'action 1976–80. 1980. Paris: Actualités/documents, Premier ministre, Service d'information et de diffusion.

Rosa, Jean-Jacques. 1981. "The New French Reality." *Journal of Contemporary Studies* (Fall).

Ross, George, and Jensen, Jane. 1983. "Crisis and France's 'Third Way.'" *Studies in Political Economy* (Summer).

Safran, William. 1985. *The French Policy.* 2d ed. New York: Longman.

Salais, Robert. 1978. "Redresser l'emploi: relance et politique structurelle." *Projet,* no. 123.

Vernholes, Alain. 1984. "Le Chant des sirènes: dix-huit mois de rigueur." *Le Monde* (January 19).

Vinocur, John. 1984a. "French Socialism May Be Suffering an Indentity Crisis." *New York Times* (Review Section) (April 22).

———. 1984b. "Mitterrand's Changes: Giving Socialism a New Centrist Look." *New York Times* (July 21).

Will, George. 1983. "The Comeback of Capitalism in France." *Washington Post* (October 15).

10 WEST GERMAN CRISIS MANAGEMENT: STABILITY AND CHANGE IN THE POST-KEYNESIAN AGE

Jeremiah M. Riemer

Not too long ago, the economy of the Federal Republic of Germany (FRG) was an object of international envy and a source of national pride. West Germany, like most countries, did not remain immune to the worldwide recession of 1974–75. And its recovery from that slump was much less vigorous than the FRG's comeback from a previous recession in 1966–67. But while the Federal Republic had its share of crises, West Germans could look on their economy in the 1970s as a stable island in the midst of an unstable world.

Figures on growth, unemployment, and inflation in the 1970s told the story of the Federal Republic's relative success. On average, the annual rate of growth in West Germany's per capita gross national product during the ten years from 1969 to 1978 was 3.3 percent, at least a percentage point or more above the comparable rates for the United States, Britain, and Sweden, although a good two percentage points behind Japan's decade average. Until 1974, the Federal Republic had the lowest unemployment rate of these five countries, either slightly under or slightly over one percent. Although the 1974–75 recession pushed unemployment well above 2 percent (a ceiling it had not reached, with the exception of the brief 1966–67 recession, since 1960), the number of

Portions of this article were presented at two conference panels in the fall of 1983. The author wishes to thank the panel chairpersons, Peter Gourevitch and Gary Marks.

jobless slowly but steadily declined from the vicinity of 5 percent in 1975 to something over 4 percent by 1978. Japan and Sweden, by contrast, maintained postrecessionary averages close to 2 percent unemployment, although their unemployment rolls got slightly worse, not modestly better, in each successive year. West Germany's unemployment statistics were certainly better than those in Britain and especially the United States, whose *best* set of figures for the decade (4.9 percent in 1970 and again in 1973) was roughly equal to the Federal Republic's *worst* in 1975. (The German low point was better than the American high point if the official annual statistics taken by the West German Federal Labor Office are used. Seasonally adjusted figures from other sources make West Germany look marginally worse, but not enough to make the United States' "best" record appear much better by comparison.) Most impressively of all, West Germany avoided double-digit inflation throughout the entire decade of the 1970s. The biggest jump in prices, which happened between 1973 and 1974 (the year of the first oil shock), was just below 7 percent. In the four years following 1975, inflation stayed well under 5 percent.

American observers of the West German political and economic scene interpreted the FRG's relative success in one of two ways, each favorable. Conservatives, impressed by the unsocialist temperament of Social Democratic Chancellor Helmut Schmidt (finance minister since 1972 and head of the ruling center-left coalition from 1974 to 1982), emphasized Schmidt's businesslike style of crisis management and his insistence that monetary stability was a precondition for—not a barrier to—high employment. West Germany's ability to achieve a reasonable trade-off between inflation and unemployment at a low level for each (to avoid, in the technical jargon of economics, a rightward shifting "Phillips curve") seemed to confirm the chief lesson drawn by the authors of the conservative, post-Keynesian McCracken Report (see Keohane, 1978). In this review of economic planning in the 1970s (commissioned by the OECD), a team of international economists concluded that a cautious mixture of fiscal and monetary policies (much like West Germany's) was required if governments and economies were going to learn how they might tread along a "narrow path" of stable growth, avoiding the extremes of either too much reflation or too much austerity. Post-Keynesians further to the left, like Harvard's Robert Reich, drew a different set of lessons from the West German experience. They concluded that industrial policy, more than fiscal or monetary policy, held the key to the Federal Republic's success. By facilitating a process of industrial adjustment that promoted internationally competitive firms while phasing out technologically obsolete production, government policies meshed with business and labor practices to welcome and encourage productivity and growth.

Inside West Germany, the FRG's *relative* immunity to the worldwide recessionary climate redounded favorably on the Social Democrats, the governing party of the 1970s. Although the Christian Democratic opposition offered marginal criticisms of economic policy on issues like the growing federal deficit and a less than vigorous recovery from the 1975 recession, Chancellor Schmidt was reelected twice (in 1976 and 1980), largely on the strength of his authoritative brand of crisis management. When the Social Democrats ran on the campaign slogan "Model Germany" in 1976, they demonstrated that West Germany's reputation for stability abroad could be converted into political popularity at home.

Electoral confirmation of Social Democratic power did not mean that West Germans were entirely free of crisis anxiety. On the contrary: Surveying the West German scene in 1978, American political scientist David Calleo observed that "as the seventies progressed, a sort of low-grade crisis of confidence has afflicted the German economy" (Calleo, 1978, 190). By the end of the decade, these vague anxieties about the future of the West German economy became concrete. In 1979 the Federal Republic's balance of payments, normally buoyed by a habitual export surplus, showed a deficit on current account (the balance of trade in goods and services). The current account remained in deficit until 1982. Unemployment climbed quickly above the late 1970s' ceiling of 4 percent in 1980, reached a peak of well over 9 percent in 1983, and showed little sign of getting down into the 8 percent range by 1984. From 1980 to 1982 industrial production declined, and West Germany's third postwar recession led to the ouster of Chancellor Schmidt in the fall of 1982 and his replacement by Christian Democrat Helmut Kohl. Kohl's governing majority was strengthened by a special election held in the spring of 1983.

As the West German economy moved from "model" stability in the mid-1970s, through crisis anxiety toward the end of the decade, and into genuine crisis by the 1980s, economic opinion inside the Federal Republic became the object of uncertainty and controversy. Throughout most of the postwar period, the policy-making establishment in Bonn was united around a consensus emphasizing the primacy of monetary stability. But the economy's incomplete recovery from the 1975 recession and its crisis in the early 1980s raised doubts about the particular kind of stability-conscious course pursued by the Social Democratic–led government. Some critics (on the right) charged that the Schmidt administration had done too little to promote new business investment, while others (on the left) maintained that the government had been too cautious about stimulating the economy through even more deficit spending. Still other concerned observers, convinced that all traditional policies designed to stabilize the business cycle had become obsolete by the 1970s, believed that the policy-making establishment needed to come to terms with a new reality, which they called a "structural crisis." By structural crisis these new critics meant a long-term and sectorally differentiated crisis, different in scope and character from the short-term, cyclical crises of the 1960s and early 1970s. As a result of all these criticisms, which predated (and perhaps anticipated) the recession of the 1980s, politicians and their economist-advisers seemed to confront a somewhat wider, and certainly more disorienting, range of public policy choices at the start of the new decade.

Traditionally in the Federal Republic, the professional politician interested in legitimating a public position and the student of political economy trying to explain public policy could draw on a narrow, clearly defined range of choices. The clarity of policy choices in the FRG derived in part from the existence of programmatic parties there: on the right, the conservative Christian Democratic Union (CDU) and its Bavarian sister party, the Christian Social Union (CSU), have been the traditional defenders of the propertied classes (small business, big industry, and farmers), while drawing additional support from some (usually Catholic) workers; on the left, the Social Democratic party (SPD) has always enjoyed close ties to the labor movement, although its appeal (especially to university graduates and the "floating voter" in the 1960s and 1970s) has become much broader than the traditional Social Democratic base among the Protestant and northern working class. At times, each of these big parties on either end of the political spectrum has enjoyed a special appeal to society and the electorate at large. The CDU/CSU has always flourished when public opinion seems to favor making business investment and close ties to the United States the highest domestic and international priorities. Thus, in the 1950s and 1960s, the Cold War and rebuilding a war-torn economy were issues tailor-made for a long period of Christian Democratic predominance. (The same combination of economic and foreign policy concerns, though on a smaller scale, helped bring the Christian Democrats back to power in 1982.) The SPD seems to do better when capitalist prosperity at home is combined with East-West understanding abroad, as in the recent era of affluence and détente. Although the 1970s marked the high point of Social Democratic influence, in only one federal election (1972) did the SPD actually outpoll the Christian Democrats and become the majority party in the Bundestag (West Germany's parliament). Throughout most of the Federal Republic's history, both major parties have been forced to govern in coalition with one or more smaller parties.

In between the major parties, and at various times coalition partner to either one of them, the tiny Free Democratic party (FDP) speaks up strongly for that section of the business community which is more liberal on foreign policy and civil liberties issues than the Christian Democrats but more conservative on economic issues than the SPD. Although the FDP is small, its economic policy clout is large. Partly because the business community has close ties to the Free Democrats, and partly because many voters support the FDP as a centrist "brake" on the leftward and rightward tendencies of the major parties, the influence of the FDP over economic policy is out of proportion to the party's small size. (West Germany's youngest party, the Green and Alternative List [GAL], is not included here because this antinuclear party has concentrated on such issues as peace and the environment and has barely developed a coherent economic program.) Even today, the range of policy choices in the FRG is narrower than in many other countries because, while German history has been rich in economic and political variation, the only part of this history relevant to current policy debates is the three and a half decades since World War II.

In the contest leading up to the West German general election of March 1983, the major political parties drew on the memories and experiences of these three decades for their campaign themes. On the political right, Chancellor Helmut Kohl of the CDU was quite explicit about his nostalgic admiration for the Christian Democratic chancellor of the 1950s, Konrad Adenauer. Kohl's Free Democratic economics minister, Otto Lambsdorff, appeared to be modeling himself after the chief economic policy maker of the 1950s, Ludwig Erhard. Erhard, widely regarded as the principal author of that decade's "economic miracle" (the mythical label applied to West Germany's postwar recovery), was a Christian Democrat by virtue of his party membership, but closer to the Free Democrats in his economic philosophy.

Whereas the CDU–FDP governing coalition (which had been in power since the fall of 1982, when Free Democrats like Lambsdorff abandoned their longstanding coalition with Helmut Schmidt's Social Democrats) shared a common nostalgia for the 1950s, the Social Democratic party entered the 1983 election campaign in greater disarray about their party's economic past and future. Looking backward, the Social Democrats could justly be proud of their accomplishments in the 1960s and (although perhaps to a lesser extent) 1970s. Late in 1966, when Chancellor Erhard (who had succeeded Adenauer as chief executive in 1963) resigned in the midst of a minor recession and fiscal crisis, the Social Democrats picked up the pieces of political responsibility for the economy. The SPD remained in power until 1982. The first Social Democratic economics minister in postwar Germany, Karl Schiller, introduced modern Keynesian planning into the Federal Republic by getting the Bundestag to pass a Stability and Growth Act in 1967. With the aid of this powerful law (which won the approval of all three major political groupings in the Bundestag), Social Democratic–led governments were subsequently able to cope with more severe trials than the 1966–67 recession—such as the oil crisis of 1973 and the worldwide recession of 1975. Although the Social Democrats handed over the Economics Ministry to the Free Democrats in 1972, the SPD retained substantial influence over economic policy during the 1970s through its control of the Finance Ministry, as well as through the personal authority and expertise of Chancellor Schmidt (a trained economist who briefly served out Schiller's term as economics-finance "superminister" in 1972 and stayed on as finance minister until becoming chancellor in 1974).

Although SPD Chancellors Willy Brandt (1969–74) and Helmut Schmidt (1974–82) presided over more than a decade of prosperity and successful crisis management, the parties to the Social-Liberal (SPD–FDP) coalition were unable to find a mutually agreeable path out of the FRG's third recession in 1981–82. As early as the recession of 1975, younger party members and labor interests in the SPD had been registering their dissatisfaction with Helmut Schmidt's conservative style of crisis management. Convinced that West Germany in the 1970s was going through a "structural crisis"—different in scope and character from the "cyclical crisis" of 1966–67—these dissenting Social Democrats initiated a debate about "structural policy" very similar to the current discussion of "industrial policy" in the United States. Freed from the constraints of the Free Democrats and the authority of ex-Chancellor Schmidt (who stepped down as chancellor candidate in favor of the current opposition leader, Hans-Jochen Vogel), the Social Democrats in 1983 made a last-minute effort to update their economic policy and appeal to new electoral groups (such as ecologists and young people tempted to vote for the Greens). But as the decline of SPD support among voters in the "smokestack" regions of the industrial north may have indicated, the Social Democratic turnaround in economic policy was either too hasty or too poorly conceived to prove effective in time for the critical March elections. Unlike the CDU and FDP, both of whom knew how to capitalize on nostalgia for the mythically trouble-free 1950s, the SPD was not able to take credit for its accomplishments in the 1960s. Nor could the Social Democrats demonstrate that they had moved successfully into the future during the 1970s.

The second part of this chapter will look behind the major partisan interpretations of West Germany's economic heritage to review the images of political economy informing these interpretations. In particular, three different views of the relationship between the state and the economy—the "embattled state," the "expert state," and the "strategically capable state"—will be reviewed. The third part examines the details of the FRG's economic adjustment by drawing on the insights of these different images of the state while discarding some of their simplifying assumptions about the roles of interest politics, economic advice, and policy-making institutions. The fourth part concludes with an assessment of the current situation in Bonn—the problem of engineering a recovery facing the Kohl government and the problem of rethinking economic policy preoccupying the Social Democratic opposition.

THREE IMAGES OF THE WEST GERMAN POLITICAL ECONOMY

To the student of comparative politics, the competing campaign positions of the 1983 federal election are interesting for their similarity to competing models of political economy. Christian Democratic nostalgia for the 1950s, the all-party consensus of the mid-1960s, and the left–Social Democratic position that began to emerge in the late 1970s all bear a strong resemblance to different social science images of how the modern representative state relates to the contemporary capitalist economy. These different images correspond to different interpretations of how the relationship between the state and the economy has changed across the postwar era and to different proposals for the direction that relationship must take if countries like West Germany are to overcome their current economic difficulties. The images of the state implied in each model of political economy may be described as the "embattled state" (idealizing the 1950s), the "expert state" (fixated on the reforms of the 1960s), and the "strategically capable state" (focusing on the opportunities, missed and fulfilled, of the 1970s). Each of these images, while applicable to any advanced capitalist country, is also associated with some distinctively West German attitudes about the character and direction of policy change:

1. A distinctively West German definition of what constitutes a strong or adequate economic policy.
2. A specific attitude (positive, negative, or mixed) toward the major watershed in West German economic policy making, the "Keynesian revolution" that accompanied the Stability and Growth Act of 1967 (Küster, 1974).
3. A crisis interpretation or theory of what has gone wrong with West German economic policy during and between the three critical recessionary trials of the Social Democratic era (1966–82).

The Embattled—or Overextended—State and the Crisis of Claims

Among the various twentieth-century models of political economy, the "embattled state" comes closest to the nineteenth-century image of the "nightwatchman" state. According to this classical liberal view, the state was meant to restrict its role in the capitalist economy to a few functions of essential public oversight. Government was supposed to use its central bank to regulate the money supply, its courts to ensure the sanctity of private contracts, its police to maintain public order, and its taxes to finance indispensable public services. In essence, the state was to act as a security guard for capitalist society.

The "embattled (or overextended) state" is an image of modern government that many conservatives and a few public choice theorists have come to favor as a reaction to the Keynesian reforms of the 1960s. Political economists of this school are chiefly concerned with defining (and, in recent years, limiting) the public budget according to strict criteria of economic rationality. Since the 1970s, their major worries have been inflation and the mounting claims of private interests on the strained resources of the public sector. Talk of an "overloaded" state and of "ungovernability" has become a standard lament in the litany of the embattled state. Nostalgia for the supposedly less meddlesome state of the 1950s is expressed in such neoconservative proposals as lower taxes, a balanced budget, and the reprivatization of public services.

In the FRG, the image of the embattled state may be found in the writings of conservative thinkers who go by the name *neoliberal.* The term *neoliberal* means something very different from what it has recently come to signify in the United States. German neoliberalism (a philosophy more commonly known inside West Germany as the "social market economy") is a market-oriented ideology going back to the 1950s (MacLennan, Forsyth, and Denton, 1968, 18–24, 34–78). The official doctrine of the CDU and FDP in Erhard's day, neoliberalism has enjoyed something of a revival among economists associated with the "new political economy" (a German-language branch of public choice theory) and on the (once Keynesian) Council of Experts, a nonpartisan body of economists that advises the Bonn government.

Together with their English-speaking colleagues, German conservatives share a fondness for reprivatization and a longing for the leaner state of an earlier era. They draw inspiration from such legendary acts of conservative principle as Ludwig Erhard's sale of state shares in the semipublic company that manufactures Volkswagen automobiles. But whereas Anglo-Americans in sympathy with the embattled state long for a *minimal* state, the corresponding German tradition stresses a state that is *strong*—strong enough, at least, to resist the onslaught of lobbies and special interest politics. Unlike the advocates of the "strategically capable state" (see below), these conservatives are not likely to look favorably on well-organized unions and powerful trade associations (the *Verbände*) as substitutes for the strong state. Nor do they believe that Keynesian planning has proven itself as an acceptable substitute for the guiding mechanisms of the market.

The crisis theory of the embattled state's defenders may be described as a "crisis of claims" *(Anspruchskrise)*. According to this interpretation of West German economic policy, the economy went into crisis because the public sector did not put up effective, sustained resistance to an avalanche of private sector claims that cascaded in the 1970s, with Social Democratic complicity or support. The attack on the embattled state started in the 1960s, when the Social Democrats were becoming such an effective opposition to the faction-ridden CDU that the Christian Democrats were forced to abandon their chancellor (Erhard) and form a Grand Coalition with the SPD (lasting from 1966 to 1969). Although the Grand Coalition sponsored a successful recovery, the strong economy that emerged from the recession eventually betrayed its political sponsors.

The economy's inflationary response to policies that nurtured economic growth in the 1950s and restored growth after 1966 did not become really serious until after the election of 1969, when the SPD rode into office on the prestige of Economics Minister Schiller and Foreign Minister (later Chancellor) Willy Brandt. Throughout the 1960s, distributive conflict—i.e., the struggle between wage earners and businesses for shares of the gross national product—had been fueling a slow inflationary trend in the economy. Now, in the 1970s under Social Democratic leadership, the federal government itself became fully implicated in this inflationary distributive struggle. As the nation's largest employer and as the guarantor of full employment under a weak Keynesian regime, successive SPD-led governments gave in to demand-pull and cost-push inflation.

According to the crisis of claims model, the Erhard era of the 1950s, when economic policy was dominated by the neoliberal philosophy of the "Freiburg" (free market) school, was clearly West Germany's most stable (if not most prosperous) period. The reforms of the 1960s, in which Karl Schiller sought to synthesize the Freiburg tradition with Keynesian economics, were intended to buy more stability but unintentionally promoted a dangerous prosperity. In this view, Schiller's moderate Keynesian revolution proved to be a mere way station on the path toward an extreme form of "Keynesian imperialism" (the full employment economy) that weakened Germany's economic position in the ensuing decade.

The Expert State and the Crisis of Economic Theory

A major increase in the state's capacity for intervening in the economy came with the Keynesian revolution and the institutionalization of professional economic advice. The economist replaced the "nightwatchman" as the defender of the capitalist economy. When Keynesianism (which originated in the Great Depression but was not fully implemented in many countries until the postwar period) came into its own during the 1960s, the image of the "expert state" emerged. According to this image of the modern interventionist state, what matters is the advice that policy makers get from professional economists. Policy making is a question of getting and interpreting information—establishing quantitative indicators of national welfare, obtaining reliable statistics on the state of the economy, and constructing economic models to match data with analysis. Government becomes very much an intellectual enterprise.

As with other countries, the FRG has gone through an almost standard sequence of intellectual fashions since the 1960s—from Keynesianism, through monetarism, to post-Keynesian perspectives like industrial policy. But, distinctively for West Germany, these changes of fashion occurred in rapid succession within a compact period of time. In 1963, when the five-member Council of Experts was set up to advise the government on economic policy, neoliberalism was still the official doctrine of the CDU state. Three years later, when the Bundestag passed a liberal version of the Growth and Stability Act, Keynesianism replaced neoliberalism as the dominant economic philosophy. By 1975 Keynesianism seemed to have fallen out of fashion among government economists, while monetarism came into fashion and "structural policy" was already being debated. The quick change of fashions has frequently blurred the lines of debate for those political economists who take these changes in economic schools of thought seriously. During the 1970s, left-Keynesian economists who had become critical of orthodox (i.e. centrist) Keynesianism nonetheless found themselves advocating some very orthodox Keynesian positions, such as the call for more deficit spending. These "post-Keynesians" rose to the defense of "old-fashioned" Keynesianism because the quick rise of the monetarist attack on beleaguered Keynesian policies worried them much more than the declining appeal of Keynesian-style analysis (Baisch et al., 1977; Arbeitsgruppe "Alternative Wirtschaftspolitik," 1978).

The proliferation of economic philosophies over the last two decades has dramatized the contribution made by professional economists to economic crisis management since the recession of 1966–67. The rapid turnover in economic policy prescriptions has also produced a distinctive definition and theory of economic crises in the Keynesian era. Each economic crisis—from the recession of 1966–67, through the recession of 1975, to the "structural crisis" of the late 1970s—has been interpreted as a "crisis of economic theory" (Markmann and Simmert, 1978). According to political economists who think that trends in economic advice are decisive, the economy is unable to recover from a crisis whenever the government cannot find the appropriate crisis diagnosis and therapy for the particular type of crisis it faces.

Finding the proper match between crisis diagnosis and crisis prescription has been of special interest to left-Keynesian economists who are sympathetic to trade unions and the Social Democratic party. Their account of what was done correctly and what went wrong during the entire Keynesian era runs something like this: Keynesianism was an appropriate, progressive solution to recession in the low-inflation 1960s, while monetarism was an ill-conceived, conservative response to greater economic instability in the 1970s. But the Bonn government has yet to formulate, much less act upon, a suitable post-Keynesian perspective. Such an up-to-date perspective would emphasize maintaining sufficient levels of investment in an economy undergoing structural change. Structural policy, rather than a traditional macroeconomic policy of the right or the left, is considered the key because the proper crisis diagnosis has become a structural diagnosis. According to this view, West Germany no longer faces a stabilization crisis, as it did in 1966–67 or from 1973 to 1975. Each such stabilization crisis occurred when the Bundesbank, the Federal Republic's central bank, deliberately induced a recession in order to squeeze inflation out of the economy. Recession quickly followed upon Bundesbank restraint in 1966. But the central bank's attempt to cool the economy in 1973 did not produce a recession until the worldwide economic downturn of 1974–75 intervened. These earlier recessions were cyclical—rather than structural—in character. They were downturns in the business cycle that affected the entire economy. But the structural crisis typical of the late 1970s and early 1980s was a crisis of unemployment concentrated in specific sectors.

The conservative policies of the current Kohl government have not been much of a mystery to those Social Democratic Keynesians who view economic policy as an affair of the expert state and who interpret crisis management as a crisis of economic theory. Kohl has been more than explicit about his government's intentions and ideas. Together with the liberal Free Democrats, the CDU has been trying to engineer a political *Wende*—literally, a turnabout from the direction economic policy was taking under Brandt and Schmidt. The CDU–FDP coalition has been trying to reduce the federal budget deficit, which grew immensely in the 1970s, to increase profits and restore business confidence, and to resist the pressure of the trade union confederation (the Deutsche Gewerkschaftsbund, or DGB) for a thirty-five-hour work week. The pro-business tilt of the Free Democrats has also been easy for left-of-center Keynesian Social Democrats to interpret. Many Social Democrats blamed the FDP, which has run the Economics Ministry since December 1972, for the conservative turn of economic policy since the oil crisis of 1973 and the recession of 1975. Most SPD party members identified Count Otto Lambsdorff as the principal villain of the 1982 *Wende*—the man who betrayed the electoral commitments of the Social–Liberal coalition (which had been returned to power in the general election of 1980) and the person most responsible for bringing down the government of Helmut Schmidt. In the late 1970s, a number of Social Democrats were also frustrated by the way that the Free Democrats contributed to the authority of Chancellor Schmidt over his own party, the SPD. Whenever the authoritative chancellor wanted to defeat the Keynesian proposals of the party's left wing, Schmidt's Free Democratic coalition partner on the right provided a convenient excuse for party discipline.

Somewhat more puzzling than the probusiness attitude of the CDU, FDP, and Schmidt was the economic orientation of the governing SPD in the late 1970s. Why did the party which had introduced Keynesianism into the Federal Republic seem to renounce its Keynesian heritage without arriving at a more up-to-date, post-Keynesian perspective? Some left-Keynesian Social Democrats, confident that a proper crisis diagnosis of the FRG's economic ills was available in the form of structural policy, blamed a neoconservative change of ideological fashion—a *Tendenzwende*—for the government's inability to make appropriate changes in economic policy. For these critics, who saw a direct line leading from the *Tendenzwende* of the late 1970s to the *Wende* of 1982–83, the "expert state" in Social Democratic hands was also a misinformed state. Other critics of government policy during the 1970s, less certain about the direction in which economic policy should have been heading, characterized Social–Liberal policies as disoriented. Interestingly, the German word for "disoriented" is *ratlos,* which literally means "at a loss for advice." In either interpretation of the crisis of economic theory during the 1970s—the misinformed state or the disoriented state—the crucial variable was the state of expert opinion on economic policy.

The Strategically Capable State and the Institutional Crisis

Whereas the image of the embattled state focuses on the nightwatchman who protects the economic order, while the image of the expert state draws attention to the advice that governments get from professional economists, a third model of political economy pictures the guardianship of public welfare in strategic terms. Like the expert state, although unlike the embattled state, the "strategically capable state" is a state that is committed to economic planning. But unlike the expert state, the strategically capable state plans in a long-range fashion.

In the literature on corporatism and economic planning (Schmitter and Lehmbruch, 1979; Shonfield, 1969; Reich and Magaziner, 1982), the strategically capable state is typically a strong state with the institutional capacity to steer an organized capitalist economy in a planned direction. The history of West German economic policy meets these general criteria, but with some special nuances. Since the Federal Republic has not always conformed to the image of a strong state overseeing a planned economy, the German version of the strategically capable state has focused on powerful institutions that were said to plan in spite of the postwar order's ideological bias against planning. Some of these strong institutions, most notably the Bundesbank, are public. Others, like the major German banks (especially the big three: Deutsche, Dresdner, and Commerz) may be private but are said to occupy strategic positions in the economy by virtue of their control over shareholder proxies and corporate boards of directors. Yet another type of powerful private institution is one for which there is a special German word—the *Spitzenverband*—literally, a "peak association" of interests, like a trade union or an employers' federation. Finally, one authority on the FRG (Katzenstein, 1982) has identified a set of strategically capable institutions there neither wholly public nor completely private but rather "parapublic" in nature.

Regardless of their status in society or government, all these organizations are considered important because of their economic steering capacity. Whether public, private, or parapublic, each of these institutions purportedly possesses an administrative or managerial capability to move the economy along the path of a well-defined growth strategy. According to some experienced observers, the postwar growth strategy of the West German economy has been dictated by the country's success at exporting high quality (or high value-added) goods at reasonable prices. The pattern of export-oriented growth has sometimes been labeled "neomercantilistic" (Hankel, 1975; Riese, 1975; Kreile, 1978) because of the way that the West German government and economy have usually been able to generate a large trade surplus (Kindleberger, 1965), build up a substantial foreign exchange reserve, and promote a strong currency (the deutsche mark, or DM).

Like the adherents to the model of the expert state, proponents of the strategically capable state tend to believe that West Germany must fashion a coherent post-Keynesian industrial policy for the 1980s. However, instead of emphasizing changing schools of economic thought, these post-Keynesian strategists view institutional innovation as the critical variable. Most observers would agree that West German policy makers went a long way toward strengthening and expanding their country's institutional capabilities in the 1960s, especially with the passage of the Stability and Growth Act in 1967. Prior to that legislation, the only public institution equipped to act on a strategic outlook was the Deutsche Bundesbank, West Germany's powerful federal reserve bank. But opinion is divided on how far the Federal Republic then moved in the direction of a more coherent, long-term growth strategy during the 1970s. By implication, it is not entirely clear whether West Germany's strong government or parapublic institutions will be able to cope with whatever crisis conditions arise in the present decade. The more pessimistic observers (usually from the Social Democratic left) have been warning since the 1970s about the need for more corporatist institution building. These prophets of post-Keynesian crisis management want the Bonn government to create a new set of cooperative arrangements among government, business, and labor that will facilitate a high-level consensus on industrial policy goals. More optimistic analyses of the West German economy in the 1970s (usually carried out by foreign—e.g., American—admirers of the "German model") came to the opposite conclusion: West Germany already has an impressive industrial policy based on solid corporatist foundations.

Most prominent among the American admirers of German industrial policy have been Robert Reich and Ira Magaziner. In *Minding America's Business,* they observed: "The most direct government efforts to promote new products and processes are found in the Federal Republic of Germany." The authors drew attention to four special features of the government's effort to promote industrial change: (1) an increase in the federal share of business research and development funding (from 14 percent to 20 percent); (2) a switch in the method of promoting research, away from general tax incentives and toward selective, direct cash grants; (3) an emphasis on funding engineering industries (mechanical, electric, and electronic); and (4) a focus "on building strong business positions in businesses that can support a high wage rate" (Reich and Magaziner, 1982, 279–82). This overall shift toward a more concentrated style of targeting growth happened during the 1970s, a decade of Social Democratic–led governments, and was presided over by the newly created Ministry of Research and Technology (BMFT—Bundesministerium für Forschung und Technologie).

At the same time that, according to Reich and Magaziner, a Social Democratic research policy was enhancing the international competitiveness of German industry, policy analysts in the SPD were becoming interested in industrial policy as an instrument of domestic crisis management. By American standards, an economy with an unemployment rate ranging between 4 and 5 percent for most of the 1970s was in good shape. By West Germans' more exacting standards, however, more than 3 percent unemployment meant a crisis. In 1975 the parliamentary state secretary at the Research Ministry (Volker Hauff) teamed up with a political scientist (Fritz Scharpf) to write a book about the need for an industrial policy that could effectively combat the recession that year. Using language and argument strikingly similar to Reich's later critique of American economic policy (Reich, 1983), Hauff and Scharpf pleaded for a "strategy of active structural adjustment" and warned against adopting a "strategy of preservation" for the West German economy (Hauff and Scharpf, 1975; Narr and Offe, 1976).

Structural policy as an innovation to enhance Helmut Schmidt's repertoire of crisis management techniques became a standard theme of policy analysis within the Social Democratic party, especially as the SPD prepared to write a new party program in 1975 and campaign for reelection in 1976 (Oertzen, Ehmke, and Ehrenberg, 1974; Sarrazin, 1976). During Schmidt's second term in office, a number of young Social Democratic economists and freshman members of the Bundestag hoped that structural policy would be integrated into the Social–Liberal coalition's effort to achieve more than a lukewarm recovery from the recession of 1975. Their case for institutional innovations in industrial policy sounded much like the left-Keynesian perspective on the expert state, but with an emphasis on economic strategy alongside the attention given to economic advice. Since the SPD had successfully used new Keynesian ideas to combat the relatively mild recession of 1966–67, these Social Democrats reasoned, why not implement an innovative post-Keynesian strategy at a time when the economic crisis was more serious? The party that gave West Germany a successful stabilization policy for the comparatively trivial stabilization crisis of the 1960s should be able to fashion a durable strategy of structural adjustment for the persistent structural crises of the 1970s and 1980s.

In short, foreign observers and domestic participants came to opposite conclusions about industrial policy in the FRG. According to American admirers of German policies, West German research and technology policy in the 1970s made for an effective strategy of "active" structural adjustment. The German model as managed by the Social Democratic Research Ministry offered much worth emulating as far as America's late-blooming high-tech corporatists, the so-called Atari Democrats, were concerned. But according to the Social Democrats who were administering this model "strategy," much more was needed in the way of an active structural policy if West Germany was going to master future crises as effectively as it had overcome recession in the past.

POLICY ADJUSTMENT IN THE FEDERAL REPUBLIC: THE ROLES OF ECONOMIC ADVICE, INTEREST POLITICS, AND INDUSTRIAL STRATEGY

Each of the above models or images of the state in the capitalist economy draws attention to some important feature of West German economic policy during the Keynesian era. But each image is partial. None alone can explain the record of change over the last two decades. Nor can any one of these models accurately predict the future of the West German economy.

As in the United States, economic thinking in the FRG has undergone a general shift from Keynesian "demand-side" economics to various kinds of "supply-side" economics (whether monetarism on the right or industrial policy further to the left). It is one thing to note and document these changes in fashionable economic philosophies, but it is quite another thing to leap to the conclusion that these changes have had an overwhelming impact on economic policy. For characterizations like "Keynesian revolution," "monetarist counterrevolution," or "structural policy for a structural crisis" do not adequately capture the record of policy change in the FRG.

The "Keynesian" economists who inspired the Stability and Growth Act were very much concerned with monetary stability. The recovery programs they authored in 1967 combined a very limited amount of deficit spending with equal amounts of budgetary cutbacks. The same pattern of fiscal stimulation matched by fiscal consolidation was applied after the recession of 1975. The government practiced a conservative kind of compensatory finance, using federal spending as a temporary substitute for lost private demand and trying hard not to distort the export-oriented demand structure of the West German economy in the process.

The government's recovery strategy of 1975–77 *looked* like an abandonment of Keynesianism only because the government was not practicing the kind of deficit spending that it had never practiced in the first place but that Keynesian economists now thought was necessary: the state was not *over*compensating for lost private demand. Monetarist influence *appeared* to be at its height only because of the Bundesbank's new and more public preoccupation with monetary indicators. This preoccupation had less to do with the economics of Milton Friedman and more to do with the obsolescence of a monetary indicator that predated the high domestic inflation and international monetary turbulence of the 1970s. The Bundesbank did undertake drastic steps to make its new indicators work, but the reasons for its Draconian policy were more institutional than ideological.

Finally, the debate over a new structural policy had little to do with the merits of any structural crisis diagnosis. Not only was the post-Keynesian emphasis on industrial policy far from commanding a consensus among economists, but there was not even a single view of structural policy with which one could agree or disagree. "Structural policy" meant different things to different people. Liberals and conservatives emphasized those aspects of structural policy most consistent with market principles and a low-profile state. Social Democrats had in mind a structural policy to be based either on a technocratic consensus or on trade union participation. What "structural policy" meant depended very much on where one stood in relation to the Social–Liberal policy-making establishment.

Does this mean that terms like *Keynesian, monetarist,* and *structural* were completely meaningless in the Social Democratic era? Not exactly. These economic doctrines and the public philosophies associated with them have meant something, but only if one ignores what they represent as academic schools of thought. Keynesian, monetarist, and structural perspectives have been important ideas because of the way they have regulated the relationship between proposed institutional innovations and the types of interest politics associated with these innovations. Each school of economic thought has made its contribution not as a crisis diagnosis but as an ideology of political intervention into the economy—as a set of ideas about the proper division of responsibilities between the public and private halves of "organized capitalism" in the FRG.

Thus, Keynesianism was a key component of the switch to "global guidance"—as Karl Schiller's brand of government intervention was called—because of the way Schiller used one important aspect of Keynes's thought: the distinction between microeconomics (the economics of individual, competing firms) and macroeconomics (the economics of large national aggregates). Schiller used the distinction to justify a more interventionist state, to show that planning (at the macro level) could be made safe for the "market" (at the micro level). In this way Schiller also demonstrated that he had no intention of harming the holiest cow of West German capitalism, the autonomy of collective bargaining (Tarifautonomie), i.e., the freedom of private sector wage and price determination from direct government control.

The Social Democratic economics minister wanted to show that he was against *direct* wage and price controls because another major component of his global guidance package was a program of *indirect* wage restraint. Schiller and the Keynesian economists of the 1960s hoped that unions, businesses, and government could reach agreement on a set of guidelines for moderate growth in wages, prices, and government spending. Schiller called this social contract of labor, capital, and the state a "concerted action" in order to underline its voluntary character. It was hoped that these self-regulating (or indicative) guidelines would stop inflation before the Bundesbank was forced to intervene and deliberately induce a recession or "stabilization crisis" in order to cool an overheated economy.

The increased emphasis on monetary matters in the 1970s did not fundamentally alter the way that global guidance divided responsibility for economic welfare between an aggregate-regulating (macroeconomic) state and an otherwise self-regulating (microeconomic) private sector. Stricter monetary guidelines were intended to highlight the limits to— and contours of—this not always clear-cut division of responsibilities. The concerted action was supplemented by a new kind of indicative incomes policy, dubbed the "monetary mantle" in order to stress the government's seriousness about limiting income growth via a strictly controlled money supply.

Structural policy occupied an untidy no-man's-land between the market and the state. For, as economists like Joan Robinson pointed out quite early in the 1970s (Robinson, 1972), the left-Keynesian perspective typically associated with structural policy raised issues that threatened to explode the division between the macroeconomic state and the microeconomic institutions of the labor and commodity markets. Even more important than the undetermined accuracy of any structural crisis diagnosis was the unpreparedness of West German politics for the ideology of state intervention that went along with a high-level structural policy. Within the SPD, structural policy came to prominence as part of a controversy over investment guidance *(Investionslenkung)*. As far as most businesspeople were concerned, investment guidance was a red flag. Even union leaders could be scared into thinking that investment guidance would spell the end of free collective bargaining.

Another reason that the corporatist vision of an "active structural policy" favored by some Social Democrats never got very far during the 1970s was that the SPD left's program for obtaining a consensus on industrial policy was overambitious. The program, which depended on the creation of "structural councils" representing business and labor, struck no sympathetic chord within the inner circles of the Bonn establishment—the Economics and Finance ministries, the FDP, and the right-of-center Social Democrats around Schmidt. After a lukewarm recovery from the recession of 1975, the Social–Liberal government headed by Schmidt realized that the economic expectations of most Germans had been dampened by the oil crisis and a perception that the economic crisis of the 1970s was international, not solely German. Only left-of-center Social Democrats and the relatively powerless Research Ministry worried about forging a high-level consensus on issues of structural change. Some union economists, representing sectors with special problems like overcapacity, also had a strong interest in structural policy. But these union spokesmen could not speak for the entire DGB (West Germany's trade union confederation). Nor could proposed innovations like the structural councils—an essentially sectoral approach to planning—replace the unions' overriding interest in seeking greater influence via codetermination, or union representation on the company boards of individual enterprises. German business and its political sponsors in the FDP and CDU had very little interest in a new industrial policy.

Finally, by the late 1970s, the policy-making establishment was coping unexpectedly well with the FRG's comparatively mild economic crisis. The Social–Liberal government was therefore unreceptive to innovative proposals on industrial policy emanating from the Social Democratic left and the SPD-controlled Research Ministry. In spite of the growing importance of industrial policy, the centers of policy making in Bonn and Frankfurt (West Germany's financial capital) remained what they were in the 1960s—the Bundesbank, the Economics Ministry, and the Finance Ministry. Although the Research Ministry's status was upgraded somewhat by the Brandt and Schmidt administrations, West Germany has still not acquired the kind of technocratic planning apparatus that has long been characteristic of French or Japanese industrial policy.

WEST GERMANY'S POST-KEYNESIAN FUTURE: THE LIMITS TO INDUSTRIAL CORPORATISM

The record of policy choice and change in the FRG betrays the political establishment's overriding concern with economic stability as well as Bonn's occasional willingness to sponsor innovations that promote peaceful coexistence between the state's most powerful policy-making institutions and the private sector's most important peak associations. Over the last thirty years, this stable arrangement has proved compatible with a variety of styles in interest group bargaining, economic ideas, and institutional accommodations. But prior to 1980, stability-conscious "Model Germany" never had to confront such serious problems—jobless rates refusing to get under 8 or 9 percent, industrial production falling for more than two years in a row, less secure international markets for the goods West Germany has traditionally excelled at exporting, and a possibly severe technological lag behind Japan and the United States. The success of past stabilization policy combined with the uncertainty of future industrial adjustment has raised a new set of questions for the government and opposition in the changed political constellation of the 1980s. What is the future of West German economic policy now that the era of Keynesian intervention and Social Democratic reforms has come to a definitive end, while a new period of Christian Democratic emphasis on capitalist "basics" is under way? Will the enthusiasm of the CDU and FDP for free market solutions lead the Kohl government to the extremes of Margaret Thatcher and Ronald Reagan? Or will West Germany, in spite of its ideologically conservative leadership, have to move closer toward a corporatist industrial policy?

As the Federal Republic moved rapidly from Schmidt's second reelection triumph in 1980 toward the serious economic and political crisis that brought Kohl to power, post-Keynesian perspectives on the West German economy became disoriented in a manner that upset almost everyone's expectations about the future of the German model. It appears as though foreign admirers of West German industrial policy had underestimated the impact of economic crisis on what they saw as the Federal Republic's successful strategy of industrial competitiveness. At the same time, the Social Democratic left seems to have overestimated the responsiveness of the crisis-managing establishment to new economic crisis diagnoses.

After the political *Wende* of 1982–83, the Kohl government came to power with a commitment to reverse the course set by the SPD for a decade. The Christian Democrat who took control of the Research Ministry decided to cut back on the sort of direct aid and project-oriented research and development funding admired by America's "Atari Democrats." The CDU set about replacing direct government subsidies of specific R&D projects with more indirect, general incentives, like tax breaks. In specific sectors—steel, electronics, and shipbuilding—the Kohl government has avoided promoting "winners" and easing out "losers" as would be required by an active industrial policy.

To a large extent, the Christian Democratic coalition is simply following habits already practiced by the previous government, which had the same economics minister, Otto Lambsdorff. It was the Schmidt government that hesitated to bail out the failing electronics firm AEG. With respect to shipbuilding on the Bremen wharves and steel in the Ruhr industrial basin, the current government has encouraged industrial restructuring in the same manner that the previous government facilitated the orderly collapse of AEG: it has encouraged crisis-ridden companies, together with their unions and banks, to consolidate using their own resources. The shipbuilding industry has been urged to cut back on excess capacity; steel companies have been asked to merge into larger units. Where required by EEC authorities (such as the Common Market's Davignon Commission) to reduce overcapacity and exports in steel, the Germans have done so under protest that their steel firms are less heavily subsidized. The German Cartel Office (the FRG's antitrust authority) frustrated the French plan to carve out a special European (i.e. non-Japanese) niche for video electronics when it blocked the acquisition of a controlling share in Grundig by the state-owned French firm Thompson-Brandt. In short, recent research policy and sectoral policy have been moving in the direction of a lower government profile, especially since the political turnabout of 1982–83. The trend toward privatization quickened as the West German economy edged closer toward a severe economic crisis. This has been disappointing to those advocates of an active structural policy who expected that a deeper structural crisis would demand a more comprehensive industrial policy.

The striking thing about structural crisis management in the late 1970s and early 1980s was that industrial policy came to mean entirely different things to different people. Free trade liberals believed that West

Germany was undergoing a structural crisis only to the extent that the country's unusual industrial structure ("overindustrialization" and an "underdeveloped" service sector) had been distorted by the effects of a currency that had been priced under its market value for too long. Social Democratic technocrats in the Research Ministry wanted a policy of "active structural adjustment" along the lines of Hauff and Scharpf. Some socialist and trade union economists favored industrial policies designed to make sure that West Germany remained a high-wage country. The Free Democratic Economics Ministry believed that businesses and their trade associations were the best judges of sectoral trends. The Council of Experts thought that it was wrong for the state and the unions to force the pace of structural change via high wages.

The limits to structural policy suggest that there are limits to high-level corporatism in the Federal Republic. Both the Kohl and Schmidt governments appreciated that a corporatist consensus of capital and labor is easier for the government to manage when the major actors are limited to specific economic sectors—companies, banks, trade associations, and unions. In a country like West Germany, where capitalism is organized into peak associations that are more highly aggregated than Britain's but not as centralized as Austria's or Sweden's, it is easier for the government to delegate industrial policy to industrial sectors than for the state itself to forge a national consensus on winners and losers. And in a country with a defensive parliamentary establishment, a powerful central bank but not so powerful Research Ministry, and a system of collective bargaining that jealously guards its autonomy, it is hard to legitimate the kind of technocratic public philosophy that goes along with an active structural policy.

Two increasingly important constraints on the Bonn government's ability to pursue corporatist policies for West German industry are the limitations imposed by labor costs and the world economy. When the Keynesian revolution began in the mid-1960s, both wages and the international value of the currency (the DM) were relatively low. Low wages and an undervalued DM gave policy makers in Bonn unusual flexibility as they set about reforming economic policy and trying to reconcile stability with growth. But early in the 1970s, labor costs began to rise, while the DM moved within a few short years from being chronically undervalued to its present status (somewhat tarnished by the dollar's comeback in the early 1980s) as a strong, highly coveted currency. The successes of German wage earners and the currency in which they were paid made it more difficult for the Federal Republic to maintain its international competitive edge in the 1970s. The economy of the FRG did hold on to its relatively strong position as a leading exporter, but only at the cost of greater vigilance in the fight against inflation and wage demands. The supporters of an active structural policy have refused to bow to the internal constraint of higher labor costs and the external constraint of a more competitive, more crisis-ridden world economy. They hope that, by redefining West Germany as a high-wage country producing and exporting high value-added products within a new worldwide division of labor, the FRG can overcome the constraints of German wages and the international economy.

This political vision of an activist future for industrial policy is unlikely to encounter much sympathy from the Christian Democrats and Free Democrats in the current Bonn government. And it remains to be seen whether the entire SPD in opposition will fully embrace this post-Keynesian future, now that the FDP and Schmidt no longer mediate between Social Democratic principles and capitalist realities. The first year of economic policy under Kohl and Lambsdorff was a lackluster year, characterized by relatively uncontroversial budgetary cutbacks and cautious conservatism. Although the Social Democrats, like their counterparts in the American Democratic party, attacked the government on the "fairness" issue, the SPD was not able to formulate effective counterproposals in time for the March 1983 elections. Accordingly, West German economic policy since the *Wende* has proceeded within a programmatic vacuum.

However, the lack of meaningful alternatives on the right and left of the West German political spectrum need not last throughout the 1980s. There is at least one economic issue that may reignite genuine controversy between the government and the opposition. The trade union proposal for a thirty-five-hour week has elicited support from the SPD and resistance from the government parties (who came up with a counterproposal emphasizing the early retirement of older workers). And it is possible that industrial policy, a dormant issue in the first year of the *Wende,* may experience a political revival. The revival of the structural policy issue could come from one of two directions.

In the *Länder* (provinces) of southern Germany, most notably in Baden-Wurtemberg, Christian Democratic provincial governments have been somewhat more concerned about industrial policy than the Kohl government in Bonn. Like the American "Sunbelt," some of the south German *Länder* have developed modern industries that are less dependent on the intensive use of energy and less prone to economic obsolescence than the traditional smokestack industries of the north. But unlike their conservative counterparts in the American southwest, entrepreneurs and Christian Democratic politicians from the Black Forest and Bavaria are not averse to interventionist state policies that will help their electronics and machine tool manufacturers stand up to intensified Japanese (and American) competition. Whether the Kohl government takes note of the call for a more active industrial policy will depend on the extent of economic recovery in the early 1980s and on possible changes in the composition and governing style of the CDU–FDP coalition.

During his first year in office, Chancellor Kohl (who, unlike his predecessor Schmidt, has no special expertise in economics) delegated responsibility for economic policy to other cabinet members (Economics Minister Lambsdorff from the FDP, Finance Minister Gerhard Stolten-berg, and Labor Minister Norbert Blüm from the CDU). Kohl's style of governing has been low-key, in contrast to the authoritative manner of former Chancellor Schmidt. Unlike both Schmidt and Karl Schiller, the dominant personalities in the wake of the 1975 and 1966–67 recessions, Kohl has not equipped his government with a distinctive strategy for economic recovery. Serious economic strategy has fallen by default to those central bankers and business leaders who since at least 1980 have been calling for higher profits, tax relief, less welfare spending, and a government willing to tough it out until the West German economy becomes competitive again. Instead of dictating and enforcing policy guidelines designed to go along with this conservative prescription, Kohl has been more concerned with promoting collegial harmony in the Chris-tian–Liberal coalition and with reviving conservative values in the coun-try at large.

Yet it is possible that a combination of slow economic revival, coali-tion politics, and a political rebellion against Kohl within the CDU could lead to changes in the government's economic policy and governing style. One possibility is that Franz-Josef Strauss, the ambitious but controversial leader of the right-wing Bavarian CSU (and finance minister from 1966 to 1969), will engineer his way into the Bonn government and take charge of economic policy in a way that Kohl has been unwilling to do. One oppor-tunity for Strauss came and went in June 1984, when Economics Minister Lambsdorff, long under investigation on a bribery and corruption charge involving the Flick corporation, was formally indicted and resigned his office. Although Kohl outmaneuvered Strauss by replacing Lambsdorff with another Free Democrat, Martin Bangemann, this appointment did not entirely put the issue of economic policy leadership to rest. Unlike either Lambsdorff or Strauss, Bangemann has little experience in eco-nomic affairs and no following in the business community. As an addi-tional handicap, the liberal Free Democrats appear to have become a dying party. Unable to get a required 5 percent of the votes in several recent elections, the FDP now lives at the mercy of sympathetic Chris-tian Democrats like Kohl. Should the Free Democrats fail to enter the Bundestag in the next general elections scheduled for 1987, their disap-pearance would mean more than a victory for right-wing politicians like

Strauss. It would also represent a loss for the neoliberal market ideology that has long served as a bulwark against the interventionist tendencies of both major parties.

Meanwhile, the Social Democratic party may get a chance to sort out its own post-Keynesian future in the opposition. During the 1983 election campaign, the new Social Democratic chancellor candidate, Hans-Jochen Vogel, and his economic adviser, Hans-Jürgen Krupp, devised a last-minute economic platform emphasizing job creation in public service and ecological projects. The low cost of the Krupp–Vogel plan helped the SPD to skirt the issue of high budget deficits, while the plan's emphasis on the long-term unemployed and its ecological accent constituted an appeal to younger voters who were leaning toward the Greens in 1983. After the March 1983 elections, the SPD became less constrained by the fiscal legacy of the 1981 recession and by the pull of the Green and Alternative List on younger voters. Ever since the Social Democrats came out firmly against the stationing of new U.S. missiles at a party convention late in 1983, the SPD has not had to worry as much about the Greens (who have been in disarray over what to do now that the new missiles are in place on German territory). The SPD is today in a better position to concentrate on cultivating its traditional party base, the blue collar workers of the industrial north, who in 1983 felt neglected by their party and switched over to the CDU.

It remains to be seen whether a revived Social Democratic opposition or a recast Christian Democratic government will focus their economic attention on finding a new, high-level direction for industrial policy. From an intellectual point of view, the West German government badly needs a suitable post-Keynesian perspective for the 1980s. Yet, for all the limitations of traditional Keynesian economics, the very idea of a coherent industrial policy may destroy the one thing that the Keynesian philosophy was good at—drawing a clear-cut division of responsibilities between public (or political) and private (or economic) responsibilities for national welfare. By focusing on specific growth sectors of the economy, the post-Keynesian perspective of structural policy has broken down Keynes's distinction between macro- and microeconomics. In so doing, structural policy threatens to disturb the stable truce that has held West Germany's political and economic establishments together since the 1960s. The two establishments of "Model Germany," which have a strong stake in stability but have also demonstrated a limited capacity for reform, discovered that they needed each other in the stabilization crises of the past. But the state and organized capitalism in the FRG have yet to reach an institutional and ideological accommodation that would resolve the crisis of post-Keynesian political economy.

REFERENCES

Arbeitsgruppe "Alternative Wirtschaftspolitik." 1978. *Memorandum: Alternativen der Wirtschaftspolitik.* Cologne: Bund.

Baisch, H., et al. 1977. "Die Wirtschaftskrise in der BRD." *Leviathan* 2.

Calleo, D. 1978. *The German Problem Reconsidered.* Cambridge: Cambridge University Press.

Hankel, W. 1975. *Der Ausweg aus der Krise.* Düsseldorf: Econ.

Hauff, V., and Scharpf, F. 1975. *Modernisierung der Volkswirtschaft: Technologiepolitik als Strukturpolitik.* Frankfurt: EVA.

Katzenstein, P. 1982. "West Germany as Number Two: Reflections on the German Model." In *The Political Economy of West Germany,* ed. A. Markovits. New York: Praeger.

Katzenstein, P., ed. 1978. *Between Power and Plenty: Foreign Economic Policies of Advanced Industrial States.* Madison: University of Wisconsin Press.

Keohane, R. 1978. "Economics, Inflation, and the Role of the State." *World Politics* 31:108–28.

Kindleberger, C. 1965. "Germany's Persistent Balance-of-Payments Disequilibrium." In *Trade, Growth and the Balance of Payments,* ed. R. E. Baldwin et al. Chicago: Rand McNally.

Kreile, M. 1978. "West Germany: The Dynamics of Expansion." In *Between Power and Plenty,* ed. P. Katzenstein. Madison: University of Wisconsin Press.

Küster, G. H. 1974. "Germany." In *Big Business and the State: Changing Relations in Western Europe,* by R. Vernon. Cambridge: Harvard University Press.

MacLennan, M., Forsyth, M., and Denton, G. 1968. *Economic Planning and Policies in Britain, France, and Germany.* New York: Praeger.

Markmann, H., and Simmert, D. B., eds. 1978. *Krise der Wirtschaftspolitik: Krise der ökonomischen Theorie?* Cologne: Bund.

Markovits, A., ed. 1982. *The Political Economy of West Germany: Modell Deutschland.* New York: Praeger.

Narr, W.-D., and Offe, C. 1976. "Was heisst hier Strukturpolitik? Neokorporativismus als Rettung aus der Krise?" In *Technologie und Politik, Aktuell-Magazin 6,* ed. F. Duve. Reinbek bei Hamburg: Rowohlt.

Oertzen, P. von, Ehmke, H., and Ehrenberg, H. 1974 *Thema: Wirtschaftspolitik.* Bonn-Bad Godesberg: Verlag Neue Gesellschaft.

Reich, R. 1983. "Beyond Free Trade." *Foreign Affairs* 61, no. 4.

Reich, R., and Magaziner, I. 1982. *Minding America's Business: The Decline and Rise of the American Economy.* New York: Harcourt Brace Jovanovich.

Riemer, J. 1982. "Alterations in the Design of Model Germany: Critical Innovations in the Policy Machinery for Economic Steering." In *The Political Economy of West Germany,* ed. A. Markovits. New York: Praeger.

Riese, H. 1975. *Wohlfahrt und Wirtschaftspolitik.* Reinbek bei Hamburg: Rowohlt.

Robinson, J. 1972. "The Second Crisis of Economic Theory." *American Economic Review* 62 (May).

Sarrazin, T., ed. 1976. *Investionslenkung.* Bonn-Bad Godesberg: Verlag Neue Gesellschaft.

Schmitter, P., and Lehmbruch, G., eds. 1979. *Trends Toward Corporatist Intermediation.* Beverly Hills, Calif.: Sage.

Shonfield, A. 1969. *Modern Capitalism.* New York: Oxford University Press.

ECONOMIC CONDITIONS
AND POLITICAL BEHAVIOR

To what extent are governments judged on the basis of economic performance? A sizable body of research has accumulated in the past fifteen years on the economic determinants of government popularity and voting behavior. Political scientists and economists have formulated increasingly sophisticated econometric models for estimating the political significance of such factors as real income growth, unemployment, and inflation rates. They have also attempted to relate government policy making to electoral requisites by postulating and testing for the existence of "political business cycles"—i.e., deliberate manipulation of the economy by incumbent authorities to enhance their chances for reelection. Are these theories validated by recent experience? Or is there evidence that governments may now be evaluated differently than in the past?

In their study of public support for the Thatcher and Reagan administrations (Chapter 11), Steven Schier and Norman Vig find that both leaders came to power largely as a result of negative restrospective judgments about previous administrations rather than because of any ideological shift in the electorate. But the authors find striking differences in the relevance of economic factors to the continuing popularity of the two governments and conclude that unintended and unforeseen events have had a major influence in both cases. Why was Reagan's economic strategy more attuned to the electoral cycle than Thatcher's? Can these governments maintain public support given the new problems they face?

The election of a Socialist president and government in France in 1981 stood in marked contrast to the rightward trend in Britain and the United States.

In Chapter 12, Michael Lewis-Beck notes that, as in the 1980 American presidential election, negative retrospective evaluations of the incumbent produced the margin necessary to elect François Mitterrand. This shift resulted from a direct link many voters saw between their personal economic situations and governmental policies, as well as their negative views of national economic conditions. These patterns also seem to explain the declining popularity of Socialist rule as economic conditions deteriorated and the recent efforts of President Mitterrand to recapture middle-class support by appointing a new cabinet that excludes the Communists. Must Mitterrand also hope for unforeseen events to boost his popularity? Has his government fatally overstepped the bounds of popular legitimacy in enforcing tough economic policies?

The most involved and extensive studies of the relationships of economic opinions to voting choice have focused on American national elections. In Chapter 13, D. Roderick Kiewiet summarizes much of the theory resulting from these studies and applies it in an investigation of survey data on presidential voting from 1960 to 1980. Kiewiet finds evidence that voters employ a number of decision rules when evaluating candidates and their policies. In particular, he argues that although voters judge the incumbents retrospectively, they do not simply act on the basis of their recent personal experience but make broader assessments of the national economy and government policies. This is in contrast to the strong relation of personal assessments to voting choice that Lewis-Beck discovered in France. Which framework of evaluation seems more appropriate for popular judgment? What lessons for understanding recent American elections are found in Kiewiet's analysis?

The selections point to the wide variety of influences upon public opinion formation and voting behavior, which require complex modes of analysis if they are to be fully understood. An important goal of this research is to sort out the enduring, short-term, and unpredictable influences of economic phenomena upon mass evaluations of governments and individual leaders. These relationships fully merit the careful attention they receive in the following chapters, for at issue here are the fundamental democratic components of a nation's political economy.

11 ECONOMIC PERFORMANCE AND MASS SUPPORT: THE THATCHER AND REAGAN REGIMES

Steven E. Schier and Norman J. Vig

For the first time in half a century, British and American governments are attempting to revive their economies by cutting public spending and vigorously controlling the money supply. In the 1930s, governments following deflationary, budget-balancing policies were discredited by massive unemployment, and Keynesian "pump priming" gradually replaced the old fiscal orthodoxy. After World War II, macroeconomic management to stabilize business cycles and promote full employment and growth provided the basis for a new political consensus. But when both inflation and unemployment began accelerating in the 1970s and wage-price controls and other government interventions failed to stem the tide, neoconservatives demanding a return to monetary discipline and laissez-faire principles gained ascendancy once again. Prime Minister Thatcher and President Reagan came into office determined to halt inflation, limit the size and scope of government, and restore incentives for private enterprise.

Beyond these similarities, there were some important differences between "Thatcherism" and "Reaganomics" (see Chapter 8). The Thatcher government has adopted a rigid monetarist strategy aimed at wringing inflation out of the economy as a precondition for long-term recovery and growth. The massive unemployment and bankruptcies that followed have been justified as part of a painful but necessary transition to a more competitive economy; indeed, Mrs. Thatcher has made a virtue out of sticking to her policies despite continuing economic adversity.

Reaganomics, on the other hand, was an unusual blend of monetary restraint and a highly expansionary fiscal policy. While the Federal Reserve Board controlled inflation, the historic 1981 tax reduction promised to stimulate investment and output on the "supply side" of the economy. Reagan's strategy was risky because of potential conflicts between its monetary and fiscal components and because it promised a quick and relatively painless turnaround in the American economy. But it represented a positive alternative that had greater political appeal than Thatcher's austere brand of capitalism.

To some extent Reagan and Thatcher have succeeded in their objectives. Although government spending has increased rather than decreased, its rate of growth has slowed down. In both countries the inflation rate was cut by more than half by 1983. But the deflation was accompanied by the worst recession and highest unemployment rates since the 1930s. When Mrs. Thatcher won reelection in June 1983, 12.4 percent of the British labor force was out of work and national output was lower than when she had taken office four years earlier. In the United States unemployment also peaked at over 10 percent in 1982, and real interest rates remained at historically high levels. The large tax cuts contributed to a vigorous recovery in 1983–84 but also produced enormous budget deficits that threatened long-term stability and growth. Yet in 1984 President Reagan won reelection by a landslide.

This chapter focuses on the *political* success of the Thatcher and Reagan governments—specifically, on whether their mass political support can be attributed to their economic policies and performance. A sizable literature on the economic determinants of voting behavior and presidential or governmental popularity has developed over the past decade, and part of our purpose is to evaluate the relevance of such theories to the surprising strength of the new conservative regimes. In the next section we briefly discuss formal economic support models and in the following two sections go on to the British and American case studies. Finally, we attempt to draw some comparative conclusions about the relationship between economic policy and political support in the two countries.

THE MUDDLE OF MODELS

It has long been suspected that the popularity of leaders rises and falls with the state of the economy. Since 1970 a great deal of effort has been put into attempts to specify, in quantitative terms, the relationships between government (or presidential) support and economic conditions. Early research (Goodhart and Bhansali, 1970; Mueller, 1970; Kramer,

1971) suggested that government popularity and hence voting behavior could be modeled as a function of a few variables such as real income, unemployment, and inflation. Criticisms of the initial models stimulated the development of more complex regression equations, some of which statistically explained 70 percent or more of the past variation in governmental or presidential popularity (e.g. Frey, 1978; Pissarides, 1980; Kernell, 1978; Ostrom and Simon, 1984). These models were applied to several of the advanced capitalist democracies (Whitely, 1980).

If government popularity was shown to vary closely with economic performance, it was only a short step to the conclusion that incumbents would attempt to manipulate the business cycle to maximize support at election time. In the United States, Nordhaus (1975), Tufte (1978), and others presented evidence of a regular "political business cycle" by which administrations pumped up the economy in election years to improve their popularity. Frey and Schneider (1978) tried to close the circle by developing larger models in which government policies were a function of the size of the incumbent party's lead over the opposition, which in turn reflected the government's success in managing the economy.

It has been difficult to formulate micro-level hypotheses linking individual behavior to the aggregate outcomes that are statistically "explained." Most of the existing models assume that people respond directly to their current economic situation (or act "as if" they do). Voters are thus seen as short-sighted utility maximizers who reward or punish the incumbent authorities according to whether their personal financial condition has improved or deteriorated in the period just prior to the election. However, scholars such as Kinder and Kiewiet (1981), Chappell (1983), and Ursprung (1984) have posited a number of alternative behavioral models that suggest more sophisticated assessment of government economic performance (see Chapter 13 by Kiewiet in this volume). On the government side, existence of the political business cycle has also been called into question, especially as applied to Britain (Alt and Chrystal, 1983).

Thus, rather than attempting to apply a specific model, we will examine a broad range of empirical data on support for the Thatcher and Reagan regimes and seek to draw some comparative conclusions that point toward more useful theoretical approaches.

SUPPORT FOR THE THATCHER GOVERNMENT

Before considering Mrs. Thatcher's electoral success, it is important to put her victories in rough perspective. Figure 11.1 shows the level of support for British governments since 1970 (as indicated by responses to the monthly Gallup Poll question, "If there were a general election to-morrow, which party would you support?"). It is evident that Mrs. Thatcher's support has been less stable than her predecessors'. Her government experienced an abnormally steep popularity loss and recovery. At the midterm low, in December 1981, only 20 percent of Gallup respondents approved of the government's handling of economic and financial affairs (68 percent disapproved), and only 23 percent said they would vote for the Conservatives if an election were held then (Figure 11.2). In fact, the Conservative share of the popular vote in 1979 (43.9 percent) was lower than in any Tory victory since the war, and actually declined 1.5 percent further in the "landslide" of 1983. The gain of fifty-eight parliamentary seats in June 1983 was due not to increased support but to a divided opposition and redistricting of seats (Crewe, 1983).

Nevertheless, Mrs. Thatcher's successful appeal to "stay the course" in 1983 was a remarkable achievement. No full-term British government had gained reelection since 1959, when Harold Macmillan won a third Conservative victory on a program of "You never had it so good." Mrs. Thatcher could scarcely make such claims, with the highest levels of unemployment and the worst economic growth record since the Great Depression. Furthermore, it had become more difficult for any government to maintain support as party "dealignment" had produced an increasingly volatile electorate prone to negative voting (Särlvik and Crewe, 1983). As in the United States, numerous opinion surveys indicated declining confidence in government as economic crises came to dominate the political agenda in the 1970s (Alt, 1979). Yet the prime minister was able to gain another five years to carry out her conservative economic experiment. How can we explain this, especially given the state of the British economy?

An Ideological Mandate?

One possible explanation for political support in the absence of specific achievement is that the government has won a broader ideological mandate. Some have argued that Thatcher's election signals a fundamental ideological shift to the right in the British electorate—or at least a major departure from the postwar Keynesian welfare state consensus (Wattenberg, 1979; Butt, 1983). But most students of public attitudes give a different answer. Ivor Crewe, in analyses of survey data collected during the 1979 and 1983 elections, concludes that in both cases the Conservative victory was much more attributable to negative voting against Labour than to popular embrace of Thatcher's economic doctrines (Crewe, 1981, 1983). He reports that in 1983 "59 percent of all voters—and 73 percent of those deciding during the campaign—said they disliked the other party

Figure 11.1
Government Support in Britain, 1970–1983

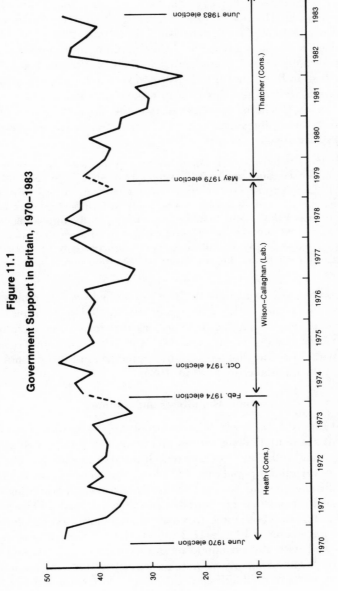

*Percent saying they would vote for the party in office if an election were held tomorrow in Gallup poll monthly surveys (end of quarter observations, adjusted to exclude "Don't Knows"). Dotted lines indicate change of party.

Source: Webb and Wybrow, 1981, and Monthly Gallup Political Indexes.

(ies) more than they liked their own" (Crewe, 1983, 58). Vernon Bogdanor states that the government's electoral support "was fundamentally negative—fear of Labour—rather than positive—support for a Conservative counterrevolution. The result of the election, therefore, can in no way be construed as a mandate for 'Thatcherism'" (Bogdanor, 1983, 17).

Nor do surveys show any major change in public attitudes toward the role of government. For example, polls taken in 1979 and at regular intervals since indicate that the British people would rather pay higher taxes than see welfare services cut. In an analysis based on a detailed Marplan survey, Richard Rose argues that the majority of the British support *both* the capitalist free market to generate wealth *and* state programs to ensure welfare.

> Unlike Mrs. Thatcher and President Reagan, who often rail against government as necessarily bad, ordinary voters are pro-market but not antistate. . . . Whereas most Americans would probably regard British government as claiming too large a share of the national product in taxation, most Britons think that it is too small. . . . Notwithstanding its electoral success, the Thatcher government has failed to secure popular support for an effective tax-cutting policy, which can only be carried through by cutting spending on major welfare state programs (Rose, 1983, 14).

Or, as Everett Carll Ladd puts it, "The public had become ambivalent about government, not hostile to it" (Ladd, 1983b, 6). On the other hand, public opinion was strongly antisocialist, as that term is understood in Britain. In 1979, and even more so in 1983, the British electorate rejected socialism without embracing laissez-faire capitalism; but this did not represent any fundamental change (Rose, 1983).

Economic Conditions and Support

A glance at Figure 11.2, in which indicators of support for Mrs. Thatcher's government are plotted along with economic performance variables (unemployment and inflation rates and real disposable income), might suggest that government popularity (A) closely reflects approval for its handling of economic and financial affairs (B). However, covariation does not necessarily mean that one variable has a causal relationship to the other, and in this case both indicators may be responding to other factors.

Closer inspection of Figure 11.2 reveals that neither support rating correlates well with the economic indicators (C, D, E). Although the inflation rate declined sharply from its peak in early 1980, the unemployment rate more than doubled, and real disposable income fell and then inched up only slightly in the year before the election. This scarcely has the appearance of a successful political business cycle (nor, probably, was

Figure 11.2

British Government Support and Economic Performance 1979–1983

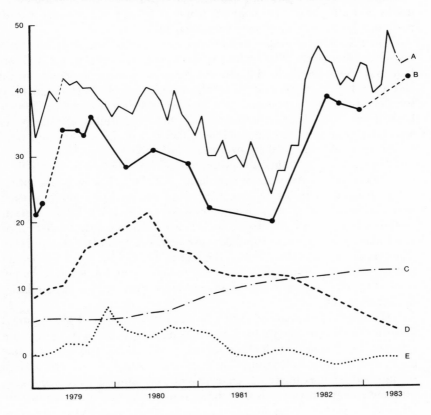

A = Government support (percent stating they would vote for
    the government in Gallup survey).
B = Economic policy approval (percent approving government handling
    of economic and financial affairs in Gallup surveys).
C = Unemployment rate. Source: CSO, *Economic Trends.*
D = Inflation rate (consumer price index, all items).
    Source: CSO, *Economic Trends.*
E = Real per capita disposable income (percentage change).
    Source: CSO, *Economic Trends.*

that Mrs. Thatcher's intent). Unless the inflation rate is the only economic
variable that counts, one can hardly explain the government's dramatic
political recovery in terms of current economic performance.

Econometric support models developed prior to 1979 do not predict
well for the Thatcher government. Most would indicate that the Conservatives should have been trailing the oppostion by a wide margin in
1982–83, given Thatcher's economic record (see, e.g., Figure 11.3).

There are two obvious reasons for this misfit: the quantitative relation-ships between government popularity and such factors as the inflation and unemployment rates are not stable over time; and prior models were predicated on a two-party contest, whereas Britain had genuine three-party competition during the period 1981–83.

The first of these problems had been discussed earlier by James Alt in his perceptive study, *The Politics of Economic Decline.* He pointed out that "unprecedentedly high levels of inflation and unemployment during and after 1974 suggest that whatever magnitudes of effect might have been attributed to these economic variables in earlier years will no longer hold" (Alt, 1979, 116). In other words, the magnitudes of the effects associated with any variable such as inflation will differ from one time period to another as public perceptions and expectations change. When problems such as inflation are perceived as reaching "crisis" levels they may indeed affect government popularity, but the public may also antici-pate and discount trends or otherwise adapt to changing conditions such as higher levels of inflation or unemployment (Alt, 1979, 120ff). In fact, neither Chrystal and Alt (1981) nor Pissarides (1980) found inflation or unemployment to be very significant predictors of government popularity when models were extended into the late 1970s. Certainly neither would suggest that the trade-off of higher unemployment for lower inflation worked by Mrs. Thatcher would account for her resurgence in popularity during 1982–83.

The second problem had not really been addressed, as it was assumed that the incumbent party's lead over the main opposition party was the relevant determinant of electoral outcomes (since third parties won few parliamentary seats in Britain's winner-take-all system). Thus, virtually all models had been estimated as government "lead" functions (i.e. the gov-ernment's share of responses to "how would you vote" polls minus the other major party's share, as in Figure 11.3). However, with the formation of the new Social Democratic party (SDP) in January 1981 and emergence of the Alliance (with the Liberals) later that year, a credible third-party alternative came into existence. While a model pitting the government against the combined opposition might have had some validity, those computed on the basis of the government's lead over the main opposition party were not applicable to a three-party situation.[1] As Figure 11.3 shows, the Conservatives gained sharply vis-à-vis Labour during 1981 at the same time as their overall popularity was declining, suggesting that defeat of the main opposition had little to do with the success of the government's economic policies (the recession being at its worst in that year).

The one area in which the government could claim unequivocal suc-cess was in cutting the inflation rate from double digits to about 4 percent

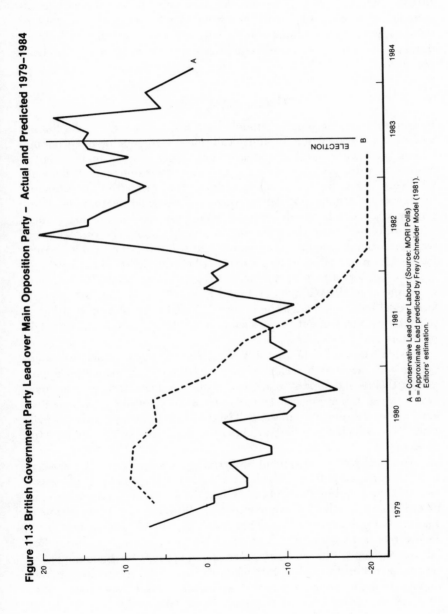

Figure 11.3 British Government Party Lead over Main Opposition Party – Actual and Predicted 1979–1984

A = Conservative Lead over Labour (Source: MORI Polls)
B = Approximate Lead predicted by Frey/Schneider Model (1981).
    Editors' estimation.

265

by early 1983. There is some evidence (to be discussed later) that controlling inflation was more important than reducing unemployment to the
British voters in 1983. However, the massive shift from Labour to Alliance opposition in 1981, and then from Alliance opposition to government support in the first half of 1982, suggests that something much more
dramatic than macroeconomic conditions was affecting Mrs. Thatcher's
popularity.

The Impact of Events

British government support models have not contained terms (dummy
variables) to account for the impact of major economic or noneconomic
events (as have several presidential popularity models in the United
States). In retrospect this must be seen as a major omission. It does not
take very much sophistication to observe that instead of governments
undergoing a regular popularity cycle with marginal fluctuations determined by economic trends, unusual events can account for major inter-
party shifts that make the difference at election time. The breakdown of
wage control policies and subsequent large-scale strikes probably account
for the sharp pre-election losses that marked the defeat of both Edward
Heath's Conservative government in 1974 and James Callaghan's Labour
government in 1979 (Figure 11.1; and King, 1981). Another steep popularity decline accompanied the severe financial crisis of 1976 that forced
the Labour government to seek emergency IMF loans and adopt tight
monetary and fiscal policies.

Examination of data for the years 1979–83 suggests that two major
events may account for most of the variation in government support
during this period: a party realignment that produced a sharp temporary
swing to the Liberal–Social Democratic Alliance during 1981; and Britain's successful recapture of the Falkland Islands from Argentina in April–
June 1982, which generated an unprecedented popularity rally for Mrs.
Thatcher.

The 1981 party realignment occurred in response to both the government's economic policies (which were highly unpopular in the first two
years, as indicated in Figure 11.2) and, at the same time, a disastrous loss
of credibility by the Labour opposition. Michael Foot's succession as
Labour party leader in November 1980, the breakaway of the Social
Democrats in January 1981, and the subsequent attempt by the radical
left to gain control of the party organization account for Labour's loss of
twenty points in the polls—just when the government reached its own
popularity nadir. Alliance support, on the other hand, was heavily *negative*, reflecting the extreme unpopularity of *both* major parties by late
1981.

The Falklands War was, without question, the decisive event in Mrs.

Thatcher's resurgence. MORI polls indicate that support for Mrs. Thatcher's handling of the issue increased from 60 percent in early April to 84 percent by the end of May (*Economist,* May 29, 1982, 22). Some 20 percent of the public that had expressed an intention to vote for the Alliance in late 1981 now swung back to the government, while Labour support remained about the same. As a result, Mrs. Thatcher regained all of the support she had lost over the first thirty months of her administration (and then some) in the second quarter of 1982. Party support then stabilized at about this level over the year before the election, with only a slight decline for Mrs. Thatcher from her Falklands peak.

To summarize, then, the 1979–83 period can be subdivided into four phases that highlight these shifts:

First, in the first eighteen months, the Conservative government lost popularity to the Labour opposition as traditional models would predict. By the end of 1980 the Conservatives trailed Labour in the polls by fourteen to sixteen points. This especially sharp downswing accompanied and no doubt reflected the onset of recession in the British economy.

Second, in the next twelve months, the period of realignment from January to December 1981, the government lost further ground to the combined opposition; but because Labour lost almost half of its total support to the Alliance, it ended up even with the Conservatives. The Alliance ballooned to over 40 percent in the polls.

Third, in the next six months support for the Alliance faded rapidly, and in the second quarter the Falklands rally produced an avalanche of support for the government. When Argentina occupied Port Stanley on April 2, the three parties were running about evenly in the polls. By May 25, after the successful Falklands landing, Mrs. Thatcher's party had jumped to 51 percent, and Labour and the Alliance had fallen to 25 percent and 22 percent, respectively.

Fourth, in the twelve-month runup to the reelection, government support stabilized at near its 1979 electoral level, Labour gained nothing, and the Alliance remained a credible third party that kept the opposition divided.

These shifts were dramatic enough to belie any simple correlation between economic conditions and government popularity. It is also instructive that such indicators as support for the government's handling of the economy, economic expectations for the next twelve months, and even retrospective assessments of whether the economy had gotten better or worse in the *past* twelve months all turned sharply upward and followed the trajectory of Mrs. Thatcher's popularity surge in the second quarter of 1982. This suggests that public economic evaluations can be highly "subjective" or sensitive to political influences, rather than vice versa.

Ivor Crewe has contended that the Falklands factor was relatively insignificant for the election, since by then only 1.4 percent of voters said that it influenced their vote (Crewe, 1983, 59). However, it is impossible to explain the massive swing to Mrs. Thatcher a year earlier without reference to the crisis, and it is likely that her military success had substantial indirect effects on the election. As one commentator explained,

> It was not the war that came to people's minds as a reason for casting a Conservative vote but a picture of the prime minister as someone who would gain respect for Britain abroad, had good judgment in a crisis, and offered a vision of where she wanted to lead the country. (Sackett, 1983, 38)

The Economist went even further in its assessment just prior to the 1983 election:

> The impact of the Falklands war on Mrs. Thatcher and the course of her government cannot be overstated. Had it not occurred, it is probable that pressure from within and outside the government would by late summer have driven Mrs. Thatcher into a major reflationary package or into resignation. . . . She had spent three years wrestling with the complexity of economics, failing and yet having to defend that failure in public. . . . War is simple. Where economics tore government and people apart, the war brought them together in organic unity. . . . The Falklands war transformed Mrs. Thatcher from an electoral liability into an indispensable asset. (*The Economist*, May 21, 1983, 26)

Issues, Expectations, and Support

Crewe points out that on two of the issues considered most important to the electorate—defense and inflation—the Conservative party was preferred over the opposition by a wide margin. Partly in response to the Falklands venture, defense was a far more important issue in 1983 than in 1979 (being mentioned by 39 percent of the voters, compared to only 2 percent in 1979), and the Conservative position was preferred by a 54 percent margin over Labour's (Crewe, 1983, 59). The Labour proposals for unilateral nuclear disarmament, removal of American missile bases, and withdrawal of Britain from the European Economic Community won little popular support (O'Sullivan, 1983).

But the critical factor, in Crewe's opinion, was that the Conservatives had reversed Labour's 1979 advantage and in fact opened up a wide lead (+40 percent) over Labour on control of inflation, while preference for Labour on the jobs issue had actually declined from +20 to +16 (Crewe, 1983, 58–59). Thus, even though unemployment had replaced inflation as the issue of widest public concern and Labour was still seen as the party best able to provide jobs, Labour failed to capitalize on the fact that over 3 million were out of work because it did not have a credible alternative economic program. "As a result, unemployment damaged the Conservative vote without repairing Labour's; at best it prevented Labour's disaster from turning into catastrophe" (Crewe, 1983, 59).

Another explanation is that people did not necessarily blame the government for unemployment. One poll found that 57 percent of the unemployed themselves attributed it to other causes: "They blamed various factors such as the world slump, labor unions, and 'nobody'" (O'Sullivan, 1983, 50). At the same time, there is evidence that more people felt personally threatened by inflation than by unemployment. A Harris Poll taken just before the election asked, "Which matters most to you and your family, reducing unemployment or keeping down inflation?" Only 38 percent chose "reducing unemployment" compared to 56 percent who said "keeping down inflation" (Ladd, 1983b, 5). It is thus likely that the government got some reward for its anti-inflationary success, but this cannot account for the backswing in 1982, since at that time expectations of rising prices were still very high. Furthermore, the largest swing to the Conservatives in 1983 occurred not among the middle-class voters, who are considered most sensitive to inflation, but rather among working-class people, who deserted their party for other reasons.

Indeed, the continuing erosion of the traditional class bases of parties was another important feature of the 1983 election. Only 38 percent of manual workers voted Labour, compared to 50 percent in 1979 and 69 percent in 1966 (Crewe, 1983, 56). This massive electoral fluidity—fully 37 percent of Labour's 1979 voters deserted it in 1983—indicates that social change may be working to the benefit of the Conservatives (and potentially the Alliance) if they can offer populist solutions.

Are Mrs. Thatcher's economic policies a case in point? Despite all of the foregoing arguments, it is hard to deny that the government has won a large measure of respect for adopting a different course and sticking to it. It appears that, in Britain as well as the United States, a substantial segment of the public believes that current policies are a necessary corrective to past failures and will pay off in the future. Ladd speaks of a "willingness to bear some considerable short-term discomfort to see government launched securely along a new path" and an "impulse to 'stay the course' long before any such campaign slogans appeared" (1983b, 5–6).

Data on economic expectations support this contention to some extent. In March 1983, 50 percent of the respondents to a MORI survey agreed with the statement, "In the long term this government's policies will improve Britain's economy"; however, during 1981 clear pluralities had disagreed in similar surveys (*Public Opinion*, June–July 1983, 25). Expectations of improvement in the national economy over the next twelve months went up gradually from early 1980, but remained heavily negative until the Falklands war changed the political climate. Even then, economic expectations remained considerably less positive than in the United States, and in early 1983 almost as many people still thought that the economy would get worse as thought it would get better. Thus, at best, British public opinion remained sharply divided over the potential success of Thatcher's economic regime.

Summary

Unlike her predecessors, Mrs. Thatcher benefited greatly from two major noneconomic events: the self-destruction of the Labour opposition; and winning a war (of course, the prime minister deserves the credit for the latter). We cannot determine how much of a backswing to the government would have occurred without these developments, but no economic model that we know of would suggest that it would have been sufficient to reelect Mrs. Thatcher in 1983. Evidence of negative voting suggests that the Conservatives were returned *in spite of,* not because of, their economic policies. Continuing economic hardship may have led British voters to expect even less of their government in the 1980s than in the past.

REAGAN'S BUSINESS CYCLE

Manipulation of economic policies to achieve political ends has seemed especially prevalent in the United States, where elections are frequent and parties are weak. It has been considered politically necessary for incumbent presidents to raise disposable income and get unemployment down in election years. However, President Carter's administration followed the reverse pattern as he stimulated expansion during the first half of his term and ultimately suffered the electoral consequences of a rising "misery index" in the last year of his presidency. By then it was no longer evident that any administration could effectively manipulate the economy, but Carter's timing was most unfortunate. Ronald Reagan faced an even stiffer challenge since he promised to cut taxes, increase defense spending, eliminate inflation, and balance the budget all at the same time. How could he implement what candidate George Bush called "voodoo economics" in such a way as to ensure his reelection?

The 1980 Verdict

Ronald Reagan's election in 1980 seemed to portend as many dramatic changes in the conduct of government as did Mrs. Thatcher's. Much analysis has since been devoted to explaining what motivated this electoral verdict. Investigations of the election's substantive meaning focused upon two alternative explanations: did Reagan's victory reflect a broadly based rightward shift in public opinion, or did it represent a rejection of Jimmy Carter's conduct of the presidency?

The first explanation does possess a superficial plausibility. The election of the most conservative president since Herbert Hoover could indeed logically result from an ideologically conservative tide in the populace. But this requires evidence that the American people were more likely to view themselves as conservative in 1980 than in years past and that Reagan's conservatism was mentioned as a preponderant reason for voting for him.

However, in 1980 the ideology of the general public showed nonexistent or very small shifts toward self-described conservatism in comparison to 1978, ranging from a 4 percent increase in the University of Michigan's surveys to a 2 percent *drop* in the Gallup Poll (Hibbs, 1982, 403). The CBS News/New York Times exit polls of actual voters registered 32 percent as self-described conservatives in 1976 and 31 percent in 1980. Self-described liberals declined by 2 percent—from 20 to 18 percent of the electorate (Frankovic, 1981, 114). A careful analysis of the 1980 National Election Study of the Michigan Center for Political Studies (CPS) by Abramson, Aldrich, and Rohde did find respondents preferred more conservative policies in a number of areas (1982, 126). The public nonetheless placed itself on average about midway between what they perceived to be Carter's and Reagan's positions on these issues, but closer on average to Carter in terms of ideology (Center for Political Studies, 1980).

Miller and Shanks, in another analysis of the CPS surveys, claimed that "majority preferences for a conservative shift in federal policy take credit for a substantial contribution" to Reagan's victory. However, the scale of this shift was small, leading them to conclude,

> The contribution made by preferences for a more conservative direction in federal policies in no way provides a mandate for President Reagan's specific positions on all policy issues . . . popular support for a change in the direction of federal policy may turn to opposition if the new policies go substantially "further" than their electoral supporters had intended. (1982, 353)

In most issue areas, popular majorities continued to support the liberal position in 1980, but by reduced margins.

If the public did desire somewhat more conservative policies in 1980, was this a dominant reason for the choice made by Reagan voters? The CBS/New York Times exit poll asked those who voted for Reagan to pick two reasons for their vote from a list of eight. Only 11 percent indicated they chose Reagan because "he's a real conservative." Thirty-eight percent chose to explain their choice as "it's time for a change," and 21 percent because Reagan was a "strong leader," both more performance-related reasons (Pierce and Hagstrom, 1980, 1877).

The evidence is more supportive of the second explanation for Reagan's victory—the alleged failings of Jimmy Carter as incumbent. Kathleen Frankovic (1981, 103) found in exit polls that disapproval and dislike of the incumbent outweighed any other single explanation for supporting Ronald Reagan. Several studies have demonstrated that retrospective evaluations of economic and foreign policy trends influenced the votes of many and aided Reagan in the election. Douglas Hibbs labeled the economy the "dominant issue" of the election and argued:

> Since both the cumulative and election year economic records of the Carter administration in 1980 were less favorable than the Nixon–Ford records of 1976, fewer voters felt better off (18% versus 23%) and more voters felt worse off (38% versus 28%) during the Carter–Reagan contest than during the Ford–Carter race. And this is the main reason that Reagan defeated Carter by a margin larger than Carter's victory over Ford four years earlier (Hibbs, 1982, 406).

Abramson, Aldrich, and Rohde (1982, 154–57) find both prospective and retrospective aspects in 1980 voters' candidate performance evaluations and identify independents and weak party members as having anti-Carter retrospective evaluations and pro-Reagan prospective evaluations which contributed importantly to Reagan's victory.

The 1980 presidential verdict was, then, evidence not of an ideological sea-change toward conservatism but rather primarily of a negative retrospective judgment on the Carter presidency and a belief that Ronald Reagan, in spite of his greater ideological distance from the average voter, would perform better in the presidency than Carter. Crucial voting blocs seemed ready to accept Reagan for his leadership and probable performance. Thus the Reagan presidency, like that of its predecessors, would depend for its popular support in large part on retrospective and prospective judgments of its conduct in office. This would particularly be the case if the 1980 election did not entail broad popular movement toward Reagan's ideological position. Has any such movement occurred in the wake of the election?

Public Opinion and Presidential Popularity Since 1980

In a recent review of public opinion trends from 1978 to 1983, Everett Carll Ladd summarized his findings by noting "how little the nation's values and attitudes have shifted in the face of kaleidoscopic changes in the political setting." Very little change in the patterns of party and ideological identification had surfaced. "The public's views of the country, its prospects, and its central institutions have changed hardly at all. Attitudes toward government, and taxing and spending, have shown great stability. So have a broad array of social and cultural values" (Ladd, 1983a, 41).

Some changes in public opinion on specific policies have occurred since Reagan's inauguration, but not in the way the president would have desired. The percentage believing Reagan was going "too far" in increasing military spending rose from 19 percent in April 1981 to 52 percent in August 1983. Those believing he was going too far in cutting government social programs increased from 34 to 52 percent over this same period. The public also preferred cuts in defense spending to further cuts in social programs as a way to reduce the federal deficit by a three-to-two margin in 1983, in direct opposition to the announced preferences of the administration. Overall, public opinion concerning the proper size of government has remained unchanged since the middle 1970s (Goodman, 1984, 34–39). One could hardly view these tendencies as evidence of a pronounced conservative shift in the electorate.

The overall stability in political attitudes in recent years suggests that public support for President Reagan may follow the traditional pattern noted in public opinion polls. Pollster Burns Roper identified the following sequence over the course of the past seven presidencies:

> A president's approval rating tends to rise for two or three months after he takes office. From that point on his approval rating is inclined to drop, drop, drop—though with a number of zigs and zags caused by specific events. In the event of a domestic crisis, regardless of what the president does or does not do, his approval rating almost invariably drops. In the event of an international crisis, regardless of what a president does or does not do, the immediate effect is for his approval rating to rise. If the long-term effect of the international crisis is bad, then his approval rating reverses and drops sharply. In about January of his fourth year, the president's rating decline halts and thereafter begins to rise again—whether he is running for reelection or retiring (Roper, 1983, 42).

Political scientists and economists have attempted to supplement observation of such cyclical patterns with econometric models. These models estimate the relationship between popular support for presidents and variables representing economic trends (real personal income, inflation, unemployment), major public events (such as Vietnam, Watergate, or the Iranian hostage crisis), and other influences (e.g. legislative success, natural erosion of support over time). Figure 11.4 illustrates the actual pattern of presidential support in Gallup Polls from 1981 to 1984 and the average predicted pattern of support derived from a recent model (Ostrom and Simon, 1984). Reagan's pattern conforms reasonably closely to the forecasts of both Roper and this model.

Figure 11.4

Actual and Predicted Support for Ronald Reagan 1981–1983

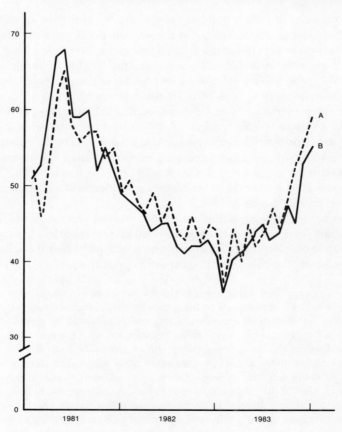

A = Monthly Gallup poll support percentages. Source: Gallup Surveys.
B = Predicted support from Ostrom and Simon model (1984).

Possible reasons for this overall conformity with the predictions are suggested in Figure 11.5, which graphs Reagan's popular support in relation to economic trends and public opinion about the government's economic policy. As unemployment climbed upward throughout late 1981 and 1982, Reagan's popularity correspondingly eroded. Yet despite the deepest recession of the postwar era, public support for government economic policies never reached the lows of the Carter administration in 1979 and 1980. This probably reflects public faith that in the "long run" the nation's economic situation would be better because of Reagan's economic policies.

Figure 11.5

Support for U.S. Presidents and Economic Performance 1979–1984

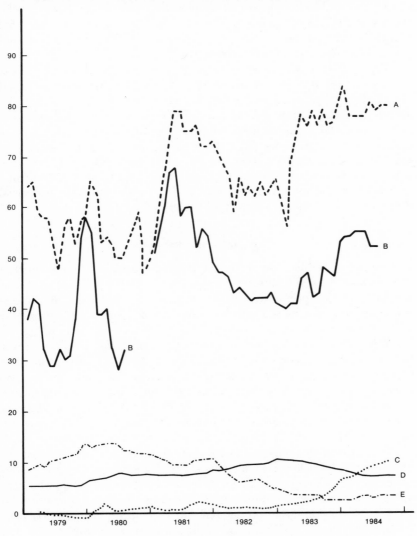

A = Support for government's economic policy (percent stating government is doing a good or fair job).
  Source: *SCA Redbook*, Institute for Social Research, University of Michigan.
B = Support for the president (percent indicating approval of the handling of the job).
  Source: Gallup Surveys. Note: question was not asked September–December 1980.
C = Percent increase in real disposable income per capita from the level of 1978 fourth quarter.
  Source: *Economic Report of the President* and *Economic Indicators*.
D = Unemployment rate.
  Source: *Economic Report of the President* and *Economic Indicators*.
E = Inflation rate (consumer Price Index, all items).
  Source: *Economic Report of the President* and *Economic Indicators*.

In 1982, though, the erosion of popular support for Reagan as president seemed severe. At the end of his twenty-fourth month in office, Reagan enjoyed lower support in the polls than any of his postwar predecessors at comparable points in their terms. His popularity rebounded sharply from that point, however, and by mid-1984 he ranked considerably above Carter's level of mid-1980.

What accounts for this comeback? Reagan's popularity climbed as the recovery from the 1981–82 recession proceeded. Although this trend included an unsustained peak when Americans briefly rallied around the leader after the "successful" Grenada invasion, overall it followed the pattern of macroeconomic improvement (in contrast to Britain). Figure 11.5 shows the concurrent fall in unemployment, rise in disposable personal income, and stabilization of inflation during 1983–84. Public support for the government's economic policy also steadily climbed, reaching by late 1983 the highest levels recorded since the Institute for Social Research began asking this question in 1961.

Explaining the Pattern

Two aspects of public support for the Reagan presidency require further explanation: What broader explanation for the *relative* degree of public support for the president can be suggested? Why has the public evidenced unprecedented *absolute* levels of support for his economic policies since the onset of recovery? First, a broader explanation.

Edward Tufte in his book, *Political Control of the Economy,* posits that an "electoral economic" or "political business" cycle can often be observed in the economies of capitalist democracies. Tufte explains the cycle this way: "An incumbent administration, while operating within political and economic constraints and limited by the usual uncertainties in successfully implementing economic policy, may manipulate the short-run course of the national economy in order to improve its party's standing in upcoming elections and to repay political debts" (Tufte, 1980, 3–4). Alt and Chrystal (1983, 122) describe four behavioral rules for authorities implicit in Tufte's approach: (1) support your core clients; (2) do whatever the public finds most important; (3) get unemployment down for the presidential election; and (4) get real incomes up for any election. The actual behavior of the Reagan administration conforms well to the first three rules, as it does in 1984 (but not in 1982) to the fourth rule.

One important group of core clients for the Reagan administration are those Americans with annual incomes of more than $50,000. In 1983, fully 44 percent of this group described themselves as Republicans, the largest percentage of any demographic subgroup in the population. Numerous studies have indicated that the various changes in the tax system since

1980 have disproportionately benefited this group (for example, see Palmer and Sawhill, 1984, chap. 10). The administration explains its policy as necessary for stimulating growth through investment on the "supply side" of the economy. Regardless of the merits of this argument, this policy also rewards an important core component of the Republican party. David Stockman, in an incautious moment, suggested that the real administration goal in the 1981 tax changes was to reduce the maximum marginal tax rates of high-income individuals from 70 percent to 50 percent: "Kemp-Roth was always a Trojan Horse to bring down the top rate" (Greider, 1982, 49). Mr. Tufte would be hard pressed to manufacture evidence that supports his theory as well.

Public economic worries in recent years have focused on the problems of inflation and unemployment. When Mr. Reagan took office in 1981, 56 percent saw inflation as causing the more serious economic hardship, while only 34 percent viewed unemployment in this way. Tight monetary policies originally adopted by the Federal Reserve Board in October 1979 and continued with the full support of the Reagan administration contributed to the onset of the recession of 1981–82 and concurrent decline of the inflation rate from 12.4 percent in 1980 to 3.2 percent in 1983 and 4.3 percent in 1984. With the advent of the recession came increasing public concern about unemployment; by November 1982 public identification of it as the most important problem peaked at 76 percent, compared to 16 percent mentioning inflation. The unemployment rate then trended downward from 10.6 percent in November 1982 to 7.1 percent in November 1984.

The economic record of the Reagan administration indicates action to address, at least in the short term, the economic problems cited as most serious by the public. The degree to which this action was consciously planned is at best unclear; certainly the administration did not anticipate the historically high budget deficits which at least temporarily stimulated the economy in 1983 and 1984. Nevertheless, the actions taken have ameliorated the problems the public found most important, in conformity with Tufte's model. By mid-1984 unemployment stood at the lowest level since mid-1980, with the annual rate of inflation at 4.2 percent, compared with 12.4 percent in 1980. Real disposable income per capita, in accordance with Tufte's prescription, rose steadily between the third quarter of 1982 and the third quarter of 1984, increasing by 8.9 percent during that time and by 10.6 percent since the fourth quarter of 1980.

The administration did not, however, succeed in raising disposable income appreciably in time for the 1982 congressional elections. It increased an anemic 0.3 percent from the first quarter of 1981 to the fourth quarter of 1982. The administration's failure to raise real incomes in 1982 resulted from the difficulty of combatting high unemployment and inflation simultaneously, especially given the restrictive monetary policies practiced by the Federal Reserve in the early 1980s. A corresponding electoral price was paid as Republicans lost twenty-six House seats. The deep recession did not result in as serious a loss, though, as Tufte's econometric model predicted it would. Over fifty seats should have fallen due to low growth in disposable income and lagging presidential popularity at the time of the election. Gary Jacobson and Sam Kernell explain this less-than-expected loss as resulting from a financial advantage held by Republican candidates contesting the elections (1982, 428–30).

Douglas Hibbs Jr. has developed a simple regression model that accurately predicts the popular vote outcome of every presidential election since 1952 and is also theoretically congruent with Tufte's analysis. The model holds that the percentage of the vote achieved by an incumbent running for reelection is a linear function of the change in average per capita disposable income discounted over time (Hibbs, 1982, 394). This model predicted Reagan would receive 58.6 percent of the popular vote in 1984—extremely close to his actual percentage (58.9). A related model by Hibbs correctly predicted a Republican gain of 14 seats in the House of Representatives in 1984. These results confirm the importance of economic performance in the 1984 elections.

The question remains as to why the Reagan political business cycle is accompanied by unprecedentedly high public support for the government's economic policies. This pattern is evident throughout the Reagan presidency in comparison with that of Carter at similar points in their terms. In late 1983 and throughout 1984, percentages supported the government's policy equal to those during the reign of optimism accompanying Reagan's first months in office. A corresponding increase occurred in the percentage of Americans viewing the Republicans as the "party of prosperity." In September 1984, 50 percent concurred with this statement, the highest level of agreement since Gallup began asking the question over thirty years ago, while only 33 percent picked the Democrats. This is a marked reversal of the traditional perceptions of the parties. These trends accompany persistently high levels of belief since 1980 that the long-term effects of Reaganomics will benefit the country. In early 1984, 44 percent of respondents to an Institute for Social Research survey thought good times would persist for five years, the highest percentage in thirty years (Curtin, 1984). It seems logical to conclude that policy support derives from a belief that the overall direction of economic policy is appropriate for the long term.

This perception strongly influenced presidential voting choices in 1984. As William Schneider (1984) put it:

> The electorate was not, to any exceptional degree, driven by greed. Yes, people who felt better off voted for the incumbent and those who felt worse off voted for the challenger. But that was no more true this year

than in 1980, or in 1976, or in any previous election. Moreover, voters' assessment of the nation's economy had a stronger and more consistent impact on their vote than their evaluation of their own personal well-being. People who felt that the country was beginning a long-term recovery voted for Reagan by a wide margin, no matter how they themselves had fared. And those who saw no improvement in the economy voted overwhelmingly for Mondale, even if they had become better off.

Should this optimism persist, some observers foresee a major party realignment that will make Republicans the "normal" majority party (Sussman, 1984; Schneider, 1984). The Democratic party had by 1984 lost its traditional reputation as the party better able to manage the economy. Further, though exit polls from the election indicated that on many issues the voters were closer to the position of Walter Mondale, they perceived Reagan to be closer on most issues. Why the discrepancy? Apparently people thought they agreed with Reagan because his policies were perceived to be working. The implication is that public support could swing back to the Democrats if the economy falters.

However, a Gallup Poll taken just after the 1984 election indicated that the percentage of people who classified their ideological beliefs as "right of center" was 36 percent, compared to 32 percent in 1980 and 31 percent in 1976 (Gallup, 1984). This may portend a gradual realignment, but it is too early to tell.

Summary

By accident or by design of the Reagan administration, the course of economic policy and presidential popularity during 1981–84 conforms to Edward Tufte's political business cycle explanation. Put simply, the policies led to economic stimulus as the 1984 election neared, and the recovery generated a strong rebound in presidential popularity. However, popular support for Reaganomics was remarkably resilient even in the depths of the 1982 recession, apparently due to consistently favorable expectations of its long-term results. The implication is that public support for an incumbent administration is significantly based on prospective assessments of its policies as well as on retrospective or current economic performance. Consequently the Reagan approach has been given considerable time to prove itself. Living up to such expectations may be the most formidable task of all.

CONCLUSION

We noted at the beginning that, despite many similarities, there have been some notable differences in the macroeconomic policies of Margaret Thatcher and Ronald Reagan. Thatcher's campaign to revive British capitalism promised few short-term benefits, whereas Reagan attempted to stimulate rapid growth at the same time as inflation was brought down. It is not surprising, then, that public opinion would respond somewhat differently to the two regimes. But the lessons for political economy are far from clear. In the case of Britain, it appears that extraneous events and rejection of the opposition account for an electoral verdict that had little to do with the success of Mrs. Thatcher's economic "counterrevolution." In America, on the other hand, economic recovery appeared to be Reagan's strongest electoral asset.

What then can be said about the economic determinants of voting?

The first point is that short-term economic trends are *not necessarily* the overriding factor in national elections: in the case of Britain in 1983, Mrs. Thatcher's image as a "resolute" leader owed far more to her laurels in the Falklands and the incompetence and divisions of the opposition than to her meager economic achievements. Support for her economic policies has tended to follow rather than lead her general popularity ratings. By contrast, it is clear that economic success (as perceived by the public) contributed mightily to Ronald Reagan's image as a strong and effective president in 1984—while at the same time deflecting and discrediting the attacks of the Democratic opposition. In the absence of critical external events on the scale of the Iranian hostage crisis of 1980 or the Vietnam War in 1968, the economic climate overshadowed other issues in the 1984 election.

We are thus led to the conclusion that short-term economic performance is one of several key variables that *may* decisively influence the leadership image of the incumbent chief executive—which in an age of weak political parties and television politics is likely to determine the electoral outcome. (Since parties choose leaders between elections in Britain, there is always an incumbent prime minister at general election. When the incumbent president does not stand for reelection in the United States—as in 1952, 1960, and 1968—the opposition party fares much better, a fact to keep in mind for 1988.)

Secondly, when we look more closely at individual motivations the relevance of various hypotheses remains uncertain. For example, the 1984 verdict in America initially might seem to confirm the dominant theory of "pocketbook voting"—that voters are myopic personal utility maximizers who respond retrospectively to changes in their financial condition in the year or so before the election. Thus many people who had experienced financial losses or even unemployment during the recession of 1982 had become Reagan voters by 1984. However, there is also evidence that even during 1982 people had remarkably high expectations that Reagan's policies would eventually succeed, suggesting that future expectations for the health of the national economy are also important in explaining Reagan's popularity. Margaret Thatcher's government, to the contrary, has consciously tried to lower economic expectations, which perhaps accounts for the tolerance her policies have thus far received. In both cases, then, public expectations have been corroborated by results, whereas in the 1970s rising expectations were frustrated by stagnation and declining real incomes.

But it is doubtful that these governments can retain support on this basis in the future. In the United States high expectations could well be dashed by the continuing deficit crisis or another steep recession. Nor will a democratic electorate indefinitely accept an unemployment rate reminiscent of the 1920s, if not the Great Depression, in Britain. The future of these conservative experiments thus remains very much in question.

NOTE

1. Borooah and van der Ploeg have developed a multiparty econometric model which has been estimated for the three parties in Britain to 1979. But it is difficult to see how this model could capture the effect of the Liberal–SDP Alliance either, and the authors indicate that it is likely that parameters have changed as "Mrs. Thatcher has altered the nature of the economic debate by downgrading high employment and upgrading low inflation rates as objectives in economic policy" (1983, 57).

REFERENCES

Abramson, P. R., Aldrich, J. H., and Rohde, D. W. 1982. *Change and Continuity in the 1980 Elections*. Washington, D.C.: Congressional Quarterly Press.

Alt, J. E. 1979. *The Politics of Economic Decline*. Cambridge: Cambridge University Press.

Alt, J. E., and Chrystal, K. A. 1983. *Political Economics*. Berkeley: University of California Press.

Bogdanor, V. 1983. "The Meaning of Mrs. Thatcher's Victory—In a Long Perspective." *Encounter* (September–October):14–19.

Borooah, V. K., and van der Ploeg, F. 1983. *Political Aspects of the Economy*. Cambridge: Cambridge University Press.

Butt, R. 1983. "The Politics of Thatcherism." *Policy Review* (Fall): 30–35.

Center for Political Studies. 1980. Unpublished chart summaries of the 1980 National Election Studies. Ann Arbor: Institute for Social Research.

Chappell, H. W. 1983. "Presidential Popularity and Macroeconomic Performance: Are Voters Really So Naive?" *Review of Economics and Statistics* 65: 385–92.

Chrystal, K. A., and Alt, J. E. 1981. "Some Problems in Formulating and Testing a

Politico-Economic Model of the United Kingdom." *Economic Journal* 91: 730–36.

Crewe, I. 1981. "Why the Conservatives Won." In *Britain at the Polls, 1979*, ed. H. R. Penniman. Washington, D.C.: American Enterprise Institute.

———. 1983. "Why Labour Lost the British Elections." *Public Opinion* (June–July): 7–9, 56–60.

Curtin, R. T. 1984. "The Reign of Optimism." *Economic Outlook USA* 11: 31–34.

Economist. 1982. "Rally Round the Tory Flag." *Economist* (May 29): 22.

———. 1983. "The Thatcher Style: The Trials and Triumphs of a Party Ideologue." *Economist* (May 21): 21–28.

Frankovic, K. A. 1981. "Public Opinion Trends." In *The Election of 1980*, ed. M. Pomper. Chatham, N.J.: Chatham House.

Frey, B. S. 1978. *Modern Political Economy*. New York: Wiley.

Frey, B. S., and Schneider, F. 1978. "A Politico-Economic Model of the United Kingdom." *Economic Journal* 88: 243–53.

———. 1981. "A Politico-Economic Model of the U.K.: New Estimates and Predictions." *Economic Journal* 91: 737–40.

Gallup, G. 1984. "Poll of Political Ideologies Finds a Trend to the Right." *Washington Post* (Dec. 2).

Goodhart, C. A. E., and Bhansali, R. J. 1970. "Political Economy." *Political Studies* 18: 43–106.

Goodman, J. L., Jr. 1983. *Public Opinion During the Reagan Administration*. Washington, D.C.: Urban Institute Press.

Greider, W. 1982. *The Education of David Stockman and Other Americans*. New York: Dutton.

Hibbs, D. A. 1982. "President Reagan's Mandate from the 1980 Elections: A Shift to the Right?" *American Politics Quarterly* 10: 387–420.

Jacobson, G. C., and Kernell, S. 1982. "Strategy and Choice in the 1982 Congressional Elections." *PS* 15: 423–30.

Kernell, S. 1978. "Explaining Presidential Popularity." *American Political Science Review* 72: 506–22.

Kinder, D. R., and Kiewiet, D. R. 1981. "Sociotropic Politics: The American Case." *British Journal of Political Science* 11: 129–61.

King, A. 1981. "Politics, Economics, and the Trade Unions, 1974–1979." In *Britain at the Polls, 1979*, ed. H. R. Penniman. Washington, D.C.: American Enterprise Institute.

Kramer, G. H. 1971. "Short-Term Fluctuations in U.S. Voting Behavior, 1896–1964." *American Political Science Review* 65: 131–43.

Ladd, E. C. 1983a. "Public Opinion: Questions at the Quinquennial." *Public Opinion* (April–May): 20–41.

———. 1983b. "Converging Currents in British and American Politics." *Public Opinion* (June–July): 4–6, 55–56.

MacKuen, M. B. 1983. "Political Drama, Economic Conditions, and the Dynamics of Presidential Popularity." *American Journal of Political Science* 27: 165–92.

Miller, W. E., and Shanks, J. M. 1982. "Policy Directions and Presidential Leadership: Alternative Interpretations of the 1980 Presidential Election." *British Journal of Political Science* 12: 299–356.

Mueller, D. C. 1970. "Presidential Popularity from Truman to Johnson." *American Political Science Review* 64: 18–34.

Nordhaus, W. 1975. "The Political Business Cycle." *Review of Economic Studies* 42: 169–90.

Ostrom, C. W., and Simon, D. M. 1984. "Promise and Performance: A Dynamic Model of Presidential Popularity." Paper presented at the 1984 Annual Meeting of the Midwest Political Science Association, Chicago, April 11–15.

O'Sullivan, J. 1983. "Thatcherization (Cont'd)." *Commentary* (September): 47–54.

Paldam, M. 1981. "A Preliminary Survey of the Theories and Findings on Vote and Popularity Functions." *European Journal of Political Research* 9: 181–99.

Palmer, J. S., and Sawhill, I. V. 1984. *The Reagan Record.* Cambridge, Mass.: Ballinger.

Pierce, N. R., and Hagstrom, J. 1980. "Why They Pulled the Reagan Lever." *National Journal* 45:1877.

Pissarides, C. A. 1980. "British Government Popularity and Economic Performance." *Economic Journal* 90: 569–81.

Roper, B. 1983. "Presidential Popularity: Do People Like the Actor or His Actions?" *Public Opinion* (Oct.–Nov.): 42–45.

Rose, R. 1983. "Two and One-Half Cheers for the Market in Britain." *Public Opinion* (June–July): 10–15.

Sackett, V. 1983. "The Shape of Things to Come." *Policy Review* (Fall): 37–40.

Särlvik, B., and Crewe, I. 1983. *Decade of Dealignment: The Conservative Victory of 1979 and Electoral Trends in the 1970s.* Cambridge: Cambridge University Press.

Tufte, E. 1978. *Political Control of the Economy.* Princeton: Princeton University Press.

Ursprung, H. W. 1984. "Macroeconomic Performance and Government Popularity in New Zealand." *Comparative Political Studies* 16: 457–78.

Wattenberg, B. J. 1979. "Uncle Jim and the Iron Lady." *Public Opinion* (June–July): 47–50.

Webb, N. L., and Wybrow, R. J., eds. 1981. *The Gallup Report.* London: Sphere Books.

Whitely, P., ed. 1980. *Models of Political Economy.* London: Sage.

12   ECONOMICS AND ELECTORAL BEHAVIOR IN FRANCE

Michael S. Lewis-Beck

In recent national elections—the United States (1980), France (1981), Great Britain (1979), Italy (1983)—ruling parties have not been returned to power. With regard to France in particular, President Valery Giscard d'Estaing and his Republicans, along with their allies the Gaullists, were voted out of office. It is tempting, given the state of the economy prior to these contests, to jump to the simple conclusion that voters were casting their ballots against government economic mismanagement. With regard to the United States, there is considerable evidence that economically discontented voters do tend to oppose the president and his party. For Western European countries, such as France, our knowledge about the effects of economic conditions at the voting booth is more uncertain, since much less research has been carried out. Still, some studies do exist. Below, I draw on these efforts in an attempt to account for how economics affects French voters. First, I evaluate economic influences on the popularity of the president and the prime minister. Second, I assess the role economics plays in voting for candidates to the National Assembly. Third, I suggest the ways economic hardship can explain the victory of President Mitterrand and the left in 1981. Finally, I speculate on the impact of economic voting in future elections.

ECONOMICS AND EXECUTIVE POPULARITY IN FRANCE

During the Third and Fourth Republics, the French multiparty political system was thought to be chaotic. Jacques Fauvet summed up this view:

"France contains two fundamental temperaments—that of the left and that of the right . . . three principal tendencies, if one adds the center; six spiritual families; ten parties, large or small, traversed by multiple currents; fourteen parliamentary groups without much discipline; and forty million opinions" (see Ehrmann, 1971, 197). Under this system, governments did not last long, for it was difficult to sustain the parliamentary majority necessary to rule. In the end, the profound controversies of French Common Market membership and the colonial status of Algeria provoked a constitutional crisis. To solve it, General de Gaulle was returned to power. He quickly engineered the passage of the Constitution of the Fifth Republic, by referendum in September 1958, and was immediately elected its first president. Since the creation of the Fifth Republic, the French government has operated more like a presidential system than a parliamentary system, which it was under the Fourth Republic. While the office of prime minister still exists, it is the president who exercises executive authority, in fact and in law.

How popular is the central actor in French politics? The answer, of course, depends in part on which president one is talking about. President de Gaulle is widely held to have been the most popular, for many of the same reasons President Eisenhower was regarded as so popular in the United States. This common view is confirmed by evidence from public opinion polls (Lewis-Beck, 1980b). A major French polling firm, Institut français d'opinion publique (IFOP), comparable in some ways to the Gallup organization in the United States, has regularly asked a national sample of the French public the following question: Are you satisfied or dissatisfied with X as president of the Republic? The respondents had five categories to choose from for their answer: very satisfied; rather satisfied; rather dissatisfied; very dissatisfied; and no opinion. IFOP posed this question three times in 1958 and 1959, respectively, and has asked it almost monthly since 1960. The results are quickly available in the French press and are frequently cited by journalists, politicians, and voters as a good indicator of how well the president is doing his job. No president has received higher scores in this rating than Charles de Gaulle.

Especially in the first years of his initial term, the French public was highly approving of de Gaulle, with as much as 74 percent of those polled declaring themselves "satisfied" (i.e. selecting either "very satisfied" or "rather satisfied"). Overall, across his two terms in office, de Gaulle's rating in this popularity poll averaged 58 percent, a figure unsurpassed by subsequent French presidents (on de Gaulle's popularity, see Charlot, 1971; Parodi, 1971). After de Gaulle's resignation, his prime minister, Georges Pompidou, was elected president in 1969. Pompidou, himself a Gaullist politically, never reached the peaks of mass support that his mentor attained. Still, his average popularity managed to match de Gaulle's. In contrast, President Valery Giscard d'Estaing, an Independent Republican elected in 1974, was decidedly less popular, with an average satisfaction rating below 50 percent. Indeed, of these three presidents, all located on the center-right of the political spectrum, Giscard d'Estaing's popularity fell the lowest, dropping in March 1981 to 35 percent. When the current president, Socialist François Mitterrand, assumed office, presidential popularity jumped to 54 percent (June 1981). However, since then his mass following has seriously eroded. In fact, from June 1981 to December 1983, his popularity averaged only 43 percent in these crucial monthly IFOP polls.

Hence, we observe that presidential approval has varied widely, at different times and with different presidents. Why is this so? Or, to put the question another way: What makes a president popular? Obviously, many factors influence this level of public support for a president. For example, a president may be highly regarded for a winning smile, firm leadership, honesty, an independent foreign policy, or progressive social programs. Clearly, everyone would not assign the same values to such factors. Some issues will influence few and be short-term, while others will influence many and be long-term. Moreover, with regard to the United States, it has been argued that in the long term, the president's actions will inevitably disappoint more citizens than they will satisfy. The French data are mildly compatible with this general notion of the "inexorable disillusionment" of the public with the president. As each month passes, the French president does tend to slip a tiny bit at the polls (e.g. after about twenty months in office, he can expect to have one percentage point shaved off his basic approval score; Lewis-Beck, 1980b, 314). In contrast, a major factor that might offset this decline is war, or the threat of it. The American evidence indicates that the president's decisions during wartime can greatly influence his level of public support (Kernell, 1978). For France, there is some indication that the Algerian War raised de Gaulle's popularity about three or four percentage points above what it would otherwise have been (Lewis-Beck, 1980b, 313). Thus, French presidential popularity appears to depend, in part, on the characteristics of the particular administration, the length of time in office, and whether or not the nation is at war.

But what about the influence of economic variables, which are our special concern? First, to provide some context, let us take a brief look at the French economic picture in the postwar period. Since World War II, the country has undergone substantial economic development. Peasants have left the land in great numbers, largely to take jobs in city factories, where real wages tripled between 1945 and 1970. In addition, big business has thrived on active government support initiated under de Gaulle.

From about 1970 to 1980, the overall rate of economic growth was greater than that of other European countries. Currently, per capita income in France is comparable to that in the United States.

These economic strides, real as they are, have not meant that the French economy has been untroubled. During the 1960s, the annual unemployment rate was quite low, varying between 1 and 2 percent. However, by the mid-1970s, unemployment was clearly on the rise. Since then, it has increased more or less steadily. The year before President Giscard was defeated in his 1981 reelection bid, unemployment had reached an unprecedented 7 percent of the work force. Turning to inflation, we see a similar picture. For the 1960s, there was more fluctuation in the rate of consumer price increases, but it was never too far from 3 percent a year. But by the mid-1970s, the inflation rate had begun to accelerate in earnest. For 1980, it was at 14 percent. Thus, these two central macroeconomic indicators—unemployment and inflation—have assumed very different magnitudes across the twenty-five years of the Fifth Republic. What are the consequences of these macroeconomic fluctuations for presidential popularity?

For some background, we can quickly review the U.S. results from such an inquiry. Several American studies have analyzed the relationship between these macroeconomic indicators and presidential popularity, as measured in the Gallup Poll question: Do you approve or disapprove of the way President X is handling his job as president? Unfortunately, these investigations are not in complete agreement. Some find that inflation damages the American president's popularity rating, whereas unemployment does not. In contrast, others have decided that rising unemployment lowers presidential support in the polls. However, this work is disregarded on methodological grounds by certain scholars. Different from any of these is research which indicates that inflation and unemployment together cause the president's job approval score to fall. Despite the disparity of these findings, they all point to one important conclusion: national economic downturn leads to a loss of presidential popularity in the United States. Can we reach the same conclusion for France?

There are three relevant studies for the French case. The first, by Lafay (1977), provides indirect evidence, looking at economic influences on public satisfaction with the prime minister. Technically, the Constitution of the Fifth Republic divides the executive in two (the president and the prime minister with his Cabinet), but in fact power resides with the president. As Macridis has summarized the prime minister's position, "He is the President's man" (1975, 28). Using quarterly data from 1961 to 1977, Lafay finds that the prime minister's popularity (as measured in an IFOP poll comparable to that for president) was significantly associated with real salaries, price changes, and employment requests. In another study, Hibbs and Vasilatos (1981) examine presidential popularity directly, with quarterly observations from 1969 to 1978. They decide that the economy affects his popularity through changes in the real personal disposable income growth rate.

A third piece by Lewis-Beck (1980b) explores fluctuations in the monthly IFOP poll on presidential satisfaction from 1960 to 1978. He argues that unemployment and inflation significantly reduce the French president's popularity rating. More precisely, he estimates that for each additional 100,000 workers who become unemployed, presidential popularity drops about .5 percent. And, for every 1 percent increase in the inflation rate, presidential popularity can be expected to decline almost 2 percent (Lewis-Beck, 1980, 314). Further, the popularity of the prime minister is diminished even more by these adverse economic conditions because, in addition to being a subject of the president's will, he is sometimes made a scapegoat for unpopular economic policies (Lewis-Beck, 1980, 318–20). While each of these investigations examines slightly different economic indicators, they have a common finding, which is that economic hard times translates into reduced popular support for the president (or prime minister). Certainly, they give a truthful ring to a recent (June 1983) headline in the *International Herald Tribune:* "Mitterrand Ratings Go Down With Economy." In Figure 12.1 is a summary of various poll results on the declining popularity of President Mitterrand, from 1981 to the end of 1984.

ECONOMIC CONDITIONS AND THE VOTE: AGGREGATE TIME SERIES STUDIES

As informative as these popularity studies are, they do not really tell us how economics affects the vote choice. That is, to say that I am satisfied with a president does not necessarily mean I will vote for him. I may, for instance, be still more satisfied with his opponent, and thus vote that way. Still, we might expect the connection between approval and vote to be strong, if imperfect. In the United States, the president's popularity is actually highly predictive of his November vote share (Lewis-Beck and Rice, 1982). But for France the evidence here is only impressionistic. Therefore, in order to assess the effects of economics on the vote, we must look directly at the latter. However, before doing so, a few words about the nature of the French electoral system would seem helpful (for a full review, see Pierce, 1968, chap. 6).

In France, the president is chosen by direct election, in two ballots. Victory on the first ballot requires a majority, which not even de Gaulle achieved. At the second ballot, held two weeks later, competition is lim-

Figure 12.1 Approval of President François Mitterrand, 1981–1984

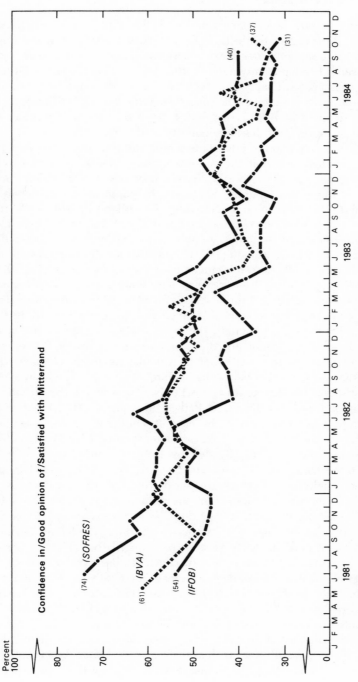

Key: Do you have complete confidence, not very much confidence, or no confidence at all in François Mitterrand to resolve the problems facing France today? (SOFRES)
What is your opinion of Mr. François Mitterrand as President of the Republic? (BVA)
Are you satisfied or dissatisfied with Mr. François Mitterrand as President of the Republic? (IFOP)

Source: *Public Opinion* (Oct./Nov. 1984):33. By permission of the American Enterprise Institute.

ited to the top two vote-getters on the first ballot, thus assuring a majority president. With regard to elections for the National Assembly, the Fifth Republic has single-member districts with two ballots. To win on the first ballot, a candidate for deputy must capture a majority of the votes. Otherwise, there is a second ballot one week later, when the candidate with the largest number of votes takes the seat. Generally, French legislative elections are decided at this second ballot, because the large number of parties makes it difficult to gain a majority on the first ballot.

The multiple parties of France often bewilder foreign observers. One source of confusion is that the same party may change its name from election to election. For example, the Gaullists, the major nonleft party for most of the Fifth Republic, have used half a dozen names between 1958 and 1981: Union pour la Nouvelle République (UNR), 1958; the UNR and the Union Démocratique du Travail (UDT), 1962; Union Démocratique pour la Cinquième République (UDVe), 1967; Union des Démocrates pour la République (UDR), 1968; Union des Républicains de Progrès (URP), 1973; Rassemblement pour la République (RPR), 1978, 1981. Besides parties with multiple names, there are also simply many parties. One way of sorting the parties is on a left–right continuum. (The terms *left* and *right* originated in France and are quite familiar to the average voter there.) On the left, the major parties are the Communists and the Socialists. Traditionally, the Communists win around 20 percent of the electorate on the first ballot of National Assembly elections, although they fell somewhat below that in 1981. (Currently, the head of the Communist party is George Marchais.) By way of contrast, the Socialists, in conjunction with the tiny Left Radical Movement (MRG), captured almost 38 percent of the vote in this contest. On the center-right are two major party organizations which are now almost equally balanced in electoral support: the Gaullists, headed by Jacques Chirac, the mayor of Paris, and the Union for French Democracy (UDF), the camp of Giscard d'Estaing. In addition, there are smaller parties, left, right, and center.

How do macroeconomic conditions influence the choice the voter must make among the parties? For the United States, many studies explore the relationship between economic indicators of inflation, income, unemployment and the party vote share in legislative elections across time. In contrast, for France, only two such studies exist, and both attempt to link national economic indicators to the total vote share of leftist parties in National Assembly elections (Rosa and Amson, 1976; Lewis-Beck and Bellucci, 1982). The fact that they lump together the parties on the left into one category is not unusual. These parties, i.e., the Communists, the Socialists, and smaller parties, have sometimes actually banded together in electoral alliance, such as the Union de la Gauche in the 1978 legislative elections. Also, the public tends to think of these parties as a unified group, "the left." The study by Rosa and Amson (1976) concludes, after looking at annual data from 1920 to 1973, that the vote percentage going to leftist parties in legislative elections increases with inflation and unemployment and decreases with heightened income. Lewis-Beck and Bellucci (1982), in their investigation of National Assembly results to 1978, find that the left vote total is largely a function of the national unemployment rate and real per capita income. Specifically, on the basis of their regression model, they assert that a 1 percent rise in the unemployment rate in the year prior to the election will increase the vote share of the left by about 5 percent. Further, a 1,000 franc decline in real per capita income the year before should strengthen the left vote by around one percentage point.

Although their model is based on only seven elections, the authors are encouraged because it successfully passes several statistical tests (of significance, normality, autocorrelation, goodness-of-fit). In particular, the model manages to forecast actual election outcomes rather well. For example, it forecast that left parties in 1978 would together receive 51.2 percent of the vote in the first ballot of National Assembly elections. This estimate was off only 1.7 percentage points from the actual total, which was 49.5 percent. What is more, this accuracy exceeds that of the last IFOP pre-election poll, which predicted these parties would gain a total of 52.1 percent, giving IFOP an error of 2.6 percentage points. Even more impressive was the model's ability to forecast the unprecedented 1981 victory of the left, before it happened. That is, based on the 1980 unemployment rate (6.7 percent) and real per capita income (31,279 francs) figures, the model predicted that the left would win with 55 percent of the vote. The real first-ballot returns awarded the left (Communists plus Socialists plus MRG) about 54 percent, giving a prediction error of only one percentage point.

From these studies relating national economic conditions and voter preference in legislative elections over time, the easy inference is that individual French citizens do take economic circumstances into account in deciding their vote. It appears, for example, that as the economy worsens (e.g. unemployment goes up or income goes down), voters punish the incumbent party coalition by voting against it (which until 1981 automatically meant a vote for a leftist party). However, this might be a spurious inference, for other mechanisms could also work to produce the observed aggregate association between economics and the vote. For instance, it may be that in bad economic years the incumbent parties risk only their weaker candidates, providing them with little campaign funding. If this were the case, then an aggregate association between economics and the vote would be generated by individual voters responding to candidate appeal and campaign spending rather than to economic issues. Hence, the inference from the aggregate results—economic issues affect individual voters—would be what is known as an ecological fallacy. To establish that individual voters actually do take economics into account, data from individuals in election surveys must be analyzed. As Fiorina, writing on the U.S. case, observes, "The existence of some relationship between the two [in the survey data] would appear to be a necessary condition for the existence of a 'true' relationship between the time series of aggregate data" (1978, 430).

ECONOMIC CONDITIONS AND THE VOTE: ELECTION SURVEYS

There are several reasons why individual French voters might not translate economic discontent into a ballot against the incumbent. For one, they might not accurately see their own economic difficulties, e.g., the nominal rise in a paycheck is mistaken for a real (deflated) rise. For another, accurate perception does not necessarily result in political action, e.g., a worker who is laid off blames himself rather than elected public officials. For yet another, even when the government is held responsible for economic hardship, it may receive backing for other policy reasons, e.g., a pensioner hurt by inflation votes for the incumbent because of his strong stance against the Soviet Union. Lastly, one might refuse to support the opposition on strict grounds of economic policy, e.g., the suffering pensioner who feels that inflation would be even worse if the current government were voted out.

Such alternative hypotheses and the main hypothesis—voters do respond to economic conditions—can be tested through the analysis of French election surveys. Since 1970, the European Community has conducted national public opinion surveys, called Euro-Barometers, in France and the other member nations. These polls, under the direction of Jacques-René Rabier and Ronald Inglehart, have regularly asked between 1,000 and 2,000 French adults their opinions on different social, economic, and political matters. The responses to these questions can serve as the data for deciding the extent of economic voting among the French electorate. In each survey, the respondents were asked, If there were a general election tomorrow, which party would you support? We can arrange these answers along a scale from leftist to rightist parties, i.e., Communist, Unified Socialist, Socialist, Left Radical, Centrist, Union for French Democracy, Gaullist. These party choices are what we wish to relate to changing economic conditions. Those readers who are unused to working with surveys might find themselves somewhat uncomfortable at this point. After all, the survey question elicits vote intention rather than actual vote. How do we know that the intentions expressed to a pollster are not wildly different from behavior at the ballot box? Fortunately, scientific election surveys generally produce vote estimates that are very close to real vote totals. For example, in France, the most extended series of Fifth Republic election surveys, by IFOP, has predicted election results quite well, with an average error of only 2 percent (Lewis-Beck, 1981, 531). Likewise, the national French surveys of the Euro-Barometer, whose scientific procedures parallel those of IFOP, will tend to reflect the true distribution of voter preferences in the French electorate.

How are these vote preferences related to the responses on the economic items? Let us look at an example from the 1978 election year survey (Euro-Barometer 9), when, in addition to the above vote question, a national sample of the French citizenry was also asked whether they had been unemployed at any time in the last three years. Among those who declared they had been unemployed over the past three years, fully 78 percent responded they would vote for a party on the left (Communist, Unified Socialist, Socialist, or Left Radical). This far exceeds the "normal" vote for left parties, which at that time averaged 45 percent in Fifth Republic first-ballot legislative elections (see Lewis-Beck, 1983, 349–50). The clear implication is that employment status influenced party choice.

This connection between unemployment and support for the left seems an expression of dissatisfaction with the economic programs of the then-ruling Center-Right Majorité of President Giscard d'Estaing. By 1978, under his leadership, the unemployment rate had risen to 5.3 percent, higher than at any previous time in the Fifth Republic. Hence, it would not appear unreasonable for the recently unemployed to hold this Majorité responsible for their plight and to declare a vote for an opposition party on the left. Such voting, then, was essentially "incumbency-oriented," focusing its evaluation on past actions of the current government. In addition, there undoubtedly were some unemployed who voiced support for the left solely on grounds of party policy. That is to say, those unemployed who believe they are better served by a leftist party, perhaps because of its working-class appeal, regardless of its current status as an "in" or "out" party. In this case, voting is essentially "policy-oriented," focusing on the promises and programs of the parties (on these distinct orientations, see especially Chapter 13 in this volume). There is some evidence that "policy-oriented" voting, as well as "incumbency-oriented" voting can be a factor in French economic voting. Prior to the 1978 contest, IFOP asked a sample of the French electorate why anyone would vote for the left. The chief reason was the problem of unemployment (with two-thirds of those sampled saying it was a "fundamental" reason for backing the left; Sondages, nos. 2 and 3 [1978]: 132–34).

The next concern, of course, is whether the relationship between these unemployment and vote variables in the 1978 survey is in any way representative of how economic conditions usually related to party preference in France. To help answer this, I located all the economic questions (55) in then-available Euro-Barometer surveys (11) from 1970 to 1978 and related each to the survey's vote question. Out of these fifty-five bivariate relationships, all were in the expected direction. That is to say, when the respondent expressed economic discontent (e.g., complained about inflation, unemployment, income), he or she was more likely to voice support for a party of the left opposition. Moreover, the average correlation for these fifty-five relationships was $r = .20$. Interestingly, the strength of this association is greater than that commonly reported from survey data on economics and congressional voting in the United States (see Kinder and Kiewiet, 1979, 503–04). This argues that the French voter is more willing than the American voter to allow economic hardship to alter a voting decision, a possibility explored further below.

Obviously, other factors besides economics determine how the French voter decides. Indeed, it is possible that these other factors are more important and perhaps can even explain away the role economics appears to play. In U.S. research, the single most important determinant of the vote is party identification, i.e. psychological attachment to a party. American voters who feel they belong to, say, the Democratic party are very likely to vote for Democratic candidates, even in the face of strong issue pressures in the other direction. Further, it may even be that Americans who claim they are voting on the economic issues are really just voting their party label. For example, suppose that blue collar laborer John Citizen says Reagan is putting people out of work and so he is going to vote for the Democratic candidate in 1984. Is he really voting for the Democratic candidate because he dislikes Reagan's unemployment policies or simply because he is a life-long Democratic party member? Luckily, by applying statistical controls in multiple regression analysis, we can provide an answer to this question.

Let us work through this same issue in the French context. As already mentioned, in France there are many parties with frequently changing names. Thus, the notion of party identification, at least as a stable, enduring link between a particular voter and a particular party, has less utility than in the United States. Still, this does not mean that the French voter operates without a party identification or something like it. This functional equivalent appears to be "ideological identification," where strong attachment to an ideology serves as an unswerving guide to vote choice (see Inglehart and Klingemann, 1976; Lewis-Beck, 1983, 351–52; 1984). In the Euro-Barometer surveys, the respondent's ideology has been assessed with the following question: In political matters people talk of "the left" and "the right." How would you place your views on this scale? (The respondent chooses from a ten-point scale ordered from "left" to "right.") Because of the historic importance of the left–right dimension in French politics, respondents seldom have trouble locating themselves on this continuum. And, what is relevant for our purposes, where they place themselves, i.e., their ideological identification, goes a long way toward determining how they will vote. In the 1978 election year survey, for example, 97 percent of those who identified themselves as ideologically on the left (chose a 1, 2, 3, or 4) went on to say they would vote for a party on the left (Communist, Unified Socialist, Socialist, Left Radical) (see Lewis-Beck, 1984). Thus, ideological identification in France appears to work much like party identification in the United States, powerfully ordering voter preferences.

Is ideological identification so important, then, that economic issues actually have no independent force of their own? For example, suppose French voters who said they disliked Giscard's unemployment policies were more likely to say they would vote against his ruling party coalition in 1978? Is this apparent causal connection between the unemployment issue and the vote actually spurious, a product of the relationship of ideological identification to both? That is, because respondents are ideologically on the left, they may be more disapproving of the administration's unemployment policies and, at the same time, more likely to vote for a leftist party. Indeed, it may be that this common influence of ideology entirely accounts for the observed association between unemployment policy evaluation and party choice. In such a case, the economic issue cannot be said to have any actual impact on the vote. To check against this possibility of spuriousness, statistical controls can be applied, using multiple regression analysis.

Such a procedure allows us to examine the impact of more than one economic variable at a time, while simultaneously separating out the impact of ideological identification. Of course, many kinds of economic variables could be considered. As indicated, the research to date has concentrated on the respondent's evaluation of three economic issues— unemployment, income, and inflation. Some hypothetical examples are, respectively, Are you unemployed? Has your financial situation been getting better? Do you think the government is doing a good job fighting inflation? Besides these substantive divisions, economic items have been categorized theoretically. For example, the respondent's evaluation may be "retrospective" or "prospective": Has your financial situation been getting better over the past year? versus Do you think your financial situation will get better next year? (see Kuklinski and West, 1981). Another division concerns whether the questions are "simple" or "mediated" (here see especially Fiorina, 1981, 80–81). With the first, the respondent is asked only to evaluate some economic condition. With the second, the respondent is asked to consider an economic condition and also government policy toward it. Examples, respectively, are as follows: Has the national economic picture improved? Looking at the national economic picture, has government policy helped improve it? A final distinction is between "personal" and "collective" evaluations (see Kinder and Kiewiet, 1979). The former, also called a "pocketbook" evaluation, involves the respondent's judgment about his or her own economic situation, e.g., Has your financial situation improved? The latter, which as well has been labeled a "sociotropic" evaluation, treats the individual's interpretation of a larger world, often the nation, e.g., Has the national economy improved?

For the U.S. case, these different categories of economic variables have provided a rich ground for exploration. Unfortunately, for the French case, there can be much less exploration, because the sources of survey data are poorer, consisting mainly of the Euro-Barometer polls. These surveys, which were designed for other purposes, contain relatively few economic questions, and these differ from one to the next. Nevertheless, there is enough to begin to see how economic conditions influence the individual French voter, quite apart from the powerful influence of ideology. During the 1970s, two National Assembly elections were held, in 1973 and 1978. A multiple regression analysis of the Euro-Barometer survey data from these years was carried out. The model which was postulated held that French voters choose among the parties according to their ideological identification, plus their personal and collective economic discontent.

The actual estimates strongly support this explanation of voting behavior for both 1973 and 1978. As expected, the voter's self-placement on a left–right ideology scale was a significant predictor of party choice. Also, economic grievance was a significant factor pushing French citizens to vote against a ruling center-right coalition. In 1973, respondents were asked a "pocketbook" question about whether they were satisfied with their income. The more dissatisfied they were, the more likely they were to declare a vote for a leftist opposition party. In addition, they were asked to make a "sociotropic" judgment on whether the country should give top priority to fighting inflation, or to some noneconomic priority. Those who felt that the inflation fight demanded top priority were, as well, more likely to favor the left opposition. For 1978, the voters had put to them the "personal" item we considered earlier as to whether they had ever been unemployed during the last three years. These multiple regression results confirm our earlier bivariate finding, which is that the recently unemployed opposed the parties of the ruling Giscardian coalition. Further, the respondents had to make a "collective" judgment about the job opportunities in the area. Interestingly, the worse they saw area job opportunities, the more they favored parties on the left. In sum, these findings indicate that the French electorate does take economic conditions into account in casting their ballots, as the aggregate time series studies had initially implied. Economic discontent in its various forms— over income, inflation, unemployment—rouses individual French citizens to vote against the incumbent party coalition. Moreover, this expression of discontent is not entirely "selfish." That is, it is not motivated only by one's own personal economic situation. Rather, the voter's grasp of how the larger community is faring is also important.

Thus, in France, both personal and collective economic concerns motivate the voter. These findings are somewhat different from the United States, where personal economic circumstances, in contrast to collective ones, have been found only faintly related to vote. Why would personal conditions have a greater effect in France? It might well be due to the cultural differences between the two nations. The economic values of the American culture emphasize individualism and self-reliance (Feldman, 1982; Kinder and Kiewiet, 1979, 522–23). In this milieu, those who are suffering economic hardship, say, unemployment, tend to blame themselves, perhaps feeling they lacked the necessary work skills or did not apply themselves while on the job. The president and his party are seen as essentially irrelevant to their financial problems and certainly not responsible for their job loss. From this point of view, to vote against them for economic reasons would simply make no sense. In France, by way of contrast, this private enterprise, rugged individualist tradition is much less vibrant. While it is true that France is fundamentally a capitalist country, traditions of government intervention to direct the economy (dirigism) are strong. For many years, political authority has been centralized in a national state which has actively involved itself in the marketplace. Given this history, it is not unreasonable for the unemployed in France to find fault with the government and vote against it in the next election.

For the French citizen in the Fifth Republic, economic considerations are important determinants of the vote. But, obviously, other factors also work to shape the voting decision. The power of ideological identification has already been mentioned. In addition, the major forces of long-standing impact are social class, religion, and region (Cerny, 1972, 445; Macridis, 1975, 60–64, 91). Some analysts would consider social class the most important issue dividing voters in Western European democracies such as France, where Marxism has a firm tradition. In repeated studies, it has been found that working-class voters are much more likely to favor parties on the left than are middle-class voters (see especially Alford, 1963; Lewis-Beck, 1981). For France, religion is also a key factor. While almost everyone is Catholic, there are large differences in the degree to which Catholicism is actually practiced. The evidence shows that the more closely tied French voters are to religion, as indicated by the extent to which they regularly practice it, the more likely they are to support political parties on the right (Michelet and Simon, 1977). The last major influence that is routinely cited is regional attachment. In France, people tend to vote according to region. For instance, the inhabitants of the northwest appear conservative when compared to the dwellers in the rest of France.

When all these pivotal factors—social class, religion, region—are considered together with ideology and economics in a multiple regression equation, the economic concerns still manage to play a significant role in party choice (Lewis-Beck, 1983, 356). Indeed, in other research, which simply compares the magnitude of the correlation coefficients among the variables, economic dissatisfaction is as strongly related to vote (average r about .20) as the celebrated variable of social class (average r also equal to about .20). And it is even more strongly related than the traditional tie of region, where the average beta is about .10. Thus, only ideology (average r of about .70) and, to a lesser extent, religion (average r of about .40) seem to exert a greater impact on the French voter than economic concerns (see Lewis-Beck, 1984). In fact, for some elections, economic discontent even appears important enough to have provided the critical margin of victory. The elections of 1981 are one such example.

ECONOMICS AND THE ELECTIONS OF 1981

In May 1981 Socialist François Mitterrand defeated incumbent president Valery Giscard d'Estaing in the second round of balloting, winning with 51.8 percent of the popular vote. The next month legislative elections were held and a Socialist-led coalition took control of the National Assembly. What brought about the victory of the left, without precedent in the history of the Fifth Republic? It is helpful, in answering this question, to consider the strength of the left in earlier elections. Under the Third and Fourth Republics, the government was sometimes directed by Socialist-dominated coalitions. During the Fifth Republic itself, the parties on the left, taken together, have always received a respectable share of the popular vote (the lowest combined first-ballot total was 41 percent in 1968). Indeed, in the National Assembly contest of 1978, it was widely believed that the Union of the Left (an alliance of the Socialists plus the Communists plus smaller parties) would actually become the majority. Hence, the left has ever been a close rival for power in contemporary France. The electoral success of Mitterrand and his followers, then, should not be viewed as a total surprise. In fact, earlier, in the 1974 presidential race,

Mitterrand had also run against Giscard and barely lost (with 49.2 percent of the vote on the second ballot). Therefore, his 1981 victory came not from massive popular upheaval but rather from a modest shift in public opinion. What caused this small, though critical, shift in his favor? First and foremost, it seems to have been brought about by the deteriorating economic conditions preceding the election. (Interestingly, a similar argument has been made for the 1980 victory of Reagan in the United States.)

The Mitterrand success is certainly not associated with a dramatic change in key traditional forces operating on the French voter (Lewis-Beck, 1984). A common view is that the Socialist rise was anticipated by an ideological shift to the left in the political thinking of the French public. But survey evidence shows such a shift never actually took place. That is, before the elections only about 30 percent of the adult population placed itself clearly on the left (i.e., chose either 1, 2, 3, or 4 on the self-placement scale previously discussed), a total similar to the average percentage of leftists reported in surveys across the Fifth Republic. Furthermore, the data do not suggest a lessening of class cleavages, expressed as an unusual defection of the middle class to parties on the left. Instead, one observes that the tug of class on the French voter exhibits essentially the same strength as it has for over twenty years.

What can account for this Socialist surge are changing economic conditions and their persistent link with the voter. The aggregate time series model considered earlier implied the importance of deteriorating economic conditions by successfully forecasting a 1981 first-ballot majority for the left, as a result of the declining real income and rising unemployment occurring before the election. The survey research just reported confirms at the level of the individual voter the importance of various kinds of economic hardship in shaping party preferences. In particular, it was established that economic discontent pushed voters to act against the incumbent coalition. During years of great prosperity, relatively few citizens would be economically dissatisfied. Hence, not many votes against the incumbent would be generated by economic grievance. During a time of recession, however, a large number of citizens would be economically dissatisfied. Such a situation, which describes France before the 1981 presidential election, would produce a lot of votes against the incumbent.

Despite Giscard's economic policy efforts, inflation had reached an annual rate of 14 percent, and the unemployment rate stood at 7 percent, figures unequaled under previous Fifth Republic presidents (but very similar to President Carter's "misery index" in the United States in 1980). Moreover, the French public perceived this sad state of the economy. In a survey regularly carried out by the European Community, consumers are asked about the "general economic situation in the country now compared to twelve months ago." Looking at the responses just before the 1981 presidential election, one observes that consumer confidence in the economy registered its lowest score ever, since the beginning of the survey in 1972 (Lewis-Beck, 1983, 357). All of these indicators point to a time of unprecedented economic difficulty in the Fifth Republic. The many who were economically discontented delivered an unusual number of votes to Mitterrand and the left, in protest against the economic policies of the Giscard government. These extra economic voters, who had not been there in 1974, transformed Mitterrand into a winner in 1981.

CONCLUSION

This essay has considered the influence of economics on French electoral behavior, in particular examining popularity and voting. Across the Fifth Republic, changing economic conditions have caused the popularity of the president (and the prime minister) to rise or fall. Specifically, decreases in macroeconomic indicators of unemployment, inflation, and income produce significant declines in the percentage of the French public who are satisfied with the president. French politicians watch these declines closely, for they suggest that the president is not doing his job well and may be vulnerable at the ballot box. What do these economic fluctuations mean in terms of actual votes? Aggregate time series analyses imply that changes in national measures of unemployment, income, and inflation are highly predictive of voter preferences in upcoming legislative elections. Unfortunately, with these studies we cannot be sure whether individual voters are responding to economic conditions or to something else related to them. To pinpoint what motivates individual voters, it is necessary to inspect survey data.

Systematic analysis of French election surveys reveals a clear relationship between economic discontent and a vote against the government and its party coalition. In particular, income dissatisfaction, inflation, and unemployment have all been shown to encourage the French to vote for an opposition party. Moreover, these economic grievances have manifested themselves as both personal and collective concerns. Beyond these key conclusions, it is difficult to be more specific because not enough data are available. For example, does income change have a bigger impact than unemployment or inflation? Are personal incentives more powerful than collective ones? Are economic votes based largely on emotion or reason? In voting against the government, do voters tend to look at past performance or future promises? The answers to these questions must await further data and research. However, despite the fact that much is still unknown, a general finding emerges from the research to date: economics is an important determinant of the vote in contemporary France. Indeed, for some elections, such as those of 1981, economic concerns are decisive.

What does the future hold? Since coming to power, President Mitterrand, with the help of his prime minister and the Socialist-led coalition in the National Assembly, has enacted sweeping reforms. Here is a sampling, from the first two years in office, of those reforms which bear on the economy: nationalization of several major companies, thereby extending government control to over 30 percent of the nation's industrial activity; greatly increased social spending, the minimum wage going up 10 percent, old-age pensions 20 percent, benefits for big families 25 percent, and housing allowances 25 percent; a fifth week of annual paid vacation granted to workers; devaluation of the franc; wage and price controls; increased taxes on business. What has been the net effect of these measures? A good deal of public reaction has been negative. Perhaps predictably, there have been outcries from the business community. For example, Henri Lepage, author of "Vive le Commerce!" (Long Live Business!) and staff member of the Institut de l'Entreprise, summarized the business viewpoint in a *Wall Street Journal* article: "France Under Mitterrand: Two Years in and Sinking" (Lepage, 1983, 29). But complaints are also coming from workers, traditionally the strongest sources of left support. Consider the recent comments of a lathe operator in a small plant in Mainvilliers who has always voted left but feels that Mitterrand's programs are hurting him financially. For the March 1983 municipal elections he decided to switch to "the old regime," remarking, "I think a lot of people like me will vote for the right" (Ulman, 1983, 1). The actual municipal election results, especially those from the first round of balloting, hint that his prediction was correct. In these local contests, which are commonly held to be a referendum on the national government's performance, the parties of the left lost ground, receiving only 46.4 percent of the vote on the first ballot (March 6).

Besides this local election setback, the popularity of President Mitterrand has fallen more or less steadily in the polls. As of May 1984, the percentage of those in the monthly IFOP poll who said they were satisfied with the president had dropped to 33 percent (the rating for Prime Minister Pierre Mauroy was even lower, at 27 percent, presaging his resignation in July). Such low levels of public support seem to have been brought about largely by the government's economic policies, which have not managed to improve the nation's macroeconomic performance. The limited success of these policies is indicated by the inflation and unemployment rate figures for 1984, which stood at about 7 percent and 10 percent, respectively. According to these estimates, then, the economy exhibits more or less the same stagflation as in Giscard's last year. And the implications for future incumbent electoral performance are equivalent. That is, on the basis of what we know about economic voting in France, the ruling left party coalition would be soundly defeated if elections were held now, just as the center-right ruling coalition was in 1981. Of course, the next legislative elections are in fact not scheduled until 1986, and the presidential elections not until 1988. Therefore, Mitterrand and his followers may have enough time to engineer an economic revival and thus avoid electoral defeat.

REFERENCES

Alford, Robert R. 1963. *Party and Society: The Anglo-American Democracies.* Chicago: Rand McNally.

Cerny, P. G. 1972. "Cleavage, Aggregation, and Change in French Politics." *British Journal of Political Science* 2:443–55.

Charlot, Jean. 1971. *Les Français et de Gaulle.* Paris: Plon.

Ehrmann, Henry W. 1971. *Politics in France.* 2nd ed. Boston: Little, Brown.

Feldman, Stanley. 1982. "Economic Self-Interest and Political Behavior." *American Journal of Political Science* 26 (August): 446–66.

Fiorina, Morris P. 1978. "Economic Retrospective Voting in American National Elections: A Micro-Analysis." *American Journal of Political Science* 22:426–43.

————. 1981. *Retrospective Voting in American National Elections.* New Haven: Yale University Press.

Hibbs, Douglas A., Jr., and Vasilatos, Nicholas. 1981. "Economics and Politics in France: Economic Performance and Political Support for Presidents Pompidou and Giscard d'Estaing." *European Journal of Political Research* 9:133–45.

Inglehart, Ronald, and Klingemann, Hans D. 1976. "Party Identification, Ideological Preference and the Left-Right Dimension Among Western Mass Publics." In *Party Identification and Beyond,* ed. Ian Budge, Ivor Crewe, and Dennis Farlie. London: Wiley.

Kernell, Samuel. 1978. "Explaining Presidential Popularity." *American Political Science Review* 72 (March): 506–22.

Kinder, Donald R., and Kiewiet, D. Roderick. 1979. "Economic Discontent and Political Behavior: The Role of Personal Grievances and Collective Economic Judgments in Congressional Voting." *American Journal of Political Science* 23:495–527.

Kuklinski, James H., and West, Darrell M. 1981. "Economic Expectations and Voting Behavior in United States Senate and House Elections." *American Political Science Review* 75:436–47.

Lafay, Jean-Dominique. 1977. "Les Consequences electorales de la conjoncture économique: Essais de prévision chiffrée pour mars 1978." *Vie et sciences économiques*, no. 75 (October):1–7.

Lepage, Henri. 1983. "France Under Mitterrand: Two Years in and Sinking." *Wall Street Journal* (May 11): 29.

Lewis-Beck, Michael S. 1980a. *Applied Regression Analysis: An Introduction.* Beverly Hills, Calif.: Sage.

———. 1980b. "Economic Conditions and Executive Popularity: The French Experience." *American Journal of Political Science* 24 (May):306–23.

———. 1981. "The Electoral Politics of the French Peasantry: 1946–1978." *Political Studies* 29 (December): 517–36.

———. 1983. "Economics and the French Voter: A Microanalysis." *Public Opinion Quarterly* 47:347–60.

———. 1984. "France: The Stalled Electorate." In *Electoral Change in Advanced Industrial Democracies: Realignment or Dealignment?* ed. Paul Allen Beck, Russell J. Dalton, and Scott C. Flanagan. Princeton: Princeton University Press.

Lewis-Beck, Michael S., and Bellucci, Paolo. 1982. "Economic Influences on Legislative Elections in Multiparty Systems: France and Italy." *Political Behavior* 4 (June):93–107.

Lewis-Beck, Michael S., and Rice, Tom W. 1982. "Presidential Popularity and Presidential Vote." *Public Opinion Quarterly* 46:534–37.

Macridis, Roy C. 1975. *French Politics in Transition: The Years After de Gaulle.* Cambridge, Mass.: Winthrop.

Michelat, Guy, and Simon, Michel. 1977. "Religion, Class, and Politics." *Comparative Politics* 10:159–84.

Parodi, Jean-Luc. 1971. "Sur deux courbes de popularité." *Revue française de science politique* 21 (February):129–51.

Pierce, Roy. 1968. *French Politics and Political Institutions.* New York: Harper & Row.

Rosa, Jean-Jacques, and Amson, Daniel. 1976. "Conditions économiques et élections: une analyse politico-économetrique (1920–1973)." *Revue française de science politique* 26 (December):1101–24.

Ulman, Neil. 1983. "French Workers Grow Increasingly Dismayed by National Policies." *Wall Street Journal* (March 1):1.

13 THE EFFECTS OF ECONOMIC ISSUES ON VOTING FOR PRESIDENT, 1956–1980

D. Roderick Kiewiet

Until recently, knowledge about just exactly how economic issues affected voting behavior was largely confined to the domain of political folk wisdom. The troubled economy of the 1970s, however, captured the attention of political scientists as well as the public, and there resulted a veritable explosion of research on the political effects of economic issues. Studies in this area range from analyses of several decades of national voting and economic statistics to intensive examinations of survey data from a single election. None has employed exactly the same set of assumptions or the same statistical models. Yet one can identify two basic dimensions running through this body of research. The first concerns voters' decision rules. According to the *incumbency-oriented* hypothesis, voters respond to all manner of economic adversity by tending to vote against the incumbent officeholders, and to any sort of economic improvement by tending to vote for them. An alternative hypothesis is that voting is *policy-oriented;* voters choose between candidates for national office on the basis of differences in the relative macroeconomic priorities of the respective parties. In particular, voters who are concerned about unemployment give greater support to Democratic candidates, and those who are relatively more averse to inflation tend to vote Republican.

A second basic dimension concerns the weight voters assign to different types of economic events, experiences, and information. As before, two general alternatives have emerged from previous research. The first, the *personal experiences* hypothesis, posits that voters react mainly to directly experienced economic conditions. According to the second, the *national assessments* hypothesis, it is their perceptions and evaluations of the nation's economy which lead them to choose one candidate over another. These two alternatives can be considered in conjunction with the two decision rule alternatives, resulting in personal experiences and national assessments versions of both incumbency-oriented and policy-oriented voting. A voter's decision to vote Democratic instead of Republican, for example, could grow out of losing his job or from the conviction that unemployment is a serious problem for the country as a whole. The resultant four hypotheses, it should be added, are not mutually exclusive. Evidence about one, either supportive or nonsupportive, does not necessarily imply anything about the others.

INCUMBENCY-ORIENTED VERSUS POLICY-ORIENTED VOTING

Following publication in 1971 of Gerald Kramer's influential study, subsequent research focused primarily upon the incumbency-oriented hypothesis. As Kramer acknowledged, the model he estimated was largely inspired by the work of Anthony Downs (1957). Voters, according to Downs, make their decisions under a high degree of uncertainty. Relevant information about the available choices, e.g., party platforms or campaign promises, is both bothersome to obtain and of questionable reliability. There is, however, one source of reliable information readily available to voters—the record of the incumbent administration. As Fiorina observes:

> Citizens are not fools. Having often observed political equivocation, if not outright lying, should they listen carefully to campaign promises? Having heard the economic, educational, sociological, defense, and foreign policy expert advisors disagree on both the effects of past policies and the prospects of future ones, should they pay close attention to policy debates? Even if concerned and competent, citizens appear to have little solid basis on which to cast their votes, save on those rare occasions when candidates take clear and differing positions on salient specific issues (e.g., busing, abortion, the Equal Rights Amendment).
>
> But are the citizens' choices actually so unclear? After all, they typically have one comparatively hard bit of data: they know what life has been like during the incumbent's administration. They need not know the precise economic or foreign policies of the incumbent administration in order to see or feel the results of those policies. (1981, 5)

As developed by Downs, Kramer, Fiorina, and others, the incumbency-oriented hypothesis posits that voting is *retrospective*—voters pay heed to what has occurred under the present incumbents, not to parties' or candidates' promises about the future. Similarly, voters are assumed to be more familiar with and concerned about the *results* produced by public policy than with the specific policy instruments themselves.

The incumbency-oriented hypothesis has received substantial empirical support in several time series analyses (including Kramer's) of U.S. economic and voting data. It is doubtful, however, that that is the whole story. Certainly voters prefer good economic conditions to bad. But prosperity is not all of one piece, and it is simply not possible for policy makers to attack all economic problems with equal fervor. In particular, the key question in economic policy during the past several years has been how much priority to assign to reducing unemployment versus reducing inflation. Unfortunately, medicine for one of these two problems is usually bane for the other: policies to reduce unemployment typically do so by seeking to stimulate aggregate demand, whereas policies to lower inflation typically seek to depress aggregate demand (Hibbs, 1979).

Over the past three decades the major political parties have differed in the priority they assign to reducing inflation versus lowering unemployment. Compared to Republican administrations, Democratic administrations have been more sensitive to unemployment and have been more willing to risk some inflation to reduce it. Republican administrations, conversely, have usually tolerated much more slack in the economy and thus unemployment to fight inflation. There is reason to believe, then, that voting in response to economic conditions is often policy-oriented: voters will give greater support to Democratic presidential and congressional candidates during periods of high unemployment but greater support to Republicans during inflationary periods. Instead of simply blaming the incumbents for any and all forms of economic difficulty, policy-oriented voters support the party which places a higher priority on attacking the particular economic problem that they are concerned about—whether or not that party is currently in power.

So construed, the policy-oriented hypothesis demands little more of voters than the incumbency-oriented hypothesis. It too holds that voters' decisions are retrospective in nature, weighing heavily their experiences of the recent past, and that they need be concerned only about the actual results of macroeconomic policies. Voters need not have a sophisticated understanding of fiscal and monetary policy instruments, nor must they believe anything in particular about the nature of the relationship between inflation and unemployment. Rather, policy-oriented voting requires only that voters (1) see either inflation or unemployment as a serious problem and want to see it alleviated, and (2) that they perceive differences between the parties in the amount of effort and/or skill they would apply in combatting that problem.[1]

PERSONAL EXPERIENCES VERSUS NATIONAL ASSESSMENTS

Evidence on the incumbency-oriented and policy-oriented hypotheses, however, would shed no light on other important facets of individual voting behavior. Above all, it would tell us little about the particular worries, perceptions, and evaluations concerning inflation, unemployment, or other economic problems which influence voters' choices in American elections.

What exactly is the nature of the economic concerns which move a voter to choose one candidate over another? According to one of the most widely held assumptions about political behavior, the answer is simple— voting in response to unemployment, inflation, or any other economic concerns is the product of direct, personally experienced conditions and events. Adopting this perspective, we can specify personal experience versions of both the incumbency-oriented and policy-oriented hypotheses. Such a version of the former hypothesis would hold that those individuals whose recent economic fortunes have been favorable would tend to support the incumbents, while those whose fortunes have soured would tend to support the opposition. Thus the incumbent party falters at the polls during economic downturns because there are more voters encountering economic difficulties in their own lives. The personal experience version of the policy-oriented hypothesis would have it that it is those individuals who are themselves out of work or threatened with unemployment who identify with and vote for the party which has stressed action against unemployment, i.e., the Democrats. Those individuals who are less susceptible to unemployment, similarly, tend to favor price stability and the Republican party.

The fundamental egocentrism of the personal experiences hypothesis is intuitively appealing. The personal experiences hypothesis (at least the incumbency-oriented version of it) has also received some empirical backing in previous voting studies. Voters' perceptions of recent trends in their families' financial situations have been linked to incumbency-oriented voting, primarily in presidential elections (Fiorina, 1978, 1981; Kinder and Kiewiet, 1981; Schlozman and Verba, 1979). Previous research concerning this version of the policy-oriented hypothesis has also provided bits of evidence suggesting that voters respond in a policy-oriented manner to personally experienced unemployment (Kiewiet, 1981; Fiorina, 1981).

Several recent studies, however, have also examined a major competing proposition concerning the way in which economic concerns affect voting decisions. This view holds that it is perceptions of national conditions and events which most heavily influence voting behavior. As before, the national assessments hypothesis can be applied to both incumbency-oriented and policy-oriented voting. In the first case, the prediction is that voters who believed the *nation's* economy was doing well would tend to support the incumbents, whereas those who believed it had worsened would tend to vote for the challengers. Similarly, such a version of the policy-oriented hypothesis posits that voters who see unemployment as a major national problem are more likely to support the Democrats, whereas those who believe the country is plagued by inflation turn instead to the Republicans. According to this hypothesis, economic problems, either in general or inflation and unemployment in particular, can exert a strong influence on policy preferences and voting decisions without being personally troublesome.

Proponents of this hypothesis concede that the condition of the nation's economy is undoubtedly of less personal relevance to most individuals than their own economic well-being. They argue, however, that national assessments are of more obvious *political relevance*. Kinder and Kiewiet (1979) contend that most people largely attribute their own economic successes and failures to purely personal or local factors, e.g., getting a raise or a better job, making an unwise career choice, or trends in local business conditions. Schlozman and Verba's survey evidence certainly backs them up. After examining the explanations of hundreds of unemployed people as to why they had lost their jobs, they report: "What may be most significant is that the explanations of one's own loss of work tend to be narrow and contingent. Our respondents do not see themselves as victims of broad social forces or governmental ineptitude but of specific events connected with their particular employment circumstance" (1979, 194).

Sniderman and Brody (1977) make a related argument against the personal experiences hypothesis. In their view, it is the "ethic of self-reliance" which diffuses the political significance of personal economic problems. Data from the 1972 and 1974 National Election Studies strongly supported the claim that most people in this country believe that they themselves (not the government) are primarily responsible for dealing with their own personal economic problems.

In contrast, according to proponents of the national assessments hypothesis, most people readily perceive trends in the nation's economy to be a product of the policies pursued by those in power. An individual may attribute a personal loss of income to unwise investments or to a cutback in overtime hours but believe a drop in GNP results from the ineptitude of the current administration. A worker who has been laid off will blame it on his or her company losing a contract to a competing firm but see a rise in the unemployment rate as the consequence of Republican macroeconomic policies. In short, trends in the nation's economy, in most people's minds, reflect directly upon the performance and policies of the governing party. Their own personal economic fortunes, in contrast, generally do not.

It should be stressed that the distinction between these hypotheses is *not* equivalent to the distinction between altruism and self-interest. True, voters choosing on the basis of personal economic experiences are surely motivated by concern for themselves and their families. Why voters might vote on the basis of national assessments, on the other hand, is less clear. Some may be acting out of an altruistic or patriotic concern for the well-being of all Americans (or at least a large subset of them). On the other hand, voting on the basis of national assessments may be motivated by self-interest. Voters may construe the performance or policies of the party in power as a public good and thus use information about the condition of the nation's economy as an indicator of the present administration's ability to promote their own economic well-being—and incidentally that of the nation as a whole.

DATA

The following analysis examines voting in American presidential elections in terms of this two-dimensional (incumbency-oriented or policy-oriented, personal experiences or national assessments) framework.[2] The survey data upon which the analysis is based come from the 1956–80 CPS National Election Studies.[3]

Evidence on the personal experiences version of the incumbency-oriented hypothesis will be derived from a question which has been included in every biennial CPS study since 1956:

We are interested in how people are getting along financially these days. Would you say that you (and your family) are better off or worse off financially than you were a year ago, or about the same?

If this hypothesis is supported, voters who believe their financial situation has recently worsened will, everything else being equal, tend to vote against the incumbent president. Voters who believe their finances have improved, in contrast, will tend to vote for him.

Most of the evidence on the personal experiences version of the policy-oriented hypothesis will be based upon the employment status of the head of the respondent's family (over 60 percent of respondents were themselves heads of households). Because previous research suggests that the effects of past experiences of unemployment decline fairly quickly, this analysis will include two separate variables for unemployment. The first will indicate that the respondent's head of household was actually unemployed at the time of the survey. The second will indicate that the family head had been out of work sometime during the previous six months but was working at the time of the interview. If policy-oriented voting in response to unemployment occurs, these variables should register pro-Democratic effects upon voting decision regardless of which party is in power. Furthermore, the effect of one's head of household being currently out of work should be stronger than the effect of unemployment experienced in the previous six months.

Data on unemployment, of course, tells us nothing about the electoral consequences of personal hardships resulting from inflation. Fortunately, in the 1972–76 surveys we can identify individuals who perceived inflation (or unemployment) to be personally troublesome by their responses to the following question:

> Let's change the subject for a moment. We like to have people tell us what sorts of problems they have to deal with in their daily lives. Can you tell me what some of the problems are that you face these days in your life? . . . Anything else?

As indicated in Table 13.1, categories of other important economic problems could also be derived from these responses. Indeed, over half the respondents referred to at least one economic problem. Although this chapter examines only voting in presidential elections, data from 1974 were also collected and reported in Table 13.1 in order to assess better the validity of the personal economic problem variables. What are reported are respondents' most important personal *economic* problems. If respondents mentioned a noneconomic problem, e.g., poor health, as their most important but also mentioned an economic problem, the economic problem was the one coded here.

As Table 13.1 shows, respondents cited *inflation* more frequently than any other economic problem. This category includes all references to high or rising prices, either for specific commodities like food or fuel oil or prices in general. Confidence that this category reflects what it is supposed to is bolstered by the fact that the percentage of respondents naming inflation their worst personal economic problem corresponded closely to the objective rate of inflation which obtained in these years (the Consumer Price Index rose by 3.3 percent in 1972, 11.0 percent in 1974, and 5.8 percent in 1976).

Many economists suspect that the public is often confused about inflation and its costs. Above all, it is *real* incomes and *real* prices which should concern people, not the nominal price level. Widespread aversion to inflation, they argue, results mainly from people confusing inflation with a declining real income. Such confusion, of course, is understandable—the typical way real incomes are reduced is for price inflation to outpace wage increases. People thus blame the mechanism (price infla-

TABLE 13.1
Most Important Personal Economic Problems, 1972–1976
(percentage)

PROBLEM REPORTED	1972	1974	1976
Inflation	14.4	30.2	22.2
Declining real income	4.8	7.1	5.9
Unemployment related	3.4	4.4	4.0
Taxes	5.5	1.3	4.1
General economic problems	18.6	19.2	19.8
Noneconomic problems	32.5	24.4	26.8
No problem mentioned	20.8	13.4	17.2
Total	100.0	100.0	100.0
N	1,109	2,523	2,415

tion) instead of the end result (a lower real income). But as Table 13.1 indicates, between 5 and 7 percent of the respondents in these surveys referred explicitly to a *declining real income.* A variety of responses were subsumed under this category, such as failure of wages to keep up with price increases, living on a fixed income, or complaints about declining purchasing power. Given that there is undoubtedly some confusion between inflation per se and real income losses, one might question the wisdom of creating these two separate categories. Recognition of a declining real income, however, could more strongly influence voting decisions for two reasons. First, respondents in this category could have been suffering more economic hardship than those who simply cited inflation. Second, these individuals may have been more sophisticated in perceiving the true nature of their problems.

The *unemployment related* category contains all respondents who felt their worst economic problem was that they (or persons close to them) were laid off, unemployed, underemployed, or worried by the threat of unemployment. Despite the breadth of this definition, surprisingly few respondents fell into this category—between 3.4. and 4.4 percent. One likely reason for this is that unemployment compensation and other programs have taken some of the sting out of joblessness. Still, unemployment is no bed of roses for most workers and their families. As Cameron (1979) points out, the unemployed come disproportionately from that segment of the labor force which is not covered by compensation programs, and benefits for those who are covered average less than half the gross earnings of the typical production worker. Whatever the case, the percentage of respondents naming unemployment their worst problem was lower than the objective rate of unemployment.

Similarly, few respondents referred to *taxes.* Lowering taxes, of course, is a frequent Republican campaign theme. Differentiating respondents in this category from the others thus allows us to examine a second policy-oriented hypothesis, i.e., that concern over taxes will produce support for Republican presidential candidates.

A residual category, *general or miscellaneous economic problems,* was composed mainly of vague references to such things as bills, money problems, or "not making enough money." As Table 13.1 shows, the size of this category was remarkably stable from year to year—around 20 percent. In fact, the size of most categories remained fairly stable from year to year; only the percentage citing inflation fluctuated much. And as indicated earlier, the size of the inflation category clearly reflected the actual rates of inflation in 1972, 1974, and 1976.

The two remaining categories are self-explanatory. People who reported literally hundreds of different types of problems ended up in the *noneconomic problems* category. Most of these were ordinary, day-to-day problems, such as not getting along with the neighbors or poor health. Respondents in the last category, finally, mentioned no problems whatsoever.

As with personal economic concerns, most research to date on national economic assessments has focused on incumbency-oriented voting. In testing this hypothesis, previous studies have relied primarily upon responses to a question included in most CPS national election studies since 1962, which asks: Now turning to business conditions in the country as a whole . . . would you say that at the present time business conditions are better or worse than they were a year ago?

This question is analogous to the family finances question described earlier. If the national assessments version of the incumbency-oriented hypothesis is supported, voters who believe that national economic conditions have recently worsened will tend to vote against the incumbent president. Voters who believe the national business climate has improved, in contrast, will tend to vote for him.

Since 1960 the CPS National Election Studies have also included national-level counterparts to the personal economic problems measures discussed earlier. Like the personal problems questions, these questions were open-ended and nondirective. Respondents were simply asked to name the problems they believed were most serious—not for themselves, in this case, but for the nation as a whole. These questions were as follows:

What do you think are the most important problems facing this *country?* (1972, 1976, 1980)

What do you personally feel are the most important problems which the government in Washington should try to take care of? (1968)

What would you personally feel are the most important problems the government should try to take care of when the new president and Congress take office in January? (1960, 1964)

As with answers to the personal problems questions, it was possible to distinguish references to other economic problems in addition to unemployment and inflation. The resultant coding scheme and marginal frequencies for each year are presented in Table 13.2. As before, if a noneconomic problem, e.g., crime, was deemed most important, but an economic problem was also mentioned, the economic problem was the one coded here.

The *inflation* category includes all those who named high or rising prices the most troublesome national economic problem. Occasionally they referred to particular goods or services, but most referred to prices in general. Included under *unemployment* are respondents who felt the government should create more jobs, provide job retraining, or grant aid to depressed areas; most, though, simply cited unemployment. As Table 13.2 shows, the size of these two categories closely tracked the actual inflation and unemployment rates in these years. As was seen earlier, the frequency with which inflation and unemployment were cited as personal problems also moved up and down with the objective rates (see Table 13.1).

As at the personal level, few respondents felt that *taxes* were the most important national economic problem. The next two categories each subsumed a wide range of responses. Under the heading of *need more government programs* were respondents who believed that the federal government should do more to alleviate social problems. Most advocated new or enlarged federal programs in particular areas: education, social security, etc. Whatever the specific social ill respondents cited, what put them in this category was their belief that the role of the public sector should be expanded in order to remedy it.

Individuals in the next category, however, believed that a growing public sector was precisely what was wrong with this country. A variety of responses fell under the rubric of *need less government spending*—the

TABLE 13.2
Most Important National Economic Problems, 1960–1980
(percentage)

PROBLEM REPORTED	1960	1964	1968	1972	1976	1980
Inflation	3.7	1.2	2.6	20.0	30.3	40.4
Unemployment	11.6	6.9	2.3	6.3	32.1	12.4
Taxes	4.7	4.3	3.7	5.5	1.6	2.1
More government programs	20.3	27.3	16.1	10.9	4.2	10.1
Less government spending	3.5	3.6	2.5	3.3	2.3	5.2
General economic problems	2.9	0.6	0.8	8.0	14.1	11.8
Noneconomic problems	42.1	37.9	69.4	42.7	9.3	15.2
No problem mentioned	11.2	18.2	2.6	3.3	6.1	2.8
N	1,514	1,571	1,557	1,109	1,217	1,391

federal government's budget deficits, waste and inefficiency in the bureaucracy, etc. What respondents in this category shared, then, was the desire to see the government's power—especially its spending power—reduced.

The central policy-oriented hypotheses to be tested here, of course, concern inflation and unemployment: voters who believe that the former is the most important national economic problem are predicted to give relatively greater support to Republican contenders; those concerned about the latter should tend to support Democrats. An auxiliary policy-oriented hypothesis—that concern over high taxes would lead voters to support Republicans—was posed in the discussion of personal economic problems, and, as the presence of the taxes category in Table 13.2 implies, an analogous national level version of it can be tested. Another traditional point of contention between parties of the left and right, however, concerns the proper size of the public sector: parties of the left favor its expansion; parties of the right oppose it. Tufte (1978) argues that even the "ideologically bland" parties of the United States differ on this score. The national economic problems data can be used to determine whether this difference is also present in the parties' electoral bases of support. The following analysis, then, will examine the hypotheses that voters who believe more government programs are needed to remedy serious national problems give greater support to Democrats, whereas Republican candidates garner relatively more support from voters who believe that the nation's worst problem is too much government.

Most respondents in the next category, *general or miscellaneous economic problems,* were subsumed under the "general" heading, referring simply to "the economy." The miscellany included those who cited interest rates, a bearish stock market, or a few other specific problems. As was the case at the personal level, no policy-oriented hypotheses can be made about the voting behavior of respondents in this category. *Noneconomic problems* include everything else: crime in the streets, the Vietnam War, foreign affairs, and a host of other things. Not surprisingly, this catch-all category was largest in the tumultuous but prosperous year of 1968, smallest in the peaceful but economically troubled period after 1972.

ANALYSIS

This analysis is designed to estimate the effects of several independent variables—the various economic concerns and perceptions discussed above—upon voters' choices in American presidential elections. Because of the dichotomous nature of the dependent variable (voters choose to vote either Democratic or Republican), the statistical technique employed here is probit analysis. Although this technique is somewhat different from ordinary regression, it is possible to understand and interpret the results produced by probit analysis without knowledge of its mathematical derivation. For a detailed discussion of this and related techniques, see almost any current econometrics text.

It is also the case that the independent variables can take on only a few discrete values. Respondents' perceptions of national business conditions, for example, can be registered in only one of three separate ways—better, same, or worse. The various economic variables are thus specified as "dummy" variables, which take on only the values of 1 or 0. A voter who felt national business conditions had improved during the previous year, for example, would have a value of 1 on the "business conditions better" variable but 0 on the "business conditions worse" variable. Construction of dummy variables in this manner requires that one category in each battery of responses be left out of the equation.[4] In the current example the suppressed reference category would be "business conditions same," and the effects of perceptions of either improving or worsening conditions would be measured in reference to it.

Dummy variables were thus created for the family finances better and worse categories, with voters who felt their family's financial situation had stayed the same forming the reference group. Similarly, national business conditions better and worse variables were created, with those who felt conditions had stayed the same again forming a reference group. (Although the family finances question was asked in every survey between 1960 and 1980, data on perceptions of national business conditions are available only for 1968 on.) The equations for all election years other than 1972 and 1976 also include the two head of household unemployment variables, while the 1972 and 1976 equations include instead dummy variables for each of the five categories of personal economic problems reported in Table 13.1. All equations include dummy variables for the six types of perceived national economic problems reported in Table 13.2. For both the personal and national level economic problem variables a reference group was formed by voters who either failed to cite an economic problem or who reported no problems at all.

Finally, the probit equations estimated here also include dummy variables which reflect voters' partisan predispositions. In the 1960 and 1976 equations the "Democratic" and "Republican" dummy variables reflect the party of the candidate the voter had supported in the previous presidential election, i.e., 1956 and 1972. The reference group is thus composed of those individuals who four years earlier reported that they had not voted for president. In all other years respondents had not been interviewed at the time of previous elections. What the "Democratic" and "Republican" dummy variables in these years reflect instead is the respondents' answers to the standard party identification question: Generally speaking, do you usually think of yourself as a Democrat, a Republican, an Independent, or what? Those voters who replied that they were Independents thus form the reference group.

The results of this analysis are presented in Table 13.3. The left number in each entry is the probit estimates, and the number in parentheses to the right is the standard error.[5] Democratic votes were coded 0 and Republican votes 1, so negative signs are pro-Democratic and positive signs pro-Republican.

Probably the first thing which should be noted about the results is the strength of the effects associated with the partisanship variables. Registered by either the party identification measures or, in 1960 and 1976, the respondent's vote in the previous election, the probit estimates for these variables are indicative of a large degree of continuity in voting behavior. If a voter supported the Democratic nominee in one election, there is a strong probability that he or she will do so in the next election (Campbell et al., 1960).

As in most previous studies of presidential elections, the personal experiences version of the incumbency-oriented hypothesis received some empirical support. Coefficients of eleven of the twelve family finances "better" and "worse" dummies were in the predicted direction—compared to voters who felt their financial situation had stayed the same during the previous year, those who felt they were better off gave greater support to the incumbent, and those who felt worse off gave him less. In two of the elections at least one of the terms was statistically significant; in two others (1960 and 1980), although neither were significantly different from the reference group in the middle, the difference between the better and worse terms was statistically significant ($p < .05$). Given that the average difference between the pair was .28, feeling that one's financial situation had improved recently instead of worsened could, everything else being equal, increase a voter's probability of opting for the incumbent by as much as 11 percent.

The entries in Table 13.3 also show that the personal experience version of the policy-oriented hypothesis also received some empirical backing. In all elections except 1968, coefficients of the personal level unemployment terms all bore a negative (pro-Democratic) sign. But while the pro-Democratic direction of this support is fairly impressive in consistency, it is often not impressive in magnitude. Four coefficients exceed .5, but three are less than .1. The difference between these effects is substantial. If there is a 50 percent probability that a certain voter will vote Democratic, an estimate of $-.5$ on the unemployment term would, everything else being equal, increase his probability of voting Democratic to 69 percent; an estimate of $-.1$ would move it up to only 54 percent. So although voters from families injured by unemployment nearly always gave greater support to Democratic candidates in this series of elections, the magnitude of this support was often quite modest.

Looking more closely at the results reported in Table 13.3, we see that the pro-Democratic influence of unemployment upon voters' choices was generally much greater when their head of household was currently unemployed than when they had been recently unemployed but were currently working. This pattern of effects would obviously limit the electoral impact of personally experienced unemployment. In arguing *for* the political potency of unemployment, Okun (1973) pointed out that although only a small percentage of people are jobless at any one time (usually), many times that number have been out of work during the previous year or so. (This fact is reflected in the relative sizes of the two unemployment categories in these surveys.) If, however, the effects of personally encountered unemployment upon voting decisions are dissipated as rapidly as these figures suggest, these difficulties would necessarily have only a very small impact upon the outcomes of presidential elections.

The evidence also tends to be supportive on the inflation side of the hypothesis. The personal-level inflation coefficients in both 1972 and 1976 were more positive and thus more pro-Republican than estimates for the unemployment terms. The 1972 evidence is very strong. Those individuals who felt that inflation was their worst economic problem were much more likely than other voters to back Nixon. The influence registered by the .27 coefficient would increase the probability of a person voting Republican, all else being equal, from 50 percent to 61 percent. This effect is even more impressive when the strong support Nixon received from the electorate as a whole is taken into account.

Distinguishing between references to inflation per se and declining real income appears to have been a good idea. Although the probit estimates for these variables were identical in 1976, in 1972 the effect associated with declining real income was significantly less Republican (or more Democratic) than that associated with inflation. For the remaining sets of problems there is little to be said. All four coeficients of the personal-level taxes or general economic problems cluster closely around zero.

To a large extent, then, these findings back up those of most previous analyses. Voters in presidential elections clearly respond in an incumbency-oriented fashion to perceived changes in their (family's) financial situation. Individuals who personally experience unemployment or unemployment-related problems vote in a policy-oriented manner by throwing more support to the Democratic nominee. And although very little evidence can be brought to bear on the inflation side, voters who

TABLE 13.3

Economic Concerns and Voting in Presidential Elections, 1960–1980

VARIABLE	1960	1964	1968[a]	1972	1976	1980[a]
Constant	−.04/(.09)	−.57/(.18)**	.52/(.18)**	.69/(.17)**	−.25/(.19)	.57/(.22)
Republican	.59/(.09)**	1.29/(.19)**	1.02/(.19)**	.72/(.19)**	.67/(.13)**	.80/(.19)**
Democrat	−1.07/(.11)**	−.53/(.18)**	−1.26/(.17)**	−.82/(.17)**	−.73/(.15)**	−1.26/(.17)**
Personal economic experiences						
Family finances better	.14/(.09)	−.03/(.10)	−.33/(.12)**	.05/(.12)	−.02/(.11)	−.15/(.14)
Family finances worse	−.05/(.12)	.18/(.15)	14/(.15)	−.30/(.14)*	−.19/(.12)	.13/(.14)
Head unemployed currently	−.61/(.31)*	−.83/(.70)	.05/(.47)	—	—	−.85/(.32)**
Head unemployed last year	−.24/(.19)	−.56/(.34)*	.02/(.37)	—	—	−.04/(.18)
Inflation	—	—	—	.27/(.16)*	−.01/(.12)	—
Declining real income	—	—	—	−.09/(.23)	−.01/(.21)	—
Unemployment	—	—	—	−.35/(.30)	−.24/(.27)	—
Taxes	—	—	—	.07/(.23)	.02/(.23)	—
General economic problems	—	—	—	.07/(.14)	−.08/(.13)	—

National economic assessments

Business conditions better	—	—	.10/(.12)	.25/(.12)*	.53/(.11)**	−.14/(.19)
Business conditions worse	—	—	.30/(.19)	−.26/(.17)	−.15/(.13)	.33/(.14)**
Unemployment	−.24/(.14)*	−.22/(.19)	.28/(.29)	.02/(.22)	−.40/(.15)**	−.50/(.20)**
Inflation	.38/(.23)*	.51/(.49)	−.03/(.24)	.04/(.14)	.08/(.15)	−.05/(.15)
Taxes	.07/(.20)	.21/(.20)	.43/(.22)*	.36/(.26)	−.04/(−.41)	.50/(.44)
More government programs	−.06/(.10)	−.52/(.11)**	−.20/(.12)*	−.07/(.18)	.15/(.27)	−.34/(.21)*
Less government spending	−.17/(.21)	.36/(.22)*	.73/(.32)*	.20/(.31)	.22/(.34)	−.07/(.25)
General economic problems	.09/(.22)	b	b	−.42/(.20)*	−.03/(.17)	−.16/(.19)
R^2	.34	.48	.58	.40	.40	.54
N	1,149	1,111	911	827	923	877

*$p < .05$
**$p < .01$
[a]Wallace voters in 1968 and Anderson voters in 1980 were excluded from the analysis.
[b]Not included in the equation because of very low n.

319

were personally concerned about inflation were considerably more likely than other voters to choose Nixon over McGovern.

In short, the results reported in Table 13.3 give some backing to the personal experiences version of both the incumbency-oriented and policy-oriented hypotheses. With few exceptions, however, the survey data analyzed here are much more supportive of the national assessments version of both hypotheses. First, seven of the eight coefficients of the national business conditions terms (all but the 1968 "better" term) were in accord with the hypothesis that the more favorably individuals rated the recent course of the economy, the more likely they were to vote for incumbent presidential candidates. (And although the aberrant estimate of the 1968 "better" term was more anti-incumbent than the reference group, it was still more pro-incumbent than the coefficient of the "worse" term.) The average difference between each pair of business conditions better and worse terms was .47, and in all surveys except for 1968 at least one of the coefficients was significantly different from the reference group. An effect of this magnitude (.47) would increase the probability that an individual would vote for (or against) the incumbent from 50 percent to 68 percent. This difference is also considerably larger than the average .28 difference between the better and worse family finances terms. General assessments of the national economy thus exert a stronger incumbency-oriented influence upon individual voters' decisions than do perceived trends in their own economic conditions.

The national assessments version of the policy-oriented hypothesis also fared well in this analysis. In 1960, 1976, and 1980, those who believed that the nation's most important economic problem was unemployment voted significantly more Democratic than did those who believed it was inflation. These were all years in which unemployment and/or inflation was serious enough to be cited as a national problem by a large segment of the voting public. Conversely, in the prosperous year of 1968, when fewer than 3 percent of the voters referred to each of these problems, the hypothesis fared poorly. To be sure, there was little difference between estimates of the national-level inflation and unemployment terms in 1972, even though these problems were cited by fairly large percentages of voters. In general, though, in years in which unemployment and/or inflation were high on the national agenda, these issues influenced voters' choices for president in the manner predicted by the policy-oriented hypothesis.

The results also gave some empirical backing to the hypotheses concerning the proper size and scope of the public sector. With a couple of exceptions (the 1960 "less government spending" term and the 1968 "taxes" term), those who believed new or expanded government programs were needed to attack serious national problems voted Democratic more often than individuals who believed that either too *much* government spending or taxation was the most important problem facing the nation. As was the case with the unemployment-inflation hypothesis, the public sector hypothesis made its strongest showing in the election years in which a large segment of the electorate fell into the relevant categories—1964 and 1968. In 1964 the -.52 probit estimate associated with the "more government programs" term means that falling into this category would, other things being being equal, increase the probability of an individual voting for Johnson from 50 percent to 70 percent. Holding the opposite opinion, that the nation's worst economic problem was too *much* government spending, would likewise lower the probability of an individual voting for Johnson, everything else being equal, from 50 percent to 36 percent.[6]

The final category in Table 13.3 to be considered was composed of voters who cited either the economy in general or a miscellany of other specific economic problems. For the most part the behavior of these voters did not differ from that of the reference group. In 1964 and 1968 this category was too small even to be specified in the probit equation. In 1972, though, voters in this category gave significantly more support than did those in the reference group to the Democratic challenger McGovern. Given the vague, general nature of the perceptions which fell into this category, it probably makes sense to view this one isolated effect as augmenting the incumbency-oriented voting registered by the national business conditions terms.

DISCUSSION

In interpreting the results of this analysis it should be kept in mind that economic issues are not the only factors which influence voters' choices among candidates for president. Moral and cultural issues, foreign policy positions, or a candidate's character and integrity often come into play in presidential election campaigns. This is the reason, of course, why the preceding discussion of the results so often included the caveat "everything else being equal."

Still, as the findings here and in dozens of other studies have shown, the state of the economy is a powerful influence upon the outcomes of presidential elections. It would require foreign policy reversals or personal scandals of great magnitude to undo completely the advantage to the incumbent president of a strong economy going into election day. Conversely, a president saddled with a poorly performing economy will probably not find a great deal of consolation in the fact that the United States is not at war or that he is perceived to be an honest man.

It is thus important to ascertain exactly how economic issues influence voters' decisions. The present study investigated four interlocking hypotheses and succeeded in finding at least some empirical support for each of them. First, there was strong evidence of incumbency-oriented voting: the more favorably voters assessed recent trends in the nation's economy or in their own financial situation, the more likely they were to support the incumbent. The results reported in Table 13.3 also provide support for the inflation-unemployment policy-oriented hypothesis. In those years in which large portions of the electorate believed the nation's most serious economic problem was either inflation or unemployment, voters who were concerned about the former problem were much more likely to support the Republican candidate for president than were voters worried about the latter problem. With few exceptions, voters whose family head was currently or had been out of work gave greater than average support to Democratic candidates. Finally, in one of the two years in which the requisite data were available (1972), voters who reported that their most important personal economic problem was inflation were considerably more likely than other voters to choose Nixon over McGovern.

It was the case, then, that the voting analyses generated some evidence in support of the personal experiences and national assessments versions of both the incumbency-oriented and policy-oriented hypotheses. That voters take into account both personal experiences and their assessments of national conditions and events seems eminently reasonable; the strong points of one type of economic information complement the shortcomings of the other. Personally encountered economic conditions are, above all, immediate and tangible; they are as Fiorina puts it, particularly hard pieces of data. Moreover, Adam Smith's characterization of human nature—"Every man feels his own pleasures and his own pains more sensibly than those of other people"—would appear to remain at least a good first approximation. There is a certain poignancy about receiving a pink slip which cannot be conveyed by a news story that unemployment rose .3 percent in the previous month.

There are, on the other hand, important factors which act to deflect the impact of personal economic experiences upon voting decisions. As indicated earlier, several studies have shown that Americans tend to attribute their own economic fortunes to forces which are not directly related to national economic trends or to the government's macroeconomic policies (Schlozman and Verba, 1979; Feldman, 1982; Kiewiet, 1983). Similarly, the National Election Studies survey data evince an enduring commitment to the ethic of self-reliance. When asked in the 1972 CPS election study who, if anybody, should be helping them with their most serious personal problems, only a small minority of respondents referred to the government in general or to a particular public agency. Instead, most felt that they themselves were primarily responsible for dealing with their problems as best they could (Sniderman and Brody, 1977).

As a result of these factors, the impact of personally experienced economic conditions, despite their salience and immediacy, is not nearly as strong as we might have expected. And as indicated in Table 13.3, assessments of national economic conditions and perceptions of important national economic problems exerted considerably more influence upon voters' decisions. Above all, estimates of the incumbency-oriented effect associated with the national business conditions measures were much larger than the respective estimates of the family finances terms.

Conditions in the nation's economy, of course, are probably not as personally salient to most individuals as their own financial situation. But national economic assessments are, by definition, of general, widespread phenomena. Findings reported by Kiewiet (1983) provide very strong evidence on this point: regardless of the particular problem respondents in the 1976 NES survey cited as the most important facing the nation, the overwhelming majority believed that the government bore a great deal of responsibility for solving it. Consequently, in most people's minds national economic conditions reflect upon the performance and policies of the incumbent administration much more directly than the conditions of their own lives. Thus what national economic assessments lack in personal relevance, they make up for by being of more obvious political relevance.

In sum, the performance of the nation's economy in the year or so prior to the election weighs very heavily in the decision of American voters to either support or reject the incumbent president. Although the data series analyzed in this chapter ended with 1980, the events of 1984 strongly indicate that there is no reason to modify this conclusion. To be sure, as of this writing a number of serious problems—high real interest rates, the collapse of the agricultural sector, huge government and foreign trade deficits—pose a serious threat to the nation's prosperity. The political consequence of future economic conditions, however, will be felt in future elections. What mattered for the contest between Reagan and Mondale was the fact that the recovery which began in 1983 had gathered tremendous steam by the second quarter of 1984, pushing unemployment down rapidly with little price inflation. American voters were by and large aware of the major upturn in the nation's economy, gave Ronald Reagan a large measure of credit for it, and reelected him by a landslide.

NOTES

1. Policy-oriented voting would seem to present those in power with perverse incentives. It appears to imply that when in office the Republicans could

help themselves by allowing a high rate of inflation, while the Democrats could bolster their prospects for reelection by running up a high unemployment rate. Consideration of long-term consequences, however, strongly suggests that an incumbent party's strategy of deliberately exacerbating the economic problem it is supposed to be more adept at handling (or, less flagrantly, of attempting to protect a weak electoral flank by shifting into a vigorous attack on the problem it is supposed to be relatively less adept at handling) would be counterproductive. Not only would a flip-flop on economic priorities betray the party's key constituent groups and alienate its most dependable supporters, but the resultant uncertainty as to what the party could be expected to do in office would also frighten away many others (Downs, 1957).

2. A large amount of research on economic conditions and voting has concerned congressional elections. The results derived from running the analyses described in this paper upon congressional election data are reported in Kiewiet (1983).

3. Data from these surveys were made available by the Inter-University Consortium for Political and Social Research. Neither the original collectors of the data nor the Consortium bear any responsibility for the analyses or interpretations presented here.

4. The reason why one category in each response battery must be left out of the probit equation is because it adds no additional information. In the current example, for instance, we know that a respondent who had a value of 0 on the "business conditions better" variable and 0 on the "business conditions worse" variable had to have answered that business conditions had stayed the same. There is thus no need to include a "business conditions same" dummy (1 or 0) variable. Indeed, doing so would create a "dummy variable error" and thus make it impossible to estimate the equation.

5. The standard error is an indicator of how exact the probit estimate for a given variable is. The larger the ratio of the probit estimate to the standard error, the more confidence we can have that the probit estimate is actually different from 0 (0 indicates that the variable has no effect on the dependent variable). When this ratio exceeds a certain level, the estimate is said to be statistically significant, meaning that there is a very low probability that the probit estimate could have been produced purely by chance. The criterion of statistical significance used here ($p < .05$) means that if the true effect of a variable were actually 0, there is only a 5 percent probability that a probit estimate as large as that which was obtained could have occurred purely by chance.

6. Goldwater's call for a major reduction in the role of the federal government in the American economy came, however, at a strikingly unpropitious time. According to the evidence presented back in Table 13.2, in 1964 the number of voters who believed serious national problems necessitated an expansion of the public sector was nearly eight times greater than the number who believed it was crucial to reduce government spending.

REFERENCES

Brody, R. A., and Sniderman, P. M. 1977. "From Life Space to Polling Place: The Relevance of Personal Concerns for Voting Behavior." *British Journal of Political Science* 7: 337–60.

Cameron, D. 1979. "Economic Inequality in the United States." Manuscript. Yale University.

Campbell, A., et al. 1960. *The American Voter*. New York: Wiley.

Downs, A. 1957. *An Economic Theory of Democracy*. New York: Harper & Row.

Fair, R. C. 1978. "The Effect of Economic Events on Votes for President." *Review of Economics and Statistics* 60:159–73.

Feldman, S. 1982. "Economic Self-Interest and Political Behavior." *American Journal of Political Science* 26: 446–66.

Fiorina, M. P. 1978. "Economic Retrospective Voting in American National Elections: A Micro-Analysis." *American Journal of Political Science* 22: 426–43.

———. 1981. *Retrospective Voting in American National Elections*. New Haven: Yale University Press.

Hibbs, D. A. 1979. "The Mass Public and Macroeconomic Policy: The Dynamics of Public Opinion Toward Unemployment and Inflation." *American Journal of Political Science* 23: 705–31.

Kiewiet, D. R. 1981. "Policy-Oriented Voting in Response to Economic Issues." *American Political Science Review* 75: 448–59.

———. 1983. *Macroeconomics and Micropolitics*. Chicago: University of Chicago Press.

Kinder, D. R., and Kiewiet, D. R. 1979. "Economic Discontent and Political Behavior: The Role of Personal Grievances and Collective Economic Judgments in Congressional Voting." *American Journal of Political Science* 23: 495–517.

———. 1981. "Sociotropic Politics: The American Case." *British Journal of Political Science* 11: 129–61.

Kramer, G. 1971. "Short-Term Fluctuations in U. S. Voting Behavior, 1896–1964." *American Political Science Review* 65: 131–43.

Schlozman, K., and Verba, S. 1979. *Injury to Insult*. Cambridge: Harvard University Press.

Sniderman, P. M., and Brody, R. A. 1977. "Coping: The Ethic of Self-Reliance." *American Journal of Political Science* 21: 501–21.

Tufte, E. R. 1978. *Political Control of the Economy*. Princeton: Princeton University Press.

NOTES ON CONTRIBUTORS

ALEXANDER HICKS is Assistant Professor of Political Science and Sociology at Northwestern University. He has recently published articles on political economy in such journals as *American Journal of Political Science, American Journal of Sociology, American Sociological Review, Comparative Political Studies,* and *Policy Studies Journal.*

D. RODERICK KIEWIET is Associate Professor of Political Science at California Institute of Technology. He is author of *Macroeconomics & Micropolitics: The Electoral Effects of Economic Issues* and has contributed to such journals as *American Political Science Review* and *British Journal of Political Science.*

MICHAEL S. LEWIS-BECK is Professor of Political Science at the University of Iowa. He has published in, among others, *American Political Science Review, American Journal of Sociology, American Journal of Political Science, Journal of Politics,* and *Public Opinion Quarterly.* He is also author of *Applied Regression: An Introduction.*

GARY W. MARKS is Assistant Professor of Government and Foreign Affairs at the University of Virginia. He is the author of a forthcoming book on the development of union political activity in Britain, Germany, and the United States and is writing a book on the politics of economic policy in Western democracies.

B. GUY PETERS is Maurice Falk Professor of American Government at the University of Pittsburgh and former Director of the Center for Public Policy Studies at Tulane University. His publications include *Can Government Go Bankrupt?* (with Richard Rose), *Policy Dynamics* (with Brian Hogwood), and *The Politics of Bureaucracy.*

ADAM PRZEWORSKI is Professor of Political Science at the University of Chicago. Recent publications include *Capitalism and Social Democracy* and, with John Sprague, *Paper Stones: A History of Electoral Socialism.*

He is currently working, with Michael Wallerstein, on the political determinants of investment policy.

JEREMIAH M. RIEMER is Assistant Professor of Government at Oberlin College. A contributor to *The Political Economy of West Germany*, edited by Andrei Markovits, he has research interests that include comparative labor movements and political parties. He is currently completing a project on economic politics in the "not quite corporatist" state.

WILLIAM SAFRAN is Professor of Political Science at the University of Colorado at Boulder. He has written *Veto-Group Politics* and *The French Polity*, is coauthor of *Ideology and Politics: The Socialist Party of France* and *Comparative Politics*, and has contributed to numerous books and journals on comparative politics. His current research interests are French public policy and ethnic politics.

STEVEN E. SCHIER is Assistant Professor of Political Science and Director of the political economy program at Carleton College. He is author of *The Rules and the Game* and several articles in *American Politics Quarterly* and other journals, and is currently writing a book on macroeconomic policy making in the U. S. Congress.

MANFRED G. SCHMIDT is Professor of Political Science at the Free University of Berlin. His books include *CDU und SPD an der Regierung, Wohlfahrtsstaatliche Politik unter bürgerlichen und sozialdemokratischen Regierungen,* and *Der schweizerlische Weg zur Vollbeschäftigung.* He is also coediting *Politics and Policy-Making in the Federal Republic of Germany* with Klaus von Beyme.

DUANE H. SWANK is Assistant Professor of Political Science at Marquette University. His research interests include the determinants and consequences of state social and economic policies in industrialized democracies. He has published articles on these topics in *American Behavioral Scientist, Comparative Political Studies,* and *American Journal of Political Science.*

NORMAN J. VIG is Professor of Political Science at Carleton College. He is author of *Science and Technology in British Politics;* coeditor of *Politics in Advanced Nations* and *Environmental Policy in the 1980s: Reagan's New Agenda;* and has published in numerous journals including *World Politics, Political Science Quarterly,* and *Parliamentary Affairs.*

MICHAEL WALLERSTEIN is Assistant Professor of Political Science at the

University of California, Los Angeles. His current work concerns the organization of the union movement in democratic capitalist societies. He is also working, with Adam Przeworski, on the political determinants of investment policy.

CATHERINE H. ZUCKERT is Associate Professor of Political Science at Carleton College. She has published articles on political philosophy in *Polity, Review of Politics, Interpretation, Feminist Studies,* and *Political Theory.* Currently she is working on literary critiques of American political principles, contemporary rereadings of Plato, and the politics of the regime.